CHALLENGING ISSUES IN CHILD CUSTODY DISPUTES:

A Guide for Legal and Mental Health Professionals

Barbara Jo Fidler, Ph.D, C.Psych, Acc.FM
Nicholas Bala, B.A., LL.B., LL.M.
Rachel Birnbaum, Ph.D, RSW, LL.M.
Katherine Kavassalis, B.A., LL.B

A cataloguing record for this publication is available from Library and Archives Canada.

ISBN 978-0-7798-1758-0

Composition: Computer Composition of Canada Inc.

THOMSON CARSWELL

One Corporate Plaze, 2075 Kennedy Road, Scarborough, Ontario M1T 3V4
Customer Care:
Toronto: 1-416-609-3800
Elsewhere in Canada/US: 1-800-387-5164
Fax: 1-416-298-5094

Acknowledgements

Writing this book has involved many who have supported us in our efforts. A special thank you to O'Neil Smith at ThomsonReuters Carswell Publishing for his support and guidance. We are most grateful to our copy editor, Carol Pollock, for her editorial work and to Matt Hodgson and Alex Fidler-Wener for their administrative assistance. Our appreciation is extended to Christine Galea, articling student at Walker, Head, for her legal research assistance. Our utmost appreciation and gratitude is extended to Justice Emile Kruzick, Dr. Peter Jaffe, and Dr. Richard Warshak for their time, helpful direction, insight, and editorial comments. Rachel Birnbaum and Nicholas Bala would also like to acknowledge funding support for their work from the Social Sciences and Humanities Research Council. We thank our families, colleagues and friends for their continuing patience, encouragement, and attentive ears.

Some parts of this book are based on revised excerpts from previous papers co-authored by Prof. Bala; thanks go to his colleagues on these projects: Claire Crooks, Dan Goldberg, Joanne Harris, Claire Houston, Peter Jaffe, Mindy Mitnick, and, Nico Trocmé.

We especially thank once again our families and friends, who provided us with support and humility along the way. One of the themes of this book is that parents have a central formative role in the lives of their children, and all of the authors recognize that their present success in life reflects the love and guidance provided by their own parents. The lead author of this project, Barbara, wishes to acknowledge her late father for instilling curiosity, drive and a love of learning and her mother for listening and supporting.

About the Authors

Barbara Jo Fidler, Ph.D., C.Psych., Acc.FM., is a registered psychologist and accredited mediator practising in Ontario, Canada. She received her Ph.D. from York University (Toronto) in 1986. Dr. Fidler maintains a private practice and is a founding member of Family Solutions. She provides mediation, arbitration, parenting coordination, consultation, expert court testimony and custody/access assessment critiques. Her practice also includes marital, individual and family therapy, including reunification therapy. Dr. Fidler provides training and supervision for parenting plan assessments (custody/access), parenting coordination, mediation, and parent-child contact problems, including child alienation, and has published in these and other areas. She has been actively involved in the development of parenting coordination services and was appointed to the AFCC Task Force charged with developing guidelines and standards of practice for parenting coordination. She is currently a member of the High Conflict Forum in Toronto and a frequent presenter on high-conflict families and related topics.

Nicholas Bala, B.A., LL.B., LL.M. has been a Professor at the Faculty of Law at Queen's University since 1980, and was the Academic Director of the Family Law part time LL.M. program at Osgoode Hall Law School from 2006 to 2008. Prof. Bala's primary area of teaching and research interest is Family and Children's Law, focusing on such issues as parental rights and responsibilities after divorce, spousal abuse and its effects on children, support obligations, the legal definition of the family, young offenders, child welfare law and child witnesses. Much of his research work has interdisciplinary aspects, and he has collaborated on research projects with psychologists, social workers, psychiatrists, criminologists and sociologists. His work is often cited by all levels of courts, including the Supreme Court of Canada. He is frequently invited to present at professional education programs for judges, lawyers, social workers, psychologists and other professionals, and he has worked with the National Judicial Institute in planning education programs for judges.

Rachel Birnbaum, Ph.D., RSW, LL.M, is an associate professor at King's University College at the University of Western Ontario. Her primary areas of teaching focus on children and families, ethics and the law, and research methods. Dr. Birnbaum has extensive clinical practice and research experience in working with children and families of separation and/or divorce. She has authored several papers for the Department of Justice Canada on children's participation in separation and/or divorce. Dr. Birnbaum continues to publish in this area and presents both nationally and internationally at workshops and conferences on children and the law, working with high conflict families and collaboration between law and social work. She has co-authored several books regarding children and post separation and/or divorce, as well as, *Law for Social Workers* with Thomson Carswell. She has been the President of the College of Social Workers and Social Service Workers since 2005.

Katherine Kavassalis, B.A., LL.B., is a practising member of the Ontario bar. She received her B.A. from the University of Waterloo in 1979 and her LL.B. from the University of Windsor in 1982. She has practised family law since her call to the bar in 1984. In 2004, she joined the in-house legal staff of the Office of the Children's Lawyer, Ministry of the Attorney General, in Toronto, Canada, where she represents children in family law matters. In addition to her practical experience of working with families and children in separation and divorce matters, Ms Kavassalis has published in this area and has presented both locally and internationally. She has taught at various institutions, including the University of Western Ontario. She is currently a member of several law-related organizations, including the Family Law Advisory Committee to Legal Aid Ontario, the Family Bar Advisory Committee on Domestic Violence, and the Advocates Society.

Preface

This is a companion to the recently published book, *Child Custody Assessments: A Resource Guide for Legal and Mental Health Professionals*, which provides the building blocks for practitioners involved in child custody and access disputes and assessments. Included in our first book is a detailed description of assessment methodology, from intake and referral to report writing, along with an analysis of the use of critiques and second opinions in the courts, and a discussion of the practical and ethical dilemmas faced by mental health professionals involved in family law disputes. That book discusses practice considerations for making recommendations pertaining to parenting time schedules and the decision-making protocols, the two primary aspects of any parenting plan. The earlier work also provides a summary of the literature on sole, joint, and parallel parenting from both the social science and legal perspectives.

In this book we discuss in depth four challenging, albeit common, issues in custody and access disputes and assessments: relocation, domestic violence, sexual abuse allegations, and child alienation. Except for sexual abuse allegations, two chapters are devoted to each of these topics, the first focusing on historical context and theory, and the second on practice from both the mental health and legal perspectives. We address sexual abuse allegations in one chapter since, while assessors and family lawyers need to understand this type of case when making and considering parenting plan recommendations, the front-end responsibility for the investigation of these allegations typically rests with child welfare workers and police. For each topic, we summarize the relevant social science and research literature, consider best practice issues for assessors, and discuss how Canadian courts approach and address these cases, through a discussion of illustrative case law and leading precedents. We begin the book with an Introduction that reminds readers of the basic principles of custody and access law in Canada, a topic discussed in greater depth in the first book.

The four topics that are the focus of this book are among the most frequently encountered and controversial issues facing legal and mental health practitioners who work with high-conflict separating and divorcing parents. In fact, most assessments require that an assessor investigate at least one, and often more of these issues. While such concerns may commonly arise, conducting a comprehensive and competent custody and access assessment in such cases is complex and challenging, even for a seasoned practitioner. In addition to knowing about assessment methodology more generally, assessors need to be familiar with the large social science literature and the case law relevant to these areas. Ethical and practice dilemmas are frequently encountered, adding further to the complexity of this work.

The literature and case law reviewed for these topics is extensive, making the writing of this book daunting, but nonetheless necessary. As noted in our first book, there is little empirical research supporting one assessment methodology over another, or on outcomes relating to matching up parenting plans with different sets of family circumstances. Conducting such research is difficult, if not impossible in some areas, given the ethical constraints and methodological challenges. Much can be gained, however, from the substantial theoretical and clinical literature that does exist. In terms of outcome research, in addition to some empirical studies, we have the benefit of a significant body of literature on the impact of separation, divorce, and parental conflict on children, and on other related subjects such as attachment, child development, memory, and parenting, all of which can be extrapolated to our work with high-conflict separating and divorcing families.

As educators in both the private and public sectors, we are concerned about the lack of comprehensive training courses on child custody assessments in universities and colleges. To help address these problems, our objective in this book, as with the companion book, has been to provide a comprehensive resource guide for both beginning and seasoned practitioners, including current and thorough information relating to the social science and research literature, best practice considerations and clinical protocols, and relevant case law and legal themes.

The discussion of case law in this book considers leading Canadian precedents and judgments that are illustrative of judicial approaches or situations commonly before the courts. The treatment of case law is not, however, exhaustive, and there are many reported decisions in each of the areas that are not mentioned. This text may serve as a useful starting point for legal and social science research, particularly for the mental health professional conducting child custody assessments. Readers are cautioned that the case law is always evolving and the social science literature is growing. Those with cases before the courts must ensure that their research is current and relevant to their particular jurisdiction.

We hope that the reader finds this book informative and practical in the complex, challenging and often controversial work that custody assessments entail. However, and notwithstanding its contribution, it is equally important to recognize the knowledge gaps and debates that continue in the field. In many respects there is still much to learn about children and families after separation and divorce.

Contents

List of Tables

Table of Cases

Table of Legislation

Introduction

Canadian Law Governing Custody, Access and Assessments

The laws governing care of children have dramatically evolved over the past two hundred years, reflecting ever-changing patterns of family living, societal values, and social understandings. Until the twentieth century, the patriarchal common law provided that in the event of separation, a rare event at that time, the father was viewed as the "natural guardian" and had the legal right to custody of his children; the mother did not even have a the right to visitation, regardless of the fact she left her husband because he was abusive or had committed adultery. Throughout much of the twentieth century, the courts followed the "tender years" doctrine, with a strong presumption that the mother would be granted custody of the children in the event of separation, with the father usually only having a limited right of visitation, unless the mother demonstrated "moral unfitness" by committing adultery, in which case she would forfeit her claim to custody.

There has been enormous change in gender roles and patterns of family living in Canada over the past half century, and this has been reflected in significant legal changes. Women are marrying later, having fewer children and much more likely to be in the labour force. Fathers are now much more involved in the care of children than a generation ago. On average, though, they still do less childcare than mothers do. Unmarried cohabitation is more common today than in the past, and the divorce rate has climbed so that more than one in three marriages end in divorce, though the divorce rate seems to have stabilized over the past decade. The law has also had to respond to new issues posed by parenting in same-sex relationships and because of the development of artificial reproductive technology.

The laws and legal processes governing child-related disputes in the event of parental separation remain contentious and there is a range of different proposals for law reform. A number of jurisdictions have undertaken ambitious projects to change the way that they deal with these issues. In Canada, Alberta's *Family Law Act* has discarded the concepts of "custody" and "access" and now uses the terminology of "parenting orders". In this book, we continue to use the terms "custody" and "access," which are used in the *Divorce Act* and most provincial legislation. We do this not because we think that these terms are preferable; indeed we prefer other more child-focused terminology, such as "parenting time", "parent-child contact" and "parenting plans", which we also use. We use the present *Divorce Act* terminology because this book is intended to help understand and improve professional practice in the context of existing laws and legal structures, and does not address law reform issues that should be undertaken by governments.

Since 1985, section 16(1) of the *Divorce Act* has provided that child custody and access decisions are to be based on determination of the "best interests" of the child before the court.[1] Section 16(9) provides that the "past conduct" of a person shall not be taken into consideration unless the conduct is relevant to a person's ability to parent. This precludes consideration of such purely marital misconduct as adultery. However, while spousal abuse was long ignored and viewed as "private matter" not relevant to post-separation parenting, it is now accepted that spousal abuse should be taken into consideration when determining the best interests of a child.[2] Section 16(10) specifies that a child should have "as much contact with each [parent] . . . as is consistent with the best interests of the child and, for that purpose, shall take into consideration the willingness of the person for whom custody is sought to facilitate such contact." The view that it is generally in the best interests of children to have regular and frequent contact with both parents is supported by the social science literature which concludes that children's psychological well-being is generally enhanced by maintaining contact with both parents after separation (Amato, 1994; Kelly & Emery, 2003). However, others have argued that the value of maintaining relationships with both parents is not as clear for children from violent and highly conflicted homes (Sturge & Glaser, 2000; Wolfe, Zak, Wilson & Jaffe, 1986; Jaffe, Lemon & Poisson, 2003).

In Canada, the federal *Divorce Act*[3] governs cases where parents are divorcing. The provincial legislation governs cases where parents are separating without a divorce, perhaps because they were not married. While there are differences between the provinces in how

---

[1] The reader should consult the legislation on child custody and access matters in their own provincial jurisdiction. Access to this information can be found on each government website, or alternatively through the Canadian Legal Information Institute website, referred to as Canlii that can be found at: www.canlii.org.

[2] See Appendix A for the specific legislation outlining the factors in each province that a court is obligated to consider regarding domestic violence and abuse.

[3] R.S.C. 1985 c. 3 (2nd Supp.), as amended, R.S.C. 1985 c. 27 (2nd Supp.)

some family law matters are resolved, in particular property issues, and although the wording of the statutes governing disputes related to children varies between provinces, the law, as articulated in legislation and appellate judgments, is now effectively the same across Canada. This is not to say that there will be uniformity on how the law will be applied. There may be significant differences even within the same city, in how individual judges apply the vague "best interests" of the child test to specific cases. (See Appendix A for survey of Canadian legislation.)

There is a broad movement in many countries towards involving both parents in the lives of their children in the event of separation, with close to half of divorcing parents in Canada now making arrangements for some form of joint legal custody of their children (though usually continuing to reside primarily with mothers). After separation, parents are also encouraged to make their own arrangements for the care of their children, with the establishment of programs of parenting education and the encouragement of mediation and collaborative family law to help parents resolve their disagreements in a non-adversarial fashion. While the majority of separating parents do make their own arrangements for the care of their children without involving legal or mental health professionals, the sizeable minority who are unable to resolve their differences must involve lawyers, judges, mediators, assessors, arbitrators, and parenting coordinators to help them resolve their disagreements. Even amongst those separated parents who seek these types of professional assistance, only a small minority actually go to trial about custody or access issues. These cases, however, are settled "in the shadow of the law," with the threat that there will be a trial if the parents cannot settle, and the settlement is affected by the perception of the likely outcome of litigation.

In all Canadian jurisdictions, legislation or rules of the court allow the courts to order an "assessment", "investigation" or "homestudy" in family law cases.[4] Government funded services are available

---

4 Alberta, *Rules of Court*, Alta. Reg. 390/68, Rule 218; British Columbia, *Family Relations Act,* R.S.B.C 1996, c. 128, s. 15; Manitoba, *The Family Maintenance Act,* C.C.S.M. c. F20, s. 3 and *Court of Queen's Bench Act,* C.C.S.M. c. C280, s. 49; New Brunswick, *Judicature Act,* R.S.N.B. 1973, c. J-2, s. 11.4; Newfoundland, *Children's Law Act*, R.S.N. 1990, c. C-13, s. 36; Northwest Territories, *Children's Law Act,* S.N.W.T. 1997, c. 14, s. 29; Nova Scotia, *Judicature Act,* R.S.N.S. 1990, c. J-4, s. 32F and *Maintenance and Custody Act,* R.S.N.S. 1989, c. 160, s. 19; Ontario, *Children's Law Reform Act,* R.S.O. 1990, c. C.12, s. 30 and *Courts of Justice Act,* R.S.O. 1990, c C.12, s. 112; Prince Edward Island, *Custody Jurisdiction and Enforcement Act,* R.S.PE.I., c C-33, s. 4.1; Yukon, *Children's Act*, R.S.Y. 1986, c. 22, s. 43. It has also been held that a superior court has an inherent jurisdiction to order an assessment:

in most of these jurisdictions, however these resources are limited. The schemes for determining which cases will have access to which particular service vary considerably across jurisdictions. Consequently, it is not uncommon for parties to have little choice but to independently fund services.

In many of the high conflict cases that are resolved without trial, the recommendations of the assessor often help to shape the settlement, and if the case does go to trial, the assessor's evidence will often be very influential, provided that the assessment was properly conducted.

Cillis v. Cillis, 1980 CarswellOnt 315, 20 R.F.L. (2d) 208 (Ont. H.C.). We discuss the two different types of court-ordered assessments available in Ontario more fully in our companion book (Birnbaum, Fidler & Kavassalis, 2008). See also a comparison of the two types of assessment (Fidler & Birnbaum, 2006).

Chapter 1

Understanding Residential Moves and Relocation: The Impact on Children and their Families

Few, if any, issues cause reasonable and cooperative parents to resort to litigation as does mobility of children. While most types of family law disputes are amenable to some form of resolution prior to trial, mobility cases leave little room for compromise. Two committed parents may be faced with the prospect that either, one will be disappointed in not being able to progress with their future life in a new community, or one will be disappointed in not being able to maintain the same involvement in the children's lives.

Justice Ingram (*Drury v. Drury*, 2006)[1]

One of the most frequently litigated types of family law cases are those in which parental relocation is at issue, reflecting the reality that, with changes in the economy, transportation, communication, and familial relations, Canada is an increasingly mobile society, and that, after separation, former spouses are especially likely to move to different locations (Thomson, 2004). Such moves can be made for a number of reasons, including better employment or more affordable housing, to gain proximity to family and social supports, or re-partnering. Cases in which parents have separated and one parent seeks to relocate[2] with the children pose great challenges for judges and lawyers, as well for the parents and children involved. Separated parents who have settled into reasonably amicable, long-term co-parenting arrangements sometimes become mired in conflict and adversarial processes when one parent proposes to move away. These cases are much more difficult to settle than other family law cases, as there may be no middle ground for a compromise, and a significant

[1] *Drury v. Drury*, 2006 CarswellOnt 1233, [2006] O.J. No. 833 (Ont. S.C.J.), at para. 1.

[2] In the United States, these cases are referred to as "relocation" or "move-away" cases, while in Canada they are frequently referred to as "mobility" cases. In this chapter the terms are used interchangeably.

portion of all family law cases that go to trial feature relocation as the central issue.

Further, the test which Canadian courts use to decide whether to permit a parent to relocate with children—the "best interests of the child"—gives trial judges substantial discretion to examine and assess all of the circumstances of a case, making outcomes difficult to predict and settlements hard to negotiate. It is not only individual cases that are contentious. Relocation has been controversial in the broader public sphere, with fathers' rights groups battling feminist groups about the appropriate legal rules to govern these cases. Social science researchers and clinicians have also engaged in the debate over the effects of parental relocation on children, and about how to apply the bests interests test in this particular context.

Commentators suggest that while relocation cases are among the most frequently litigated family disputes, it would appear that there is a lower likelihood of litigants seeking an assessment in this type of case than in other child-related disputes (Thompson, 2004; Bala & Harris, 2006; McLeod, 2004). The late law professor James McLeod argued that "courts finally seem to accept that mobility is a legal issue, not a mental health issue."[3] While Austin (2000a, 2008a, 2008b) argues that, for children of divorce, relocation is an established general risk factor for long-term negative behavioural outcomes similar to those arising from divorce itself, the value of obtaining an assessment in a relocation case is often overshadowed by the practical considerations of the expense and delay to the proceedings that result from an assessment.

Child custody assessors find relocation disputes difficult to assess due to the complexity of the factors and issues involved. However, Austin (2000a, 2000c, 2005b, 2006, 2007, 2008a, 2008b) provides direction for the clinician assessing relocation disputes to assist in developing parenting plans; in this chapter and the next, we particularly focus on his approaches. It is equally challenging to ascertain how best to handle these cases from a legal perspective, due to the wide variations in the application of the best interests test. With a lack of clear rules making outcomes unpredictable and often seemingly arbitrary, these cases are also difficult to settle out of court. Justice Carmody, an American judge writing about relocation decisions, stated the difficulty quite eloquently and accurately:

---

[3] James G. McLeod, "Relocation for Dummies" (Paper presented to the Law Society of Upper Canada, Six Minute Family Law Lawyer, Continuing Legal Education Program, November 30, 2004), 10-14.

> Best interests are values, not facts. They are not susceptible to scientific demonstration or conclusive proof. The same body of evidence may produce opposite but nevertheless reasonable conclusions from different judges. There is not always one right answer.[4]

There is little direct empirical data on the impact of relocation on children and adolescents. Conducting well-designed control group studies of child adjustment in relocation cases would be impossible, since ethical and practical concerns prevent random assignment. Long term follow-up of cases that were litigated could be done, but would be expensive and presents with further methodological challenges. However, it is possible to develop some good working hypotheses about the effects of relocation by extrapolating from the large related literature, including survey, cross-sectional, longitudinal and retrospective studies, as well as studies using meta-analysis (examining data sets from other researchers, combining the data and conducting statistical analysis on the expanded data set), that investigates the short- and long-term impact of separation or divorce on children and adolescents.[5] In addition, important findings are available from the limited literature on military, migrant/seasonal, and professional families who experience relocation because of employment. These latter studies provide important information on a child's long-term adjustment (i.e., school, emotional behavior, relationships with friends, etc.).

In this chapter we begin with a brief overview of the historical development of the law concerning relocation cases. We then turn to the social science literature. Given the limited research to date regarding the impact of post-separation relocation on children, we start with a summary of the more general social science and research literature on the impact of separation and divorce on children, which will assist both the legal and mental health professional to understand the context of the issues related to relocation. We then discuss the social science literature on the impact of residential mobility in non-divorced families, the literature specific to relocation in divorced families, and that related more generally to the impact of separation and divorce on children.[6] In Chapter 2, we focus on practice issues

---

[4] Carmody, Hon. Justice Tim, "Child Relocation: An Intractable International Family Law Problem" (2007) 45: 2 Fam. Ct. Rev. 214 at 215.

[5] See for example, Amato and Keith (2001), Amato (2000), Bauserman (2002), Hetherington and Kelly (2002), Fabricius (2000), Fabricius (2003), Kelly and Emery (2003), and Warshak, (2000b).

[6] Our review of the more general literature on the impact of separation and divorce on children is applicable to situations involving domestic violence, sexual abuse allegations and parent-child contact problems.

and discuss assessment frameworks, factors requiring consideration when making recommendations, and the legal trends illustrated by case law.

Historical Overview

Historically, in Canada and elsewhere, throughout the twentieth century, the well-being of a child was considered to be fundamentally interrelated with the well-being of the mother. Prior to the 1990's, it was widely believed, both by the public and in the psychological literature of the day (Goldstein, Freud & Solnit, 1973, 1986) that the primary caregiver, almost always the mother, was the best person to make decisions affecting the child, and the courts, for the most part accepted this premise. This approach was consistent with the tender years doctrine, which gave mothers a presumptive right to custody of children after separation. Further, before the 1990s the courts generally recognized a presumptive right of the custodial parent to relocate, at least in the absence of a non-removal clause in a separation agreement or court order. In the 1973 Ontario Court of Appeal decision in *Wright v. Wright*,[7] for example, the Court held that the mother was free to move as long as the change was made in good faith and was not unreasonable. The burden of proof was placed on the non-custodial parent opposing the relocation of the child to establish that the move was either unreasonable or being undertaken for the purposes of denying him access.

The position of the Court of Appeal in Ontario, in its 1995 decision in *MacGyver v. Richards,*[8] marked a jurisprudential high point in Canada of the presumptive right of custodial parents to move with their children.[9] Justice Abella, in delivering the judgment of the Court in *MacGyver v. Richards*, agreed that the overriding consideration in child-related disputes is the best interests of the child, but held that the views of the custodial parent are entitled to "presumptive deference" and "overwhelming respect" in determining what are the child's best interests. Justice Abella wrote:

> Deciding what is best for a child is uniquely delicate. . .
>
> The speculative nature of the task clearly cannot absolve judges from responsibility for exercising their judgment about what, according to the

[7] 1973 CarswellOnt 148, 12 R.F.L. 200 (Ont. C.A.).

[8] 1995 CarswellOnt 90, 22 O.R. (3d) 481, 123 D.L.R. (4th) 562, 11 R.F.L. (4th) 432 (Ont. C.A.).

[9] In its 1990 decision in *Carter v. Brooks*, 1990 CarswellOnt 317, 2 O.R. (3d) 321, the Ontario Court of Appeal adopted a best interests approach without any presumptions, but that approach was overruled five years later in *MacGyver.*

> evidence, augurs best at that point for the balance of the childhood. It can, however, and should, in deciding the incidents of custody, give pause about the extent to which judges interpose themselves between the child and the parent responsible for exercising, on a daily basis, the kind of judgment a judge is called upon to make only once. . .
>
> This argues, it seems to me, for particular sensitivity and a presumptive deference to the needs of the responsible custodial parent who, in the final analysis, lives the reality, not the speculation, of decisions dealing with the incidents of custody. . .
>
> In this facilitative, rehabilitative model, the custodial parent must be understood as bearing a disproportionate amount of responsibility. The reality and constancy of that responsibility cannot be said to be the same as the responsibilities imposed on the parent who exercises access and sees the child intermittently. During those days or hours when parents without custody are not with their child, they are largely free to conduct their lives in any way they choose. (Paras. 29-33)

Justice Abella concluded that the promotion of the well-being of the custodial parent by allowing a move should generally be given priority to a child than having frequent contact with the non-custodial parent:

> Custody is an enormous undertaking which ought to be preeminently recognized by the courts in deciding disputed issues incidental to that custody, including mobility. The right or wish to see a child every weekend or two may be of genuine benefit to a child; but it cannot begin to approach the benefit to a child of someone who takes care of him or her every day. The scales used to weigh a child's best interests are not evenly balanced between two parents when one is an occasional and the other a constant presence. (Para. 34)

Although Abella J.A. (as she then was) did not articulate an absolute legal rule in favour of the custodial parent, this decision established that the non-custodial parent had the onus of demonstrating to the court that the custodial parent was acting in an unreasonable fashion in seeking to relocate with the child and that the move would impair the child's best interests. The Court of Appeal held that "mere impairment of access" was not enough to satisfy the burden. If the non-custodial parent was unable to satisfy the onus, then the court would not examine the motive for the move. Thompson (2004) reports that the Ontario courts approved moves in ten of the eleven cases in the year following *MacGyver v. Richards*.

In many American states in the 1990s there was also a presumption in favour of allowing a custodial parent move with a child, often with a focus on the "rights" of custodial parents. This "rights" based approach was exemplified in the 1996 California decision of *In Re*

Marriage of Burgess,[10] where the state Supreme Court held that that a custodial parent had the right to change the residence of a child, subject to the power of the court to prohibit a move if satisfied that such a move would prejudice the rights or welfare of the child. Although a number of states have moved away from this rights based approach, the courts in a few states, such as Wyoming[11] continue to have a presumption in favour of the right of the custodial parent to relocate with the children, unless there was clear evidence that the move would have a detrimental effect on the children. Conversely there are a few American states such as North Dakota, where legislation, typically enacted due to pressure from father's rights groups, requires a custodial parent to obtain judicial permission to relocate the child if the access parent does not consent to the move. As observed by the North Dakota Supreme Court, this statute is intended "to safeguard the visitation rights of the non-custodial parent, and to thereby maintain and promote the parent-child relationship. . . the burden of proof is on the custodial parent to show that removal of the child is consistent with the best interests of the child."[12]

Canadian courts, along with those in many American states, have moved to a more flexible child-focused approach—a best interests test—to determine the issue of relocation. In its 1996 decision in *Gordon v. Goertz*,[13] the Supreme Court of Canada rejected the idea that there should be presumptions in these cases, with McLachilin J. writing that:

> The [*Divorce Act*] contemplates individual justice. The judge is obliged to consider the best interests of the particular child in the particular circumstances of the case. Had Parliament wished to impose general rules at the expense of individual justice, it could have done so. It did not.

The Supreme Court suggested that "the custodial parent's reason for moving" should be considered "only in the exceptional case where it is relevant to that parent's ability to meet the needs of the child." While that particular statement has largely been ignored by Canadian judges, since *Gordon v. Goertz,* courts in this country have adopted a best interests approach to relocation cases, without any presumptions.

---

[10] 913 P.2d 473 (Ca., 1996).

[11] *Watt v. Watt*, 971 P.2d 608 (Wyo., 1999).

[12] See *Stout v. Stout,* 560 N.W.2d 903 (N.D., 1997).,

[13] 1996 CarswellSask 199, [1996] 2 S.C.R. 27, 134 D.L.R. (4th) 321, 19 R.F.L. (4th) 177 (S.C.C.).

A similar best interests approach was adopted in the 1996 New York Court of Appeals decision in *Tropea v. Tropea*,[14] where the Court held that "all the relevant facts and circumstances" must be considered in deciding the issue of relocation. Unlike *Gordon v. Goertz*, however, the Court in *Tropea* (like all American courts that have adopted this approach) explicitly stated that the reason for the move as one of the relevant factors in deciding the child's best interests. In its 2004 decision in *In re Marriage of LaMusga*,[15] the California court grappled with determining the appropriate criteria to apply in deciding a relocation case. *Amicus curiae* briefs prepared by leading mental health professionals were presented on both sides of the case. On the side of the mother, who wanted to relocate, were those advocating that the well-being of the primary caregiver was the best way to promote the well-being of children. On the side supporting the position of the father were briefs arguing that the issue of relocation should be decided on the basis of the best interests of the child without any presumptions. The California court ultimately favoured a best interests approach, determining that each case must be dealt with based on its own facts, and stating that "bright-line rules in this area are inappropriate"[16] as these types of cases are not amenable to inflexible rules.

The *Gordon v. Goertz* case and the best interests test have been criticized for being vague and promoting uncertainty. However, since the decision was rendered in 1996, the Supreme Court of Canada has refused to hear appeals from court of appeal decisions in a number of relocation cases. In Chapter 2, we will more fully review the factors that Canadian courts consider important in making best interests based decisions about relocation. While there are trends that are apparent in the case law, it must also be recognized that this is a highly discretionary area of judicial decision-making, which makes it difficult to predict how individual judges will deal with specific cases. The difficulty in predicting outcomes also makes the settlement of these cases more difficult.

The Impact of Parental Separation on Children: An Overview

A review of the literature clearly shows that parental separation increases the risk for adjustment difficulties in children and adolescents compared with their counterparts who have parents who con-

---

14 87 N.Y.2d 727, 665 N.E.2d 145, 642 N.Y.2d 575 (C.A., 1996).

15 32 Cal. (4th) 1072 (2004).

16 *Ibid.*, at 1090, para. 91

tinuously reside together (Amato, 2001; Amato & Gilbreth, 1999; Clarke-Stewart, Vandell, McCartney, Owen & Booth, 2000; Hetherington, Bridges & Insabella, 1998; Kelly & Emery, 2003; Leon, 2003; McLanahan, 1999). Further, the adjustment patterns of children whose parents are separated and live as single parents are similar to those whose parents repartner (Amato & Keith, 1991; Furstenberg & Cherlin, 1991; Cherlin, *et al.*, 1991). Summarizing the literature in broad strokes, children from separated, divorced and remarried families are more likely to exhibit cognitive limitations, poorer academic achievement, and psychological maladjustment, including externalizing (i.e., acting out, conduct problems, aggression) and internalizing (i.e., depression, anxieties and phobias) problems. Social difficulties with siblings, peers and parents, along with poor self-concepts and self-esteem, are more common than for children from intact families. Unlike findings relating to the negative effects on older children and adolescents, those relating to younger children are less consistent, with some studies reporting greater risk (Zill, Morrison & Coiro, 1993) and others reporting less to younger children (Amato & Keith, 1991).

Studies also show that adolescents from separated and divorced families are more likely to exhibit difficulties, including delinquent behaviour, substance abuse, and higher school-dropout rates (Adam & Chase-Lansdale, 2002; Kelly, 2000). They are also more likely than those from two-parent families to become sexually active at an earlier age and to have children while unmarried (Carlson, 2006; Kelly, 2000; Menning, 2006; Stewart, 2003).

Retrospective and longitudinal studies of adults who experienced parental divorce during childhood, compared with those from continuously married families, showed that the former also scored lower on various indices relating to educational attainment, psychological adjustment, and interpersonal functioning (Amato & Cheadle, 2005; Hetherington, Bridges & Insabella, 1998; Wallerstein, Lewis & Blakeslee, 2000). In addition, studies of adult children of separation and divorce indicate less satisfaction with life, lower socio-economic attainment, a greater likelihood of being on welfare, less marital stability and higher divorce rates—up to 70 per cent—in the first five years of marriage for adult women from divorced families (Bumpass, Martin & Sweet, 1991). Remarkably, marital discord and divorce may be transmitted not only to the second generation, but also to the third (Amato & Cheadle, 2005).

The literature consistently indicates that about 20 to 25 per cent of children and adolescents from separated and divorced families have significant social and emotional problems compared with about 10 per cent of those from non-divorced families, the former being twice as likely to be at risk for psychosocial difficulties (Amato & Cheadle,

2005; Hetherington, Bridges & Insabella, 1998; Leon, 2003). However, this leaves the majority (about 75 to 80 per cent) of children whose parents have separated functioning well and without significant long term adjustment difficulties, a finding consistent with the initial writing of Wallerstein (initially with Kelly), who reported positive adjustment for 70 per cent of the children in her sample (though inconsistent with the arguments Wallerstein provided in her brief in *Burgess* (see also Wallerstein & Tanke, 1996) and then later in *LaMusga*, both of which are discussed later in this chapter.)

Notwithstanding the increased risk observed through many studies, debate exists regarding the extent and severity (i.e., the effect size) of these adjustment difficulties (Amato, 2003). Overall, differences between divorced and non-divorced groups remain relatively small. In addition, considerable overlap exists between the two groups, indicating notable variability (individual differences within groups) in children's responses (Amato & Keith, 1991; Hetherington, Bridges & Insabella, 1998). In other words, many children from divorced families do well, while many of those in non-divorced families have adjustment difficulties (Emery, 1999b).

Making sense of these studies is difficult because the impact of separation and divorce is complex. Few, if any, studies have simultaneously considered all of the variables accounting for this complexity. More specifically, outcomes are influenced by the various concomitant social, community and relationship changes (stressors) that accompany separation and divorce, along with the relocation (Amato & Cheadle, 2005; Kelly, 1994; Kelly & Emery, 2003; Leon, 2003). Austin (2008a) notes that a review of the literature indicates that outcomes relating to children's adjustment are explained mostly by moving and economic changes, primarily for mothers, with other factors contributing to a lesser degree. These other non-economic changes have been referred to as a "loss of social capital" (Coleman, 1990), a sociological concept that includes emotional and social supports and resources, such as parents, siblings, extended family, school, community groups and so on. McLanahan and Sandefur (1994) note that parental separation creates a temporary loss in social capital, while relocation places the child at risk for a further reduction in social capital (Austin, 2008a). Further, the impact of change and stressors is cumulative, not additive (Hodges, 1984; Rutter, 1979), a finding especially important to take into account in relocation cases where there are likely to be more, and different, changes than in a separation where no move is contemplated.

Additionally, changes in a custodial parent's psychological adjustment, emotional stability, and parenting effectiveness have been shown to have an impact on children's adjustment (Hetherington,

Cox & Cox, 1985; Pruett *et al.*, 2003). Re-partnering is also an important factor related to post-separation adjustment, with reports indicating that as many as two-thirds of the children whose parents separate will have a step-parent in their lives at some time (Ahrons, 2007; King, 2006). To varying degrees, child-specific factors affect adjustment as well. These include the child's gender, age at separation, temperament and adaptability. Children with easy temperaments are more adaptable and likely to cope better with stress than those with "difficult" temperaments, including that associated with separation and divorce (Hetherington & Kelly, 2002; Rutter, 1979).

Separation and divorce are not random events, but rather occur in families where there is likely to have already been a relatively high degree of marital discord. Longitudinal studies indicate that many of the reported difficulties experienced by children existed before the parents' separation, suggesting that adjustment problems may be due to factors other than the separation or divorce *per se* (Amato & Booth, 1996; Amato & Keith, 1991; Cherlin *et al.,* 1991; Hetherington, Bridges & Insabella, 1998; Kelly & Emery, 2003). In particular, before a separation, such children may have been exposed to parental stress and conflict, parenting deficiencies, or mental health problems. Conversely, a child's pre-existing emotional and behavioural problems may contribute, in part, to their parents' marital problems and subsequent separation.

Factors Mediating Adjustment to Divorce

Parental Conflict

The short- and long-term negative effects of parental conflict on child, adolescent and adult adjustment in divorced and continuously married families are well-documented (Amato, 2000; Amato & Afifi, 2006; Amato & Booth, 1996; Ayoub, Deutsch & Maraganore, 1999; Buchanan, Maccoby & Dornbusch, 1991; Cummings & Davis, 1994; Emery, 1999c; Grych, 2005; Hetherington & Kelly, 2002; Johnston & Roseby, 1997; Kline, Johnston & Tschann, 1991). More specifically, children raised in high-conflict, divorced and non-divorced families are at an increased risk for psychosocial adjustment problems compared with their counterparts in low-conflict, divorced and non-divorced families, indicating that it is the interparental relationship and not the marital status or structure of the family (mother-headed, father-headed, joint-custody) that is most predictive of outcome (Amato & Keith, 1991). Troxel and Matthews (2004) reported on a study which suggests that parental conflict and divorce can affect children's long-term physical health as well.

Research efforts to "unpack" parental conflict suggest that conflict alone is not necessarily harmful to children. As Kelly (2000) aptly notes, conflict between parents is common when trying to resolve important child-related matters. Moreover, while high levels of parental conflict are damaging for children, some parental conflicts may not be destructive, in particular parental conflicts that children are not aware of, or those that are appropriately resolved, may have no effect on them, or may even have positive effects (Grych, 2005). What is critical, then, is *how* parents express, manage and resolve their conflicts. Studies have found that the *quantity* and *frequency* of parental conflict is not as predictive of negative outcomes as is the *quality* (intensity and focus) of the conflict and *how* children are involved (Cummings & Davies, 1994; Grych, 2005; Johnston, 1994; Kelly, 2000; Kelly & Emery, 2003). However, as there is little empirical research differentiating levels of parental conflict or their corresponding impacts on children, it is difficult to know the extent to which conflict is harmful to children (Kelly, 2000). In other words, we cannot locate the precise tipping point or threshold at which conflict changes from being potentially helpful or having no negative impact to being harmful, but it is clear that higher levels of conflict increase risk.

More specifically, witnessing unresolved parental aggression and hostility (in particular that related to children) is a risk factor for children in both divorced and non-divorced families (Grych, 2005). Conflict can be overt or covert. In intact families, when children and adolescents are exposed to parents badmouthing each other, or are pressured to take sides—effectively caught in the middle and experiencing loyalty conflicts—they are more likely to be maladjusted than those who are not actively involved in parental conflict (Buchanan, Maccoby & Dornbusch, 1991; Grych, 2005; Johnston, 1993; Maccoby & Mnookin, 1992). Similar results have also been found relating to adults whose parents separated when they were children (Amato & Affifi, 2006).

Of further interest are findings which suggest that children exposed to high levels of marital conflict may do better after separation than those exposed to lower levels of conflict during the marriage (Amato & Cheadle, 2005; Amato, Loomis & Booth, 1995). These findings suggest that couples remaining together in a low-conflict, unhappy marriage may be better for children than divorcing, provided children are protected from parental conflict, but that in high conflict marriages, separation may improve long-term outcomes for the children.

Changes to the Parent-Child Relationship

Examining the impact of the previously mentioned family-process variables (i.e., parenting competency, quality of parent-child relationship, degree and nature of parental conflict, etc.), Pruett *et al.* (2003) report that neither parental conflict nor parent adjustment *directly* predicts children's post-separation behavioural problems. These researchers concluded that it was the impact of parental conflict *and* parent adjustment on the *parent-child relationship* that more directly predicted negative outcomes for children.

Losses and changes in the quality of children's relationships with *both* their mothers and their fathers are typical during separation or divorce, and these changes affect adjustment (Adam & Chase-Lansdale, 2002; Amato & Cheadle, 2005; Amato & Gilbreth, 1999; Kelly & Emery, 2003; Leon, 2003). Mothers, for example, may either return to work outside the home or work more, thus spending less time with their children and having less opportunity than previously to provide them with guidance and supervision (Hetherington & Kelly, 2002). Maternal adjustment and symptomatology were found to be the best predictors of negative changes in the post-separation mother-child relationship (Hetherington & Kelly, 2002; Pruett *et al.*, 2003).

In their study of a sample of adolescent girls, Adam and Chase-Lansdale (2002) found that as the number of separations from parent figures increased, scores on an adjustment index measuring cognitive, emotional, academic, and behavioral well-being declined significantly. Separations from both mothers and fathers were independently and significantly related to the girls' patterns of adjustment. Separations from temporary (less than two years) and long-term (more than two years) caregivers, and especially those occurring during early and middle childhood or adolescence, had significant negative effects on adjustment. The effects of separations were independent of family demographics and the quality of current relationships with parents and peers, as well as of neighbourhood environments.

Children of divorce will do reasonably well if they have a good relationship with one consistent caregiver (Kelly & Emery, 2003). Further, the research findings consistently show that children in both divorced and non-divorced families are better off psychologically and developmentally when they have warm and positive relationships with two involved parents and where the children's exposure to parental conflict is low (Amato, 2000; Amato & Gilbreth, 1999; Amato, Loomis & Booth, 1995; Dunn, Cheng, O'Connor & Bridges, 2004; Emery, 1988; Hetherington & Kelly, 2002; Hetherington, Bridges & Insabella, 1998; Lamb, 1999, 2002; Lamb, Sternberg & Thompson, 1997; Selzer, 1994). Having good relationships with two involved parents mitigates the negative effects of divorce (Kelly & Emery, 2003; Maccoby & Mnookin, 1992).

Father Absence and Involvement

The frequency, consistency and quality of contact with non-custodial parents—usually fathers—is another important factor that affects outcomes for some children after divorce (Amato & Gilbreth, 1999; King, 1994; Dunn, Cheng, O'Connor & Bridges, 2004). Examining the role fathers play in children's lives, and the possible impact if fathers are absent, is key to understanding the impact of relocation on children. Earlier studies in the 1970s began to address the importance of the post-separation role of fathers,[17] although many of these studies lacked refinement and had methodological weaknesses (i.e., mother reports only), making it difficult to come to definitive conclusions. Over the past few decades, the research has become more sophisticated and in turn produced some noteworthy findings most relevant not only to the impact of separation and divorce on children, but also to the possible impacts of relocation.

It is not uncommon for children to have less regular or frequent contact with their fathers, who often become less involved in their day-to-day care, after separation (Kelly & Emery, 2003). The effects of father loss in such circumstances are greater than the effects of father absence due to parental death (Amato & Keith, 1991). Not surprisingly, studies have found that the level of parental conflict predicts father involvement, with lower levels associated with greater father involvement (Kelly, 2000; Pruett *et al.*, 2003; Whiteside & Becker, 2000).

While there has been a growing recognition of the vital role that non-custodial fathers play in the post-divorce adjustment of children and adolescents (Clarke-Stewart & Hayward, 1996; Amato & Gilbreth, 1999; Hetherington, Cox & Cox, 1982), some have questioned the extent of the importance of fathers, as the frequency of contact alone has not been found to be a good predictor of adjustment or father-child closeness (Buchanan, Maccoby & Dornbusch, 1996; King, 1994; King & Heard, 1999; Whiteside & Becker, 2000). These findings were relied upon by Wallerstein and her colleagues to support claims for a presumption in favour of the custodial parent who wishes to relocate (Wallerstein, 1995; Wallerstein & Tanke, 1996), and more generally, to argue against joint custody.

Studies from the early 1980s indicate that as many as 50 per cent of fathers had no contact with their children two to three years after

[17] See Biller (1993) and Lamb (1997).

divorce, while more recent research suggests that by the middle to late 1990s there was an increase of involvement by non-custodial fathers, so that only 18 and 26 per cent of fathers lost all contact with their children two to three years after divorce (Furstenberg, Nord, Peterson & Zill, 1983; Maccoby & Mnookin, 1992; Smyth, 2005). Commentators have noted that findings indicating a weak statistical association between the frequency of father contact and outcomes are not surprising, given the significant changes in fathers' involvement in parenting in both divorced and non-divorced families since the 1970s and 1980s, when much of the data reported in these early studies were collected (King, 2006; Warshak, 1992, 2000b).

Amongst other considerations is the reality that frequency of father contact does not reflect the quality of parenting or the duration (length) of each contact (Kelly, 2007). As previously noted, methodological limitations are also likely to contribute to findings showing a weak relationship between frequency of contact and positive outcomes, as important variables, such as remarriage and the presence of a stepfather, are less frequently studied (Ahrons, 2007; King, 2006; White & Gilbreth, 2001).

Similar to findings related to parental conflict, it is the *quality* and *consistency* of non-custodial father's involvement and the *types* of activities during visits, not the *frequency or duration* of contact, that are most relevant when assessing short- and long-term outcomes (Simons & Conger, 2007; Stewart, 2003). Earlier studies relied on non-specific measures of father involvement, which is likely to explain, in part, the lack of findings in this regard. In their meta-analysis of 63 studies, Amato and Gilbreth (1999) found a positive impact on children's adjustment when non-residential parents remain actively involved, are competent, and provide authoritative parenting. These findings are consistent with earlier research, unrelated to divorce, on the effects of different types of parenting practices (Baumrind, 1971)[18] and to more recently reported results from longitudinal studies (Dunn *et al.*, 2004; King & Sobolewski, 2006; Sobolewski & King, 2005). Vogel, Bradley, Raikes, Boller and Shears (2007) found that outcomes are more positive for children whose non-resident parents remained involved compared with those who had unstable and

[18] Using the dimension of parental control, Baumrind (1971) identifies three styles of parenting: permissive (indulgent); authoritative; and authoritarian. This was expanded by Maccoby and Martin (1983), who added responsiveness as a second dimension. Parents who are high on both dimensions are categorized as authoritative. Warmth and support with enforcement of rules and use of consequences when necessary characterize these parents. Studies consistently indicate that children do better when parented with an authoritative style of parenting compared with an authoritarian or permissive style.

transient relationships with non-resident parents, a finding that may be especially relevant to relocation cases. More specifically, active, involved and competent parenting, coupled with good and close father-child relationships, have been associated with fewer internalizing and externalizing problems, lower school-dropout rates, and higher academic achievement (Carlson, 2006; Dunn *et al.*, 2004; Hetherington, Bridges & Insabella, 1998; King & Sobolewski, 2006; Maccoby & Mnookin, 1992; Menning, 2006).

As is the case with parental conflict, more recent studies have begun to "unpack" father involvement. Elements of parental involvement include: (a) emotional closeness; (b) monitoring and discipline; (c) communication; (d) guidance; (e) social, recreational; and (f) school and education. King and Sobolewski (2006) studied dimensions of non-resident father involvement, including how important the father appears to be in the child's life, how often the father considers the child's viewpoint and explains reasons for parental decisions, and how likely the child would be to talk to the father if the child were depressed. These dimensions were associated with positive social, academic and behavioural adjustment. The researchers note that while leisure activities constitute contact—even warm and supportive contact—such activities may not allow sufficiently for the responsive and authoritative parenting practices linked to positive child outcomes. Others have also reported that leisure activities alone do not have an impact on child adolescent adjustment (Amato & Gilbreth, 1999; Stewart, 2003).

A recent American study, which relied on two waves of data collected in the middle to late 1990s by the National Longitudinal Study of Adolescent Health (Menning, 2006), found that non-resident fathers' involvement which increased over time, especially through discussion of schoolwork, grades and other activities at school, predicted less school failure and better academic performance among adolescents. A national survey of close to 17,000 children reported that non-resident father involvement in children's schools, especially for those in grades six through 12, is likely to reduce suspensions, expulsions, and grade repetition (Nord, Brimhall & West, 1997). Similar findings relating to the importance of fathers in the school lives of their children has been reported by others (Carlson, 2006; Clarke-Stewart & Hayward, 1996; Simons & Conger, 2007).

Although the quality of contact is more predictive of child outcomes than frequency or duration, some time is needed after a divorce to provide opportunities for parenting and for developing and keeping healthy and long-lasting relationships between fathers and their children (Kelly & Emery, 2003; King & Sobolewski, 2006). Contact, then, is necessary but not sufficient to ensure a positive impact on children's adjustment to parental separation.

Of further interest, Menning (2006) reported that adolescents whose parents have separated and who are completely uninvolved with their fathers might fare better than those who experience low or even moderate levels of involvement. These results may support findings indicating that parental conflict and other dynamics relating to the parents' relationship are important risk/resiliency factors. Other studies report that when parental conflict is low, frequent and regular contact is associated with more positive adjustment for children (Amato & Rezac, 1994; Carlson, 2006; Wallerstein & Kelly, 1980), while in high-conflict situations frequent contact is associated with poor adjustment (Buchanan, Maccoby & Dornbush, 1991; Johnston, 1995b).

However, Fabricius and Luecken (2007) found that young adults who had more time with their non-resident fathers had better long-term relationships, irrespective of the level of parental conflict. More specifically, more time with fathers was beneficial to children in both high- and low-conflict conditions, while more exposure to parental conflict was harmful (i.e., distress about their parents' divorce and quality of relationship with father), irrespective of the amount of time—little or great—with fathers. In addition, they concluded that these negative effects were associated with poorer physical health in young adults. These researchers suggest that the combined effect of high conflict and minimal time with fathers is likely to be more of a risk factor for long-term physical problems than either one of these factors alone.

Fabricius and Luecken (2007) emphasize the challenge these findings present for policies that are based on the simple conclusion that a high level of parental conflict warrants minimal contact with the non-custodial parent, usually the father. In the view of these researchers, this conclusion ignores the more complex interplay between two important variables—parental conflict and time with the non-custodial parent. They suggest that while having less time may lower conflict and thus counter any impact of high conflict, the benefits of reduced conflict might be cancelled out by less time with the non-custodial parent. They further note studies reporting that conflict dissipates over time, while compromised relationships between divorced fathers and their children continue into adulthood.

In addition, advocating for minimal contact in the face of higher levels of parental conflict assumes that more time with the non-custodial parent necessarily means more exposure to high conflict. This is not always the case.

Another consideration relevant to outcomes in separation and divorce in general, and to relocation specifically, is that a good and close relationship with the less involved, non-custodial parent may buffer the impact of a compromised relationship with the custodial parent resulting from marginal parenting or mental illness, like depression (Kelly & Emery, 2003; King & Sobolewski, 2005; Hetherington & Kelly, 2002). Similar findings have been reported in married families (Simons & Conger, 2007). More specifically, a poor mother-child relationship, accompanied by strong ties to the non-custodial father, are associated with fewer internalizing problems and less acting out in school compared with those who have weaker ties with both parents. A child living with the less emotionally healthy custodial parent in a relocation case may be at greater risk when the potential buffering effects provided by a non-custodial parent are less accessible.

Notwithstanding the small effect size (differences between the children of separated and intact families) and the resiliency of the majority of children who experience separation, children's expressions of loss and longing for more time with their fathers, as well as feelings of loss of control, are reported both at the time of separation and years later in retrospective accounts of young adults (Ahrons & Tanner, 2003; Amato, 1987; Fabricius & Hall, 2000; Fabricius, 2003; Hetherington, Cox & Cox, 1982; Laumann-Billings & Emery, 2000; Parkinson, Cashmore & Single, 2005; Parkinson & Smyth, 2004; Wallerstein & Kelly, 1980).

For example, Fabricius and Hall (2000) report on a study of university students in an introductory psychology course at a large southwestern state university. The sample of those whose parents had separated included 344 male and 485 female participants, with an average age of 20 at time of testing. Eighty per cent of the students reported living primarily with their mothers, eight per cent equally with each parent, and 12 per cent primarily with their fathers. The results indicated that 70 per cent of the respondents wished they had spent more time with their non-custodial parents, believing that equal or near-equal time would have been preferable to what they had experienced while growing up. Only seven per cent of those living primarily in their mother's custody felt that their mothers had wanted them to spend equal amounts of time with each parent, whereas 44 per cent reported that their fathers had wanted them to live equally with each parent. Similar sentiments were reported by those who had and those who did not have an equal-time residential schedule, a result the researchers stated shows that the findings are not due to the student reports being influenced by the "grass is always greener" phenomena. The 30 per cent who did not want equal time believed children should have a substantial number of overnights with the non-custodial parent. Those who spent more time with their fathers felt closer to them, perceived more emotional support from their fathers, as well as receiving more financial support from their fathers. Fabricius and Hall (2000) replicated these results in a second sample of low-income young adults not attending college, suggesting wider applicability of their findings.

Other studies of post-separation adult children similarly report that those who had more time with their fathers felt closer to them, perceived more emotional support, had less intense feelings of loss and abandonment (Laumann-Billings & Emery, 2000), and received more financial support from them (Fabricius, Braver & Deneau, 2003). In addition, studies indicate an association between payment of child support and positive child outcomes (Fabricius, Braver & Deneau, 2003; Selzer, 1994). Young adults who had less time with their fathers reported more painful and negative memories, coupled with feelings of blame towards themselves for the divorce, and anger towards their mothers, whom they blamed for their having had insufficient time with their fathers. The more time children had with their fathers, the closer they felt to them. Fabricius (2003) notes that adolescents who felt closer to their non-custodial fathers also felt closer to their custodial mothers, reinforcing the evidence that the relationship the child has with one parent is intertwined with the relationship he or she has with the other parent.

Schwartz and Finley (2005) and Finley and Schwartz (2007) reported similar findings in their study of 1,989 ethnically diverse American university students whose parents had separated. The fathering variables studied were nurturing involvement, expressive involvement, instrumental involvement, and mentoring/advising involvement. The young adults from divorced families indicated less nurturing by and involvement with their fathers compared to those from the non-divorced group. Furthermore, consistent with other research, the majority of those from divorced families expressed a desire for more father involvement than they had received, and in particular for more instrumental involvement (i.e., day-to-day tasks, discipline, monitoring schoolwork, and protection). The researchers note that determining parenting time schedules for children and adolescents of divorce needs to take into account the "voices" of young adults from several studies revealing sentiments of "emotional longing" and "missed opportunities" where their fathers are concerned.

Smith, Taylor and Tapp (2003) reported that while about half (52 per cent) of the children whom they interviewed thought the frequency of time with their non-custodial parent was "just right", the other half wanted to see that parent "more often" (34.7 per cent) or "a lot more often" (11 per cent). These researchers noted that children valued "affection, emotional support and their parents taking an interest and an active involvement in their lives in meaningful ways". Sources of the children's anger and hurt included resentment for the non-residential parent's lack of involvement in their lives and feelings of rejection.

On one end of the spectrum writers maintain that children of separation and divorce are overwhelmingly resilient and fare reasonably well (Hetherington & Kelly, 2002; Kelly & Emery, 2003), while on the other end, reports indicate that these children are at substantial risk (Wallerstein, Lewis & Blakeslee, 2000). In an effort to reconcile the opposing perspectives on children's adjustment after divorce, Emery (2004) notes that notwithstanding their resiliency, retrospective reports of adults whose parents were separated reveal feelings of substantial and continuing distress and pain, thereby indicating that pain and resilience are not mutually exclusive (Laumann-Billings & Emery, 2000). These writers assert that while pain is important to consider and address, it is not necessarily equivalent to pathology. Emery believes that the divergent results are an artifact of different research paradigms and varying methodology. More specifically, the empirical mental health measures tend to overlook emotional pain, while the clinical measures tend to emphasize pain and overlook positive functioning.

Kelly (2003) also observes that the presence of painful feelings about divorce have been interpreted—and in her view sometimes misinterpreted—as pathology. She notes that children will necessarily face challenges and adversity, and it is in fact such experiences that will assist them in learning how to cope more effectively with life.

Gatekeeping and Support of the Child's Relationship with the Other Parent

A good and cooperative relationship between custodial mothers and non-custodial fathers is associated with more and better quality father involvement and, in turn, positive outcomes, including feelings of closeness to their fathers, in children, adolescents, and adult children of divorce (Ahrons & Tanner, 2003; Aquilino, 2006; Buchanan, Maccoby & Dornbush, 1996; Maccoby & Mnookin, 1992; Pruett *et al.*, 2003; Sobolewski & King, 2005; Whiteside & Becker, 2000). Consistent with the studies of maternal gatekeeping[19] in intact families,

[19] Mothers are typically identified as the gatekeepers, given their primary role in caring for children (see Pleck (1997)). Gatekeeping refers to attitudes and behav-

where the more mothers perceive fathers as incompetent, the more they exhibit gatekeeping behaviours (Allen & Hawkins, 1999; Fagan & Barnett, 2003), positive maternal attitudes toward fathers involvement are associated with better child adjustment (Pruett *et al.*, 2003). When fathers feel the support of the children's mothers, they are more likely to be involved, develop parenting competence, and remain involved in their children's lives (Buchanan, Maccoby & Dornbusch, 1996; Maccoby & Mnookin, 1992; Pruett *et al.*, 2003). When fathers do not feel marginalized as parents and spend more time with their children, they are more likely to remain committed to their children, not only in terms of emotional and practical involvement but also through financial contributions (Aquilino, 2006; Fabricius, Braver & Deneau, 2003; Gunnoe & Braver, 2001; Maccoby & Mnookin, 1992). Furthermore, fathers who remain involved at the time of separation are more likely to remain involved than fathers who are not as involved when separation occurs (King, 1994; King & Heard, 1999; Juby, Le Bourdais & Marcil-Gratton, 2005). Evidence of restrictive gatekeeping is an especially important factor in relocation cases, given that in the event of a move it will be challenging to maintain the child's relationship with the non-moving parent in the best of circumstances, let alone when one parent is attempting to keep the child from the other parent. We will return to this discussion more fully in Chapter 2.

In summary, the literature shows that father involvement in the lives of their children is as important as the role of mothers. Therefore, long-distance relationships pose challenges for the father-child relationship just as it does for the mother-child relationship. At a minimum, long-distance relationships diminish the ability of a parent to be involved in the child's life on a day-to-day basis, to participate in school events (i.e., recitals, practices, games), help with school projects, attend parent-teacher meetings, or provide emotional support. Moreover, the child loses the influence related to the role that gender plays in parenting.

Development of Attachment

The literature on attachment provides another window through which we can examine the impact of relocation on children, especially younger ones. Reviewing the extant literature, Kelly and Emery (2003) conclude that children can and do form multiple attachments, some as early as six months of age, even when they have spent con-

---

iours that either facilitate or restrict the other parent's opportunity to parent and develop close relationships with their children.

siderably more or less time with one caregiver than the other. Still, contact is needed for attachment, which develops over time. A preference for one caregiver, especially in times of stress and illness (i.e., sometimes referred to as a hierarchy of attachments), is common. This preference for a particular caregiver usually dissipates by the time the child is about 18 months old (Kelly & Lamb, 2003). In addition, while there may be a preferred parent, the other attachment figures continue to be sought out to fulfill the child's social and emotional needs.

The literature indicates that given a child's developing cognitive capacities, including their sense of time, space and the development of object permanency (the ability to hold images in the mind in the absence of the object), the young child requires frequent contacts of shorter duration with their caregivers (Kelly, 2007; Kelly & Lamb, 2000). As they mature and their attachments solidify, children can keep the absent parent present in their minds and tolerate longer absences without affecting the relationship. Still, transition difficulties (i.e., separation anxiety) are to be expected, especially when the child is attached to both parents. In these situations, the child who has a positive attachment can usually settle in reasonably soon after the transition has been made.

Consequently, attachment is more fragile in the early years, a point of particular relevance in relocation cases involving younger children (Kelly & Lamb, 2003). As one might expect, distance and face-to-face contact are strongly related—the greater the distance, the less contact there is (Maccoby & Mnookin, 1992). Furthermore, the greater the distance between the parents, the greater the time, effort and money required to facilitate ongoing parent-child contact. Given the central role of parents as attachment figures, and the distress that accompanies even short-term separations from important caregivers (Ainsworth, Blehar, Waters & Wall, 1978; Bowlby, 1969), a history of frequent separations from important parent figures may be particularly detrimental to a child's well-being (Adam & Chase-Lansdale, 2002).

Kelly and Lamb (2000) warn that repeated separations from a non-moving parent may weaken the developing attachments and furthermore may even extinguish those that exist. The negative, long-term effects of separation, coupled with repeated separations from a parent, may affect the development of security, independence, and self-esteem in a child. As previously discussed, risks related to feelings of loss, abandonment and rejection are evident, with the resolution of these issues affecting adult functioning, including the development of relationships (Fabricius, 2003; Fabricius & Hall, 2000; Laumann-Billings & Emery, 2000).

The risk to developing attachment and maintaining healthy relationships apply not only to the non-moving parent, but also to the custodial parent who moves, since the child may undergo repeated and often lengthy separations from that parent when the child spends extended time with the non-moving parent (Kelly & Lamb, 2003). In the face of insurmountable practical and economic circumstances, contacts/separations of longer durations from the custodial parent may be agreed to by the parents, recommended by assessors, and ordered by the court, despite being contraindicated from a developmental and attachment perspective.

Military, Migrant/Seasonal Workers and Professional Families

In assessing the potential impact of moving on children after separation or divorce, child custody assessors can draw on substantial research on children whose families have moved for other reasons. Taken as a whole, this literature indicates that children's emotional, academic, behavioural, and social adjustment is negatively impacted by repeated moves. "Children fear separation and abandonment, so moving recreates these fears" (Jalongo, 1994).

Research suggests that children can experience moving as a loss of their familiar surroundings, even if relocation does not involve great distances. Simpson and Fowler (1994) analyzed data from the 1988 National Health Interview Survey of Child Health, which included data on health and demographic characteristics, emotional and behavioural variables, school functioning, and geographic mobility for 10,362 school-aged children in the U.S. They concluded that a child who moves more than three times is at risk of experiencing behavioural or emotional problems and troubles at school. Haour-Knipe (1989) concludes that the emotional problems can stem from a sense of loss of a friend or familiar surroundings or from difficulties in adjusting to a new school or social ties. Diler, Avci and Seydaoglu (2003) surveyed 526 children (60 per cent of whom were boys, and 40 per cent girls), with an average age of 11.23, at five schools in Turkey; 182 of the children (35 per cent) were migrants and 344 (65 per cent) were non-migrants. They found that the migrant children had significantly lower self-esteem and higher depression and anxiety scores compared to their non-migrant counterparts.

Moving often means changing schools and, for a child, dealing with a new curriculum, set of academic standards, and peer network. Several studies reveal that children's academic performance suffers when they move frequently (Buerkle, 1997; Diler, Avci & Seydaoglu, 2003; Ingersoll, Scamman & Eckerling, 1989; Jalongo, 1994; Wood,

Halfon, Scarlata, Newacheck & Nessim, 1993). Rumberger (2003) concludes that moving not only affects the student involved, but affects the school setting. As a body, a class needs to adjust to students who come or go during the school year, potentially creating disruption and adjustment difficulties for the other children.

Simmon, Burgeson, Carlton-Ford and Blyth (1987) reported negative effects of geographic mobility of families when examining academic achievement among girls in sixth and seventh grade. Ingersoll, Scamman and Eckerling (1989) also reported negative effects of geographic mobility on student achievement. Buerkle (1997) found that children from non-mobile families have better attendance records compared with children who moved. Children who did not change schools attained better math scores than those who changed schools. Wood *et al.* (1993) found that 23 per cent of children who moved frequently had repeated a grade, compared with the 12 per cent who never or infrequently moved. Ingersoll, Scammer and Eckerling (1989) also found that academic achievement of the stable student population was consistently higher than that of mobile student populations. Haveman, Wolfe and Spaulding (1991) conducted a longitudinal study to explore the effects of a variety of childhood events on high school completion rates. They found that the number of moves made in childhood was negatively associated with a likelihood of not graduating from high school.

In addition to experiencing significant changes, which can be experienced as loss of one parent, children of separation and divorce also experience losses in relation to friends and social networks, some at a time when peer relationships are of developmental importance (Jalongo, 1994). For children who move, even in intact families, Haour-Knipe (1989) reports that the negative impact of losing old friends can be compounded by the fear of making new friends, both of these events occurring at the same time. Anderzen, Arnetz, Soderstrom and Soderman (1997) found evidence that children who travelled abroad suffered from a loss of identity because they were no longer connected to their usual social networks. As well, a reduction in extracurricular activities while they were abroad may have perpetuated feelings of social isolation in these children. In a study comparing 36 mobile and 37 non-mobile adolescents, Vernberg (1990) found that in the year following a move, the mobile students reported fewer contacts with friends and experienced less intimacy and sharing in their relationships with their new best friends than did their non-mobile counterparts. In addition, this study reported that males who moved experienced more rejection from peers than did their female counterparts. Swanson and Schneider (1999) maintain that disruptions in peer relationships can have serious negative implications throughout childhood and into adolescence. They further point out that when youths move late in high school for the potential benefits of residential and educational opportunities, these benefits tend to be counteracted by disruptions to social support networks in the home, neighbourhood and school.

Wood *et al.* (1993) completed a national study of 9,915 school-aged children, placing them in two groups based on parental reports of total number of moves experienced by the child: never or infrequent moves; and frequent moves. Results show a strong negative relationship between frequent moves and child dysfunction. Specifically, frequent movers were 77 per cent more likely to have four or more behavioural problems and 35 per cent more likely to have failed a grade. These findings are informative, as the researchers controlled for potentially confounding variables, including poverty, ethnicity, parental employment and education, urban or rural residence, the child's health status and gender, and family structure. Nelson, Simoni and Adelman (1996) reported that significantly more students who did not move or moved only once experienced fewer behavioural difficulties compared with students who moved two or more times.

In a study conducted to determine if geographic relocation had an impact on the onset of drug use and subsequent drug-related problems, DeWit (1998) obtained 3,700 surveys from young adults ranging in age from 18 to 35. He found that for most of the respondents, there was a steady increase in the prevalence of drug use and drug-related problems corresponding to an increasing number of childhood moves. He concluded that those who had moved as children were much more likely than non-movers to be introduced to drug use at an earlier age. The drugs included marijuana, hallucinogens, crack/cocaine, and prescribed drugs, but not alcohol.

As revealed in the literature regarding children of migrant workers and other families who move, significant short- and long-term consequences result for children emotionally, behaviourally, and academically because of not just one move but multiple moves. For children of separation and divorce, there is often at least one initial move as a result of parental separation, and negative effects as a result of a significant relocation are additional to the losses and other negative effects they may already be experiencing.

Literature Specific to Relocation in Post-Separation Families

Depending on the circumstances, relocation may have serious, long-lasting consequences for children and non-moving parents (Kelly & Lamb, 2003; Ricci, 1997). Gindes (1998) concludes that in both divorced and non-divorced families, relocation has both positive and negative effects on a child's overall adjustment. In non-divorced families, factors such as the distance and frequency of the moves, parental attitude toward the moves, children's prior adjustment, parental satisfaction and self-confidence, and any special needs of children should be considered when assessing the effects of a move on a child. In post-divorce families, factors such as a change in environment or school, and the custodial parent's (usually the mother's) starting or resuming work are all likely to affect a child's adjustment to one extent or another (Adam & Chase-Lansdale, 2002; Stolberg & Ankers, 1983; Stolberg, Camplair, Currier & Wells, 1987).

From the moment parents physically separate, there is a geographic distance between a child and the non-custodial parent, and their relationship changes qualitatively (Clarke-Stewart & Hayward, 1996). Austin (2008a) and Turkat (1996) posit that relocation poses a new problem because the physical distance between non-custodial parent and child can become a serious impediment to their relationship. While moves of a significant distance are likely to impact parent-child relationships, even moves of less than one hour travel time may have negative effects on children and their relationship to the non-custodial parent, depending on the reasons for the move, and the family circumstances and routines. Hetherington and Kelly (2002) reported that a move of 75 miles often was associated with the non-moving parent dropping out of their child's life. Shear (1996) argues that if parents live even twenty minutes apart, a child's life becomes fragmented in terms of spending time with the non-custodial parent; while this claim may seem extreme, such fragmentation is likely to occur with relocations one or more hours of travel away.

Residential moves following separation and divorce are common. Reports indicate that children of divorce, including step-families, move more frequently than those from non-divorced families (Hetherington & Kelly, 2002; McLanahan & Sandefur, 1994; Tucker *et al.*, 1998). Further, a first move by a custodial parent has been associated with repeated subsequent moves, with reports indicating that 50 per cent of those who move once will relocate again (Wood, *et al.*, 1993). Kelly and Lamb (2003) note that we do not have data on the number of moves—in other words, the threshold—that is likely to have an impact on a child's adjustment. Further, parents who choose to move and make significant changes in their lives may not be as well-adjusted to begin with and in turn are less sensitive to their children's needs (Kelly & Lamb, 2003). In some cases frequent moves may be due to economic or social conditions that are beyond the custodial parent's control but will impact negatively on their children.

Braver, Ellman and Fabricius (2003) conducted a retrospective survey—of which a subset of questions was related to separation/divorce—of over 2,000 American students enrolled in an introductory psychology course. This study was completed by 602 students, representing 29 per cent of the total sample, whose parents had divorced. More than half (61 per cent) reported having experienced at least one move of more than one hour's drive away from either their mother or their father. One quarter of the students had moved with their mothers away from their fathers, 26 per cent had stayed with their mothers when their fathers moved away, eight per cent had stayed with their fathers when their mothers moved away, and four per cent had moved with their fathers away from their mothers. Moves were common in the sole-custody families (70 to 75 per cent), while much less frequent in the joint legal custody families (48 per cent).

The results of this preliminary study indicated that a residential move from either parent—whether the result of moving away with one parent, or having a parent move away—were associated with negative outcomes on 11 of the 14 variables, including financial and emotional outcomes in adulthood, compared with those whose parents had remained in close proximity (Braver, Ellman & Fabricius, 2003). Specifically, children whose primary residence was more than an hour's drive from the non-custodial parent received less financial support from that parent while at university, worried more about that support, felt more anger, and experienced more distress about the divorce. In addition, these adult children rated their parents' relationships more negatively and perceived themselves as having poorer physical health, lower life satisfaction and poorer personal and emotional adjustment. They also felt that they received less emotional support from the distant parent, whether they had moved away from the parent or the parent had moved away from them.

These results are based on correlations and therefore do not allow us to make conclusions about causality (i.e., that a move caused negative consequences). In other words, it is possible that the results are due to the effects of the move itself, or to the predisposing factors associated with the move, such as premarital conflict or other family or individual dysfunctions. The researchers conclude:

> Ultimately, however, our data cannot establish with certainty that moves cause children substantial harm. They do allow us to say, however, that there is no empirical basis on which to justify a legal presumption that a move by a custodial parent to a destination she plausibly believes will improve her life will necessarily confer benefits on the children she takes with her (p. 215).

The researchers further argue that the onus to demonstrate that a move is beneficial for a child should probably lie with the custodial parent seeking to relocate, rather than with the objecting, non-custodial parent. Notwithstanding their acknowledgment of the various limitations of their study, these findings drew strong criticism from Wallerstein (2003).[20]

In a follow-up study to address these criticisms, Fabricius and Braver (2006) re-analyzed the data to see if the findings could be attributed to pre-existing levels of parental conflict or domestic violence. The results indicated that relocation was associated with negative outcomes when conflict and domestic violence, as reported by the grown children, were controlled. The researchers argued that their new findings supported the original recommendations as noted above (Braver, Fabricius & Ellman, 2003). They reiterated that relocation is a risk factor for children, separate from the risks associated with conflict and domestic violence, and further noted a tentative finding that moves reduced levels of parental conflict. Fabricius and Braver caution that moves may benefit mothers who have been victims of domestic violence.

Controversy in California: Primary Parent vs. Best Interests

In the United States, the controversy among clinicians and researchers in the mental health community about the effects of relocation on children spilled into the courts, as different professionals took sides in the dispute over the appropriate legal test for cases in which the custodial parent wants to move with the child and the non-custodial parent seeks to prevent the move. The controversy was especially intense in California; a consideration of the course of the debate is instructive for Canadian readers, and the *amicus curiae*[21]

[20] Bruch (2002) and Wallerstein *et al.* (2004) had each filed *amicus curiae* briefs, which in turn were met with rebuttal by Warshak *et al.* (2004), before the Supreme Court of the State of California in the case of the *Marriage of LaMusga*. We return to a discussion of these briefs later.

[21] It is a common practice in the United States for professionals and advocates with an interest in the outcome of an important appeal case to file *amicus curiae* [Latin for "friend of the court"] briefs with the court. These briefs summarize the views of those who prepare the briefs; the briefs are available from the courts and are often published or available on the internet. In Canada, the scope for non-parties to obtain "intervenor" status in important appeal cases is narrower than the scope for filing *amicus curiae* briefs in the USA. It is very rare for non-parties to obtain standing to intervene in custody cases in Canada, although this did occur in the leading case of *Gordon v. Goertz,* where the Ontario Office of the Children's Lawyer was given permission to intervene in a case from Saskatchewan; the Children's Lawyer ad-

briefs in those cases provide useful summaries of literature in this controversial area.

American psychologists Wallerstein and Tanke have been important advocates in the United States for a rebuttable presumption in favour of the custodial parent, usually the mother, who wants to move. They had some early success in influencing the California Supreme Court to adopt this position in its 1996 decision *In re Marriage of Burgess*,[22] and subsequently in New Jersey in the 2001 decision *Baures v. Lewis*.[23] Emphasizing the importance of the primary parent in the lives of children, both *Burgess* and *Baures* stand for the principle that, save for in joint physical custody situations, the primary custodial parent should have the right to change the residence of the child, subject to the power of the court to restrain a removal that would prejudice the rights or welfare of the child. The importance of the custodial parent, usually the mother, to the child's positive development and adjustment was emphasized in the writing of Wallerstein and her colleagues, while the value of the non-custodial parent, usually the father, was minimized.

The California Supreme Court, as noted earlier, essentially overturned the 1996 decision in *Burgess* eight years later in the 2004 decision *In re Marriage of LaMusga*.[24] The *amicus curiae* brief of Wallerstein and her supporters (Wallerstein *et al.*, 2004; see also Bruch, 2002) in *LaMusga* argued that the courts, in order to promote the welfare of children, should generally make their decisions in a manner that enhances the well-being of the primary caregiver.[25] With Richard Warshak (Warshak *et al.*, 2004; see also Warshak, 2000b) as the lead author, a multidisciplinary group of 18 social science researchers and 10 mental health forensic practitioners provided a consensual *amicus curiae* brief to the California Supreme Court, which rebutted the position of Wallerstein. Warshak *et al.* (2004) argued that the Wallerstein brief offered "a skewed and misleading account of the social science evidence" relevant to the case. They urged the

---

vocated for the adoption of a best interests test, a position accepted by the Court. In Canada, the term *amicus curiae* is different from in the USA; it refers to a lawyer appointed to present evidence and argument that would be helpful and is not otherwise available for the court, for example in a serious criminal case where the accused refuses to be represented by counsel and the judge wants to ensure that there is a fair trial.

22 *Supra*, at note 10.

23 *Baures v. Lewis*, 167 H.J. 91, 770 A.2d 214 (N.J., 2001).

24 *Supra*, at note 15.

25 In 2004, Wallerstein and five other mental health professionals (two psychiatrists, two psychologists and one registered nurse) also filed a brief in *LaMusga* in favour of the appellant mother, who wished to relocate with the children, and who had strained relations with their father.

court to adopt a "best interests" test to replace the rebuttable presumption in favour of the custodial parent. As previously noted, the California Supreme Court in *LaMusga* adopted a best interests approach, and that is now the dominant legal approach to relocation cases in North America, and is also followed in countries like England and Australia.

Of note, is that the views of Wallerstein and her colleagues, first in the *Burgess* brief and related article (Wallerstein & Tanke, 1996) and then in the *LaMusga* brief, were primarily based on a 25-year longitudinal study of 131 children from 60 divorced families. The results have been reported in various articles and three books (Wallerstein & Blakesee, 1989; Wallerstein, Lewis & Blakeslee, 2000; Wallerstein & Kelly, 1980). The children ranged from three to 18 years of age when the study began; many of them were re-interviewed over the years. Six of the sixty families relocated during the course of the study; out of the six mobile families, three mothers, and no fathers, were interviewed (Pasahow, 2005).

The Wallerstein group concluded that there is substantial risk to children of separation and divorce (see also Bruch & Bowmaster, 1996). These findings were then extrapolated to the circumstances of relocation. Based on retrospective self-report data, Wallerstein and Tanke (1996) maintained that a child's capacity for travel has limits, and that children should not be forced to spend their growing years in continual travel in order to visit a distant, non-custodial parent. Wallerstein and Lewis (1998) reported that many of the children found the visitation schedules with their fathers disruptive and inflexible, and consequently they received little enjoyment or benefit from the visitation. They concluded that the children neither needed nor wanted more time with their fathers, many of whom eventually dropped out of their lives in any case. In hindsight, as adults, they reported that their wishes should have been taken into account; they continued to remain angry and resentful about having their feelings disregarded. Wallerstein and Tanke (1996) concluded that the "guiding principle" in relocation cases should be to protect "the stability and integrity of the post-divorce family unit, in which the key relationship is the one between the child and their primary custodial parent" (p. 26).

Wallerstein and Lewis (1998) further reported that the results of their study were consistent whether custody and visitation arrangements were negotiated, mediated, or court-ordered. Further, the authors stated that the children of divorce, reporting as adults, would have been "astonished to learn that any judge, attorney, mediator, or indeed, anyone at all in the entire community had spent a moment considering their best interests or wishes" (p. 371). The authors concluded that their research demonstrates that a father-child relationship largely depends on the father's sense of success or failure in other parts of his life, and that those who had life troubles had difficulty maintaining regular contact with their children.

These remarks and conclusions are strong, especially given the significant limitations of the research upon which it is apparently based. Consequently, caution must be exercised when interpreting these data, both as they relate generally to the impact of separation and divorce, and more specifically to the impact of relocation on children. The methodological limitations of the study include the following: (1) the study sample size was small (60 families), clinical, and thus unrepresentative (counselling had been offered in exchange for participation); (2) there was no comparison group of non-divorced families; (3) there was only one joint-custodial family in the group; and (4) the data was limited to subjective reports using non-standardized measures. At the time of the legal brief provided to support a presumption in favour of the custodial parent's moving, there was not a single study reported in the literature, including that of Wallerstein, directly examining the effects of parental relocation on children.

Not surprisingly, the Wallerstein brief in *Burgess* met with strong objections. In an article critiquing her brief in that case, Warshak (2000b) reviewed more than 75 articles, including empirical and non-empirical studies as well as data pooled from numerous studies that examine the same issue and share similar methods (also referred to as meta-analyses). In addition to the methodological limitations previously mentioned, Warshak notes that Wallerstein cited only ten references supporting her brief, seven of which involved her own work. This is of significant concern given the plethora of relevant studies that also could have been cited and which Warshak went on to summarize.

Warshak provided specific examples in which information included in the Wallerstein brief, noting the damaging effects of separation and divorce on children, actually ignored or contradicted the author's own five- and 10-year follow-up data previously reported by her and her colleagues. Particularly telling were the statements in Wallerstein's work noting the importance of good father-child relationships, including regular and frequent contact, for positive child outcomes, and children's reports of loneliness, desire and intense longing for the non-custodial parent.

In assessing Wallerstein's work, it is important to recognize that fathers' involvement with their children has changed markedly since the 1970s when the first wave of the Wallerstein and Kelly (1980) data was collected (Amato, 2003; Emery, 2004; Warshak, 2000b). The weak findings about the effect of post-separation father involvement may have been due to limited pre- and post-separation engagement of fathers in the study compared to fathers in later studies (Furstenberg & Cherlin, 1991).[26] It is reasonable to expect that a father's impact on his children and their adjustment will be greater if the father is more, rather than less, involved with them, both during marriage and after separation, the former being more the case now than when Wallerstein undertook the research that she relied upon for her brief. A related point is that much of the earlier research about the effects of separation on children was based exclusively on the reports of mothers, giving incomplete and possibly biased perspectives relating to both mothers' and fathers' involvement with their children.

In a letter to the Chief Justice of the California Supreme Court prior to the arguing of *LaMusga*, Warshak[27] made the critical point that the emphasis on stability by Wallerstein ignores the child's reality when faced with a move; Warshak pointed out that permitting a custodial parent to move with a child does not promote "stability", given the inevitable environmental changes that will occur. Warshak states:

> First, although *Burgess* correctly underscored the importance of protecting children's critical psychological attachments, it is a mistake to assume that the maintenance of the legal status of the designated custody parent is equivalent to preserving the existing "environment" and custodial "arrangements." This fails to recognize the children's reality. From the children's vantage point, the existing environment and the existing custodial arrangements consist of their home with their mother and their home with their father and their experiences of each parent's involvement in their life. Any relocation necessarily alters the status quo and undermines the environment stability as far as the child is concerned (p. 2).

While controversy continues among advocates and mental health professionals about the effects of relocation, courts in Canada and most American states have adopted the "best interests" approach. As will be discussed further in Chapter 2, in theory, courts adopting this approach have no presumptions in relocation cases, but it would appear that in the years since the Supreme Court of Canada adopted

---

26 Citing McLanahan and Sanefur (1994), Austin (2008b) notes that studies have uncovered two groups—involved and uninvolved fathers. Averaging results from the two groups may make it seem like there was no effect to father involvement.

27 Letter Re: *In re Marriage of LaMusga* to Chief Justice, Honorable Ronald M. George, dated July 10, 2002.

this approach, courts in this country have tended to more closely scrutinize applications to allow relocation, and have been somewhat less inclined to allow custodial parents to move if this will undermine a strong and healthy relationship of the child with the other parent.

Relocation in Violent and High-Conflict Cases

Some families remain embroiled in conflict many years after a couple's separation, which can result in a custodial parent wanting to move away, while for others, the desire to move precipitates conflict in what was an otherwise reasonably amicable parental relationship. In a high-conflict situation, one parent may want to move in order to keep the child from the other parent; in other situations, parents may understandably want to move to ensure safety and to absent themselves from ongoing domestic violence.

When children have a distant or disturbed relationship with a non-resident parent, or there is ongoing domestic violence, deficient parenting, a mentally ill parent, or a substance-abusing parent, a move away from such a parent, thereby minimizing risk, may well be in the child's best interest (Fabricius & Braver, 2006; Kelly & Lamb, 2003). A relocation will shield the children from the abuse or violence, and may permit better parenting by the custodial parent (Austin, 2008b). Where children are in the middle of extreme levels of parental conflict, relocation may enhance their well-being (Kelly & Lamb, 2003; Wallerstein & Tanke, 1996). The following cases illustrate these issues.[28]

In the 1998 Ontario case of *Matthews v. Matthews*,[29] the mother applied for sole custody of the three children along with the right to relocate with them to England, where she planned to move with her new husband. The separation had been highly conflicted and each parent alleged that the other party had physically abused the children. The children corroborated the evidence of the mother concerning the abuse by the father. The children were afraid of their father and since the separation had not wanted to see him. Since separating, the father's behaviour had become erratic. A number of mental health professionals had been involved with the family, and a complete court ordered assessment had been conducted, including the preparation of an interim report which resulted in the father having only supervised access. Justice Granger concluded that the father would do what he could to turn the children against their mother, and that he had few parenting skills and was a risk to the children. The evidence led

[28] We discuss the issue of domestic violence as a factor in custody assessments and the specialized risk assessment more generally in Chapters 3 and 4.

[29] 1998 CarswellOnt 1419, [1998] O.J. No. 1424 (Ont. Gen. Div.)

at trial indicated that the family had been dysfunctional prior to separation, with all of the children exhibiting behavioural difficulties and lack of control. After separation, in conjunction with her new spouse, the mother had made progress towards improving her parenting skills. The father, his animosity towards the mother having escalated after separation, had engaged in a pattern of inappropriate conduct during supervised access. He was diagnosed as having several personality disorders and being severely learning disabled; his emotional difficulties were believed by almost all the experts involved to be detrimental to the emotional and physical health of the children. The Court ordered that the mother have sole custody of the children and that she be permitted to move to England with them. The father was not permitted any access to the children. The judge noted that the mother had a well-thought-out plan for the children's future while living in England with her new partner, whereas the father had nothing but a vague plan for raising the children.

In the 2006 Ontario case of *Takenaka v. Kaleta*,[30] the mother of a six-year-old sought custody of her daughter and permission to move with her to Japan. Justice Croll ordered sole custody to the mother and granted her permission to move, as she had been the main caregiver of her daughter since birth and the daughter had a stronger connection with her. The child's first language was Japanese and she spoke little English. After the child's birth, mother and daughter travelled to Japan eight times; as a result, the daughter had strong bonds with the mother's family in Japan. Further, there was evidence that the father had an obsessive relationship with his daughter and that the daughter had had little contact with his extended family. The father had been emotionally abusive to the mother and the judge concluded that there was little hope that his proposed parenting plan, which included frequent consultation with the mother, would work.

In some cases, a significant geographical separation of the parents may be the best way to allow animosity to dissipate, or at least to reduce its effect on the children, and the court allows the primary caregiver to move with the children, even if the court concludes that the conflict is not wholly the fault of the non-custodial parent.[31] In the 1998 Ontario case of *Elliott v. Elliott*,[32] the Court allowed the mother to move with the child from Barrie to Toronto (an hour drive) in the hope that this would help to reduce the level of conflict between

---

30 2006 CarswellOnt 907, 28 R.F.L. (6th) 119 (Ont. S.C.J.)

31 See *Noble v. Boutilier*, 2005 CarswellOnt 4340, 2005 ONCJ 251 (Ont. C.J.), *per* McSorley J.; and *Laturnus v. Laturnus*, 2004 CarswellSask 485, 2004 SKQB 298, 252 Sask. R. 76 (Sask. Q.B.), *per* Matheson J.

32 1998 CarswellOnt 4470, [1998] O.J. No. 4827 (Ont. Gen. Div.), *per* Wood J.

the parents. The father had been seeing the six-year-old child daily, and at the exchange of the child there were frequently arguments, use of profane language, "and demonstrations of outright hatred which cannot but have had a devastating effect" on the child. Justice Wood observed that neither party was blameless, but that the father caused the majority of the difficulty the parties experienced. The judge concluded that "the absence of daily contact between the child and [her father]. . . will actually benefit her by removing her from the conflict between the parties."

A move out of the jurisdiction by the custodial parent and children may be a concern if it is a high conflict situation and the custodial parent is not supportive of the child's relationship with the other parent and seems likely to become a restrictive gatekeeper (Austin, 2008b; Warshak, 2000b). Kelly (2007) explains that not all couples who are characterized as "high conflict" involve two equally dysfunctional, competing and hostile parents, or raise issues of domestic violence. She notes that legal and mental-health practitioners have frequently observed that one parent may be more emotionally disengaged and desirous of avoiding litigation and conflict, while the other parent remains more heavily invested in vengeance, anger, control and pursuit of litigation (Friedman, 2004). When parents live at a considerable distance, greater effort is needed to maintain a child's tie with the non-custodial parent between visits, which are likely to be more infrequent, and the degree of support that the custodial parent will provide for the relationship with the other parent should be a significant factor in determining whether the move should be permitted.

As mentioned previously, parental conflict is an important predictor of father involvement, with high conflict being associated with less paternal involvement (Pruett *et al.*, 2003). Researchers have recognized that the custodial parent might act as a gatekeeper, impeding the non-custodial parent's time and involvement with the child. Lehr and MacMillan (2001) found that fathers reported considerable difficulty maintaining meaningful contact with their children after a divorce if there is high conflict with their ex-partner. Similarly, Kelly (2000) observes that the frequency and pattern of contact between fathers and children after a divorce are related to marital and post-divorce conflict, including legal disputes. It is reasonable to assume that a relocation coupled with parental conflict is likely to contribute to greater difficulties in maintaining a child's relationship with a non-moving parent than a move in families in which the parents have an amicable relationship.

Warshak (2000b) observes that the maintenance of stability and continuity with a custodial parent will only benefit a child if that relationship is a healthy one. In high conflict cases in which the custodial parent is attempting to alienate the child from the other parent, the relationship with the alienating parent is not emotionally healthy (Lamb & Kelly, 2003; Warshak, 2000b). Effective parenting is compromised by alienating parents who have difficulty separating their needs from their child's, or who over-identify with the child's feelings, negatively affecting individuation and autonomy. If treatment intended to ameliorate these concerns is interrupted by relocation, children are deprived of the opportunity to resolve the problems. Moreover, without regular contact between the child and the non-custodial parent, even more challenging pathological alienation can result.[33]

Warshak (2000b) summarizes the concerns about alienation when relocation is also an issue:

> When the children are physically isolated from the target, the chances of preventing or reversing alienation are slim. As long as the children are exclusively dependent on the parent doing the bad-mouthing, there is little hope that they will be able to resist maneuvers to estrange them from the other parent. The most effective means of resisting and reversing such programming is to provide them with opportunities to be with that parent and to experience his or her love and attention. If too much time goes by before contact is reestablished, the damage to the relationship is much harder to repair. In view of the above, when the parent who requests relocation denigrates and devalues the other parent, even if the children have not succumbed to alienation, the psychologist [conducting an assessment] should consider the risks of alienation taking root or becoming further entrenched if the children are relocated away from the target parent.
>
> Custodial parents who are intent on undermining their children's relationship with the other parent will often try to obstruct visits. Although this occurs when parents live in close proximity, relocation magnifies the custodial parent's power to accomplish visitation interference. The custodial parent can easily thwart visits by not taking the child to the airport or arriving late and missing the flight, or by not having the child at home when the other parent arrives from out-of-town. (p. 108).

Summary

As discussed in this chapter, there is little empirical research that deals directly with the impact of relocation on children whose parents have separated. What research is available must be viewed as prelim-

---

[33] For further elaboration on this issue, see Chapters 6 and 7 in this book on alienation as well as our companion book on assessments more generally (Birnbaum, Fidler & Kavassalis, 2008).

inary. There is, however, a large and relevant literature that we can draw upon when considering whether a move is likely to be in a child's best interest, or more appropriately, the least detrimental alternative. This includes research on residential mobility of non-divorced families of various types, as well as on the risk and resilience factors related to children's adjustment to divorce, and the development of attachment.

Austin (2008a) reminds us that while the research literature provides convincing evidence that residential mobility has negative effects for children from divorced and non-divorced homes, and thus is a general risk factor, the aggregate results of these studies should not be used as a basis for bias or creating presumptions against such moves. Rather, the data should be used as a "starting point" for the assessor. Austin explains that while the existing research is valuable for developing hypotheses, it alone cannot be used to predict the short- and long-term impact of a relocation on a particular child in a particular set of circumstances. As the studies show, there is great variability in children's adjustment to divorce and to moving; the impact of relocation on an individual child will depend on the combination of the risk and protective or buffering factors. Each case requires a individualized assessment where all of the various factors need to be investigated and weighed by the custody assessor, who when making parenting plan recommendations, provides a prediction of the potential risks and benefits of the various alternatives. In addition, when a relocation is recommended because on balance the benefits are greater than the risks, the assessor must make specific recommendations as to what measures can be taken to minimize the potential harm associated with the move while considering the various changes to the child's relationship with both parents.

In Chapter 2, we shall discuss issues relevant to assessments in relocation cases, the many factors requiring investigation, and various harm reduction strategies. We also summarize the legal trends in Canada as illustrated by case law.

Chapter 2

Relocation Disputes: Assessment Considerations, Factors and Legal Trends

Children's needs in relocation cases are not mere corollaries of parental desires. Each child's relocation case requires individualized assessment of the risks, benefits and consequences of the proposed move, and the possible parenting plans for the child. Shortcuts will shortchange children.

Leslie Ellen Shear (2004)[1]

Assessment Considerations

Notwithstanding the previously noted lack of research on outcomes in relocation cases, and the debate in the Canadian jurisprudence as to whether relocation involves "clinical" or "mental health" issues necessitating an assessment, custody and access assessors continue to be called upon to provide information and opinions to assist the courts in making these decisions.

There is also controversy about whether or not assessors should be making recommendations to the court in any custody and access cases.[2] Some of those who generally support assessors making recommendations nevertheless suggest that in relocation cases assessors should limit their role and avoid making recommendations, leaving the final decision to the courts (Stahl, 2006; Austin & Gould, 2006). According to this view, after summarizing all of the information obtained, assessors should limit their conclusions to a discussion of the potential risks and benefits of several alternatives in the context of the relevant factors found in the literature and the law in their jurisdiction. This approach is based on the view that children are likely to be subject to emotional harm, to one extent or or another, in each available option in a relocation case. Thus, it is the court's responsibility, and not the assessor's, to determine which type of harm would be least detrimental to the child in the long term. In effect, the court, not the assessor, needs to balance two or more types of harm? (Austin & Gould, 2006).

---

[1] Shear, L.E. (2004). *Amici curiae* brief, *In re Marriage of LaMusga*, Supreme Court of California, p. 1.

[2] See volumes 42(2) and (4) of the 2005 *Family Court Review*.

While at least short-term emotional harm may occur regardless of which option is chosen by the court, in many cases it is possible to predict the likelihood of different types of risk and predict which option is likely to be least detrimental to the child. If the matter does proceed to an assessment, a thorough investigation involving a multi-method, multi-source approach consistent with best practice guidelines is required.[3] We support the view that in appropriate relocation cases assessors may provide a recommendation, albeit using the language of probabilities—of the risks and benefits for the child. Having said that, there may be cases where the assessor is more comfortable delineating each option and discussing the risks and benefits of each (Austin, 2008b; Austin & Gould, 2006). Assessors in Canada continue to make recommendations about the ultimate issue in relocations; judges continue to receive this evidence and, in appropriate cases, give it significant weight.[4]

An assessor in a relocation case, essentially making predictions, is sometimes faced with assessing the likely benefits and risks to the child of two stark alternatives: (1) allowing the child to relocate with the moving parent; (2) having custody changed and allowing the child to remain with the non-moving parent in the same community, while the other parent moves. In some cases there may be more options, including; (3) having the child remain in the custody of a parent whose wish to relocate has been disallowed by the court (preserving the status quo); and (4) allowing relocation with the moving parent while the other parent also moves to the new location. A fifth option that might be possible in some cases involves having the custodial parent's new partner move to the custodial parent's community instead of the parent moving to live with the new partner in their community (Thompson, 2004).[5]

There has been considerable discussion in the legal and mental health communities about whether custodial parents should be asked if they intend to move without the child in the event the court does

---

[3] We elaborate more fully on best practice assessment methodology in our companion book (Birnbaum, Fidler & Kavassalis, 2008).

[4] For a examples of cases where assessors made recommendations and the judges appeared to give them significant weight, see *Datars v. Graham*, 2007 CarswellOnt 5257, 41 R.F.L. (6th) 51 (Ont. S.C.J.), *per* Quigley J.; *Noble v. Boutilier*, 2005 CarswellOnt 4340, [2005] O.J. 3825 (Ont. C.J.), *per* McSorley J.; and *Boukema v. Boukema*, 1997 CarswellOnt 3115, [1997] O.J. 2903 (Ont. Gen. Div.)

[5] See *Burns v. Burns*, 2000 CarswellNS 2, [2000] N.S.J. No.2, 2000 N.S,C.A. 1, 183 D.L.R. (4th) 60, 182 N.S.R. (2d) 101, 3 R.F.L. (5th) 189 (N.S.C.A.); *Whalen v. Whalen*, 2005 CarswellNfld 161, [2005] N.J. No. 196, 2005 N.L.C.A. 35, 247 Nfld. & P.E.I.R. 344, 18 R.F.L. (6th) 215 (N.L.C.A.); *Rockwell v. Rockwell*, 1998 CarswellBC 2580, [1998] B.C.J. No. 2718, 167 D.L.R. (4th) 293, B.C.L.R. (3d) 380, 43 R.F.L. (4th) 450 (B.C.C.A.)

not allow a move with the child. While some assessors have noted that it is important to know whether this is a possible plan to be evaluated and suggest that the question is necessarily important and part of the usual protocol of questions (Austin & Gould, 2006), Canadian courts have suggested that this is an unfair question. In *MacPhail v. Karasek*[6] the Alberta Court of Appeal observed:

> The trial judge found that the Mother's stated position at trial, that she would not move back to Medicine Hat [where the child had lived before the move], was an "egregious example of manipulation" by the Mother. But the Mother was caught in a quandary at this point. If she did not take this position, the court might avoid making the difficult decision it is compelled to make in mobility cases. She was in the "classic double bind" as that conundrum was described by this court in *Spencer v. Spencer*, [2005] A.J. No. 934, 2005 ABCA 262 (Alta. C.A.), at para. 18:
>
> > [I]t is problematic to rely on representations by the custodial parent that he or she will not move without the children should the application to relocate be denied. The effect of such an inquiry places the parent seeking to relocate in a classic double bind. If the answer is that the parent is not willing to remain behind with the children, he or she raises the prospect of being regarded as self interested and discounting the children's best interests in favour of his or her own. On the other hand, advising the court that the parent is prepared to forgo the requested move if unsuccessful, undermines the submissions in favour of relocation by suggesting that such a move is not critical to the parent's well-being or to that of the children.

Thompson (2007) argues that the answer is usually known by the time a case goes to court, and thus there is no information lost if the question remains unasked in court. He adds that it is unfair to put a parent in this double bind and asserts it is better to ask the parent who is opposed to the move whether they would relocate to maintain a close relationship with the child if the move is permitted; as the answer to this question is generally not known, may be significant, and should be available to the court. The practical reality is that most parents who oppose a move are not able to move to the new locale to maintain their relationship with the child, and even if they are, they may be reluctant to admit this during litigation as they will still have this option if the child is permitted to move.

While the 1996 decision of the Supreme Court of Canada in *Gordon v. Goertz*,[7] suggested that it is only in the "exceptional case" that

---

6 2006 CarswellAlta 1035, 30 R.F.L. (6th) 324, 273 D.L.R. (4th) 151 (Alta. C.A.), at para 51.

7 1996 CarswellSask 199, [1996] 2 S.C.R. 27 (S.C.C.), at para. 49.

reasons for the move will be significant, judges often consider the proposed reasons to be significant to making decisions in relocation cases. Further, it is often impossible to disentangle an assessment of the effect of the move on a child from consideration of the reasons for the move. It is accordingly important for an assessor to address and investigate the reasons for the proposed move in order to be able to provide the court with a comprehensive risk/benefit analysis of the various alternatives. The reasons for which the non-moving parent is opposing the move are also important for the assessor to consider.

Assessors may over-predict harm (a false positive) or under-predict harm (a false negative). As professionals, we must do what we can to minimize both of these types of prediction errors. A thorough assessment that includes different types and sources of information, including material from collateral sources, will assist towards this end. Given the various allegations and proposals being presented, an assessment of the parents' credibility is imperative (Association of Family and Conciliation Courts, 2004, revised 2007). Austin and Kirkpatrick (2004) and others have suggested that there is an investigative function to an assessment, and that efforts should be made to find at least two corroborating sources to support parents' claims and reports. In relocation cases these may include, to name a few, an official document, public record, or income information from tax returns to establish an ability to afford the added costs of visits that may result from a move, and other collateral sources reporting the same piece of information (Austin & Gould, 2006). The assessor then examines all of the data obtained, looking for confirming and disconfirming information, taking into account the relevant social science literature and case law that supports or does not support the conclusions and recommendations.

Factors Requiring Consideration

In considering the effects of a proposed move on a child, an assessor must consider numerous complex and interacting factors. Austin (2000a, 2000c, 2008b) describes a research-based predictive and hierarchical risk assessment model known as the Relocation Risk Assessment (RRA) in which the assessor starts from a baseline assumption that a move necessarily means the child will experience some degree of short-term distress. To that baseline are introduced both the risk and modulating factors. These numerous and relevant factors can be grouped into four categories related to:

(1) the child;

(2) the immediate family;

(3) the extended family and social supports; and

(4) the context of the proposed move, including the willingness and ability of the moving parent to facilitate contact with the non-moving parent.[8]

The *child-related* factors include:

(a) age;

(b) gender;

(c) temperament;

(d) nature and extent of attachments;

(e) social, emotional, and academic adjustment;

(f) adaptability and resiliency; and

(g) the presence of any special needs.

Additionally, it is important to consider the length of time since the parental separation and the child's age at the time of the separation. The effects of stress and change are cumulative (Hodges, 1984; Rutter, 1979). Hence the effect of a move on a child who is coping with a recent parental separation, and the increase in conflict that this entails, compromise parenting and disruption to the child (Hetherington & Kelly, 2002). This is very different from coping with a move after a period of adjustment to a separation.

Factors requiring consideration related to *family* factors include:

(1) the quality of the parent-child relationships before and after the separation;

(2) each parent's pre-separation parenting (degree and nature of involvement);

(3) each parent's parenting strengths and challenges, including the parenting style (i.e., authoritative, authoritarian, permissive);

(4) each parent's psychological stability and coping skills;

(5) the nature, degree and intensity of parental conflict;

---

[8] In his recent article, Austin (2008b) provides a review of the specific research findings he purports to support his RRA. Austin cautions that the RRA model is not a scientific instrument, but rather a framework that assists the assessor to organize the data obtained during the assessment and in turn; make predictions with respect to the risks and benefits of the various alternatives.

(6) the extent and manner of the child's involvement in the conflict;

(7) the history of domestic abuse and violence (degree and type);

(8) the child's relationships and involvement with step-parents (or step-parent figures) and step-siblings;

(9) the ability and willingness of the relocating parent to support the child's relationship with the other parent after the move; and

(10) the ability of the non-moving parent to relocate to the new community.

Children's Wishes and Preferences

A child's wishes are significant for a court to consider in making a best interest decision. For example, in its 2002 decision in *Rushinko v. Rushinko*,[9] the Ontario Court of Appeal ruled that the trial judge had erred in transferring custody to the father as the custodial mother planned to move regardless of whether the children could move with her. The appeal court held that the trial judge had placed undue emphasis on the effect that leaving their community would have on the children and insufficient consideration of the harm the children would suffer if the mother was no longer the custodial parent. Perhaps most important in that case, the appeal court ruled that the trial judge gave insufficient weight to the "stated preferences" of the children, as expressed through their lawyer, to relocate with their mother, who was their primary caregiver.

Because of the importance of a child's perceptions and wishes, interviews with the child are an important part of the assessment process. Consideration of the preferences of the child requires that the child has the cognitive maturity to be able to consider future possibilities, including having a realistic view of the consequences of both moving from and remaining in their community. Younger children may not be able to consider the effects of living arrangements that they have not experienced, but they may still express a preference for living with a certain parent. Some older children may have concerns about moving and leaving friends and school, coupled with anxiety about having to start at a new school and making new friends. While some children may want to move, others may be ambivalent. It is important, if possible, to obtain the child's preferences and to evaluate and interpret these in terms of whether they have been influenced by one of their parents.

---

[9] 2006 CarswellOnt 2898, 27 R.F.L. (6th) 44 (Ont. C.A.).

Nevertheless, a child's preferences are clearly not determinative of a best interest decision, especially if the child is choosing between options that have not actually been experienced by the child. The concerns about placing emphasis on the wishes of a child about a proposed move are heightened if the child has been subjected to pressure or alienation (a topic expanded on in chapters 6 and 7).

The concerns about not placing weight on the views of a child who has been influenced by a parent are illustrated the 1997 Ontario decision of *Boukema v. Boukema*,[10] a case in which the mother wanted her 11-year-old daughter to move with her from Toronto to New Jersey, where the mother had relocated so that she could live with her new husband. At the time of the application, the child had her primary residence with her father in Toronto pursuant to a joint custody arrangement based on a separation agreement. After a six-week holiday with her mother, the child expressed a wish to live with her in New Jersey. The mother claimed that the child's desire to live with her was a material change in circumstances justifying new custody and access arrangements. Taking into account an assessment and the representations of the child's lawyer, the judge concluded that the child's views were not formed independently, and for this reason the Court gave little weight to those views and ordered the child to remain in the sole custody of her father in Toronto, with visits to the mother. *Boukema* established an important legal precedent, particularly about the role of the lawyer for the child, when the lawyer declined to advocate the child's views without putting before the court detailed evidence of all the factors that have influenced those views. The case is also illustrative of the fact that as children become adolescents their views will have greater weight, not only with judges but also with parents, as two years after the court decision was made the parents agreed that the girl, then 13 years of age, could move to New Jersey to live with her mother.

Maintaining a Relationship with Both Parents

As previously mentioned, given the benefits of positive and active paternal involvement, the assessor needs to consider the risk to the child of restrictive gatekeeping and pathological (irrational) alienation, especially in situations of high conflict, which in turn would diminish the many benefits from the father's involvement. Of course, protective gatekeeping and realistic estrangement (rational or justified alienation) must also be considered. Consequently, it is imperative to assess the moving parent's concrete plans for the child's on-

[10] *Supra*, at note 4.

going post-separation relationship with the other parent. The following issues, for example, need to be canvassed:

(1) post-separation behaviour with respect to promoting the child's relationship with the other parent;

(2) past behaviour with respect to willingness and ability to communicate with the other parent about the child;

(3) previous compliance with the parenting plan and court orders to date;

(4) ability and willingness to promote the child's relationship with the other parent once a relocation occurs; and

(5) ability of the parents to separate their own needs and feelings about each other from the child's needs and feelings.

As we discussed more fully in Chapter 1, the extent to which the custodial parent is a responsible (protective) or irresponsible (restrictive) gatekeeper to a relationship with the other parent is especially important to investigate in relocation cases, where maintaining the child's contact with the non-moving parent will take a concerted effort on the part of the moving parent.

Social and Context Factors

The effects of moving, positive and negative, on the family's social capital, the child's social relationships, and on extended family relationships in both the proposed and current environments are also important considerations that require an assessor's investigation. These include:

(1) extended family involvement;

(2) social supports for the child; and

(3) child-care arrangements, including who will be caring for the child, the caregiver's parenting capacity, and the child's relationship, if any, with these potential caregivers.

The context-related factors for consideration include the new community, neighbourhood and school, and the extent to which these fit the child's needs. Austin and Gould (2006) suggest the assessor go beyond the surface by investigating:

(1) the quality of the proposed new educational program for the child;

(2) the availability of daycare or child-care options in the new community;

(3) proposed new employment and alternatives in the current community;

(4) community comparisons (i.e., urban vs. rural); and

(5) the stability of the custodial parent's new relationship as well as the new partner's individual stability and relationship with the child.

Some of these same considerations need to be looked at in the event that the non-moving parent proposes a change to the status quo in terms of neighbourhood and school, or if they are introducing a new partner.

Other context-related factors include the geographical distance and travel time of the proposed move and the extent to which meaningful contact and relationships can be maintained, taking into account both economic and logistical implications. Does the family have the economical resources to permit travel and possibly frequent travel? Can the child travel alone, or will she or he need to be accompanied, and if so, for how long? Can the non-moving parent realistically take time off work to travel to the child's new location? What are the effects, if any, on the child of the travel itself? Will an older child who is more likely to have significant peer and community involvement want to travel as frequently as suggested in the possible recommendations?

Kelly and Lamb (2003) suggest that if a resident parent is competent *and* relocation improves his or her educational, career or partnering opportunities, the children may benefit from that parent's enhanced well-being, especially if the children are able to maintain a meaningful relationship with their non-resident parent through regular contact. They go on to observe that more commonly, however, in cases in which children have a meaningful relationship with both parents, the relative costs and benefits of relocation are far more difficult to evaluate. Moves that allow the socio-economic status to rise to above the poverty level are likely to be associated with positive outcomes in children (Emery, 1988). In the final analysis, relocation will create obvious financial and travel burdens on the family (Waldron, 2005).

Austin (2000a, 2000c, 2000d) summarizes criteria, as outlined below, indicating when greater harm is more likely to occur and when less harm is likely subsequent to relocation.

Table 1: Criteria for Determining Degree of Harm

Greater harm likely:	Less harm occurs if:
(1) for a younger child who is developing attachments; (2) if the non-custodial parent has been actively involved in warm parenting; (3) if the child has fewer individual coping resources; (4) if the residential parent has poor coping and parenting skills; (5) if the residential parent is unstable and/or character-disordered; (6) the greater the geographical distance; and (7) if the separation has been recent.	(1) the child is older; (2) the relationship with the non-moving parent is troubled and/or not solid; (3) the parents have a good relationship characterized by low conflict; (4) the child is resilient (i.e., has good coping skills and individual resources); (5) the residential parent has good coping and parenting skills; (6) the geographical distance is shorter; and (7) more time has passed since the separation.

In writing about the risks associated with having young children relocate, Austin and Gould (2006) conclude that:

> In light of the knowledge gleaned from attachment theory (Ainsworth, Blehar, Waters & Wall, 1979), and the young child's limited sense of time and lack of a sense of object permanence concerning the left-behind parent (Kelly & Lamb, 2003), there is probably a scientific and empirical basis for a *de facto* presumption against relocation in the instance of two involved parents and a very young child (p.100).

Younger Children

The developmental and attachment literature note that secure attachments require not only for the child and caregiver to spend time together, but also for the child to have experiences across domains of parenting (Kelly & Lamb, 2000; Lamb & Kelly, 2001). Extrapolating from these findings, we can conclude that, in relocation cases, the younger the child, the greater the potential harm to the child's relationship with the non-moving parent (Kelly & Lamb, 2003; Austin, 2008a). Note that harm is also likely to occur to the child's relationship with the moving parent if the child is separated for longer durations than appropriate in an effort to have long visits to compensate for the move (Lamb & Kelly, 2003). Consequently, some writers argue that if a child is to have a meaningful relationship with both parents, a move, if it is to occur at all, should be postponed until the child is about five or six years old (Kelly & Lamb, 2003). While not without risks, in most cases the child by this age will have acquired object permanence, language development and sustainable attachments, which in turn will mitigate to some extent the inevitable risks associated with relocation (Austin & Gould, 2006; Kelly & Lamb, 2003; Warshak, 2000b). With their language and cognitive capabilities, school-aged and older children are better prepared for the many changes they will have to undergo. They are also more likely to cope better with extended absences and the various other logistics involved when life involves living in two homes in different geographical jurisdictions. In addition, these children will be more able than younger children to participate meaningfully in telephone contact and other long-distance communication. It would be a mistake, however, to conclude that extended contacts over summer and other holidays will have the same impact on the parent-child relationship as more regular and frequent contact.

As a child accomplishes certain developmental tasks, the development of others that have yet to be mastered may be at risk after relocation. As we elaborated in our companion book, the formulation of parenting plans requires careful consideration of the competing needs of children (Birnbaum, Fidler & Kavassalis, 2008). For example, children between 5 and 10 years of age are not as dependent as older children on their external social circumstances. A move may pose less risk for younger children, whose development and adjustment are less closely tied to peers, school, and other community activities. However, these younger children need more frequent contacts with the non-moving parent in order to develop and sustain meaningful attachments.

Notwithstanding the negative effects that a move may have on the development of a child's relationship with a non-custodial parent, there recently seems to be more willingness in Ontario for judges to allow relocation for children of pre-school age (under 6 years of age) than for school age children (6-11 years of age). This is due to the view that younger children are less likely to have significant ties to their schools and communities (Bala & Harris, 2006).[11] Very young children

[11] Thompson (2004) offers an assessment of cases decided between 1996 and 2003 throughout Canada, concluding that for children aged 6 to 11 years, a move is more often permitted than for children less than 6 years of age. For children 12 or older the child's preferences strongly influence the decision. Professor Thompson provides a number of suggestions why these findings exist:

- younger children experience more recent separations and interim moves;
- shared parenting is showing up more often amongst the younger age group;
- the older children are more capable of adjusting to longer periods of block

may not have significant psychological ties to adults unless they have lived with them or spent significant time with them, and they are less affected by a move than an older child who is more likely to miss the relationship with an absent parent. There are a number of recent relocation cases in which courts have allowed custodial mothers to relocate with very young children (under 1 year), even though it may be difficult for fathers to maintain strong and meaningful relationships with these children after the moves. Typically, in these cases there were strong employment or economic reasons for allowing the mother to move, and a recognition of the "reality of the parenting and childcare arrangements" with the mother providing almost all the young child's care.[12]

Older Children

As children become older, their wishes become much more important. Older children may be able to spend relatively large blocks of time with a parent who lives at some distance. They may also more easily maintain a relationship with a distant parent, for example by phone and email, so that living farther from a parent will be less disruptive to the relationship between parent and child.

While adolescents are able to manage longer stretches of time away from one parent or the other, in some cases relocation may not be consistent with their developmental needs. It has been noted by some mental health professionals that relocating when a child reaches adolescence raises special concerns (Austin, 2000a). While some adolescents may be eager to move, many object because they do not want to leave their life as they have come to know it, which for them is dominated by friends and activities. They may experience trepidation at the thought of having to reestablish themselves socially and in a new school environment. The assessor will have to consider carefully the risks and benefits in this regard, taking into account the importance of continuity in peer relationships, academic programs and extracurricular activities, which for some older children are top priorities (Austin & Gould, 2006). In some cases, recommendations may include separating siblings because of differing developmental

---

access, or at least judges seems to think so; and

- the older group may involve more distance from separation, more drift toward increased maternal caregiving, and reduced access, thereby easing the relocation decision.

[12] *Hassan v. Mufti*, 2008 CarswellOnt 3622, [2008] O.J. 2422 (Ont. S.C.J.), at para. 57, *per* Lalonde J. (5 month old child permitted to move from Toronto to Saudi Arabia). See also *Nyari v. Velasco*, 2008 CarswellOnt 3540, [2008] O.J. 2383 (Ont. C.J.), *per* Sherr J. (7 month old permitted to relocate from Toronto to Ottawa with mother).

needs and varying preferences (Rotman, Tomkins, Schwartz & Samuels, 2000).

Cases involving older children who express clear and consistent views about the possibility of moving to a new jurisdiction are not frequently litigated, as parents usually settle such cases based on their children's wishes. While any expression of preference by a child in a relocation case will usually require that the child speculate about future living arrangements that have not been experienced, the courts tend to give significant weight to the wishes of older children in such cases.[13] Nevertheless, our experiences as parents and clinicians reveal that adolescents do not always make decisions that are in their own long-term best interests. Further, there is research showing that positive and active father involvement is especially important for positive adolescent adjustment (King & Sobolewski, 2006; Allen & Daley, 2007), raising concerns about the effects of post-separation relocation.

Parenting Plans: Reducing Risks in the Move

Parenting plan recommendations can include suggestions for steps a moving parent should take prior to relocation to facilitate the child's transition to and involvement in a new environment. This may involve visiting the new home and school in advance, looking at community-centre activity programs, and attempting to establish connections with friends and relatives prior to the move. Moving parents can also assist their child's transition by taking concrete steps to maintain contacts in the current community. In addition to communication through telephone, email and online chat rooms, visits to the child's former community can be arranged to coincide with important social events (Waldron, 2005). The ties with the former network are likely to weaken over time, but maintaining these at least for a while may assist with the transition to the new community and promote the child's psychological well-being.

In relocation cases, consideration is frequently given to an unequal division of the school holidays and summer. Older children may balk at leaving their new home community for extended periods. While it may not always be suitable for them to have prolonged time away from the community where they reside and have important peer attachments—and it may not be possible or desirable to force them to do so—there are steps that parents can take early on to help the older child continue a strong relationship with the non-moving parent

---

[13] See *Wilkinson v. Edward*, 2004 CarswellOnt 3715, [2004] O.J. No. 3796 (Ont. S.C.J.).

through adolescence. Summer activities, including vacations with the non-moving parent, camp attendance and summer employment, can be scheduled so that the older child can plan for and look forward to extended periods with the non-moving parent. Such planning may serve as incentive for the child to accept the move with a positive attitude. For some children, the desire to spend time with the other parent continues and the ties with friends and community do not weaken. These children acclimatize more easily to sustaining two environments, one during the school year in the new community and the other in the community of origin during the majority of the time out of school.

As we have discussed more generally (Birnbaum, Fidler & Kavassalis, 2008), the higher the level of parental conflict, the more specific and structured the parenting plan needs to be. This is especially important in relocation cases. To ensure smooth implementation of the parenting time schedule, it is advisable for the recommended parenting plan to include terms for the many implementation-related matters that can arise, especially when higher-conflict parents are involved. For example, it is important to include specific terms in a parenting plan related to the provision of documentation required for travel (birth certificate, passports, or notarized letters authorizing border crossings), and clear protocols for travel and exchanges.

In addition to the specifics surrounding parenting time, recommendations for the child's age-appropriate contact—how and when—with the other parent between scheduled parenting times need to be included. Options include telephone communications, virtual parenting time (web-cam), email and instant messaging, and audio and video recordings (Gottfried, 2002; Shefts, 2002). Critics note that while virtual contacts may be an improvement over telephone and written communications, these should not be equated with face-to-face contact, hugs, the ability to show school work and awards, attendance at activities and the like (Waldron, 2005). Providing detail about these communication methods will assist the courts in determining how the associated costs are managed between the parents. Younger children may not communicate well on the phone or other electronic means of communication, and the parent with care of the child may need to support such communication. While children 12 years and older are likely to work out their communication with the non-custodial parent independently, without needing to have it documented in the parenting plan, there may be cases where such provisions will be required.

Transportation is another significant implementation issue that the assessor needs to address. When can the child travel alone by air, train and/or by bus? If the parents are driving, to what extent is the driving shared, and how? Does one parent deliver the child while the other returns the child? Do the parents meet half way? If so, where? Or, do the parents alternate responsibility for driving? Identifying the nature and extent of the transportation involved will assist a court in its determination with respect to associated costs.

Parenting time schedules almost inevitably change over time as children mature and circumstances change. This may be especially relevant in relocation cases. For example, the suitable duration of parenting time in the summer is likely to vary for children of different ages, and most plans will evolve over time to accommodate this change. While parenting time for the non-custodial parent may increase with the school-aged child, it may decline once the child reaches 16 or 17 years of age. It is advisable for the recommended parenting plan to include an explicit statement that parenting time is likely to require change over time, along with a dispute resolution mechanism specifying how disputes will be resolved in the event they cannot come to an agreement on their own. For example, will the parents return to their assessor? Alternatively, will the parents return to court if they cannot come to a mutual agreement? Has a mediator or parenting coordinator been identified in the parenting plan in advance of a potential dispute? In addition to addressing any future changes to the parenting time schedule, a professional may assist the parents in more effectively implementing their entire parenting plan, including their communication and information exchange, temporary changes to the schedules, and other issues that may arise.

As discussed in Chapter 1, studies show that a primary determinant of children's post-separation well-being is their relationship with their custodial parent. Studies also show that children do better when they have good relationships with both parents, providing they are protected from parental conflict that involves the children. More recently, research has shown the importance of having fathers remain actively involved in all aspects of their children's lives, including school, extracurricular activities, and peers, as well as setting limits and having expectations. As time spent with a child is not enough involvement in itself, it is important for recommendations for a parenting plan to include protocols for active participation, even from a distance, as it relates to homework, parent-teacher meetings, and decisions affecting education, school and extracurricular activities. Recommendations for the non-moving parent to spend time in the child's new/primary home environment, with opportunities to participate actively in the child's day-to-day life by attending school functions, meeting teachers, attending sports events or recitals, meeting the child's friends, etc., may mitigate negative effects of adjustment to relocation as well.

Protocols for information-sharing between parents, and parent involvement in both day-to-day and major decision-making, should be recommended by the assessor, with more specific plans included for higher-conflict families. In an effort to keep the parent-child relationship current and alive, there can be expectations placed upon the custodial parent to provide regular and detailed updates to the other parent about the child's day-to-day activities and functioning at home, at school, and in the community. This information may be even more important to share when relocation occurs than when parents live in close proximity and the child is seeing both of them regularly and frequently. Joint legal custody may be indicated to mandate the non-moving parent's involvement in major child-related decisions.

Trends in Canadian Jurisprudence

In addition to knowing the relevant social science literature and research and conducting a thorough investigation of the various alternatives for care of each child, the assessor needs to take into account best interests factors required by legislation and identified in the case law. The Supreme Court of Canada decision in *Gordon v. Goertz* is the leading precedent on relocation in this country, adopting the best interests of the child as the fundamental test for the resolution of these cases. It articulates the principle that each case must be determined based on its own unique circumstances and that the focus of the court's inquiry must be the child's best interests, and not the rights of either parent. There is no legal presumption in favour of the right of a custodial parent to move, although the views of that parent are entitled to "great respect". Rather, both parents bear the evidentiary burden of demonstrating where the best interests of the child lie. In a statement generally consistent with factors identified in the social science literature, Justice McLachlin summarized the law in an oft-quoted passage: "The focus is on the best interests of the child, not the interests and rights of the parents."[14]

More particularly, the judge should consider, *inter alia*:

a) the existing custody arrangement and relationship between the child and the custodial parent;

b) the existing access arrangement and the relationship between the child and the access parent;

---

[14] *Supra*, at note 7, para. 49.

c) the desirability of maximizing contact between the child and both parents;

d) the views of the child;

e) the custodial parent's reason for moving, only in the exceptional case where it is relevant to that parent's ability to meet the needs of the child;

f) disruption to the child of a change in custody;

g) disruption to the child consequent on removal from family, schools, and the community he or she has come to know.

Justice McLachlin concluded that, in the end, the importance of having the child remain in the new location with the parent to whose custody they were accustomed must be weighed against the continuance of full contact with the child's access parent, extended family, and community. The primary question is what is in the best interests of the child in all circumstances, considering both the previous patterns of parenting and the range of options for the future.

In the years immediately following the 1996 Supreme Court decision in *Gordon v. Goertz,* a majority of applications for relocation were successful (Thompson, 2004). More recently, however, the courts seem to have been somewhat more sensitive to the importance of maintaining a relationship with the non-custodial parent, and there has been a rough balance between cases where an application is allowed and those where it is denied (Bala & Harris, 2006; Thompson, 2007). Relocation decisions require judicial assessment of all of the circumstances of the case and give trial judges considerable discretion in how they weigh factors, so it can be difficult to predict outcomes, or even to be certain after a decision is made which factors were determinative. A review of the jurisprudence, however, reveals some factors that are frequently important in relocation cases. We turn now to a discussion of these factors.

Relationship of Children with the Parents

One of the most significant factors in relocation cases involves an assessment of the comparative importance of the child's relationship with each parent, and consideration of how suitable each would be as the custodial parent. If both parents have close relationships with the child and are in a "true shared parenting" situation, the court will be reluctant to permit a move, as this will result in a pronounced emotional loss to the child. In a true "shared parenting" situation, the court will be reluctant to allow the move even if the effect of this will be to require a change in the child's "primary caregiver".[15] The mere fact that the parent who wants to move is characterized by the court as the "primary caregiver" does not mean that the court will allow the move.[16] However, if the child has only limited involvement with the "access parent", the court is much more likely to allow the child to move.[17] It is, for example, more common for a father to have limited involvement in a child's life if the child was born to a single mother and the access father has never lived with the child; in these cases relocation is more likely to be permitted.[18]

If the children have had only a limited relationship with an access parent, such as access every second weekend, and the custodial parent has a good reason to relocate, the court is unlikely to order a change in custody to the non-moving parent. In its 2006 decision in *MacPhail v. Karasek*[19] the Alberta Court of Appeal reversed the decision of a trial judge, who transferred custody to a father because the custodial mother had moved with the child to a community about three hours drive away, even though the mother was the primary caregiver and "wonderful mother", and the father had been exercising access every second weekend and was still able to do so. The trial judge concluded that the move would not be in the child's "best interests", and that if the mother was not prepared to return, custody should be awarded to the father. In reversing the trial decision, the Court of Appeal observed:

> According to this logic, parents cannot move unless the move is calculated to further the best interests of their children. Custodial parents cannot be limited in this way. Canadians are mobile and the courts are not the arbiters of the reasonableness of every decision a custodial parent makes. Custodial parents cannot be held hostage to the place the access parent lives. Certainly access parents are not. Moreover, it is not an option to conclude that a child's best interests are best served by both parties living in the same place any more than it is an option to consider that it is in a child's best interest that their parents remain together.
>
> Canadians have the right to choose to separate and divorce, and they have the right to relocate, and it is not for the courts to determine whether they like or agree with the reason for separating or moving. Custodial

---

[15] See *Young v. Young*, 2003 CarswellOnt 63, [2003] O.J. No. 67 (Ont. C.A.).

[16] See *Wilkinson v. Edward*, *supra*, at note 13; and *Zunti v. McIntosh*, 2004 CarswellOnt 406, [2004] O.J. No. 473 (Ont. S.C.J.), *per* Howden J.

[17] See *Roberts v. Young*, 2004 CarswellOnt 1700, [2004] O.J. No. 1786 (Ont. S.C.J.), *per* Wildman J.; and *Nitkin v. Nitkin*, 2004 CarswellOnt 3256, [2004] O.J. 3295 (Ont. S.C.J.), *per* Wilson J.

[18] See *Nyari v. Velasco*, *supra*, at note 12, *per* Sherr J.; and *Williams v. Boutler*, [2004] O.J. 352 (Ont. S.C.J.), *per* Marnager J.

[19] *Supra*, at note 6, at para. 44-47.

> parents should not be faced with a potential loss of custody simply because they choose to move. Nor should a decision to move be seen automatically as a negative factor in the ability to parent.
>
> . . . The court should also be careful not to assume that a move away from the place where an access parent lives is a deliberate attempt to thwart contact with the access parent. Any move by a custodial parent, away from the place where an access parent lives, will inevitably make exercising access more difficult. That does not mean, however, that the parent has decided to move to produce this effect.

It may be significant in this case, that the mother actually had moved some two years before the case came to trial, and although the matter was before the courts, there had been no order preventing her from relocating. By the time the matter came to trial, the mother, her husband and the child, as well another child, had a settled life and the mother had employment in the new community.

The Moving Parent: The "Badly Behaved Parent" vs. the "Co-operative Parent"

A significant factor to consider in relocation cases is the attitude and behaviour of the parent who is seeking to relocate away from the other parent. If the parent who wishes to move can demonstrate that she has been supportive of the child having a strong relationship with the other parent, there will be an expectation that she will continue to be supportive after the move.[20] Conversely, if the parent who is seeking to relocate has been hostile and had undermined the child's relationship with the other parent, there will be a concern that this behaviour will become more pronounced after the move and the relationship with the other parent will effectively be severed.[21]

In a number of cases, one parent engaging in "bad conduct" was a major concern to the court. A particular concern is a custodial parent who has engaged in unilateral conduct in relation to relocation without notification to the other parent or permission of the court. Sometimes this conduct is combined with dishonesty towards the other parent, and perhaps towards the children; for example when a mother marries a new partner who lives at a distance and does not tell the children about her remarriage. This type of conduct usually results in the courts not permitting the custodial parent to relocate with the child.[22] The stated reason for refusing to allow the move does not stem

---

20 Almost all of the reported Canadian cases involve custodial mothers who want to relocate.

21 See *Elliott v. Elliott,* [2008] O.J. 2204 (Ont. S.C.J.), *per* Gunsolus J

22 *Gibb v. Ottaway*, 2004 CarswellOnt 5533, [2004] O.J. 5209 (Ont. S.C.J.), *per* Howden

from a desire to punish the custodial mother for her conduct, but rather a concern that a parent who engages in this type of conduct demonstrates a lack of commitment to the welfare of her children, and will be unreliable in carrying out commitments to support a relationship between the children and their distant father after a move.

In some cases it was established that the custodial mother had been misleading or dishonest with the courts about her plans or circumstances. This type of conduct is always condemned by the court and sometimes appears to influence the decision not to allow the mother to relocate.[23] In other cases, the dishonesty of the mother results in her being penalized with court costs, though in assessing all of the circumstances the court may still allow her to move, because the court is satisfied that she will continue to support a relationship with the father. [24]

Conversely, if the court is satisfied that the parent who wants to relocate is "co-operative" and likely to support the relationship of the children with the other parent after the move, the court is more likely to allow the relocation. A co-operative attitude can be demonstrated by conduct after separation, as well as by presenting the court with a detailed parenting plan that has generous provisions for maintaining the relationship between the other parent and the child.

The reality is that it is difficult to enforce access orders if both parents live in the same jurisdiction; it is virtually impossible for a parent to enforce an access order if a custodial parent is permitted to relocate to another jurisdiction. Consequently, it is appropriate for courts to take into account how co-operative a parent who wants to relocate is likely to be.

Relationship of Child to New Partners

Judges are very concerned about the relationship of children with the new partners of their parents, especially about their relationship with the new partner of the parent who plans to move, as the children are likely to be spending a lot of time with that person if the relocation is approved. If the new partner has not spent much time with the

---

J. (mother did not tell child or former husband about remarriage until after it occurred); *McMurray v. Gerow*, 2004 CarswellOnt 3199, 9 R.F.L. (6th) 431 (Ont. S.C.J.), *per* Eberhard J. (mother moved child from Ontario to Connecticut contrary to court order prohibiting relocation without court permission).

23 See *Pike v. Cook*, 2005 CarswellOnt 297, [2005] O.J. 248 (Ont. S.C.J.), *per* C.T. Hackland J.

24 *Johnstone v. Brighton*, 2004 CarswellOnt 3420, [2004] O.J. No. 3477 (Ont. S.C.J.) *per* Campbell J.

children or there are concerns about his character, such as history of alcohol abuse, the court is less likely to allow the move.[25]

Conversely, when the child has a good relationship with a step-parent, especially the new partner of the mother, this is likely to be a factor in allowing the move.[26]

Reasons for the Move

In *Gordon v. Goertz*, Madam Justice McLachlin stated that "barring an improper motive", such as a desire to disrupt the relationship with the other parent, "the custodial parent's reason for moving, [is to be considered] only in the exceptional case where it is relevant to that parent's ability to meet the needs of the child."[27] Despite this general statement, judges in both the appeal and trial courts generally do consider the reasons for the move, as these will often have an impact on the welfare of the child.

When there are strong economic reasons for a move, for example, this will be a good reason to allow the relocation. Thus, in *Gravelle v. Gravelle*, Eberhard J. allowed the mother, who had been on social assistance in Ontario, to relocate to Newfoundland, where she could get a good job and housing support from her parents, even though the father had been regularly caring for the children. Due to the very limited means of the family, there would be very few visits after the relocation. The judge observed that the move would allow the mother to "lift herself and her children out of poverty, insecurity. . . hopelessness and desperation."[28]

The courts also accept that if the mother is the primary caregiver and living with a new partner who is required by his employer to relocate, or whose employment and income prospects will be substantially improved by moving, this is a strong argument in favor of permitting relocation, as the child's standard of living will be significantly improved by the move.[29]

Courts not only consider the economic reasons for moving, but the social and psychological well-being of the custodial parent, and hence the child. An improvement in the mother's general social and economic circumstances is most likely to be the basis for allowing her

---

25 See *Sloss v. Forget*, 2004 CarswellOnt 3923, [2004] O.J. 3960 (Ont. S.C.J.).

26 See *Norris v. Norris*, 2004 CarswellOnt 3298, [2004] O.J. No. 3336, 9 R.F.L. (6th) 446 (Ont. S.C.J.), *per* Gordon J.; see also *Noble v. Boutilier*, *supra*, at note 4, *per* McSorley J.

27 *Supra*, at note 7, at para 48-49.

28 2004 CarswellOnt 3159, [2004] O.J. 3166 (Ont. S.C.J.), *per* Eberhard J., at para. 25.

29 See *Jackpine v. Grasby,* 2004 CarswellOnt 407, [2004] O.J. 301 (Ont. C.J.), *per* Bishop J.

and the child to relocate if she moved to the jurisdiction after becoming pregnant, and the child is still very young. In these cases, the mother never really had significant social and economic ties to the jurisdiction, and wants to return "home" after the relationship with the father "did not work out". In *Sheikh v. Sheikh* the mother became pregnant in England and immigrated to Canada to live with her husband; the parties only cohabited 20 months.[30] The mother, who had had a good job in England, never found employment in Ontario. Although the child was born in Ontario, the mother had much stronger family and social supports in England, and much better employment prospects there. Justice Gordon concluded that by returning to England the mother would "become financially self supporting [and] . . .regain her confidence and her emotional, psychological, social and economic well being" (para. 75). To support this conclusion the judge quoted from the Ontario Court of Appeal in a similar situation of a mother seeking to return to her home with a young child: "In this case, the child's best interests are best served and better achieved by a well-functioning and happy custodial parent, operating at her full potential."[31]

Conversely, when the custodial parent has significant ties to the community where she and the children reside, and she does not have strong social or economic reasons for moving, the courts are not sympathetic to relocation.[32]

One of the common reasons for wanting to relocate is that the custodial mother has a new partner who lives in another place, and he cannot obtain employment in the place where the mother and father live. In some of the more poignant cases, the mother is pregnant with her new partner, and informs the court that she will move even if this means that custody of the child will be transferred to the father. The courts sometimes allow the children to relocate in these cases, especially if the children have a positive relationship with the step-father.[33] However, in cases where the children have a strong tie to their father or their communities, the court may transfer custody to

---

[30] 2005 CarswellOnt 1690, [2005] O.J. 1712 (Ont. S.C.J.), *per* Gordon J. See also *Waite v. Waite*, 2005 CarswellOnt 7432, [2005] O.J. 5536 (Ont. C.J.), *per* Baldock J. (mother and children entered Canada as visitor and continued presence in Canada unlawful); and *Hassan v. Mufti*, 2008 CarswellOnt 3622, [2008] O.J. 2422 (Ont. S.C.J.), *per* Lalonde J. (mother permitted to move from Ontario to Saudi Arabia with 5 month old child; move necessitated by expiry of her work permit in Canada).

[31] *Bjornson v. Creighton*, 2002 CarswellOnt 3866, [2002] O.J. 236 (Ont. C.A.), at para. 28, quoted in *Sheikh v. Sheikh, supra*, at note 30, para. 74.

[32] See *Paquet v. Clarke*, 2004 CarswellNS 439, [2004] N.S.J. 407 (N.S.S.C.); and *Pike v. Cook, supra*, at note 23, *per* Hackland J.

[33] See *Norris v. Norris, supra*, at note 26, *per* Gordon J.

the father and the mother may be forced to move without the children.[34]

Wishes of the Child

The wishes of children who are the subject of a relocation dispute will often be an important factor in determining the outcome of litigation, though many relocation cases involve younger children who are unable to express preferences, or older children who are unwilling to "take sides" and express their views. Cases involving older children who express clear and consistent views about relocation are not frequently litigated, as the parents will likely settle the case based on their children's views. While any expression of preference by a child in a relocation case will almost always require a child to speculate about future living arrangements that have not been experienced, the courts tend to give significant weight to the wishes of children in relocation cases.

Most commonly in cases involving older children for whom friendships and peer groups are becoming important, the children are reluctant to move, make new friends and attend a new school. These are cases in which the courts will refuse to allow relocation, or will change custody to the parent who will remain in the community where the children were raised.[35] There are, however, cases in which children have a strong attachment to the parent who is moving and express a desire to relocate with that parent; these views are also entitled to significant respect.[36]

The expressed wishes of children are not determinative of relocation decisions, however, especially in cases in which there is evidence from an assessor to indicate that a child's stated preference may be influenced by a parent or otherwise not accord with the child's best interests,[37] or in cases in which there are multiple siblings who may be expressing different views.[38]

Domestic Violence and High Conflict Separations

The courts seem reticent to acknowledge that domestic violence and high levels of conflict are important factors in relocation deci-

---

34 *Gibb v. Ottaway*, *supra*, at note 22, *per* Howden J.

35 See *Wilkinson v. Edward*, *supra*, at note 13.

36 See *Brouse v. Lillini*, 2008 CarswellOnt 3438, [2008] O.J. 2322 (Ont. S.C.J.), *per* Lalonde J.; *Rushinko v. Rushinko*, 2002 CarswellOnt 1997, [2002] O.J. 2477 (Ont. C.A.)

37 *Datars v. Graham*, *supra*, at note 4, *per* Quigley J.

38 *Sloss v. Forget*, *supra*, at note 25, *per* Linhares de Sousa J.; see also *Myketiak v. Myketiak*, 2001 CarswellSask 84, [2001] S.J. 85 (Sask. C.A.)

sions, even in situations where these issues are present and the move is allowed. The courts are more willing to acknowledge spousal abuse as a factor in allowing a move if children witness it or directly suffer its effects. There are Canadian cases in which domestic violence was cited by the court as a reason for allowing a move, in the hope that it would afford the mother and children some protection.[39]

However, allegations that there was spousal abuse during the marriage may not be sufficient to justify a relocation order. A court will only take account of allegations of spousal abuse if there is a conviction in a criminal court or if they are proven, on the civil standard of proof, and if they are related to the welfare of the children. The court will be concerned with the seriousness of the abuse, and whether the violence has continued after separation.[40] Thus, even if the court accepts that the husband forced his wife to have intercourse during the marriage, but the court does not accept that other acts of violence occurred, it may not grant her request to relocate with the children after separation.[41] If the court finds that the person making the allegations, invariably the woman, has significantly exaggerated her concerns about spousal or child abuse and concludes that there are no serious safety concerns, it is likely to dismiss a request to a move that is primarily based on this ground.[42]

In some cases, a significant geographical separation of the parents may be the best way to allow animosity to dissipate, or at least to reduce its effect on the children. Thus, the court may allow the primary caregiver to move with the children, even if the court concludes that the conflict is not wholly the fault of the non-custodial parent.[43] In *Elliott v. Elliott*, the Court allowed the mother to move with the child from Barrie to Toronto (about 100 kilometres) in the hope that this would help to reduce the level of conflict between the parents. The father had been seeing the six year old child daily, and

---

[39] *Lawless v. Lawless*, 2003 CarswellAlta 1409, 2003 ABQB 800 (Alta. Q.B.); the Court refused to order the return of the children because the mother had left to escape an abusive relationship. In the Manitoba case of *Cameron v. Cameron*, 2003 CarswellMan 268, [2003] M.J. 234, 41 R.F.L. (5th) 30 (Man. Q.B.), the mother was permitted to move with the children from Manitoba to Alberta, though the father was granted significant periods of unsupervised access. The move was allowed in large measure because of the mother's "justified fears" of her former husband because of his history of assaultive behaviour toward her.

[40] *Nyari v. Velasco*, *supra*, at note 12.

[41] *M. (T.K.) v. M. (P.S.)*, 1999 CarswellAlta 226, [1999] A.J. 284 (Alta. Q.B.), *per* Lee J.

[42] *Stead v. Stead*, 2005 CarswellOnt 7064, [2005] O.J. 5203 (Ont. S.C.J.), *per* C.F. Graham J.

[43] See *Noble v. Boutilier*, *supra*, at note 4, *per* McSorley J.; and *Laturnus v. Laturnus*, 2004 CarswellSask 485, [2004] S.J. 446 (Sask. Q.B.), *per* Matheson J.

at the exchange of the child there were frequent arguments between the parents, use of profane language, "and demonstrations of outright hatred which cannot but have had a devastating effect" on the child. Justice Wood observed that neither party was blameless, but that the father caused the majority of the difficulties that the parties experienced. The judge concluded that "the absence of daily contact between the child and [her father]. . . will actually benefit her by removing her from the conflict between the parties."[44]

In cases where the main concern is the level of conflict between the parents, there may be a greater reluctance to allow a long distance move, especially one out of the province, as maintenance of regular contact and enforcement of access may be problematic. In these cases, the court allowing the parties to live an hour or two drive from each other may be an appropriate way to reduce parental conflict, while allowing the child to have significant time with both parents, perhaps with some form of supervision during the exchange of the care of the child or with the access parent picking up and leaving the child at school at the start and end of the weekend to limit opportunities for direct contact between the parents.

Joint Custody: Legal and Physical

The existence of a joint legal custody arrangement between the parties will not be determinative of a relocation case and is generally given little weight by judges in Canada. Joint legal custody does not prevent a primary caregiver from obtaining approval for a move, and a court may even order a joint custody regime to continue after the move to signal that both parents are to have a continuing say in decisions about the child.[45] However, a regime of joint physical custody, or real "shared parenting", will militate strongly against a court permitting a move because this would have a significant disruptive effect on the child.[46]

Interim Applications

It is common for a parent seeking permission to relocate to want to have the issue dealt with expeditiously; for example, to allow the children to start the school year in the new community or because

---

[44] 1998 CarswellOnt 4470, [1998] O.J. 4827 (Ont. Gen. Div.), *per* Wood J.

[45] *Johnstone v. Brighton*, *supra*, at note 24, *per* Campbell J.; *Johnson v. Cleroux*, 2002 CarswellOnt 787, 23 R.F.L. (5th) 176, (Ont. C.A.); *Luckhurst v. Luckhurst*, 1996 CarswellOnt 1908, 20 R.F.L. (4th) 373 (Ont. C.A.); *Burgin v. Howells*, 2004 CarswellNS 59, [2004] N.S.J. No. 54, 2004 NSSC 31 (N.S.S.C.).

[46] *Young v. Young*, *supra*, at note 15; *Rotzetter v. Rotzetter*, 2003 CarswellBC 3202, 2003 BCSC 1962 (B.C.S.C.).

employment requires that parent to move before a full trial can be scheduled. As a result, it is not uncommon for the moving parent to bring an interim motion to seek a court order to allow the child to move before a full hearing; such an interim motion will usually be decided only on the basis of affidavits and other documents, including an assessment report if one has been prepared.[47] But there is generally no oral testimony or cross-examination of witnesses at the motion.

There is clearly a higher persuasive burden on a custodial parent who wants an order permitting relocation to obtain court permission on an interim motion. There is much less opportunity to present and test evidence on an interim motion and judges are aware that, if an interim order is made and the child permitted to move, it may establish a status quo that will be very difficult to change at a later date. If a parent is permitted to relocate with the child at an interim hearing, they will have to return if the order is not affirmed at a full hearing; however, in practice, if a move is permitted at an interim hearing, the parent opposed to the move often gives up and the matter does not proceed to trial. Accordingly, there must be "exceptional" or "compelling circumstances" if a court is to permit relocation on an interim motion.[48] However, judges also appreciate that, in some cases, there is an urgent need for a decision and sometimes there is "overwhelming" evidence to support the interim application to allow relocation.[49]

If the judge is satisfied that the outcome of any possible trial would be "inevitable", because the non-custodial parent has had a limited relationship with the child[50] or has been abusive to the child, then relocation may be permitted on an interim application. If there is a high conflict separation, which is clearly affecting the child's emotional well-being, the court may allow the primary caregiver for the child to relocate in order to reduce the stress on the child.[51] On the other hand, if there are conflicting affidavits and a lack of inde-

---

[47] For an interim motion where an assessment report was prepared and influential, see *Datars v. Graham*, *supra*, at note 4, *per* Quigley J

[48] *White v. Richardson*, 2005 CarswellOnt 1633, [2005] O.J. No. 1715 (Ont. S.C.J.), at para. 41, *per* Gordon J.; *Kennedy v. Hull*, 2005 CarswellOnt 5936, [2005] O.J. No. 4719 (Ont. C.J.), *per* McSorley J.; *Datars v. Graham*, *supra*, at note 4, *per* Quigley J.; and *Plumley v. Plumley*, 1999 CarswellOnt 3503 (Ont. S.C.J.), *per* Marsham J.

[49] *White v. Richardson*, 2005 CarswellOnt 4692, [2005] O.J. No. 4142 (Ont. S.C.J.), and *supra*, at note 48.

[50] See *Roberts v. Young*, *supra*, at note 17, *per* Wildman J.; *Braun v. Cousins*, 2004 CarswellOnt 3165, [2004] O.J. 3163 (Ont. S.C.J.), *per* Aitken J.

[51] *Elliot v. Elliot*, 1998 CarswellOnt 4470, [1998] O.J. 4827 (Ont. Gen. Div.), *per* Wood J.

pendent evidence,[52] or if the case for relocation is not very strong, the court is unlikely to allow the move on an interim motion despite the fact that the move is only an hour and a half away, as even this relatively short distance can have a serious effect on a child's relationship with a parent.[53]

There would seem to be an even greater reluctance to allow relocation on an interim application involving young children, as it will be more difficult for the access parent to maintain a relationship from a distance with these children.[54] Further, if there has been a unilateral removal of a child, the court will be inclined to require the parent who removed the child to return with the child pending a full hearing.[55] However, even with infants the court may permit a relocation by a custodial mother on an interim basis if the mother has no realistic alternative in terms of financial support but to move herself.[56]

Conditions on Allowing Relocation

The courts have demonstrated a willingness to impose conditions on a parent who is seeking to relocate in order to help ensure that a meaningful relationship is maintained with the other parent.

Except in cases of "undue hardship", the *Child Support Guidelines* do not explicitly allow for a reduction in child support payments to accommodate the higher visitation costs that are often imposed on a payor parent as a result of the relocation of the custodial parent. However, the courts have understandably demonstrated considerable flexibility in reducing or redirecting child support to facilitate regular visits with a parent and children who have moved, especially where the move has resulted in a significant improvement in the mother's financial position, either as a result of more lucrative employment or moving to live with a relatively affluent partner.[57] In some cases, the courts have done this by keeping child support levels unchanged, but ordering the mother to pay all of the costs for the child to visit.[58] In other cases, without any discussion of the legal basis for the order,

---

52 *M. (T.K.) v. M. (P.S.), supra*, at note 41; *Zunti v. McIntosh, supra*, at note 16, *per* Howden J.

53 *Fair v. Rutherford-Fair*, 2004 CarswellOnt 1705, [2004] O.J. 1774 (Ont. S.C.J.), *per* Fragomeni J.

54 *Terris v. Terris*, 2002 CarswellOnt 2955, [2002] O.J. 3018 (Ont. S.C.J.)

55 See *McMurray v. Gerow, supra*, at note 22, *per* Eberhard J.

56 *Nyari v. Velasco, supra*, at note 12, *per* Sherr J.

57 See *Burgin v. Howells, supra*, at note 45, for a case where the court cancelled spousal support arrears to compensate the father for increased access costs due to the mother's relocation.

58 *Norris v. Norris*, 2004 CarswellOnt 4372 (Ont. S.C.J.).

judges have simply allowed the access parent to deduct his costs of going to visit the child from child support.[59]

Conditions specifying when and how access is to occur are common, and there are often provisions for phone, email and webcam communication, as well as stipulations to place an obligation on the custodial parent to provide information about the child to the other parent. While most custodial parents will honour these orders, extra-provincial enforcement is a potential concern in many relocation cases. In some instances, the orders include provisions to ensure that the court that made the order maintains jurisdiction over the case, to be able to deal with variation or enforcement issues. In the Ontario case of *Johnstone v. Brighton*,[60] Campbell J. required the wealthy new partner of the mother to marry her before the relocation of the child with the mother to the United States was permitted to occur, and that he post a $100,000 bond to cover any possible enforcement costs if the mother failed to comply with the very detailed and generous visitation provisions in the order.

In *Norris v. Norris*,[61] Gordon J. required that the mother file with the court an agreement attorning to Ontario jurisdiction in relation to all issues of custody and access prior to being permitted to relocate with the children to California. In *Nitkin v. Nitkin*,[62] Wilson J. not only required the mother to attorn to Ontario jurisdiction as a condition of moving to New Mexico, but required the mother to register the Ontario order with the New Mexico court and specified that the move to New Mexico was approved only for a one year period, subject to review after one year by the court in Ontario.

Restrictions on Relocation and Procedural Issues

There are some potentially significant but complex procedural issues related to relocation cases, including questions related to the legal effect of a clause in an separation agreement or court order that prevents relocation. Although a detailed discussion of these issues is beyond the scope of this chapter, they can affect the outcome of cases and it is important for assessors to have a general awareness of these issues.

The issue of relocation is usually dealt with in the context of an application to vary an existing custody or access order under s. 17(5) of the *Divorce Act* or provincial legislation like s. 20(7) of the *Chil-*

---

59 *Pike v. Cook*, *supra*, at note 23; *Norris v. Norris*, *supra*, at note 26.

60 *Supra*, at note 24.

61 *Supra*, at note 26.

62 *Supra*, at note 17, *per* Wilson J.

dren's Law Reform Act. In *Gordon v. Goertz*, Supreme Court of Canada Justice McLachlin wrote about the need for a party seeking relief in a relocation case to satisfy a "threshold requirement" of establishing a "material change in circumstances":

> Relocation will always be a "change". Often, but not always, it will amount to a change which materially affects the circumstances of the child and the ability of the parent to meet them. A move to a neighbouring town might not affect the child or the parents' ability to meet its needs in any significant way. Similarly, if the child lacks a positive relationship with the access parent or extended family in the area, a move might not affect the child sufficiently to constitute a material change in its situation. *Where, as here, the child enjoyed frequent and meaningful contact with the access parent, a move that would seriously curtail that contact suffices to establish the necessary connection between the change and the needs and circumstances of the child.*[63]

In practice, the "threshold requirement" of a material change in circumstances is usually quite easy to establish, if the relocation involves any significant distance, and the major focus is the best interests inquiry.

In some cases, the parents do not have a custody order, in which instance the issue of relocation is addressed as part of an original application. In *Bjornson v. Creighton*, the Ontario Court of Appeal held that in cases where one parent wants to move with the child and there is no existing order, the court should first decide the issue of which parent should have custody, and then decide whether to allow that parent to relocate with the child.[64]

In the 2003 Ontario case of *Terris v. Terris*, Mackinnon J. observed that in situations in which there is no prior order, the issues of custody and relocation are closely related, though in theory they must be analyzed separately. She wrote:

> It would be artificial to interpret *Bjornson*. . . as requiring the court to determine custody without reference to all aspects of each parent's plan, including proposed place of residence, and only to consider the proposed place of residence as a discrete issue, at which time "great respect and the most serious consideration" is to be given to the views of the newly determined custodial parent.
>
> In my view. . . . the issue of custody is to be determined having regard to all relevant factors, including place of residence. Once legal custody

[63] *Supra*, at note 7, para. 14. Emphasis added

[64] *Supra*, at note 31, paras. 18-19.

> has been determined, the court will specifically address the relocation issue in accordance with the principles in *Gordon v. Goertz* . . . .
>
> In some cases of first instance, there will be considerable overlap between the factual context of the custody determination and that of the relocation determination. Nonetheless, the determination of one issue is not necessarily determinative of the other.[65]

Justice Mackinnon decided that the mother, who had been the primary caregiver of the two young children, should be the primary residence parent in a joint custody regime, but her request to relocate with the children from Ottawa to Australia was rejected.

It is common for court orders, including those based on mediated or negotiated settlements, to specify that the parents will both continue to reside in the same city as they lived in at the time of separation, or to require the custodial parent to provide the other parent with notification of any proposed move. Further, if a proposed move would interfere with specified access provisions of a court order or agreement, the parent seeking to move must also bring an application for judicial approval for a move and proper notice to the other parent.[66] While these clauses may affect the process by which a relocation case is brought before the courts, at least in Ontario, they do not create a presumption against removal or change the onus that would otherwise apply in a relocation case.[67] The issue in a relocation proceeding is making a decision based on the best interests of the child at the time of the application, and it is accepted that a prior order or agreement cannot be determinative about what will be, after a change in circumstances (i.e., when a move is contemplated), in the best interests of the child. Although clauses restricting relocation are never binding on the parties, courts in some jurisdictions outside Ontario place greater weight on them, either as a way of encouraging parents to enter into agreements when they separate,[68] or on account of the fact that they should be taken as indicative of the views of both parents about what was in the best interests of their children at the time of separation.[69]

---

65 2003 CarswellOnt 2685, [2003] O.J. No. 2829 (Ont. S.C.J.), at paras. 7, 12, 13.

66 *Archibald v. Archibald*, 2004 CarswellAlta 127, 2004 ABQB 116 (Alta. Q.B.). The court refused to approve an interim move where the mother did not give notice as required under the agreement.

67 *Ligate v. Richardson*, 1997 CarswellOnt 2185, 34 O.R. 3d 423 (Ont. C.A.); *Krebs v. Yarmel*, 2003 CarswellOnt 2909 (Ont. S.C.J.); and *Johnstone v. Brighton, supra*, at note 24.

68 For a non-Ontario decision that gave greater weight to a clause in a separation agreement restricting relocation, see *Hearn v. Hearn*, 2004 CarswellAlta 1861, [2004] A.J. 105 (Alta. Q.B.).

69 See *Woodhouse v. Woodhouse*, 1996 CarswellOnt 1906, 29 O.R. (3d) 417 (Ont. C.A.):

A parent who moves with a child in violation of the terms of a custody order may be required to return to the original jurisdiction pending trial, and the violation of the order may affect a court's assessment of how likely that parent will be to support a relationship with the other parent if a move is ultimately allowed. However, if the access parent does not make an application for judicial intervention soon after he learns that the restriction on relocation has been violated, or that the custodial parent plans to violate the order, he may be taken to have acquiesced to the move and it may be more difficult to persuade a court to take action later.

If there is no term in a custody order or agreement about residence, the custodial parent may, in theory, move with the child without seeking permission of the court or the other party, though a unilateral and surreptitious move may be viewed negatively by a judge. Even without an order or agreement regarding residence, if the access parent learns of the plans to move, he can seek an order to prevent the move without permission of the court. If, however, the access parent takes no action, he may be regarded as having acquiesced to the move, and a new status quo will quickly be established.

A Concluding Observation

Although the same standard—the best interests test—is used across Canada to determine relocation cases, different judges, using the same legal standard, balance the best interest factors in different ways, and may arrive at different decisions in cases that seem quite similar. Further, since *Gordon v. Goertz* was decided in 1996, appeal courts have failed to give trial judges, lawyers or assessors much guidance about how to weigh different factors in making relocation decisions. For this reason, Dalhousie Law Professor Rollie Thompson, recently wrote that "the law of relocation is a mess".[70] We share the view that it would be desirable for the courts or legislatures to give a clearer indication of how different factors should be weighed in making best interests decisions in relocation cases. However, in this chapter we have argued that there is also some degree of predictability to these cases, with courts and mental health professionals looking to many of the same types of factors in these cases and focusing on the interests of children and not the rights of parents.

"Separation agreements are not binding on the court because it is the interests of the children rather than those of the parents which are at issue . . .Nevertheless, it is reasonable to think that at the time the separation agreement was made it reflected the parties' views of the best interests of the children."

[70] Thompson, 2007.

Chapter 3

Understanding Domestic Violence and Its Impact on Families

Identical violent acts may have different meanings depending on the impact on the victim and the intent of the perpetrator. . . As a result, judicial focus on a single violent incident without consideration of its larger context is misleading and dangerously incomplete. Failure to consider context can endanger victims, embolden perpetrators and place children at risk.

Nancy Ver Steegh and Clare Dalton (2008)[1]

Concerns about domestic violence in the context of parental separation have received the attention of mental health clinicians, researchers, and child custody assessors, who are called upon to assist courts in recommending parenting plans after separation. Assessors face unique challenges, as domestic violence allegations are complex, multi-layered, and require a differentiated response (Jaffe, Johnston, Crooks & Bala, 2008). Adding to this complicated mix is the varied terminology used to describe the violence and abuse occurring in the post-separation relationship (Bancroft & Silverman, 2002; Gould & Martindale, 2007; Jaffe, Lemon & Poisson, 2003). In child custody and access disputes, parents raise concerns not only about physical violence and intimidation, but about emotionally abusive conduct and about the other's parenting ability. For example, allegations about inept parenting, drug and alcohol problems, child maltreatment (i.e., physical, verbal, emotional and/or sexual abuse), and the alienation of a child from one parent are common. Often accompanying these allegations are concerns about poor communication, lack of cooperation, and suspicions about the other parent's motives. We will use the term "domestic violence"[2] to refer to acts of physical aggression or

---

1 Ver Steegh, N and Dalton, C. (2008). Report from the Wingspread Conference on domestic violence and family courts. *Family Court Review, 46(3),* pp. 456-457.

2 Domestic violence can occur between heterosexual and same-sex partners (marital, co-habiting, dating, former, non-cohabiting partners). The terms "family violence", "spousal violence" or "intimate partner violence or abuse" are sometimes used instead of "domestic violence". Family violence tends, however, to refer to a broader

intimidation—including coercing sexual activity—between parents; these acts are not just civil wrongs, but are crimes. In adition, when using the term "domestic violence" we include emotionally abusive conduct perpetrated by one parent against the other, such as denigration, social isolation and financial control. Often, but not always, physical violence is accompanied by emotionally abusive behaviour.

Johnston (2006) aptly observes that in cases concerning the future care of children, if there are allegations of familial abuse too often the response of parents, judges, lawyers, and mental health professionals is to engage in fault-finding exercises to try to prove "who did what, when, where and why", rather than concede that abuse and mistrust compromises children's well-being and work to resolve the issues effectively.

In the following chapters, we discuss both domestic violence and child sexual abuse allegations made during child custody and access disputes. These are important topics for a custody assessor to be familiar with for several reasons. First, although in many cases violence ends with separation, for an important minority of cases violence increases after separation and the risk of spousal homicide and/or child homicide actually increases after separation (Birnbaum, 2006; Jaffe, Baker & Cunningham, 2004; Jaffe, Lemon & Poisson, 2003). Second, domestic violence exposes children to inappropriate role modelling, compromised parenting, sometimes on the part of both parents (Jaffe, Lemon, & Poisson, 2003). The non-abusive parent is often undermined. There are serious negative effects on children, who are exposed to, or witness, violence and abuse (Edleson, 1999; Edleson, Mbilinyi & Shetty, 2003; Jaffe, Lemon & Poisson, 2003; Kolbo, Blakely & Engleman, 1996; Nielson, 2001). Third, child abuse and domestic violence often overlap: perpetrators of spousal abuse are more likely to abuse their children than non-perpetrators (Bancroft & Silverman, 2002; Edelson, 1999b), and in extreme cases a parent may abduct or kill their children after separation. Fourth, new relationships may be potentially violent. Fifth, ongoing litigation is a form of on-going control and abuse.

Domestic violence and child sexual abuse allegations require specialized knowledge and assessment methodologies, in addition to the knowledge required for a comprehensive child custody and access assessment, in order to help the family and the court that ultimately adjudicates these matters (Jaffe *et al.*, 2008; Gould, 1998; Stahl, 1999). Further, screening for domestic violence is imperative even when allegations are not advanced by either party, as non-disclosure

---

scope of familial relationships, including not only partner abuse but also child maltreatment, elder abuse, and violence between siblings.

may be part of the family dynamic for a host of reasons (Jaffe, Lemon & Poisson, 2003).

In this chapter we: (1) explore the complexity of defining domestic violence; (2) review the causal factors, scope and prevalence of substantiated and unsubstantiated domestic violence allegations in child custody and access disputes; (3) summarize the literature on the effects of domestic violence on children and parenting; and (4) identify various typologies that can be used to screen and assess for domestic violence. In the next chapter, we discuss how domestic violence should be taken into account by child custody assessors, and survey how the family courts in Canada deal with domestic violence issues in custody and access cases.

Recognizing Domestic Violence

Historical Perspectives

Until the 1980s, except for the most serious cases, issues of domestic violence were largely ignored by the police, prosecutors, judges and legislators. Spousal abuse was largely viewed as a "private matter", and the police would rarely lay charges if they were called to a home for a domestic dispute. Physicians, ministers and social workers also gave little support to victims who did disclose incidents of domestic violence, typically suggesting that an abused woman should return to her husband, and sometimes blaming her for the abuse. In the family courts, spousal abuse was also largely ignored, with the view being that an abusive man might be a "bad husband but he could be a good father".

Since 1980 there have been dramatic changes in how society understands domestic violence and how the justice system deals with cases involving domestic violence. Shelters for abused women and their children have been established in many communities, along with programs to provide support for victims—especially victims of domestic violence—in the justice system. Police forces and prosecutors now have policies that require charges to be laid whenever police have reasonable grounds to believe that there has been a domestic assault. The prosecution can proceed even if the victim asks for charges to be withdrawn, recognizing that often the request from the victim is a result of intimidation or pressure from the abuser or family members. Family law legislation has been enacted to help victims of family violence to get orders for exclusive possession of the family home.

In many provinces, there is now a specific provision in legislation that recognizes domestic violence as a factor in making decisions about custody or access to children. For example, an amendment to

Ontario's *Children Law Reform Act* that came into force in 2006 provides:[3]

> 24 (4) In assessing a person's ability to act as a parent, the court shall consider whether the person has at any time committed violence or abuse against,
>
> (a) his or her spouse;
> (b) a parent of the child to whom the application relates;
> (c) a member of the person's household; or
> (d) any child.
>
> 24 (5) For the purposes of subsection (4), anything done in self-defence or to protect another person shall not be considered violence or abuse.

In jurisdictions that have not enacted this type of legislation, leading precedents generally recognize that, if domestic violence is proven, it should be a factor in making a decision about the care of children. Despite changes in the law, both legislative and the judge-made common law, there is inconsistency in how different judges assess the significance of domestic violence in the context of child custody and access disputes.

Over the past three decades, there has been much social science research about the nature and patterns of domestic violence and its effects of violence on children. Over the same period, there has been a growing body of legal, social science and feminist literature on the effect that domestic violence should have on custody and access determinations.

Current Perspectives

There are a number of challenges in defining "domestic violence" and "abuse". Some of these difficulties arise over differences in how various professionals describe and refer to these.[4] Ver Steegh (2005) suggests that one explanation for the confusion is that various professional groups (i.e., social work, shelter and community workers, psychology, psychiatry, and law) approach the problem from different viewpoints and use different sets of skills and knowledge bases when responding to allegations of domestic violence. As a result, she asserts, separate silos have been created without a clear mechanism in

---

[3] See Appendix I for the specific legislation outlining the factors in each province that a court is obligated to consider regarding domestic violence and abuse.

[4] Ver Steegh (2005) reviews the debate on competing theoretical explanations and definitions of domestic violence; and Johnson and Ferraro (2000) provide a comprehensive typology that integrates the competing and contrasting literature on domestic violence.

place to apply a comprehensive view of the problem, let alone a singular definition on which everyone can agree. Emery (1998) suggests that the underlying problem in conceptualizing and defining domestic violence is that the terms "violence" and "domestic violence" are driven inherently by social judgment, and not by empirical science.

Compounding the difficulties in defining domestic violence is the ongoing debate surrounding gender symmetry and asymmetry: are men and women equally violent? The literature reveals some contradictory data. Moloney *et al.* (2007) maintain that these differences are due to the use of different samples and measurements, in effect two different types of studies. Historically, much of the early research on domestic violence was based as crime-victimization studies (i.e., Bancroft and Silverman, 2002), with study populations derived from women's shelters, hospitals, criminal courts, and police records. These studies revealed that men, motivated by an obsessive need to control their partners and children, perpetrate violence at rates far exceeding those found for women. Another methodology is the family-conflict study (i.e., Straus & Hamby, 1996; Archer, 2000) based on large-scale community-based surveys (i.e., National Family Violence surveys cited by Dutton). Studies using this methodology tend to find that violence largely arises out of conflict situations and is initiated by men and women in roughly the same proportions.

Critics of the victimization-based studies argue that one of the limitations of some of these studies is that they have been conducted by feminist researchers, and only report on male perpetrators and female victims without ever asking about female perpetrated violence (Archer, 2000; DeKeseredy & Schwarz, 1998; Dobash, Dobash, Cavenaugh & Lewis, 1998). Dutton (2005), along with Hamel and Nicholls (2006), argue that much of the victimization-based literature to date has tended to focus on male batterers and female victims. They state that much of the data provided to demonstrate that males are more likely to be the initiators of intimate partner violence comes out of battered women's shelters and victim-abuse organizations. Dutton (2005) asserts that the work of Jaffe, Lemon and Poisson (2003), Bancroft and Silverman (2002), McCloskey, Figueredo and Koss (1995), and others, focus the attention of child custody assessors almost exclusively on males as perpetrators and females as victims. Dutton strongly argues that this approach is both inaccurate and misleading and, accordingly, reminds custody assessors that they must approach their investigations from a standpoint of gender neutrality (Dutton, 2007).

Kelly and Johnson (2008) aptly summarize this debate pertaining to gender symmetry and asymmetry:

> . . . until recently, the two groups most concerned with intimate partner violence, feminist activists/practitioners and family sociologists, have rarely intersected, and misunderstanding and acrimonious debate have interfered with a more constructive and unified approach to what remains a serious problem for intimate partners and their children (p. 477).

Based on their review of the literature, Kelly and Johnson (2008) observe that both women and men can be violent in heterosexual and same-sex intimate relationships, and that in some situations women can be more aggressive than their male partners (see also Archer, 2000). They further note that both men and women can experience fear and that while the extent of injuries is debated, both women and men can be injured.

Having said this, notwithstanding the expected under-reporting, Statistics Canada (2005) reported that female victims of spousal violence were much more likely than male victims to suffer injuries, require medical attention, lose time from work, live in fear, and worry about the safety of their children. The Homicide Survey (Dauvergne, 2003) reported that between 1993 and 2002, women were four times more likely to be killed by their spouse (eight female compared to two male homicide victims per million couples). The survey found that some of the women who killed their male partners were acting in self-defence.

Archer (2000), DeKeseredy and Schwartz (2001), and Kruttschnitt, McLaughlin and Petrie (2004) note that there is a lack of consistent definitions of domestic violence in research studies, which makes it difficult, if not impossible to measure the occurrence of different types of violence across age, gender, and culture. Mohr, Noone, Lutz, Fantuzzo and Perry (2000) have argued that there is also considerable ambiguity in the literature surrounding the definition of a witness to domestic violence as it applies to children. However, Edleson (1999a) suggests that there is more agreement in the literature regarding the ways in which children experience domestic violence (i.e., hearing, seeing, and being part of the violence) than in defining the term itself.

Kelly and Johnson (2008) argue that it is no longer ethical or acceptable to speak of domestic violence without first addressing and specifying the type of partner violence. In other words, we have moved from simple constructs of "battering" or domestic violence, based on observations from shelter or hospital populations, to a more sophisticated model that identifies and differentiates the various types of intimate partner abuse, ranging from violent acts to intimidation and abusive non-violent behaviour. This more recent differentiated approach to domestic violence opens up the research to examining important practice implications for interventions, and helps to differentiate the types of parenting plans suitable for children and families when violence and abuse are or have been present.

A number of writers have identified different categories of domestic abuse. For example, Jaffe, Lemon and Poisson (2003), Jaffe, Lemon, Sandler and Wolfe (1996), Jaffe, Crooks and Bala (2005), and Stahl (1999) refer to:

(1) physical abuse, ranging from slapping, hitting, kicking, and throwing objects to the use of deadly weapons;

(2) emotional abuse, defined as having one's psychological well-being attacked by coercion, verbal threats, or humiliation;

(3) economic abuse, in which one partner controls the finances; and

(4) sexual abuse, in which a person is forced to commit a sexual act against his/her will.

Often there will be more than one type of abuse in a relationship.

Dunford-Jackson and Jordan also offer a definition of domestic violence (2006):

> . . . an intentional pattern of coercive behaviour, including threats of harm, economic control, isolation, insults, and emotional control, within an intimate relationship in which one partner engages with the purpose of achieving power and control over the other partner (p. 3).

This latter definition provides another analysis that includes emphasis on the power and control dynamics inherent in domestic violence and abuse, thereby focusing the child custody assessor on the need to assess both parents and consider the effects of the violence on the child.

Most legal definitions of domestic violence include violent acts and fear of such acts. For the most part, however, legislative definitions of domestic violence fail to address patterns of domination, coercion, and control. Kuehnle and Walker (2003) observe that the definitions of domestic violence used by lawyers and the courts emphasize physical control or harm, while mental health professionals focus more broadly on both the physical and psychologically abusive nature of the violence. These differences reflect the fact that the courts tend to focus on provable "facts" while mental health professionals take a broader approach consistent with systems theory. That is, one part of the family is interconnected to the other part, and all parts are influenced by other systems—micro (individual level), macro (community level), and mezzo (broader structural level), as well as norms, culture, and law. Examining multiple variables and systems, rather than taking a one-dimensional approach, allows for a broader understanding of domestic violence (Belsky, 1993; Garbarino, 1977). Belsky (1980) and Whitchurch and Constantine (1993) conceptualize the parent-child relationship as nested within the spousal relationship. Therefore, utilizing a systems approach facilitates a broader understanding of domestic violence, along with its impact, the implications for parental roles, and treatment interventions.

In keeping with a recognition of the differentiated nature of domestic violence and a multi-disciplinary, systems approach, an interdisciplinary group met in February 2007 at the Wingspread Custody and Domestic Violence Conference, co-sponsored by the Association of Family and Conciliation Courts and the National Council of Juvenile and Family Court Judges, to address the critical issues and differences related to domestic violence (Salem & Dunford-Jackson, 2008). The group of 37 comprised representatives from three professional communities: domestic violence and abuse advocates (policy makers and service providers), social science and legal academics, and family law professionals (including judicial, legal, mental health mediators and evaluators). Although most of the participants were American, there were Canadians in the group, and the work is clearly influential in Canada. The Wingspread group produced a common statement and a number of papers that appeared in the July 2008 issue of the *Family Court Review*.[5] The goal was to work collaboratively towards developing a common vocabulary and a shared understanding of domestic violence. The differentiated approach they have recommended for parenting plans after separation or divorce is designed to assist child custody assessors who develop these plans and the courts that ultimately adjudicate these matters. The Wingspread group also recognized the need for further research to develop more effective instruments and procedures for assisting families experiencing domestic violence. We return to a more in depth discussion of different types and patterns of domestic abuse later in this chapter.

Distinguishing Domestic Violence and High Conflict

It is important to appreciate that domestic violence families are *not* the same as "high-conflict families",[6] though there is some overlap

[5] The reader is encouraged to review the entire *Family Court Review, 46(3)* (2008) for an excellent series of articles that resulted from the work of Wingspread Conference.

[6] High conflict is a term used by Dr. Janet Johnston since the early 1990s and now adopted by the field. She is a well-respected sociologist in the United States who has published widely on the topic of high-conflict families (see Johnston, 1994, 2006;

between the two groups. The risks associated with domestic violence and the intervention strategies required are often more complex and subtle than for other types of cases (Hardesty & Chung, 2006; Johnston, 2006; Walker, Logan, Jordan & Campbell, 2004). However, within high-conflict families there are often allegations of domestic violence (Drozd, Kuehnle & Walker, 2004; Jaffe, Lemon & Poisson, 1995; Johnston, 1994, 2006). Understanding and evaluating the validity and the context of allegations of domestic violence are crucial when providing recommendations for parenting plans (residential schedules and decision-making) and appropriate interventions for children and families involved in custody and access disputes.

Table 2 highlights some of the differences between families characterized by high conflict and those in which domestic violence is occurring (Koch & Pincolini-Ford, 2006):

Table 2: High Conflict Differentiated from Domestic Violence

High Conflict	Domestic Violence
Roughly equal balance of power; parents are not making safety-based decisions because risk is low	Inequality of power; abusing partner controls abused parent and children; abused parent's decision-making may be influenced by her concerns for her own and her children's safety
Conflict between parents does not preclude any particular child custody arrangement (sole custody, joint custody, parallel parenting)	Violence between the parents must be a factor in considering custody and access arrangements;
Both parents allege poor parenting on the part of the other and blame one another for all the family's problems	The abuser minimizes much of the maltreatment, both the violence in the spousal relationship and the impact on the children
Safety planning is not the central focus of the assessment process	Safety planning is a central priority

Johnston & Roseby, 1997). The reader is also encouraged to read the Special Edition of *Domestic Violence: Essays from the Family Court Review* (2005), which examines the debate over definitions, paradigms, and typologies used to describe and understand domestic violence and abuse.

Dalton, Carbon and Olesen (2003) assert that given the differences between high-conflict families and those in which domestic violence is present, it would be inappropriate to make the same assumptions about both.[7] Johnston (2006) also differentiates abusive relationships from high-conflict divorcing families. Abusive relationships are characterized as "a multidimensional phenomenon that derives from multiple causes about which victims' advocates, ideologues, and other scholars argue" (p. 17), with one partner—usually the male—maintaining control through the use of force and intimidation. High conflict cases are marked by "high hostility, verbal abuse, and on occasion physically violent struggles" (p. 17), and power is more balanced.

Prevalence

Population Studies

Domestic violence and abuse continues to be under-reported by female and male victims for a variety of reasons (i.e., fear of retaliation, children's safety issues, emotional and economic dependency). The phenomenon affects every social and economic group, and both heterosexual and same-sex partners. Although there may be some variation in rates by cultural, ethnic or religious group, no group is immune. While there is clearly some variation by age, intimate partner abuse occurs in all age groups. Prevalence rates, however, are difficult to determine with any certainty, given the inconsistencies of definition and the many studies and surveys relying on different samples and methodologies.

The Statistics Canada (2006a) report on family violence included the results of a telephone survey of 26,000 Canadians in 2004. This study revealed a very broad spectrum of abusive conduct, ranging from only one, relatively minor assault over the course of a relationship to situations where there was a pattern of serious repeated physical violence and emotional abuse. According to this 2004 study, 7 per cent of women and 6 per cent of men were assaulted by a present or former intimate partner in the previous five years, with 2 per cent of men and women reporting an assault in the past year. For a significant number of victims, 48 per cent of men and 40 per cent of women, there was only a single assault in the previous five years.

Only 36 per cent of the female victims and 17 per cent of male victims reported to the police, with reports more likely if incidents of

---

[7] See Dalton, Carbon and Olesen (2003) for a thoughtful comparative analysis of domestic violence and high conflict, including a discussion of differences in parenting.

violence were more frequent, more serious or witnessed by children. The rates of reporting an assault to the police were higher among victims who separated than those who stayed with their spouses (45 per cent of separated female victims versus only 22 per cent of female victims who remained with their abusive partners).

For less serious forms of spousal violence, based on self-reports by victims to Statistics Canada, rates of violence were equally perpetrated by both genders. For example, 44 per cent of female victims had something thrown at them by a partner, while 49 per cent of male victims reported something was thrown at them, and 57 per cent of male victims were slapped, while only 36 per cent of female victims reported being slapped. However, women were much more likely to be victims of serious assaults, with 19 per cent of female victims reporting being choked and only 5 per cent of males reporting being choked; 13 per cent of female victims received medical attention for injuries resulting from spousal violence, but only 2 per cent of male victims received medical attention. Among female victims, 34 per cent reported that they feared for their lives as a result of an assault by an intimate partner and 21 per cent reported 10 or more assaults, while among male victims only 10 per cent reported that they feared for their lives and 11 per cent reported being victimized by 10 or more assaults.

For many victims of spousal violence, especially female victims, the psychological effects of abuse can be destructive. According to the 2004 Statistics Canada telephone survey report, 94 per cent of female victims and 70 per cent of male victims reported psychological effects from the violence. The most common reactions were relatively mild and experienced roughly equally by men and women, including anger (37 per cent of women and 25 per cent of men) and upset or confusion (37 per cent of women and 28 per cent of men). The more serious effects were much more likely to be experienced by women, including:

(1) fear for self (30% of women and 5% of men);

(2) fear for children's safety (9% of women and 2% of men);

(3) depression or anxiety attacks (21% of women and 9% of men);

(4) decline in self-esteem (17% of women and 4% of men); and

(5) sleeping problems (15% of women and 4% of men).

The more serious psychological effects generally occur in cases where there is both physical and emotional abuse, or if the physical abuse is repeated and more severe. However, for some women even a single act of physical abuse, especially when combined with emotionally abusive or degrading conduct, can create a very intimidating, psychologically destructive environment.

Almost half of women who had separated and been physically abused in a prior relationship also reported serious emotional abuse in that relationship (i.e., denial of access to information about family finances, verbal denigration, or an excessively controlling husband). Emotional abuse is an important concept and is appropriately used by clinicians and by judges dealing with family law disputes. Further, almost an equal number of men and women in violent relationships reported emotional abuse, such as verbal denigration, by their partners.

The rate of violence in gay/lesbian intimate relationships has been reported to be twice as high as that in heterosexual relationships: 15 per cent compared with seven per cent, respectively (Statistics Canada, 2005).

Drozd and Olesen (2004) suggest that figures may be an underestimate of the actual prevalence of domestic violence, as some victims do not disclose to the researchers. Further, they note that the rates are higher among families that are having child custody disputes.

Prevalence in Custody Litigating Populations

Johnston and Roseby (1997) reviewed studies of high-conflict and entrenched custody disputes, and reported that 72 to 80 per cent of these cases involved allegations of domestic violence. In a recent study of custody litigants referred for evaluations (assessments), 77 per cent had alleged occurrences of domestic violence or child maltreatment (Johnston, Lee, Olesen & Waters, 2005).

In an American study, custody evaluators reported that domestic abuse allegations occurred in 37 per cent of their cases (Bow & Boxer, 2003). This study reported that in nearly half (46 per cent) of these cases the violence reportedly occurred only around the time of the separation, in close to one third (29 per cent) episodic violence was alleged, while in about one quarter (24 per cent) chronic violence was alleged. In another American study of partner violence in child custody assessments, Austin (2001) found that 51 per cent of the alleged perpetrators were male and 11 per cent were female, while 38 per cent involved both parents as perpetrators (bi-directional).

In a recent study of court files in Australia, allegations of spousal violence and/or child abuse were present in over half of the cases in which there were children (Moloney *et al.*, 2007). The researchers classified a majority of the allegations as "severe", (that is, suggesting significantly injurious or abusive circumstances). The most common forms of alleged spousal violence were physical abuse (actual or threatened), emotional/verbal abuse, and property damage. Allegations that children saw or heard spousal violence were more common in cases requiring a judicial determination, as opposed to those that settled. The frequency of the allegations in court documents led the researchers to conclude that domestic violence is a "core business" of the Australia family courts.

Birnbaum (2005) reviewed 500 intake files of families (250 mother's and 250 father's reports) involved in a custody and access dispute at the Ontario Office of the Children's Lawyer (a public court-related service that conducts assessments and represents the legal interests of children). She found that mothers reported that their children were exposed to parental violence in 52 per cent of the cases, while fathers reported such exposure 31 per cent of the time. In addition, violence against the children was reported by mothers 45 per cent of the time and by fathers 21 per cent of the time. While, these statistics must be considered with caution, since litigating parents make numerous allegations during child custody disputes (i.e., parental alienation, sexual abuse, abusive and poor parenting, etc), they do reflect a growing concern of the negative consequences for children who have witnessed and been exposed to domestic violence.

While there remains some controversy about prevalence rates and the gender of the alleged perpetrator, a number of sobering findings are established in the literature. First, domestic violence and abuse create safety concerns for victims and their children (Bow & Boxer, 2003; Lawson, Gardiner, Johansson & MacLaurin, 2006). Secondly, children who witness violence are at a higher risk for post-separation emotional and behavioural problems than are other children (Dalton, 1999; Jaffe *et al.*, 2003). Thirdly, these children are also at a higher risk of being victims of child abuse (Edelson, 1999b; Lemon, 1999). Fourthly, domestic violence is often associated with a poor prognosis for parental cooperation (Austin, 2000b). We will examine the issues related to the impact on victims and children later in this chapter.

Rates of Substantiated and Unsubstantiated Allegations

As we note in Chapter 5, where we discuss allegations of sexual abuse, there are very significant methodological challenges in conducting research to determine the rate of founded and false allegations of domestic violence. For example, a parent may truly believe that they were abused in the relationship even though the claim may not be proven by an assessor or judge. Alternatively, an assessor may conclude that domestic violence occurred and make recommendations on that basis, but a judge may not be convinced, on the balance of probabilities, that the allegations were true.

In addition, due to the use of different samples and methodologies, it is difficult to know with any certainty the rates of substantiated and unsubstantiated allegations of domestic violence. In examining 196 custody and access trial decisions in Canada between 1990 and 1998—cases involving child sexual and physical abuse allegations against partners—Bala and Schuman (1999) found that in only 23 per cent of the cases did the court conclude that the allegations of child abuse were proven. In another study, Shaffer and Bala (2003) reviewed reported family law cases in Canada in which there was a written decision regarding domestic violence. They found that in the 42-recorded cases over a three-year period in which domestic violence was alleged against men, 31 (or 74 per cent) of the allegations of domestic violence were regarded as substantiated by the court. They found only two cases in which allegations were made against the mother, one of which was substantiated.

In a study of 120 custody and access disputing families referred for custody evaluations in the United States, Johnston, Lee, Olesen and Walters (2005) found that allegations of domestic violence and/or child abuse occurred in 77 per cent of the cases. Allegations of domestic violence against fathers were substantiated by the clinicians in 74 per cent of the cases, and while allegations of domestic violence against mothers were substantiated in 50 per cent of the cases; allegations of child maltreatment were considered substantiated in only about a third of the cases. In their survey of custody evaluators, Bow and Boxer (2003) found that in one-third of the referrals containing allegations of domestic violence, support for these was found by the assessors in more than half (57 per cent).

In summary, although there is only limited research, all of the studies to date have found that a majority of allegations of domestic violence made in the context of custody litigation, almost all of them by women, are substantiated. Since all of the cases in these studies involve litigation, it seems safe to assume that the alleged perpetrators were denying or minimizing their abuse, and thus safe to make the assertion of Jaffe, Crooks and Bala (2005) that "denial and minimization of abuse by genuine abusers are more common than false or exaggerated claims of spousal abuse by alleged victims" (p. 2). However, it is important to emphasize that each case must be examined on its own merits, and even if a majority of allegations of domestic violence are substantiated, there is a significant rate of false and exaggerated claims.

Rates of Children Exposed to Domestic Violence

Based on a large sample telephone survey, Statistics Canada (2000) estimated that half a million children had either heard or witnessed an assault on one parent by the other in the previous five years. Based on the General Social Survey (2004), Statistics Canada estimated that the children of 394,000 spousal violence victims had seen or heard violence in the home.

The Canadian Incidence Study of Reported Child Abuse and Neglect, or CIS-2003 (Trocmé, Fallon, MacLaurin, Daciuk, Felstiner, Black, Tonmyr, Blackstock, Barter, Turcotte & Cloutier, 2003), reported that over one third of substantial reports to child welfare agencies (34 per cent) involved some form of exposure to domestic violence; 25 per cent involved only exposure to domestic violence; and 9 per cent involved both exposure to domestic violence and some other form of child abuse or neglect.[8] This study found that domestic violence was considered substantiated by the investigating worker in over 70 per cent of the cases where it was reported, and suspected in a further 16 per cent of the cases they investigated.

More significantly, as noted in the research literature, children remain at risk for serious adjustment difficulties during separation (Edleson *et al.*, 2003; Gewirtz & Edleson, 2007; McIntosh, 2003a).

Underlying Causes and Explanations

There continues to be an ongoing debate in the social science literature regarding the underlying causes of and explanations for domestic violence (Dalton, 1999; Jaffe, Crooks & Bala, 2005; Jaffe *et al.*, 1996; Johnston, 2006; Morgolin, 2005; Wolfe & Jaffe, 1999; Ver Steegh, 2005).

The 1960s literature on family violence was dominated by the psychopathology model, which portrayed both the battering husband and his victim as suffering from some form of personality disorder

---

[8] The Canadian Incidence Study is the first set of national data across Canada (excluding Quebec) collected from child welfare workers using a standard set of definitions of both domestic violence and exposure to it. For a comprehensive review of the data and analysis comparing children's exposure to domestic violence to other forms of child maltreatment, we encourage the reader to visit the Centre of Excellence for Child Welfare website at the Faculty of Social Work, University of Toronto, as well as the Public Health Agency of Canada website. The use of the terms "substantiated" and "unsubstantiated" is often difficult to define; each study uses a different interpretation and different meaning for both. However, in the child welfare context, substantiated means that the child welfare worker found the allegations of domestic violence to be valid. Having said this, substantiation of allegations by a child welfare worker does not necessarily mean that a child will be taken into care (see Black, Trocmé, Fallon & MacLaurin, 2006).

(Gelles, 1973; Schultz, 1960; Spinetta & Rigler, 1972). In the 1970s, Straus's general systems theory attempted to explain violence between spouses by viewing the family as goal-seeking and purposive. Rather than being portrayed as an individual pathology, domestic violence was viewed as a product of family systems. Systems theory suggests that domestic violence is rooted in faulty couple and family interactions, and that each individual needs to be understood in the context of the interconnections and dynamics of the family relationship.

Starting in the 1970s, feminist social scientists and lawyers began to analyze domestic violence as being rooted in unequal gender relations. Dobash and Dobash (1979), for example, wrote about domestic violence as a reflection of the patriarchal social structure; they argued that patriarchy leads to the subordination of women, which significantly contributes to systemic violence against them. This line of thinking was reflected in the work of Lenore Walker (1984), who developed the theory of "battered wife syndrome". Walker argued that women are in an inherently unequal position in terms of power and status, and that their response to battering by their partners is a situation of "learned helplessness" and an inability to leave their abusive partners or protect themselves.

Some scholars have studied the biological and neurological aspects of domestic violence, based on genetics and biochemistry; they observe that impaired neurological functioning in abusers leads to inadequate problem-solving abilities and a lack of impulse control which leads to aggression. It has also been observed that the psychological and physical trauma of repeated abuse can result in changes in brain development, for both victims and children exposed to domestic violence.[9]

Sociological theorists posit that poverty and discrimination are at the root of domestic violence. Social learning and developmental theory suggests that domestic violence is the result of learned behaviour modelled and rewarded over time and supported by the broader culture and by the family (Gelles, 1973, 1980).

Emery and Laumann-Billings (1998) cogently summarize the literature regarding many of the contributing factors related to domestic violence. They include: (1) individual personality factors; (2) family

---

[9] See the Australian website that refers to studies related to biological and neurological explanations of violence, online at: http://www.aic.gov.au/publications/vda/vda-sec08.html. Also see Berman, McCloskey and Broman-Fulks (2003) for a review of biopsychosocial theories on aggression related to domestic violence and Brennan and Raine (1997) for a review of biosocial research and the theoretical bases of antisocial behavior.

interaction patterns; (3) poverty and social disorganization; (4) acute stressors; and (5) the cultural context in which the family lives.

Moreover, it is clear that there is a range of theoretical perspectives and multiple pathways that contribute to an understanding of domestic violence. A sophisticated understanding of domestic violence requires a consideration of a complex array of interacting factors, including those relating to risk and resiliency in individuals. As Johnston (1995b) aptly points out, "Domestic violence is not a unitary syndrome with a single underlying cause, but rather a set of behaviours arising from multiple sources, which may follow different patterns for different individuals and families" (p. 24). Child custody assessors called upon to assess this complex array of factors need to consider an augmented assessment approach, referred to as a specialized risk assessment, with a view to providing differentiated parenting plan and intervention recommendations that flow from the results of their assessments.[10]

Effects of Domestic Violence on Children

Sudermann and Jaffe (1999) suggest that it is preferable to use the term "exposure" rather than "witness to" domestic violence to describe the experience of children, as "exposure" allows for a broader understanding of children who may not always be direct witnesses to domestic violence, but can suffer from its aftermath nonetheless. In a Statistics Canada study, 40 per cent of female victims of spousal violence and 25 per cent of male victims reported that their children saw or heard the violence.[11] Children were more likely to observe violence that resulted in injury or that caused a parent to fear for their lives: i.e., *a child was more likely to witness more serious spousal violence*. Further, it is likely that parents underestimate the awareness that their children have of violence in the home. Even if a child does not directly observe spousal abuse, living in a home where there is spousal abuse can have serious negative effects. Saunders (1994) states:

> Hiding in their bedrooms out of fear, the children may hear reported threats of injury, verbal assaults on their mother's character, objects hurled across the room, suicide attempts, beatings, and threats to kill. Such exposure will arouse a mixture of intense feelings in the children. These feelings include a fear that the mother will be killed, guilt that

---

[10] See Anne L. Ganley and Susan Schechter (1995), "*Domestic violence: A national curriculum for child protective services*," for a discussion of the impact of control in relation to partners sharing children after separation.

[11] See Statistics Canada, *Measuring Violence Against Women* (2006) p. 34.

> they did not stop the violence, divided loyalties, and anger to the mother for not leaving. (p. 54)

Fantuzzo, Mohr and Noone (2000) have noted that the effects of domestic violence and abuse on children largely remained "invisible" until the 1980s, when the issues related to domestic violence started to receive more attention both in the professional literature and in the popular media. Edleson (1999a) observed that children who are exposed to domestic violence had been regarded as "silent" or "unintended victims", but became "more visible" to mental health practitioners. Professionals, lawyers and advocates became more aware of the effects of domestic violence on children. We are concerned that too often children remain largely invisible when caught in custody and access disputes that raise domestic violence issues, as the focus of inquiry into the allegations of violence often takes precedence to a consideration of the needs of children.

The negative impact of domestic violence on children is now widely recognized by researchers and documented in numerous studies (Ayoub, Deutsch & Maranganore, 1999; Hester, Pearson & Harwin, 2000; Jaffe, Crooks & Wolfe, 2003; Jaffe, Crooks & Bala, 2005; Mullender, Hague, Iman, Kelly, Malos & Regan, 2003). Research studies have established an array of negative effects for children who are exposed to domestic violence in terms of behavioral, academic, physical and psychological problems (Bancroft & Silverman, 2004; Jaffe, Baker & Cunningham, 2004; Geffner, Jaffe & Suderman, 2000; Johnston, 1994; Kelly, 1993; Lemon, 1999; Thompson & Amato, 1999; Wolfe & Jaffe, 1999).

A number of studies have established that children whose parents engage in domestic abuse are also significantly more likely to be subject to maltreatment. Appel and Holden (1998) reviewed more than 30 studies examining the link between domestic violence and child maltreatment, and found a 40 per cent co-occurrence rate between the two. Straus and Gelles (1990) also found that the presence of adult domestic violence correlates with an increased risk for physical abuse of children. Edleson (1999b), Edleson *et al.* (2003), Saunders (1994), and Straus (1983) have demonstrated that when domestic violence and child maltreatment are combined, serious negative consequences are more likely for children than for domestic violence alone.

Many writers have focused on the impact of domestic violence on children at the centre of child custody disputes (Johnston & Campbell, 1993b; Johnston & Roseby, 1997; Nemark, Hartell & Salem, 1995; Jaffe, Lemon & Poisson, 2003; Dalton, Carbon & Olesen, 2003; Jaffe, Crooks & Bala, 2005). Jaffe, Lemon and Poisson (2003), among others, argue that the courts have long minimized the effects on children of being exposed to domestic violence.

Kolbo, Blakely and Engleman (1996), Fantuzzo and Mohr (1999), and McIntosh (2003a) have suggested that despite the many negative consequences found for children who witness domestic violence, our knowledge is still quite limited because of methodological limitations, reliance on untested theories, and a lack of reliable measures to assess child exposure to domestic violence. Jaffe, Lemon and Poisson (2003) have noted that while there has been considerable research over the last few decades on the negative effects for children exposed to domestic violence, questions remain as to the risk and resiliency factors that influence children's adjustment to one extent or another, both in the short and long term. Furthermore, they suggest that mental health professionals need to exercise caution when examining research reported on aggregate data, which can minimize individual differences.

Not all children experience domestic violence in the same manner. Reynolds, Wallace, Hill, Weist and Nabors (2001) refer to mediating factors, including the child's gender and age, and the nature and frequency of the violence. There are individual risk factors that may increase the likelihood of negative effects, including the presence of any parents mental health problems, parents alcohol and substance abuse problems, lack of access to resources, and family vulnerability issues. There are also resiliency factors (protective factors) that decrease risk, including having supportive parental relationships, supportive relationships with caregivers outside the immediate family, academic success, and access to resources to support the child and the family (Jaffe, Lemon & Poisson, 2003; Gewirtz & Edleson, 2003; Masten & Coastworth, 1998).

In spite of the methodological limitations discussed, in their reviews of the literature, Davis (1988), Emery (1982), Fantuzzo and Lindquist (1989), Fantuzzo and Mohr (1999), and others unanimously support the view of a positive correlation in children between those children exposed to domestic violence and those that subsequently exhibit negative development. In a systematic review of the literature, Kolbo, Blakely and Engleman (1996) found 29 articles that demonstrated that children who are exposed to domestic violence are at risk for behavioural, emotional, social, cognitive, and physical health difficulties.

These studies include research on the co-occurrence of child maltreatment and exposure to domestic violence, and examine the risk and resiliency factors on child outcomes. Fantuzzo and Mohr (1999), in their reviews of the studies from 1989 and 1996, along with Carlson (2000) and Jaffe, Lemon and Poisson (2003), found that children exposed to domestic violence demonstrated more externalized, aggressive behaviours (such as hitting, kicking, or swearing) and more internalized behaviours (anxiety, depression, low self-esteem, and somatic complaints) than did children from non-violent homes. Kilpatrick, Litt and Williams (1997) and Kilpatrick and Williams (1998) found that children exposed to domestic violence between their parents are more likely to develop post-traumatic stress disorder.

In Table 3, McIntosh (2003a) summarizes the literature on the impact on children who are witnesses to domestic violence. The table delineates the developmental and behavioral impacts on children from violent homes compared to children from non-violent homes. While these disturbances in behaviour do not specifically refer to children in families where there is a custody dispute *and* domestic-violence families, one can hypothesize that a child in highly contested custody disputes is also likely to experience some, if not many, of these disturbances.

Table 3: Major Developmental Impact on Children Who Witness Domestic Violence—McIntosh (2003a)[12]

Children from violent homes compared to children from nonviolent homes, are significantly more likely to demonstrate the following:	
Psychological and Behavioural Difficulties	➢ Clinical disturbance in emotions and behavior. In the normal population about 10 per cent of children demonstrate enduring levels of clinical disturbance (over more than a year), where in the population of children living with domestic violence, the figure is 40-50 per cent (Hughes, Graham-Bermann & Gruber, 2002; Mertin & Mohr, 2002) ➢ Disturbed patterns of emotional arousal and affect regulation, particularly through violent conflict witnessed in the pre-school years (Lieberman & Van Horn, 1998)

[12] Adapted with permission from both the author and the publisher, with minor modifications. For another excellent review of the literature regarding the short- and long-term consequences for children of witnessing domestic violence and the limitations inherent in the research: see Agar (2004) and Edleson (1999a).

	➢ Children exposed to violence experience an increase in physiological arousal in response to generalized conflict (De Bellis, 2001; McLoyd, Harper & Copeland, 2001; Pfefferbaum & Allan, 1998)
Impact on Social World	➢ Children demonstrate heightened aggression, impulsiveness and poor social skills (Darwish, Esquivel, Houtz, & Alfonso, 2001; Graham-Bermann, 2002) ➢ Children have fewer contacts with supportive others, and absence of significant supports post violence (Graham-Bermann, 2002; McCloskey & Steuwig, 2001)
Intergenerational Transmission of Violent Patterns of Relating	➢ Poor decision-making in relation to choosing partners (Carlson, 2000) ➢ More likely to repeat cycle of victimization in their adult lives (Johnston, 2002)
Co-occurring Stressors for Post-Trauma Difficulties	➢ Children blaming themselves for the violence (El-Sheikh & Hargar (2001)) ➢ Continuation of exposure to post-separation conflict between parents (Kelly, 2000; McIntosh, 2003b) ➢ A continuing co-morbidity of domestic violence and child maltreatment (Faller, 2003; Margolin & Gordis, 2000; O'Leary, Smith, Slep & O'Leary, 2000) ➢ Disruptions for children in schooling, friends, daily living and family activities (Kneale, 1999; Mullender, Kelly, Hague, Malos & Iman, 2000) ➢ Living in secrecy with respect to domestic violence (McIntosh, 2002; Peled, 1996)

While research has clearly established that children are negatively affected by living in families where there is domestic violence, there is still much that is not known about predicting effects on individual children. As we noted in Chapter 1 on the effects of parental conflict on children's adjustment, much of the research to date has not differentiated effects on children by the intensity and type of domestic violence, or studied individual risk and resilience factors. Further, the nature and degree of parental involvement and the quality of the child's relationships with both parents are two other important factors that mitigate risk to children in separated families.

Effects of Domestic Violence on Parenting

Both assessors and the courts must recognize that domestic violence is related to the short- and long-term parenting capacities of both perpetrators and victims of domestic violence (Johnston and Campbell, 1988; Jaffe *et al.*, 2008). One must consider why a perpetrator is engaging in abusive behaviour towards a partner, and what this suggests about the personality and parenting capacity of the perpetrator. Victims of domestic violence may suffer from problems that are related to their vulnerability and victimization that compromise their parenting.

Parenting deficits associated with domestic violence perpetrators are noteworthy. These may include:

(1) physical abuse, emotional abuse (i.e., isolation, put downs, name-calling, ignoring), and sexual abuse;

(2) abduction or threats to abduct;

(3) use of coercive discipline engendering fear; inconsistent parenting—vacillating between being overly permissive and authoritarian, role reversal;

(4) inability to stay child-focused—keep parent's needs separate from child's needs, denial of child's feelings and ideas in favour of own, putting child in the middle of the parental conflict (using child as go-between, weapon in communication); lack of respect, poor boundaries, sense of entitlement;

(5) acting irrationally, exhibiting poor judgment, morally corrupting child (encouraging criminal behaviour); and

(6) drug or alcohol abuse.

All of the research and writing to date on victims of spousal abuse has dealt with mothers, but it seems likely that this would apply to male victims as well. Some authors argue that domestic violence has little effect on parenting capacity. For example, Van Horn and Lieberman (2002) write:

> . . . women who live in violent relationships are remarkably similar to comparison women in their beliefs about parenting, their self-reported parenting behaviours, and their observed interactions with their children. On such variables as providing structure, showing warmth, being emotionally available, and positively reinforcing their children, mothers from violent and nonviolent homes reportedly engaged in similar behavior. (p. 83)

Most of the research in this area, however, recognizes that being a victim of domestic violence may affect parenting, but does not always do so. Some victims of domestic violence may tend to neglect or even abuse their children. Further, there may be concerns about whether a victim of domestic abuse can protect their child from an abusive partner, who may also be maltreating the child.

Osofsky (1999) observed that when mothers are victims of violence, they may be less emotionally available to care for and provide support to their children. They may become depressed and irritable, thereby leaving their child to feel that they may have done something to cause their parent's emotional distress. Edleson, Mbilinyi and Shetty (2003) suggest that battered mothers experience significantly higher levels of stress than non-battered mothers, that their parenting capacity may be compromised, and that they may be more likely use aggression against their children.[13] However, these writers acknowledge the likelihood of abuse towards their children is reduced once the mother is in a safe place. Appropriate counselling and parent education for an abused mother may also improve parenting.

Victim mothers may be both physically and emotionally exhausted (Jaffe *et al.*, 2008). Their true potential as a parent may be compromised by situational factors associated with the abuse (e.g. disruptions, litigation). They may be anxious and depressed and exhibit symptoms of Post Traumatic Stress Disorder. Having low self-esteem, these mothers may lack confidence in their own parenting. Substance abuse may occur as a coping mechanism to numb the pain of the trauma. Victim mothers may have difficulty managing their children's behaviour. For example, they may exhibit inconsistent parenting and vacillate between being overly permissive and coercive, generally showing poor judgment. Role reversal may occur when a

---

[13] The reader is also encouraged to review, Edleson, J.L., Mbilinyi, L.F. and Shetty, S. (2003). *Parenting in the context of domestic violence.* Judicial Council of California. Administrative Office of the Courts for a more thorough examination of the effects on parenting by perpetrators.

victim mother depends on her child to meet the mother's needs. Some victim's may have difficulty protecting their children, while others may be overprotective.

Therefore, it is important to assess thoroughly both parents' parenting strengths and challenges, taking into account the type of domestic violence, including the context, pattern and severity. As we discuss more fully in Chapter 4, it is important to consider the extent to which the abusive parent can assume responsibility for their behaviour and take concrete steps to rehabilitate, improve their parenting and repair their relationship with their child. Also relevant is the victim parent's willingness to accept assistance and take steps to address their vulnerabilities and improve their parenting. Many victims of domestic violence should have parenting education and counselling to increase their understanding of the effects on their children of having been exposed to domestic violence, and possibly direct abuse by the perpetrator, as well having suffered from compromised parenting by the victim.

We now turn to a discussion of the different types of domestic violence.

Differentiating Domestic Violence and High Conflict[14]

Until relatively recently, researchers, advocates for abused women and many professionals tended to characterize all domestic violence as male-perpetrated battering (see Walker, 1984), and some professionals still view the phenomenon this way. Over the past few decades, however, many researchers and practitioners have come to recognize that not all domestic violence is the same. The literature has become more sophisticated in differentiating the various types of violence, using as a basis: dynamics, context and consequences. For example, a relationship in which there is a single slap at the time of the separation is very different from a relationship in which there is a pattern of violence, control and intimidation. However, a single violent act in the context of a pattern of psychologically abusive behavior may cause sustained fear and submission. Thus, the context, pattern and significance to the victim need to be considered when understanding and differentiating domestic violence and its impact.

---

[14] It is important to note that while we review various typologies found in the social science literature, we by no means provide an exhaustive list of them. Rather, our intent is to demonstrate for the mental health professional ways to gather, conceptualize and organize the information collected during a child custody assessment and then be able to provide parenting recommendations that provide safety for the children and their parents based on an individualized approach that meets the needs of the family.

It is also important to consider the motivation of the perpetrator of the violence, within the context of custody disputes to assess the impact of domestic violence on the children.

The balance of this chapter is devoted to an exploration of the value and limitations of typologies of domestic violence, and then to discussing one of the most useful typologies developed.

Typologies of Domestic Violence: Benefits and Risks

There are benefits and risks to developing and using typologies of domestic violence. The fundamental value of using a typology is that it helps to understand and respond to a complex and differentiated range of cases. The benefits of typologies are that they allow for greater differentiation and clarity of the range of observable behavior. Differences in incidence, severity, consequences and gender will be present across types. The differentiation of types will assist with triaging these cases depending on risk and need for safety. Typologies also provide for a more tailored and differentiated response (i.e., treatment and parenting plan recommendations) based on the needs of the child and parents. Clearly, a typology is preferable to an approach that views all domestic violence as battering.

There are, however, real risks and limitations to existing typologies. One important risk is the lack of sensitive, reliable and effective screening and assessment tools to identify various types of domestic violence. There are no pure and discreet types and, therefore, cases frequently overlap categories. Use of typologies may lead to false negatives (failure to identify serious lethal violence) and false positives (placing excessive restrictions on parent-child contact, when this is not warranted). Use of typologies may also increase litigation, with lawyers and expert witnesses arguing about how to categorize a particular case.

Recognizing that there are limitations to identifying the classifications and typologies of many phenomena, including domestic violence and intimate relationships, it still seems useful to discuss the various types of domestic violence (Johnson, 2005a, 2005b; Kelly & Johnson, 2008). There are a number of different but overlapping typologies that have been developed by different researchers. Underpinning each of these typologies are issues based on gender relations, culture, and politics. However, one central theme that resonates throughout the literature and around the globe is the need for a specialized and differentiated approach to domestic violence (Jaffe, Crooks & Bala, 2005; Johnston, 2006; Jaffe *et al.*, 2008; Moloney *et al.*, 2007). Differentiation leads to more thorough child custody assessments and the ability to develop more appropriate parenting plan recommendations on behalf of children. Once child custody assessors organize their data according to the various patterns of intimate partner violence, then, and only then, can more effective and differentiated responses occur, including those related to both parenting plans and other interventions (Kelly & Johnson, 2008; Jaffe *et al.*, 2008).

Given this context and cautionary note, we now summarize the most current thinking in the field, and in particular on the 2007 Wingspread Custody and Domestic Violence Conference.

A Typology of Domestic Violence

Coercive Controlling Violence (CCV)

Coercive Controlling Violence is the pattern most consistent with the battering type of domestic violence, which was first identified and discussed in the late 1970s. It has also been associated with the Duluth "power and control wheel", a tool that is still frequently used in the educational training of professionals (Pence & Paymar, 1993). CCV involves an ongoing pattern of emotional abuse that includes reported threats, coercion, control, isolation, denigration and intimidation in combination with physical violence against the victim. This type of violence tends to be the most severe. It is often associated with injuries, and may escalate to homicidal levels when the perpetrator feels threatened by separation. In their review of the literature, Kelly and Johnson (2008) found that men are much more likely to be perpetrators of this type of violence (Johnston, 2006).[15] In the early 1990s, Michael Johnson (1993, 1995, 1996) discussed this type of domestic violence, referring to it as "patriarchal terrorism". He later changed this term to intimate terrorism, in recognition of the fact that not all coercive control is necessarily rooted in a patriarchal society and that women can also be violent (Johnson, 2005a, 2005b). Consequently, the term coercive controlling violence has replaced the previous terms. Writers point out that this type of intimate partner violence (domestic violence) is found more frequently in the cases dealt with by police, in the criminal and child welfare courts, in shelters, hospital emergency rooms and agencies treating batterers (Archer, 2000; Dutton, 2007; Kelly & Johnson, 2008).

Perpetrators of coercive controlling violence may be more likely than other abusers to also engage in child maltreatment.

---

[15] Debate exists regarding the extent to which females can and do initiate CCV, with some reporting that intimate partner violence, including the severe form, is perpetrated by women more than by men. (See debate in *Journal of Child Custody*, 2005, volume 2(4), articles by Donald Dutton and Michael Johnson and D. Dutton, *Journal of Child Custody*, 2006, volume 3(1), pp. 67-69.)

Typologies of Battering

Other researchers have focused on the battering type of domestic violence and specific typologies of batterers (Gondolf, 1988; Saunders, 1992), with the hope that understanding and delineating batterer subtypes would increase the effectiveness of interventions. For example, Holtzworth-Munroe and Stuart (1994) conducted a review of 15 batterer typologies to better understand the characteristics and types of male batterers. They proposed that batterer subtypes be classified based on: (1) the severity and frequency of marital violence in the relationship; (2) the generality of the violence inside and outside the relationship; and (3) the batterer's personality disorder or psychopathology. Using these subtypes would allow for further analysis according to: (1) family-only type batterer (with little psychopathology, predicted to be the least violent subgroup); (2) dysphoric/borderline type batterer (violence is moderate to severe toward the female partner, and these persons exhibit more psychological distress); and (3) generally violent/antisocial type batterer (most violent type and antisocial, with high levels of marital violence).

Hamberger, Lohr, Bonge and Tolin (1996) examined 204 men who were violent within their marriages. They identified three main typologies: (1) the passive-aggressive-dependent, similar to the Holtzworth-Munroe and Stuart (1994) dysphoric male, who exhibits borderline organizational patterns, depression and anxiety; (2) the antisocial (more severe levels of violence); and (3) the non-pathological, similar to the Holtzworth-Munroe and Stuart (1996) family-only typology, in which the male has lower levels of violence directed toward his partner only.

Violent Resistance (VR)

This type involves a violent response to abuse initiated by a controlling perpetrator; it is a reaction to defend, fight back and protect oneself or one's children from further injury. Both men and women engage in this reactive type of violence, but women are much more frequently cited in the literature. This type of behaviour is often associated in court with the notion of self-defence, though it may involve a response that, in law, is regarded as an "over-reaction" rather than self-defence. VR has been referred to by other writers as female resistance, resistive/reactive violence, and self-defence.

Conflict-Instigated Violence (CIV)

This pattern involves one or, more commonly, both partners engaging in acts of violence, often in the course of an escalating argument, where the violence is not being used to control or intimidate the partner but rather as an expression of anger. It has been referred to previously by different names, such as situational couple violence or common couple violence (Johnston, 2005), conflict-motivated violence (Ellis & Stuckless, 1996), common couple aggression (CCA) (Zibbell, 2005) and, more generally, as mutual, symmetrical or interactional violence or abuse. Writers tend to agree that it is the most common type of physical aggression in intimate relationships, in which both men and women in a relationship, or dating, lack adequate conflict resolution skills and may be violent towards each other (Kelly & Johnson, 2008; Strauss & Gelles, 1992). The violence tends to be of a relatively minor nature, such as shoving, pushing, and slapping. Although it sometimes continues throughout the separation process, it usually ends after the separation is complete, with time and with age. CIV does *not* include patterns of control or coercion by one partner over the other, and fear is not usually present for either partner. These individuals can speak up for themselves, and in many instances are rather feisty as opposed to fearful and submissive. It results from argumentative situations that culminate in physical violence. The extent of the violence tends to be less severe and it is less likely to escalate over time than coercive controlling violence (Kelly & Johnson, 2008).

Separation-Instigated Violence (SIV)

Separation-instigated violence (also known as separation-engendered violence) arises when either partner (or both) exhibit violence in incidents precipitated by separation. It is usually limited to one or two episodes and in reaction to the emotional trauma of separation. Fear is uncharacteristic, and there is no prior history of violence in the relationship; any violence is an uncharacteristic and unexpected loss of control associated with feelings of loss, inadequacy, and humiliation. The partner who is left may be the violent one. Typically, the violent person has some awareness of his or her wrongdoing and is remorseful. The violence usually stops after separation.

Mental Illness

Some cases of domestic violence are the result of the paranoid or psychotic state of the violent spouse; in some cases depression is a major contributor to family violence. These cases often involve unpredictable attacks by one spouse as a result of disordered thinking, and often leave the victims feeling traumatized, intimidated and fearful. A relatively small percentage of spousal violence cases are in this category, but they may pose special risks as a number of cases of parental killing of children and suicide involve severe depression; these may be perpetrated by mothers or fathers.

Some of the children in this situation are badly traumatized, while others may identify with the psychotic parent and are themselves psychotic. In these cases, if the parents are separated, visitation between the abusive spouse and children should be supervised or suspended, at least until the abuser's mental state has stabilized. If properly diagnosed and treated, however, the risk of future violence can be substantially reduced or eliminated, and the formerly violent parent may resume contact with the child or may even gain custody.

Conclusion

In this chapter we explored the complexity of attempting to define domestic violence, reviewed the scope and prevalence of domestic violence allegations in child custody disputes, summarized the social science and research literature that focuses on the effects of domestic violence on children and subsequent parenting problems, and identified a typology that can be used to differentiate the types and patterns of domestic violence. In the next chapter, we explore best practice considerations, screening and assessment protocols, and the continuum of differentiated recommendations and interventions for both parenting time and legal custody or decision-making in cases involving allegations of domestic violence.

Chapter 4

Domestic Violence in Child Custody Disputes: Differential Assessment and the Court's Perspective

Family courts have traditionally turned a blind eye to domestic violence or have minimized its significance. Custody disputes involving domestic violence have been forced into a one-size-fits-all paradigm, an erroneous and potentially life-threatening approach. What is required is a differentiated approach based on careful screening of cases for the presence of domestic violence and thoughtful consideration of the clinical and legal implications.

Jaffe, Lemon and Poisson (2003)[1]

As we have elaborated more thoroughly (Birnbaum, Fidler & Kavassalis, 2008), making recommendations regarding parenting plans requires a comprehensive assessment that relies on multiple methods and sources of information. Allegations of domestic abuse and child maltreatment are common in custody and access disputing families. When domestic violence is an issue, there must be a comprehensive assessment which includes an added layer of specialized screening and risk assessment (Austin, 2000b; Jaffe, Crooks & Bala, 2005; Jaffe, Poisson & Lemon, 2003).

In the absence of criminal charges, allegations of domestic violence may be met with skepticism, particularly if there is an on-going child custody dispute where emotions run high. There may be a suspicion that one parent is making the allegation as a tactic to minimize the other parent's involvement in the lives of their children (Jaffe, Crooks & Bala, 2005; Johnston, 2006; Moloney *et al.*, 2007). In many jurisdictions there is priority for victims of domestic violence to have access to services, such as subsidized housing or legal aid. The desire to have access to such services may be another reason why exaggerated or false claims are made. Assessing the credibility of abuse allegations is a difficult and sometimes an impossible task (Austin, 2000b; Jaffe, Crooks & Bala, 2005). Careful attention needs to be paid

---

1 Jaffe, P.G., Lemon, N.K.D. and Poisson, S.E. (2003). *Child custody & domestic violence: A call for safety and accountability*. Sage Publications, p. 16-17.

to who is making allegations, and to the nature, extent and context of the violence.

While malicious and false allegations do occur in custody-disputing families, researchers note that the frequency is less than that of either the number of genuine victims of abuse who fail to report abuse, or the number of perpetrators who deny and minimize their abusive behaviour (Jaffe, Johnston, Crooks & Bala, 2008). Further, recanting by true victims is more common than untruthfulness. Accordingly, the assessor cannot be dismissive of allegations solely because they occur in the context of a custody dispute. The priorities for the assessor must always be the child's safety and the development of recommendations for the parenting plan and arrangements that are more likely to meet the individualized needs of the specific children and family.

In this chapter we: (1) summarize several domestic violence screening and assessment frameworks, including the assessment of credibility; (2) address best practice considerations for assessment; (3) discuss principles, priorities and requirements for the assessor to consider and outline the continuum of differentiated options available for the assessor to recommend; and (4) consider case law that illustrates the judicial trends when domestic violence is alleged in the context of custody and access disputes.

Screening, Psychometric Tools and Assessment Frameworks

Screening for domestic violence and power imbalance is not a discrete or isolated process but rather needs to occur throughout the child custody assessment. For assessors, screening begins with asking each spouse if there are issues of domestic violence or abuse. If there is any disclosure, there should be questions about the nature, intensity, frequency, recency and severity of all facets of the abuse—physical, psychological, sexual and financial. Investigating the patterns and context of the violence are imperative. If there is a disclosure, the assessor must also ask the alleged perpetrator about the allegations.

The assessor must be mindful that at any time during the assessment, if a parent or child feels threatened, fearful or at risk, immediate steps may need to be taken to ensure their safety. This may involve the court, lawyers, police or child protection services. In this section, we summarize selected risk assessment tools and approaches.

As we discussed in Chapter 2 of our companion book, psychological testing can be an important source of information available to an assessor who is qualified to do this. In that book we discussed psychological testing generally, and summarized some commonly used tests.[2] In addition to tests and screening instruments assessing personality, depression, psychopathy and substance abuse and dependency, which may be useful for all assessments, there are a number of additional psychometric tools that may assist the assessor in cases of domestic violence.

For example, the Trauma Symptom Inventory (TSI) developed by John Briere (1985, 2001) is a 100-item test of post-traumatic stress and other sequelae of traumatic events, including both trauma related to physical and sexual assault as well as other traumatic events like major accidents, natural disasters, and child abuse. Briere also developed a trauma system check for children (TSCC) (1996). The TSI may be useful in domestic violence cases for assessing the effects of victimization.

Based on an extensive review of the empirical and more general social science literature, Kropp, Hart, Webster and Eaves (1995), developed the Spousal Assault Risk Assessment Guide ("SARA"). The SARA contains twenty items across four categories: criminal history, psychosocial adjustment, spousal assault history, and alleged current offense. Using all of the information obtained, an overall rating can be obtained. The SARA (and a similar Ontario instrument the "ODARA"—the Ontario Domestic Assault Risk Assessment Guide) is most commonly used by police, but it may also be useful for assessors.

In cases where there is a concern that an abusive spouse may also be maltreating a child, it may be appropriate to administer the Child Abuse Potential Inventory-VI (CAP-VI Inventory, Milner, 1986), which was designed primarily as a screening scale for physical child abuse. This 77-item scale contains six factors: distress, rigidity, unhappiness, problems with child and self, problems with family, and problems with other. The inventory includes three validity scales: a faking-good index, a faking-bad index and a random response index.

Assessing Credibility

Assessing credibility is one of the greatest challenges facing assessors and judges alike in dealing with domestic violence. In the context of private family law cases, spouses often provide very different versions about the nature and extent of any violence, or even whether violence has occurred (Bala, Jaffe & Crooks, 2007). Sometimes individuals who are abusive to partners are convincing and

---

[2] See Appendix 5, page 11 for a list of tests commonly used with children and adults in child custody assessments in Birnbaum, Fidler and Kavassalis (2008). Social workers or psychiatrists who are conducting assessments may wish to consult with a psychologist about these (and other) tests.

present very well. In such cases the abuser is highly manipulative and able to con assessors, especially those who may not be familiar with patterns of abuse.

While some people consciously lie about their experiences, more often they have distorted or limited memories. Although exaggeration and lying by (alleged) victims are legitimate concerns for those in the justice system, there is social science research which suggests that women and men may experience, perceive and remember violence in different ways.[3] Further, as discussed in Chapter 3, abusers have a strong tendency to deny or minimize domestic violence, and false denials by abusers are more common than false allegations by alleged victims. Although there are only a few published studies, and these are based on limited samples, in all of the studies a preponderance of allegations of domestic violence in family law cases were substantiated. As Jaffe *et al.* (2008) note, of the few studies that exist, 50 to 75 per cent of the allegations of domestic violence made in the context of family law cases were substantiated, although only 22 to 52 per cent of the child abuse allegations in family law disputes were substantiated (Bala & Schuman, 1999; Johnston, Lee, Olesen & Walters, 2005; Shaffer & Bala, 2003).

Jaffe *et al.* (2008), Jaffe, Lemon and Poisson (2003) and Austin (see his Six Factor Test of Credibility, 2000b), suggest a number of ways in which the mental health professional can establish some credibility to the allegations of violence. These can be summarized as considering:

(1) any directly corroborating information of the abuse (i.e., police reports, hospital and medical reports, self-admissions, eye-witness evidence; teachers, relatives);[4]

(2) the pattern of abuse complaints (both official and unofficial);

(3) any indirectly corroborating evidence by credible others that would support the allegations (i.e., teachers, childcare workers, neighbours, friends or relatives who observed injuries but not the assault);

(4) the absence of disconfirming verbal reports by credible third parties (i.e., did a relative of one party who lived in the home

---

[3] Russel P. Dobash & R. Emerson Dobash, "Women's Violence to Men in Intimate Relationships" (2004) 44 Brit. J. Crim. 324.

[4] Jaffe, Lemon & Poisson (2003) assert that although many victims of domestic violence may not have reported the assault to police or may not have been seen by a physician, this should not preclude a finding of domestic violence.

fail to confirm the reported abuse; assess for information that may not support an abuse allegation);

(5) a psychological profile and past history of abusive behaviour (personality disorders, mental illness, risk factors such as mental health issues or substance abuse);

(6) the psychological status of the alleged victim(s) (personality disorders, mental illness); and

(7) the timing of the disclosure and stage of the legal proceedings.

These factors can be used to assess the degree of credibility of abuse allegations, ranging from low to high. Moreover, the assessor can use the presence, absence or extent of each of the factors to make decisions about whether or not to consider the allegations of abuse relevant to the overall assessment process.

Assessment Frameworks and Tools

A number of different frameworks and tools are available to help assessors, other professionals and victims deal more effectively with domestic violence issues. There are advantages and disadvantages to each; all have certain common elements and are based on research, although none have been fully validated for use with different populations.

Campbell's Danger Assessment[5]

Campbell (1995, 2001) has developed the Danger Assessment model ("DA", 1995), which lists 15 risk factors that have acceptable reliability and support for convergent construct validity with the Index of Spouse Abuse (Attala, Hudson & McSweeney, 1994; Hudson & McIntosh, 1981) and the Conflict Tactics Scale (Straus & Gelles, 1990). The DA is a self-report measure that enables a woman to record each act of violence perpetrated upon her by her partner, spouse and

[5] Also see the AFCC Domestic Violence Visitation Risk Assessment prepared by the Domestic Violence Visitation Task Force of the Probate and Family Court Department of the Massachusetts Trial Court (1994), which can be obtained from the Association of Family Conciliation Courts. McGill, Deutsch and Zibell (1999) Visitation and domestic violence: A clinical model of family assessment and access planning, *Family Court Review, 37(3),* 315-334, outlines the use of this tool as well as others in addressing parenting time. Variables, including level of conflict, adult parenting capacity, child's current coping skills, the occasion and duration of the abuse, type of exposure (witness vs. victim), and how the child was involved (i.e., caught in the middle), are considered in the diagnostic decision model.

ex-partner during the preceding year. Acts of violence include physical, sexual, emotional and verbal attacks, choking, use of weapons and threats of death or suicide. The scale allows the woman to record and take note of any patterns of increasing severity and/or frequency of abuse.

Bancroft and Silverman

Bancroft and Silverman (2002b, 2004) developed an instrument to assess risk to mothers and children from an abusive male. Their instrument requires gathering information from each parent, the children, past partners of the abuser, court and police records, child protective services, medical/school personnel and other relevant third parties to determine the following:

(1) level of physical danger to the mother;

(2) history of physical abuse towards the children;

(3) history of sexual abuse or boundary violations with the children;

(4) level of psychological cruelty to the mother or children;

(5) level of coercive or manipulative control exercised during the relationship;

(6) level of entitlement and self-centredness;

(7) history of using the children as go-betweens or "weapons", and of undermining the mother's parenting;

(8) history of placing the children at physical or emotional risk while abusing their mother;

(9) history of neglectful or severely under-involved parenting;

(10) refusal to accept the end of the relationship or the mother's decision to begin a new relationship;

(11) level of risk for abduction of the children;

(12) history of substance abuse; and

(13) mental health history.

Gould and Martindale (2007) have reviewed this model and note that, while useful, it is based on information gathered from women who had sought safety in battered women's shelters, and may not be representative of the women who allege domestic violence in child custody and access disputes.

Austin

Austin (2000b, 2001, 2005a) provides specific behavioural descriptions of the various factors most relevant to communicating a risk assessment to a court dealing with custody or access issues. He argues (2005a) that while typologies are helpful, the child custody assessor's task is predictive accuracy. To this end, he proposes a multidimensional typology that lends itself to such accuracy. The six dimensions he describes are:

(1) temporal pattern of violence (is it a single incident, multiple, bidirectional, chronic, or persistent?);

(2) gender of the perpetrator and causal direction of violence (instigated by male or female, bidirectional-mutual, mostly male, mostly female);

(3) severity of physical harm (mild, moderate, severe);

(4) type of aggression (verbal or physical);

(5) presence of major risk factors (alcohol, substance abuse, ongoing mental disorder, major mental disorder); and

(6) children's exposure or non-exposure to violence.

Austin (2005a) asserts that this approach combines research-based factors with clinical skill. In turn, examining these variables provides a more efficient method of making behavioural predictions relevant to the assessment process, and for communicating them more easily to a family court.

Ellis, Stuckless and Wright (2006)

To address criticisms that mediation in cases of domestic violence situations is unsafe for women, Ellis and his colleagues (2006) developed a screening tool for mediators known as "DOVE" (Domestic Violence Evaluation). This research-based instrument identifies 19 statistically significant predictors of male partner violence and abuse against female partners after separation. The researchers state that the screening tool is aimed at "the prevention and reduction of violence and abuse against separating partners and their children" (p. 480). It relies primarily on information from the alleged victim.

Drozd, Kuehnle and Walker's Safety First Model

Drozd, Kuehnle and Walker (2004) developed the Safety First Model. They maintain that while it is not the role of a child custody assessor to draw legal conclusions, their model encompasses the best interest standard used by the court for judicial decision-making. Their six-step model involves:

(1) collecting information from each parent about the physical and psychological safety of the child (questions focus on how family violence or allegations of undocumented violence may be affecting the child's physical and emotional well-being);

(2) observing and gathering information about the child across different settings, and administering standardized tests to assess cognitive, social, and emotional development, as well as psychological conflicts and trauma;

(3) assessing each parent-child relationship (looking for issues of attachment or difficulties in each);

(4) developing multiple hypotheses to explain the allegations (examining issues of separation, exposure to family violence, child alienation, and any other developmental problems related to the children);

(5) assessing the strengths and limitations of each parent and his or her ability to meet the needs of their children; and

(6) once the validity of the report of domestic violence has been determined, developing specific child custody and access recommendations to protect the child from further harm or abuse.

Drozd (2007)

The Domestic Violence in Child Custody ("DVCC") is a self report protocol the assessor can use as a guide in assessing how partners manage conflict, including domestic violence and power imbalances. It was developed from a review of the literature on domestic violence and adapted for work with custody and access disputes, such as assessments, parenting coordination, mediation and arbitration. As Drozd aptly points out, this 152-item questionnaire is not a test for domestic violence and no definitive findings of abuse can or should be made. However, the DVCC can be used as a starting point for assessors or other mental health professionals in organizing their thinking about what questions need to be addressed to help determine whether domestic violence—physical, emotional, sexual or financial is present.

Jaffe and Colleagues

Adapted from Dutton (1992), Jaffe, Lemon and Poisson (2003) developed the Abuse Observation Checklist ("ABOC"), a questionnaire designed for use in child custody assessments. Both parties are asked a series of questions covering a wide range of behaviours they may have either experienced or exhibited. These behaviours include a range of violent acts, including physical, psychological, sexual and financial abuse. The questionnaire also queries the respondent's report of what each child observed and how often. While this screening tool has no psychometric properties, these researchers believe that when this screening tool, plus the interviews with each parent, reveals concerns related to a history of domestic violence, then the assessor should gather more information from additional interviews with relatives and collateral sources.

Table 4, developed by Jaffe, Crooks and Bala (2005) provides a useful framework for the assessor's inquiry into the nature and extent of parental conflict, from a normal to more severe level that includes domestic violence.[6] The parenting plan recommendations must then take into account the type of violence and risk of future violence, and the nature of the parental conflict and parental cooperation, which we return to in the next section. Jaffe *et al.* (2008) caution that preliminary screening and assessment needs to be undertaken by a qualified mental health professional with specialized training in domestic violence.[7]

---

[6] Tables 4 and 7 are provided with the permission in an email dated November 5, 2007, from Dr. Peter Jaffe. These tables and a discussion of parenting arrangements in cases of domestic violence can also be found on the Department of Justice website at: justice.gc.ca/en/pas/pad/reports/2005-FCY-3/chap3.html, and see Jaffe, Johnston, Crooks and Bala (2008). Also, see Gilmour, G.A. (2004) *High-conflict separation and divorce: Options for consideration.* Department of Justice, Family, Children and Youth Section, which can be accessed at: justice.gc.ca/en/ps/pad/reports/2004-FCY-1/2004-FCY-1E.pdf, that reviews the guidelines for determining custody and visitation in violent parent cases based on Janet Johnston's scholarly work.

[7] Rule 5.230 of the California Rules of the Court requires 16 hours of domestic violence training completed within a 12-month period for court-appointment child custody investigators and evaluators.

Table 4:

Jaffe, P.G. & Crooks, C.V. [2004]. Visitation and custody in cases of domestic violence. In J.L. Edleson & O.J. Williams (Eds.), Parenting by Men Who Batter. Los Altos. CA: Packard Foundation.

Recently, Jaffe *et al.* (2008) have introduced a screening model that can be used as working hypotheses to make a preliminary assessment about parenting plans in cases where there are domestic violence issues. This method is, in part, based on the typology of domestic violence developed at the Wingspread Conference, and examines factors and dimensions relative to domestic violence. The model, known as the "PPP", identifies three aspects of domestic violence:

(1) *potency* (the degree of severity, dangerousness, and potential for risk of serious injury or lethality);

(2) *pattern* (the history of using coercive control, domination and violent tactics, with isolated incidents, conflict instigated events, and a pattern of coercive controlling violence being distinguished); and

(3) *primary perpetrator of the violence* (identifying the primary perpetrator as opposed to ascertaining that the violence is mutual or jointly instigated).

The specific PPP screening questions are available in the Jaffe article.[8]

At the AFCC 2008 annual conference in Vancouver, two additional "P" factors were identified (Carbon, Dunford-Jackson, Frederick, Jaffe & Johnston, 2008):

(4) *parenting problems* (including deficits of either the perpetrator or the victim parent, which may be associated with domestic abuse or arise independently, and would include drug or alcohol problems, mental illness or a history of child maltreatment);

(5) *perspective of the child* (safely consulting with the child to hear their experiences, to obtain their input, views and preferences, evaluating these for undue influence or intimidation).

A related and important factor, which may be described as the sixth "P" is the *potential for change* for each parent. To what extent has the perpetrator been able to recognize abusive behaviour and seek appropriate assistance of counselling or intervention programs? If the parenting capacity of the victim has been compromised, is that parent undergoing treatment to deal with these issues, and what is the prognosis? Hanks (1992) provides some useful questions for the assessor to consider that will inform the likelihood the perpetrator will comply with treatment:

(1) How compliant is the perpetrator with authority figures?

(2) Does he take responsibility for his actions?

(3) Is there an absence of guilt, or presence of denial, minimization, rationalization and excuses?

(4) Is there a presence of shame or guilt?

(5) Is there a capacity for empathy with the adult and children abused or exposed to abuse?

Further, expanding on the more general need for a developmental approach to parenting plans, Bala, Jaffe, Johnston and McIntosh (2008) note that in cases of domestic violence the parent-child contact needs to be restorative. They refer to the "RRR" within the "PPP" model. This involves assessment of the perpetrator's parenting capacity for: "*reflective functioning*", "*responsibility*" and "*repair*" with

---

[8] Jaffe, P., Johnston, J., Crooks, C., and Bala, N. "Custody disputes involving allegations of domestic violence: The need for differentiated approaches to parenting plans" *Family Court Review* 46:3 (2008), at page 505.

respect to the domestic violence, and the relationship with the child.[9] As discussed previously, the presence of personality disorders, which is common in these cases may mitigate against the parent having the insight necessary to reflect, take responsibility and repair.

Jaffe and his colleagues (2008) advise all professionals in the family justice system—lawyers, judges, assessors and mediators—to screen *all* of their cases for domestic violence, even when there is no disclosure. They note that victims are often reluctant to disclose, or may not recognize that they have been victims of abuse. It may take some time for a victim to feel trusting enough to disclose. If there is any type of disclosure, these writers advise using this 5-P (or 6-P) screening model as a preliminary assessment tool. Examining the risk and protective factors evident in their approach assists the assessor to develop a working hypothesis in an effort to identify and differentiate the type of domestic violence more accurately. In turn, this differentiation better informs the more appropriate interventions and recommendations for the comprehensive parenting plan, including the parent-child contact and legal custody, or decision making protocols.

Risk assessment is integral to the model that Jaffe, Johnston and their colleagues have developed. Johnston (2006) provides a checklist for indicators of lethality, dangerousness or serious psychological abuse:

(1) threats or fantasies of homicide or suicide;

(2) availability of weapons such as guns and knives;

(3) a history of violence, especially if it is within the relationship and more frequent or severe;

(4) concurrent drug and alcohol abuse;

(5) obsessive, controlling or possessive behaviour regarding the partner, especially if it includes post-separation behavior like stalking);

(6) high degrees of depression and rage;

(7) history of mental illness;

(8) disregard and contempt for authority, or disregarding prior court orders; and

---

[9] See McIntosh, Wells, Smyth, and Long (2008) for further information on how the child's perspectives and experiences can be provided to the parents to assist them to reach a mediated settlement of the parenting plan.

(9) recent significant stressors (i.e., loss of employment, a death in the family, recent separation).

Tables 5 and 6 summarize some additional indicators for the child custody assessor to explore with both parents.[10]

Table 5: Assessment of Domestic Violence: Context is Everything

Explore the following:
1. With each party, their intent in their use of violence or abusive conduct (e.g self-defence vs expression of anger/control).
2. The context of the violence.
3. The effects of the acts on the victim.
4. How the victim perceived the act (the meaning of the act to the victim).
5. The lethality of the act and the risk of further violence (see Table 6).
6. The risk of other, non-violent abuse or intimidation of the victim.
7. The patterns of conduct and specific behaviours.
8. The frequency (single episode vs. pattern), directionality, impact, severity, dangerousness of the violence, and the fear of the victim.
9. Specifically how, when and where the children are involved in the conflict, and how much of the violence have they seen, heard or learned about?
10. The related risk factors (mental health problems, substance abuse and dependency (alcohol/drugs), antisocial behavior, extra-familial violence).

[10] Summarized from the literature (including Austin, 2005b; Bala, 2003; Campbell, 1995; Jaffe, Crooks & Bala, 2005; Jaffe, Lemon & Poisson, 2003; Johnston, 2006; LaViolette, 2005).

Table 6: Framework for Assessing Lethality

Explore the following:

1. The history of domestic violence, incident frequency, telephone calls to police and other service providers.
2. Any threats of harm, homicide or suicide.
3. Any fantasies of homicide or suicide.
4. Access to and availability of weapons.
5. Drug and alcohol abuse and dependency.
6. Level of obsession or possessiveness.
7. Stalking or hostage-taking.
8. Extent of depression and rage (higher rates being of greater concern).
9. Disregard or contempt for authority or court orders.
10. Police records for criminal convictions and reports.
11. Recent stressors (i.e., loss of employment, custody and access dispute, death of a loved one, recent separation, etc.).

In the final analysis, each of these models, while overlapping, are instructive and useful when conducting a differential assessment of domestic violence allegations in the context of child custody disputes. Every assessor will need to find their own comfort level. Some may choose to rely on one specific model or tool, while others may choose to develop their own procedures, selecting from the various tools available in the literature. We have found it is useful to have an intake questionnaire that includes domestic violence screening questions, coupled with semi-structured interview material obtained during individual meetings with each party.[11]

Noteworthy is that all of these frameworks put children's safety first. In addition, the substance of each underscores the importance of conducting a comprehensive, multi-source, multi-method assessment that relies on the assessor's consideration of rival and alternative hypotheses. We now turn to a discussion of selected best practice considerations and the continuum of options and interventions for the assessor's considerations when making recommendations.

---

[11] Also see Dalton, Drozd and Wong (2006) *Navigating custody and visitation evaluations in cases with domestic violence: A judge's guide.* National Council of Juvenile and Family Court Judges, State Justice Institute, for a guide that judges use when issues of domestic violence are alleged and how to assess the merits of an assessor's report regarding domestic violence.

Parenting Plans in Domestic Violence Cases

Children's Wishes

Consideration by the assessor of a child's wishes and preferences can be problematic in domestic violence cases. A child who is psychologically compromised by violence may state a preference to live with an abusive parent based on a fear of that parent, or alternatively, because of manipulation by the abuser or special treatment. It is not uncommon for children, and especially boys who have been exposed to domestic violence, to align themselves with the stronger and more powerful parent, to "identify with the aggressor" to the point of sometimes degrading the abused parent. In some cases, a daughter may be treated in a "princess-like" fashion by an abusive father, who she then favours over the mother. In other cases, the child may view the abused parent as weak or ineffectual and may align themselves with the stronger, more powerful, abusive parent.

Some of these children become alienated from the victim parent and are either highly resistant to seeing that parent or ultimately refuse contact altogether. An abusive spouse can be very manipulative and the denigration of the other parent may influence a child's relationship with a victim of abuse.

While assessors and the courts do and should generally give weight to children's wishes and perceptions, these are not determinative of the child's best interests. Wishes must be interpreted and weighed carefully, taking into account intimidation and manipulation as well as all the other information obtained during the assessment. Limited weight should be given to a child's wish to live with a parent when allegations of violence and abuse against that parent have been substantiated.

Differentiated Recommendations and Interventions

A number of well-respected researchers and mental health professionals have argued for a continuum of services and a variety of parenting arrangements to match different degrees and types of domestic violence and parental conflict (Bancroft & Silverman, 2002; Jaffe, Crooks & Bala, 2005; Jaffe, Lemon & Poisson, 2003; Jaffe *et al.*, 2008; Johnston, 2006; Lemon, 1999; Drozd, Kuehnle & Walker, 2004). It is recognized by these writers that we do not have research evaluating the validity of one screening model or tool over another. Further, we do not have research on the short- or long-term impact of the different parenting arrangements, when allegations of domestic violence and high conflict arise. However, this does not mean that custody assessors should abandon carefully crafted and detailed parenting plans that include both parenting time and decision-making protocols. The assessor can draw upon the large body of relevant developmental and psychological literature combined with their clinical experience and that of their colleagues to help families and courts develop post-separation parenting arrangements in domestic violence cases.

Most importantly, an assessor needs to craft a careful plan for *delivery* of the recommendations to the lawyers and parents, including consideration of who will attend the meeting, where the plan is delivered, and the framing of the content. In cases where safety is in question, carefully considered and practical protection needs to be in place *before* the recommendations are provided to the parties and the court. Appropriate monitoring needs to occur afterwards, with clear delineation of who is responsible for this role.

Principles, Priorities and Other Important Considerations

Jaffe *et al.* (2008) provide options for parenting plans that take into account the type of domestic violence and the nature and degree of associated risk. These writers propose five guiding principles that an assessor and the courts should apply when making recommendations or determining a parenting plan. Frequently, these priorities are conflicting and, as such, pose difficult dilemmas for the assessor and the courts. These principles are:

- Priority 1: protect the child from violent, abusive and neglectful parenting environments;
- Priority 2: protect the safety and support the well-being of the victim parents so that they will be better able to protect their children;
- Priority 3: respect and empower parents to direct their own lives and make their own decisions in the interests of their child;
- Priority 4: hold perpetrators of domestic violence accountable for past and future actions;
- Priority 5: allow and promote the least restrictive parent-child contact and parenting plan that benefits the child.

The lower priorities should only be addressed after all of the higher priorities are satisfied, placing the safety of the child as the most important priority.

Jaffe *et al.* (2008) place a priority on the protection and safety of children and victims of domestic violence, while recognizing as an objective wherever possible, for children to have a relationship with both parents. They discuss a range of considerations that must be taken into account when formulating a parenting plan. The more danger and risk to the child and non-violent parent who is caring for the child, the more the court and child protection services need to be involved. A thorough assessment of the nature, severity and pattern of physical violence, emotional abuse, and the parental conflict, and of the effects on the victim and children is required.

Taking into account these priorities, a risk-benefit analysis of the different parenting plan options best suited for the specific child and family is required. The parenting plan options proposed by Jaffe and his colleagues are on a continuum:

(1) co-parenting (shared legal and physical custody);

(2) parallel parenting with monitored or neutral exchange (sole or divided legal[12] and physical custody);

(3) sole custody to the victim with access and supervised exchange to the abusive partner;

(4) sole custody to the victim with only supervised access for the abusive partner; and

(5) sole custody to the victim with suspended access.

Within each of these options are a number of variations.

An important consideration for the assessor, especially in domestic violence cases, is the practicality of the parenting plan recommendations. In particular, services for victims and perpetrators are not available in many locales. The assessor must be knowledgeable about resources and services in their community and ensure that any services recommended are financially feasible and available to the family. For example, if supervised access is not available, the assessor may have to recommend against any access until a suitable and reliable supervisor is available; the child's safety (physically, emotionally and psychologically) must always come first. The more resources for support and protection of victims, and the more effective intervention available to the abuser, the more continued involvement by an

12 Divided custody permits each parent to have final decision-making authority over a different domain of parenting, such as education, health and welfare, or extracurricular activities and lessons. For a thorough review of parallel parenting and joint custody in high-conflict families, see Chapter 6 in our companion book (Birnbaum, Fidler & Kavassalis, 2008).

abusive spouse with his children may be an appropriate option to consider.

Resources and interventions that may be available range along a continuum with the nature and degree of domestic violence and abuse. For example:

(1) education, mediation, collaborative law, co- or parallel parenting are options for families that present with conflict-instigated violence ("CIV"), and separation-instigated ("SIV") violence that does not persist, and generally involves lower levels of conflict and isolated events of a less serious nature;

(2) a child custody assessment, therapy to reduce conflict, arbitration, litigation, and parallel parenting are options for families with higher levels of conflict but without domestic violence; and

(3) intervention programs for batterers, services for victims, programs for children, supervised access, and specialized risk assessments by trained assessors, along with court monitoring and for sole custody, are options for families when coercive controlling violence ("CCV") has occurred.

Counselling may be suitable for normal conflict situations, while those involving higher conflict without domestic violence may require a custody assessment, therapy to reduce conflict, arbitration, litigation, or parallel parenting. When domestic violence is present, intervention for batterers, services for victims, programs for children exposed to violence, supervised access, and specialized risk assessments by trained assessors, along with court monitoring or review hearings and orders for sole custody may be required.

While treatment options for abusers are important to consider, it is important to note that the success rate of programs for coercive controlling batterers remains low (Edleson, 1995; Edleson *et al.*, 2003; Edleson & Syers, 1990, 1991). Further, it is imperative not to underestimate the lasting and traumatic impact of domestic abuse on some children. While some batterers are responsive to individual and parent-child treatment and counselling, others may remain impervious to intervention, including orders for treatment, even when experienced clinicians provide these interventions.

Another important consideration for the assessor is the stage of the separation and legal process. Immediately after the separation may be a period of high conflict and relatively greater risk, as well as when there is limited opportunity to investigate allegations and explore intervention options, requiring a more restrictive legal approach. If there has been significant time since the separation, with no recurrence of violence, it may be appropriate to move towards a legal regime that affords both parents the opportunity for considerable involvement in the lives of the children. The fact that there may have been violence or abuse during the marriage does not always preclude some form of co-parenting, though past behaviour must be addressed before co-parenting can occur. Abusers who accept responsibility for the harm that they have caused and have sought treatment may be allowed contact with their children, if there is appropriate monitoring.

Restriction, including supervision, on contact between a parent and child are clearly appropriate if there is continuing domestic violence or child maltreatment concerns. Since long-term restrictions or supervision are not usually realistic or best interest options, any restrictions on the parent's contact, though, should include clear goals and criteria necessary for the parent and child to move to a less restrictive option. In other words, supervised visits are part of a transition phase. Further restrictions should be accompanied with a process for monitoring by the court or its delegate, and a timely review of the progress (or increased risk) (Jaffe *et al.*, 2008).

Table 7 provides a schema that summarizes the approach of Jaffe and his colleagues (2005), linking the nature and degree of the parental conflict and domestic violence, the resources and interventions available and the stage of the process, to the various options for parenting arrangements, including both residential schedules and child-related decision making.

Table 7:

Parenting Arrangements after Violence

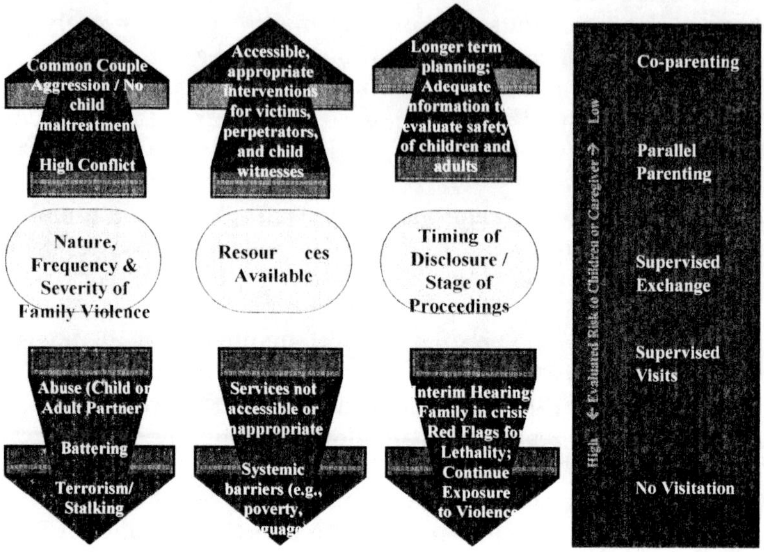

Recommendations must also consider ongoing monitoring and follow-up by the court, and where appropriate parenting coordinators and arbitrators. Case management and the careful and often challenging and time consuming coordination of services, along with follow-up and monitoring by the court, is necessary for these differential recommendations to be effective and to protect children and their parents from further domestic violence and child maltreatment when present. Jaffe, Crooks and Bala (2005) note that the court is the *only* authority that can establish an accountability mechanism with the assistance of mental health professionals. Therefore, the court may be in the best position to assist with the implementation of parenting plan recommendations by providing a monitoring role so that the perpetrator is aware that there are consequences when a court ordered parenting plan is violated.

Mears and Visher (2005) have also suggested that in order to conceptualize intervention strategies properly, there needs to be a focus on integrating interventions with the assistance of professionals from different sectors and systems. For example, they report on National Research Council ("NRC") data identifying four sources of intervention that require more integration and coordination both within and between systems:

(1) legal interventions (including the child welfare, criminal and family processes);

(2) social service interventions (shelters, advocacy and victims groups, therapists);

(3) health care interventions (screening, identification, and provision of mental health services by doctors and psychologists); and

(4) collaborative interventions (coordinated systemic responses).

We now turn to a discussion of the legal responses to family law cases raising issues of domestic violence, providing a review of case law that illustrates how courts have addressed these complex and challenging cases.

The Response of the Family Courts to Domestic Violence

Historical Development

As noted earlier, legislation and case law dealing with custody and access disputes in Canada have undergone tremendous change over the past few decades, reflecting ever-changing societal values—from patriarchal notions to standards based on the best interests of the child—and an improved understanding of domestic violence and child development issues. Until quite recently, in all but the most severe cases, the justice system gave little attention to domestic violence and its devastating effects on women and children. In recent years, considerable progress has been made in clarifying the relationship between domestic violence and child development and the relationship between domestic violence and child custody orders. For example, in 2006 amendments to Ontario's *Children's Law Reform Act*[13] (CLRA) codified case law to make clear that acts of violence or abuse committed by one parent against the other parent are relevant factors to consider in making best interest determinations regarding custody or access of a child.

[13] Subsections 24(4) and (5), as amended by S.O. 2006, c.1, s. 3(1) provide:

(4) In assessing a person's ability to act as a parent, the court shall consider whether the person has at any time committed violence or abuse against; (a) his or her spouse; (b) a parent of the child to whom the application relates; (c) a member of the person's household; or (d) any child.

(5) For the purposes of subsection (4) anything done in self-defence or to protect another person shall not be considered violence or abuse.

Until the late 1980s, the Canadian justice system ignored or significantly downplayed the importance of domestic violence in custody and access proceedings. This historical lack of concern with domestic violence as a factor in custody cases is graphically illustrated by the 1988 Nova Scotia case of *Peterson v. Peterson*.[14] At the end of their eight year marriage, upon discovering his wife and her lover in bed, the husband severely assaulted his wife and her lover using a metal bar. After the assault, while his wife lay naked and bleeding on the floor, the husband brought their 7 year old son to the door of the room and told him to look at his mother. In addition to evidence of the husband's violence towards his wife, the judge also had evidence of other incidents in which the father had assaulted the older son, including an incident when the father became angry with the boy and kicked him in the chest, and was then so agitated that he shoved his hand through a door.

The judge accepted that the husband had a predisposition to violence and had exhibited a lack of "parental wisdom" in deliberately exposing his son to his mother's "anguish and humiliation". The judge also accepted that the mother had been the primary caregiver for the children and was "an excellent mother". However, the judge concluded that "there was no evidence of intolerable cruelty" on the husband's part as "his conduct had been tolerated by Marlene Peterson through eight years of marriage and two children" (para. 8). Despite accepting the evidence of the husband's violence, in the judge's view, as a result of her acts of adultery, the mother's had "primary responsibility" for the breakup of the marriage and the termination of the children's "ideal lifestyle" and awarded interim custody to the father, emphasizing the importance to the children of having "the stabilizing factor of continuing to live in the home they are used to, with all persons of importance in their lives, excepting their mother, in the relationship they have always known" (para. 43).

In minimizing the significance of abuse in the breakdown of the marriage and awarding custody to a man with a long history of abusive conduct towards his wife and children, the court in the *Peterson* case reflected many of the deeply troubling attitudes about wife abuse that were prevalent in the Canadian judiciary and among society more broadly in 1988.

One of the earliest reported cases dealing with the effects of domestic violence in an appropriate way was *Young v. Young*,[15] a decision of one of Canada's first female judges. In that case, the parents separated after 15 years of marriage. Although the two children of

---

[14] 1988 CarswellNS 180, 85 N.S.R. (2d) 107, 216 A.P.R. 107 (N.S. Co. Ct.).

[15] 1989 CarswellOnt 225, 19 R.F.L. (3d) 227 (Ont. H.C.).

the marriage expressed a consistent wish to live with their father, Judge Janet Bolan was concerned that the father was attempting to manipulate the children during access visits. The evidence at trial clearly outlined significant physical, emotional and sexual abuse of the mother throughout the marriage, along with two physical assaults by the father after separation. There was testimony at trial by three mental health professionals retained by the mother explaining the significance of the spousal violence for the children. The judge concluded:

> The relevancy of this finding of abuse is that it goes to Mr. Young's ability to parent the children on a full-time basis. I accept the expert evidence . . . that:
>
> 1. An abuser who goes without therapy will continue to abuse in another relationship;
> 2. Children who witness abuse can become abused even though the abuse is not intentionally directed at them;
> 3. Abused male children often become abusers and abused female children may become compliant to abusers. (paras. 33-34)

The judge in *Young* awarded custody to the mother with access to the father.

In the years immediately following the *Young* decision in 1989, it was necessary for a victim of domestic violence to introduce expert evidence to persuade a judge of the significance of this violence for making a decision about the children's best interests. While it is still often helpful to have evidence from a qualified mental health professional about the effects of domestic abuse on children, it is now accepted that even without an expert witness being called, a judge may take judicial notice of the fact that domestic violence is a relevant factor in making best interest decisions. Social scientists and legal thinkers no longer accept the view that a person can be an abusive spouse but still be a loving and capable parent. The understanding that violence and abuse in a relationship ought to be considered when assessing a person's ability to exercise custody or access is now recognized in legislation in some provinces, including Alberta, Ontario and Newfoundland. However, a number of other provinces, and the federal *Divorce Act*, still do not have such statutory provisions. While leading precedents interpreting "best interest" statutes, like the *Divorce Act,* that do not have explicit reference to domestic violence, also clearly recognize that this should be a significant factor, the silence of legislation on this issue may result in some parents and professionals failing to appreciate the legal and social significance of domestic violence for children.

It is useful to be aware of the historical evolution of judicial decision-making, as the inclusion of domestic violence as a consideration in determining custody and access is a relatively recent phenomenon, and some legal professionals may still be influenced by the earlier approaches. Further, even with legislation and leading precedents requiring that domestic violence is a factor in any best interest decisions about children, in Canada there is no presumption that an abusive spouse will be disentitled to custody or access.

The cases reviewed below are not an exhaustive summary of the case law decided in Canada. Rather, they illustrate judicial approaches where domestic violence is an aspect of a case where parents are disputing over custody or access.

Interim Orders

In family law cases involving allegations of domestic violence, especially if there is a threat of the recurrence of violence, there is often a need for quick action to protect the victim of abuse and children. It is especially important that a victim is not driven out of the home without her children, as this could set up a possible *de facto*-continuity argument for custody of the children by the abuser.

Judges dealing with interim family applications for relief where there are domestic violence allegations face a real dilemma, trying to make an interim decision, often based only on affidavits that contain conflicting claims and counter-allegations.[16] A judge at an interim application may be forced to make a decision that could affect the safety and well being of parents and children, based on limited and conflicting evidence. Judges are aware of the importance of interim orders because they can provide immediate protection and have a significant impact on the outcome of a later trial. A parent with interim custody will often have a stronger claim for custody at a later trial, based on the court's preference not to disrupt the child's stability. Indeed, frequently the interim order establishes such a strong status quo that a custody case never proceeds to trial.

In the Ontario case of *Vollmer v. Vollmer*[17] each spouse alleged repeated physical assaults by the other, and each had called the police about the other once. The judge acknowledged the judicial reluctance to make an *interim* exclusive possession order in the absence of clear evidence of abuse, where that order has the effect of excluding one

---

16 If there are criminal charges, the alleged abuser will usually be required to leave the home and not contact the alleged victim as a condition of bail.

17 1998 CarswellOnt 1819 (Ont. Gen. Div.).

spouse from the home, especially if this will give the other spouse an "inappropriate advantage in terms of a claim for custody, access" or a permanent order for exclusive possession. However, in this case it was clear that the mother had been much more involved in the care of the children and would retain custody and, further, that the couple planned to sell the matrimonial home. Accordingly, there was no prejudice to the long-term interests of the husband from making an interim order. Justice Aiken recognized that the environment of "anger, stress and possible violence" had a negative effect on the children and gave the mother interim exclusive possession.

There are, however, cases in which a judge is not satisfied that there is a genuine risk to the children and may award an alleged abuser interim custody, despite the allegations. In the 2004 Nova Scotia case of *Walker v. Walker*,[18] four days after the husband allegedly assaulted his wife, she left the home taking the two children of the marriage (first to a shelter and then to live with relatives), without informing the father of where they were going. While it is common for interim orders to be made solely on the basis of affidavit and documentary evidence, the judge conducted an interim hearing over three days, including hearing testimony from the parents. In regard to the abuse allegations, Smith J. wrote:[19]

> There are few allegations more serious in a child custody case than abuse. . .
>
> I have carefully considered the evidence presented concerning the allegations of abuse. The evidence does not satisfy me, on the balance of probabilities, that [the husband] has been abusive to either [the wife] or children. I conclude that the evidence of abuse is exaggerated . . . or incomplete ("I don't remember"). . .
>
> In this case Ms. Walker's memory concerning a number of events that she now classifies as abusive is poor. Her conduct after the abuse is alleged to have occurred (including her willingness to leave the children in the care of Mr. Walker despite the suggestion that he is an abuser) calls her allegations of abuse into question.
>
> Whether someone has been verbally or emotionally abusive towards another is open to subjective interpretation. . . Controlling or jealous behaviour may be considered to be emotionally abusive by some and inappropriate behaviour by others.

The Court's decision to award the father interim custody was based on a number of factors, including the mother's unilateral removal of the children from the home without informing the father where she

---

[18] 2004 CarswellNS 167, 2004 NSSF 40, 223 N.S.R. (2d) 357, 705 A.P.R. 357 (N.S.S.C.).

[19] *Ibid.*, at para 24-28.

was taking them,[20] and the fact that in the six months prior to her departure she was frequently absent from the home ("socializing"), including several overnight stays, leaving the children with their father. The judge also considered that the father, who was a teacher, appeared to be very involved in the care of the children and was more willing than the mother to facilitate access.

If there is evidence that there is a real risk of further violence, the court is likely at this interim stage to err on the side of the protection of physical safety. In the 2005 Yukon case of *M. (H.L.) v. P. (J.J.)*,[21] the Court suspended interim access by a father to his 14 month old daughter because the father had assaulted his wife before and after separation. Justice Veale wrote:

> Applications for interim orders in family law are rarely accompanied by expert evidence on the impact of violence by a parent witnessed by a child. I take judicial notice of the fact that such violent behaviour is not in the best interests of the child. Violence between spouses, which may or may not be directly witnessed by a child, may have the following undesirable effects on a child:
>
> 1. the abuser may abuse the child;
> 2. the abuse may result in developmental and attachment difficulties;
> 3. the child may be more likely to enter an abusive relationship as an adult.
>
> There is no evidence before me that such events have occurred in this case. They are possible consequences for children whose parents have an abusive relationship.
>
> However, the onus is on the father to establish on the balance of probabilities that his access to the child is in the best interests of the child.[22]

In some cases, the period immediately after separation is especially volatile. If there are concerns that the parents may engage in verbal (or physical) altercations when care of the child is being ex-

---

20 Justice Smith acknowledged (at para. 56): "While there are occasions when a parent must take such action for the safety of him/herself and/or the children, I am not satisfied that such circumstances existed on the facts of this case."

21 2005 CarswellYukon 6, 2005 YKSC 3 (Y.T.S.C.).

22 *Ibid.*, at para. For a decision that placed greater emphasis on the "principle that the child should have as much contact with each parent as is consistent with the child's best interests" and awarded unsupervised access to the father of a 18 month old child, despite outstanding criminal charges for assaulting his wife, see *Harari v. Harari*, 2001 CarswellBC 1645, 20 R.F.L. (5th) 59 (B.C.S.C. [In Chambers]), *per* Vickers J.

changed, then supervision of the exchange of the child by a neutral party should be ordered, at least on an interim basis. In some cases, a period of supervised exchange may be needed to allow tensions to diffuse, though in other cases supervision may continue for a longer period.[23]

In a situation where there is potential for serious harm to a child by an abusive spouse, the other parent may be justified in taking immediate steps to protect a child, while making a timely application to a court for relief and protection. As stated by Justice L'Heureux-Dubé in the Supreme Court of Canada in the 1993 decision in *Young v. Young*:[24] "a custodial parent, aware of sexual or other abuse by the non-custodial parent would be remiss in his or her duty to the child not to cut off access by the abuser immediately, with or without a court order." The same principle should apply if the parents are residing together and one parent believes that it is necessary to leave in order to protect the children. This view is reinforced by s. 285 of the *Criminal Code*, which creates a defence to a prosecution for parental child abduction if action is taken to protect a child from danger of "imminent harm".

If a parent unilaterally removes children from their home, however, they will be expected to justify this action. In the 2008 Ontario case of *Donley v. Donley*,[25] the mother moved out of the house with two children, aged 7 and 10 years, without notifying the husband or seeking a court order. The couple was in court a few days later, each seeking interim custody, with the wife claiming in her affidavits that she felt that she had to act because of concerns about her husband's "anger management problem" and a number of assaults, some of which happened in the presence of the children. The husband denied the allegations and the only independent evidence was from the children's school principal who reported that the father had a warm relationship with the children. Justice Harper awarded interim custody to the father, concluding that the mother's allegations were not proven:

> On the evidence before me, it appears that Mrs. Donley was reacting to the response of counsellors and other professionals who encouraged her

---

[23] In some communities, supervision of the exchange of access is provided by community agencies. Exchange of supervision is more fully discussed below. See *D. (R.) v. D. (U.S.)*, 2001 CarswellYukon 130, 22 R.F.L. (5th) 269 (Y.T.S.C.), at 273-74 [R.F.L.], where a violent husband's right to unsupervised access was suspended at an interim hearing.

[24] 1993 CarswellBC 264, 49 R.F.L. (3d) 117 (S.C.C.), at 184 [R.F.L.], para. 130.

[25] 2008 CarswellOnt 596, 51 R.F.L. (6th) 164 (Ont. S.C.J.)

> to move out of the home with the children based on one-sided information that was provided by her and her alone.
>
> When Mr. Donley came home on January 15, 2008, he saw that many of the contents of the home were removed and that his children were gone, with only a note left by his wife that stated that the children were safe and she was doing what the OPP and the Children's Aid had advised her to do. I find that the fact that Mrs. Donley had already withdrawn the children from the only school that they have ever known is further evidence that Mrs. Donley was creating an illusion of a dangerous situation for the children in order for her to accomplish the move that she did and attempt to get the subsequent sanction of the court.
>
> There is no reason that Mrs. Donley could not have contacted her lawyer and attempted to negotiate on notice a proper resolve to the custody issue. I also find that Mrs. Donley could have, and should have, come to court first on proper notice to Mr. Donley in order to get a court order prior to uprooting the children in the dramatic way that she did.[26]

This decision illustrates the importance of a parent claiming to be a victim of domestic violence to actually be able to establish that the abuse occurred.

Family Cases: False or Exaggerated Allegations

While it seems clear that false denials of domestic violence by genuine abusers are more common than false allegations, the issue of false or exaggerated claims of domestic violence is a significant concern for the courts and assessors. More broadly, exaggeration and distortion is common in high conflict family law cases, as noted by Justice P. Smith in *Colangelo v. Colangelo*,[27] an Alberta decision dealing with domestic abuse allegations:

> it is a rare matrimonial case where the points of view of the parties coincide. I expect to see some exaggeration and colouring of the evidence on both sides. [28]

The judge in that case found each party "coloured" their evidence, but concluded that the woman's detailed allegations of spousal abuse were more convincing than the man's inconsistent denials. The mother was awarded custody with the father getting limited visits with his 11 year old daughter and "encouraged" by the judge to involve his own relatives in the visits.

---

[26] *Ibid.*, at para. 96-98

[27] 1997 CarswellAlta 350, [1997] A.J. No. 432 (Alta. Q.B.).

[28] *Ibid.*, at para. 27.

Ontario Superior Court Justice Mary Lou Benotto (1995) has also made pointed comments regarding the problem of exaggeration of claims of abuse:

> Domestic abuse is abhorrent. I have never found a judicial officer who treated physical cruelty with anything but the seriousness it deserves. *However, the term 'abuse' has been diluted beyond all proportion. There is scarcely a separated spouse who does not believe that he or she was in abusive relationship*. Abuse is a powerful term. But it is routinely used to describe shouting, badgering, voice raising, walking away when angry.

This judicial comment reflects the frustration that judges may feel in grappling with the common problem of conflicting allegations and demonstrates how important it is that victims or their counsel bring forward clear evidence that abuse has occurred, if at all possible with support for the victim's evidence from other sources.

In the Ontario case of *Brigante v. Brigante,*[29] the parties separated after six years of marriage. The mother received interim custody of their son, then three years of age, and the father obtained extensive access. The mother then met another man, and became pregnant by him; she planned to marry the man and move with him from Hamilton to Ottawa. The litigation arose about a year after the initial separation, as the mother wanted to restrict the father's access and move to Ottawa with the child. After the litigation commenced, the mother alleged for the first time that the father was physically abusing the child during access visits, and had been physically and verbally abusive of her during their cohabitation. The mother reported her concerns to the child protection authorities, who conducted an investigation of the father's alleged child abuse without contacting him. Eventually, a court ordered assessment was carried out; the assessor observed that the father and son interacted in a "normal" fashion, while the boy was "abnormally aggressive" with the mother; however, the assessor relied on the child protection agency's conclusion that the father was abusive and recommended restricted access. Justice Beckett ultimately concluded that the father had not abused his son and awarded generous access, while preventing the mother's relocation with the child. In rejecting the mother's claims of spousal abuse, the judge noted that she had made no complaints to a doctor, the police or a family member during the period of cohabitation. The judge commented:

> The allegations of severe abuse appear to have arisen during the course of this litigation and since she decided to move to Ottawa with her new

---

[29] 1991 CarswellOnt 265, 32 R.F.L. (3d) 299 (Ont. U.F.C.).

> partner. The only reason she gave for not reporting the abuse to somebody was that she thought that it had been "her fault". This Court is well aware that it is not unusual for the "battered wife" not to report to the authorities, but in the circumstances here, I have a great deal of difficulty in accepting her evidence with respect to the alleged violence. . .
>
> I have come to the conclusion that the applicant [mother] was not severely and frequently assaulted . . . as she alleges, although she may have suffered some infrequent and less serious assaultive behaviour. (paras. 6-7)

The judge was aware of the fact that abused women often do not report their victimization to the police or other authorities and that the absence of corroboration should not be fatal to such an allegation. Nevertheless, he concluded that these particular allegations were unfounded or substantially exaggerated and were advanced for strategic reasons—to permit her to move with her child.

In the 1995 Ontario case *Simpson v. Robinson*[30] the parents separated when the child was less than a year old; the father was seeking access more than a year later, while the mother sought to deny access. There was evidence that the father had been controlling and on occasion abusive of the mother; he pled guilty to criminal harassment of her as a consequence of post-separation phone calls, and was con-

---

[30] 1995 CarswellOnt 2014 (Ont. Prov. Div.). See also *Shaw v. Shaw*, 2008 CarswellOnt 1626, 2008 ONCJ 130, [2008] O.J. No. 1111 (Ont. C.J.), which illustrates how false or exaggerated allegations of spousal violence may be made to obtain tactical advantages in family litigation. One month after his wife slapped him at a social event, the husband reported the incident to the police, apparently doing so only after being advised by a lawyer that this was the cheapest and most effective way to get his wife out of the house. The mother was arrested and charged with common assault; the resulting bail conditions effectively barred her from the matrimonial home and stripped her of custodial rights. While the mother was in custody, the father sought and obtained an *ex parte* order in family court for the children's interim custody. The husband effectively used the criminal justice system to gain interim custody of the children and exclusive possession of the home. The father then claimed to have established status quo and receive interim custody. Pugsley J. directed that the children alternate between parents' residence on a weekly basis, and commented:

> The way that the criminal justice system approaches the commencement of these matters, however, often wreaks family law havoc with the family unit of the defendant and the complainant, and in particular the children of those parties . . . Routine orders excluding a party from the common home of the parties until the end of the criminal matter without thought to the consequences thereof, and without a remedy short of a bail review, place one party in a position of immediate superiority over the other party for as long as it takes (perhaps a year) for defended criminal charges to be resolved. Such rote treatment of all matters of domestic assault can lead, on the one hand, to concocted or exxagerated claims of criminal behaviour or, on the other hand, to innocent defendants pleading guilty at an early stage out of expediency or a shared desire with the complainant to start to rehabilitate the family unit.

victed of offences relating to assaults of previous partners. However, Judge Katarynych concluded that much of the mother's testimony had exaggerated incidents of abuse. She observed:

> . . . according to her evidence, she was regularly assaulted by him in the course of their altercations. . . .
>
> Over the course of my deliberations, I remained wary, but not entirely disbelieving, of Ms. Simpson's assertion that she was a typically battered woman. Conclusions drawn from stereotypes are, of course, highly suspect and I felt at times that she was constructing her testimony to fit carefully the profile advanced by the literature.
>
> . . . she was embellishing parts of her evidence on the issue of his assaultive behaviours towards her. . .
>
> Her professed "fear" of contacting the police appeared contrived and significantly inconsistent with the evidence showing that she was quite prepared to contact the police when it suited her purposes. . .
>
> Overall, it was not fear of Mr. Robinson that I detected in Ms. Simpson's testimony. It was disdain, tinged with a few vindictive touches as it became increasingly important to her to excise him from her life. (paras. 58-66)

The judge also considered the expert evidence of a "feminist marriage and family therapist" about the effect of domestic violence, but gave it little weight. There was also substantial evidence from other individuals that the father had positive involvement with other children, including a child from a previous relationship. The judge ordered supervised access and counselling for both parents, with an indication that unsupervised access should begin when the father demonstrated that he was ready.

Some lawyers may advise clients who claim to have been victims of domestic violence not to raise the issue in their court documents or in court, for fear that if they are not believed, their claims for custody or other matrimonial relief will be denied (Neilson, 2004). While a judge's assessment of the honesty and reliability of each parent is undoubtedly related to the outcome of a case, there is little evidence that judges punish parents merely for making claims about abuse that the court does not accept, on the balance of probabilities, as proven true. Judges recognize that it is common for separated spouses to have different perceptions and recollections of reality, and that it is not uncommon for witnesses to emphasize the aspects of their testimony that support their present position. Most judges are also aware that it is often difficult for a victim of abuse to provide definitive proof of events that may have occurred in private.

However, in some cases the judge will conclude that a party making an allegation of abuse is fabricating (or significantly exaggerating), and that this is directly affecting the child. In such cases, the court's decision may be affected by the judge's conclusion that an unfounded allegation of abuse was made. In some cases a custodial parent, usually the mother, will make unfounded allegations *and* alienate the children from the other parent by inducing unfounded fears in the child's mind.[31]

In the Ontario case, *S. (D.) v. S. (S.T.)*,[32] the mother alleged that her former husband had physically abused her during the marriage and sexually abused their young children during access visits. The children, who were 5 and 10 years old at the time of the trial, made some vague statements to child protection investigators that appeared to support some of these allegations, but ultimately several independent mental health professionals and a child protection investigation concluded that the incidents did not occur, and that the mother had alienated the children from their father. The experts, including an access supervisor, concluded that the allegations were unfounded and that the woman's "anger and point of view" were "transmitted" to her children, including their stated reluctance to visit their father. The Court concluded that there was a need to "reverse the process of alienation" while keeping the children in the care of the mother who was the primary caregiver and ordered structured access, as well as counselling for the parents and children; the father was awarded joint legal custody to ensure his right to access to information about the children.

It should be emphasized that the most common "defence" of genuinely abusive men is to dismiss the allegations of abuse made by their partners (or former partners) as the product of "emotional instability" or deliberate fabrication. Abusive men now also regularly assert that their children's expressed fears about contact are due to their mothers' alienating attitudes. While these assertions can be true, and each case must be assessed on its own merits, more often than not the allegations of domestic violence are founded.

Mutual Abuse

As discussed in Chapter 3, many high conflict separations can be characterized as cases of "conflict-instigated violence" (or "interactive violence", "common couple violence", "situational couple violence" or "mutual abuse", a non-clinical term that seems to be favoured by the

---

[31] For a further discussion of alienation, see Chapters 6 & 7.

[32] 1997 CarswellOnt 3973, 40 O.T.C. 321, [1997] O.J. No. 4061 (Ont. Gen. Div.), *per* Whalen J.; see also *Walker v. Walker*, *supra*, at note 18; and *A. (D.H.) v. M. (K.E.)*, 2004 CarswellYukon 10, [2004] Y.J. No. 21 (Y.T.S.C.), *per* Veale J.: concern about alienating conduct by "embittered" mother who had been victim of one assault.

legal profession). These are cases in which on different occasions either party can initiate physical aggression as part of a struggle for control, with mutual blaming and anger.[33] In general, these cases seem to have a relatively good prognosis for the reduction of violence after separation. Some reported Canadian cases clearly fit this scenario.

In the Saskatchewan case of *Derow v. Derow*[34] Justice Archambault concluded that both parents had been abusive towards one another in presence of their children, though the husband had the more serious anger problem and a greater tendency to initiate violence. The Court awarded the mother custody, but the father was to have "liberal access"; in view of the conflict between the parents, at least initially access was not to be overnight and the judge indicated that the father would be "well advised to seek counselling" for his lack of anger management.

In the Nova Scotia case of *Loughran v. Loughran*[35] Justice Goodfellow concluded:

> Both parents are lacking in objectivity in their assessment of the other and of the flare-ups that have taken place between them since separation. Mr. Loughran has on occasions allowed his frustration, the departure of his wife and her relationship with Mr. Davis, to get to him and it did not take very much for Mrs. Loughran to join in so that there was a number of instances of pushing and shoving and each contributed. Both parties, and Mr. Loughran perhaps more so, must learn to control themselves as these flare ups are totally inappropriate and have an impact on the welfare of their children. How can children learn to respect others, if they constantly see a lack of respect by their parents towards each other? (para. 7)

The Court decided that the child should continue to reside with the father, with joint legal custody shared with the mother. The decision appeared to be based on the fact the father had done more parenting, especially in the period since separation.

As indicated in Chapter 3, when considering a situation that appears to be one of "mutual abuse"—that is where each spouse has physically assaulted the other—it is important to assess whether one spouse is usually the aggressor, as well as assessing the effects of abuse on each party and the children. It is also important to distin-

---

33 See *Stackhouse v. Stackhouse*, 1997 CarswellBC 424 (B.C.S.C.), where Boyd J. referred to the "marriage as a classic power struggle" with "pushing, shoving and insulting behaviour on both parts".

34 1996 CarswellSask 162, 140 Sask. R. 241 (Sask. Q.B.).

35 2000 CarswellNS 41, [2000] N.S.J. No. 41 (N.S.S.C.).

guish between situations which are truly ones of interactive violence, and those in which the man is the stronger and more aggressive partner, with the woman's reactions being acts of self-defence or "violent resistance".[36]

In the 1995 New Brunswick case of *M. (D.A.W.) v. M. (J.A.)*,[37] there was evidence that the parties had a "stormy relationship", with the woman being physically aggressive towards her husband. At the time of initial separation, the mother obtained custody on consent, but then entered a relationship with a new man; both she and the new partner were verbally abusive to the boy and used corporal punishment extensively. The Court varied the original arrangement and gave the father custody, without any comment on the spousal conduct, and focused on the inappropriate treatment of the child by the mother and her new partner.

Separation-Instigated Violence

In some cases of domestic violence, there was no violent conduct during most of relationship, but rather the violence is confined to one or more incidents around the time of separation related to the breakdown of the marriage, and perhaps associated with the discovery of infidelity or other significant betrayals. Such situations generally have a better prognosis for future non-violent relations than cases where violence has been more pervasive. Although Canadian judges have not yet used the term "separation-instigated violence" to describe such cases, they have clearly recognized this dynamic and taken it into account in making decisions.

In the Ontario case of *Hallett v. Hallett*[38] the parents cohabited for 12 years in a relationship that was apparently free of domestic violence. During the process of separation, which lasted several months, the man assaulted the woman on three occasions, in incidents involving shoving and some hitting; one of the two children saw one of these incidents and later told an assessor that he was frightened by it. The police were called and charges were laid against the father after the third assault, and the mother and her children moved out of the matrimonial home to a shelter. While the man questioned

---

[36] See *Pavao v. Pavao*, 2000 CarswellOnt 1002, [2000] O.J. No. 1010 (Ont. C.J.), *per* Dunn, where the court concluded that the woman may have struck her husband on occasion but "her degree of violence was less than his against her, and it was likely that [the husband] . . . provoked her to retaliate." The Court awarded custody to the mother and denied access to the father.

[37] 1995 CarswellNB 118, 170 N.B.R. (2d) 186, 435 A.P.R. 186 (N.B.Q.B.).

[38] 1994 CarswellOnt 1998 (Ont. Prov. Div.), *per* Schnall J.

whether the woman should have had the advantage of a support network and long-term housing for "battered women", a worker from the shelter testified on behalf of the mother at the custody trial. Judge Schnall observed that the limited extent of the man's abuse

> does not justify his conduct by any means, but it does reflect that physical violence by the respondent was not a usual characteristic of the parties' 14 year relationship. I find that these three incidents, all of which occurred in the last two months of the relationship, were apparently out of character for the [man]. (para. 57)

The custody assessor did not consider the domestic violence to be an important factor, and did not question the children about this issue to any extent. The judge concluded that the assaults were "not relevant" to issues of custody and access, though she criticized the assessor for not exploring the issue more fully. The Court awarded sole custody to the mother, with specified access to the father on alternate week-ends and vacation periods.

In *Atkinson v. Atkinson*,[39] a 1993 Ontario decision, the trial judge had established a regime of access by the father that was significantly dependent on the mother's discretion. This was in large part due to the fact that there had been altercations between the parents during access exchange, including an incident when the father assaulted the mother. In reversing the lower court and ordering specified access on alternate weekends, Platana J. observed that there was significant evidence that the child enjoyed visits with the father. While there had been difficulties in exercising access, the judge felt that there was fault on the part of both parents and the evidence disclosed "not a history of violence but one incident . . . it is a misapprehension of the evidence to categorize one incident as a history of violence" (para. 20). Although the Court may have been correct in its assessment of the nature of the violence in this case, this was a situation in which "exchange supervision", more fully discussed below, would have been appropriate, to minimize the threat of violence, or even verbal altercation, when parents are meeting to exchange custody of the child.

Children's Wishes in Domestic Violence Cases

Although legislation and case law make clear that, in general, children's views and preferences are to be taken into account in making decisions about custody and access, the courts have stated that they are not bound by a child's wishes, especially in cases of domestic

---

39 1993 CarswellOnt 1810 (Ont. Gen. Div.).

violence.[40] In cases where there has been a high conflict separation and a history of domestic violence, a custodial mother may have significant, reasonably founded fear of the father. Even if there is no present threat to the child's safety from the abusive spouse, the child may have very negative feelings towards that parent. As recognized by Sachs J. in the 2000 Ontario case of *Roda v. Roda*:[41]

> In such cases, children can feel the need to ally with one parent at the expense of the other for two reasons—a desire to emotionally support the chosen parent and an inability to see any other way to end the intense conflict between both parents. (para. 52)

In *Roda,* the father's access to the child was terminated, based in large part on the child's fears and negative feelings, even though the fears reflected the mother's feelings rather than the child's own experiences.

On the other hand, a child's wishes can be an important factor favouring a parent who abused a partner but who appears to pose no risk of direct abuse to a child.[42] While a child's views should always be considered by a court, a child's stated desire to live with an abusive partner should have less weight in cases where there has been spousal abuse than in other contexts, though in some cases it may be determinative.

In the 1994 New Brunswick case of *Worden v. Worden*[43] the husband had a drinking problem and a history of violence towards his wife, though there was no evidence that he had abused the children. The woman left her husband after 17 years in the abusive relationship, taking the children with her to a shelter. While the 14 year old son did not get along with his father, the 10 year old daughter continued to express a desire to live with the father in the familiar home surroundings. Arguably the "familiar surroundings" and proximity of friends were critically important to the outcome in *Worden* and the decision might well have been different if the mother had initially secured exclusive possession of the family home. The judge observed that given the age of the children, they would be likely to "resist and perhaps resent situations that are thrust upon them", and ordered that the father was to have custody of the daughter on condition that

---

[40] See *Young v. Young, supra*, at note 15; and *Molloy v. Molloy*, 1996 CarswellOnt 1101 (Ont. Gen. Div.), *per* Killeen J.

[41] 2000 CarswellOnt 3558, [2000] O.J. No. 3786 (Ont. S.C.J.); see also *Kennedy v. Sinclair*, 2001 CarswellOnt 1634, 18 R.F.L. (5th) 91 (Ont. S.C.J.).

[42] See *S.P. c. J.M.*, indexed as *Droit de la famille - 1988*, 1994 CarswellQue 2257, [1994] R.D.F. 353 (Que. S.C.).

[43] 1994 CarswellNB 380, 154 N.B.R. (2d) 60, 395 A.P.R. 60 (N.B.Q.B.).

he refrain from drinking in her presence and enter counselling for his alcohol and anger management problems.

In *Brusselers v. Shirt*,[44] the parents did not cohabit after the child's birth, though they were married to each other. The father had been abusive of the child's mother during their cohabitation and there was conflict between them about access. He had been abusive of women in other relationships and the mother also had concerns about the father's parenting skills and wanted to deny him access. However, an assessor testified that the 8 year old girl expressed the wish to see her father, as she saw other children whose parents separated enjoying their relationships with their fathers. Justice Smith noted that the father was in counselling for his abuse problems and seemed to have good relations with a young son he had with another partner and ordered unsupervised access.

Joint Custody in Domestic Violence Cases

While in cases where abuse or high conflict are not concerns, it is often appropriate to consider some form of joint custody or shared parenting, this is rarely appropriate if there has been a history of spousal abuse. Indeed since joint custody requires parental cooperation, it is not appropriate if there is a high level of parental conflict or serious power imbalances even without physical abuse; there is all the more concern about joint custody if there is a history of domestic violence. (Jaffe *et al.*, 2008).

In the 2005 Ontario case of *Cameron v. MacGillivray*,[45] the Court found that the father was verbally and emotionally abusive to the mother, treating her in a threatening or demeaning manner, including in the presence of their son. The father sought joint custody, but Justice Aitken, cited the Ontario Court of Appeal decision in *Hildinger v. Carroll*,[46] in which it was noted that joint custody and parallel parenting are not appropriate parenting models in circumstances in which there is a history of intimidating or bullying behaviour. For several reasons, Justice Aitkens concluded that it would be in the child's best interests if the mother had sole custody. These reasons included the fact that the father did not recognize his own disrespectful, abusive and aggressive behaviour of the mother, that he had no insight into how destructive this sort of behaviour was to effective communication and shared parenting, and that he had continued to denigrate the mother in the child's presence. The judge set out a

---

44 1996 CarswellAlta 275, 38 Alta. L.R. (3d) 191, 183 A.R. 27 (Alta. Q.B.).

45 2005 CarswellOnt 8095, [2005] O.J. No. 5500 (Ont. S.C.J.).

46 *Hildinger v. Carroll*, 2004 CarswellOnt 444, [2004] O.J. No. 291, 2 R.F.L. (6th) 331 (Ont. C.A.).

detailed time-sharing schedule that provided both parents with significant time with the child.

There are cases in which there were one or more incidents of domestic violence, but it is nevertheless appropriate to have some form of joint custody arrangement, as it is clear that the parents are able to co-operate and there are no longer concerns about intimidation or violence, and there is a low risk of recurrence of violence. This is very unlikely to be appropriate in the immediate aftermath of separation but may be in a child's best interests if some time has elapsed since the last incident of violence, and the relationship was not marked by intimidation, control, or emotional abuse.

There are many Canadian judgments which recognize that where there is a history of significant disagreement and argument,[47] let alone abuse, joint custody is not likely to be appropriate.[48] However, there are also Canadian cases in which judges have been less sensitive to issues of domestic violence and have imposed joint custody despite a history of violence or a high conflict relationship.[49] Further, it is not uncommon for custodial mothers to feel pressured by mediators or their lawyers to settle cases on the basis of some form of "joint custody" despite ongoing issues of domestic violence (Neilson, 2004).

Custody Awarded to Spouse with History of Abuse

Although it is usually not in the best interests of a child to be placed in the care of a parent who has a history of violence, there are cases in which the courts do this. While a history of violence is a significant factor, it is not determinative. Among other factors, there must be consideration of the nature and recency of the violence, and any steps taken to address the violence or other parenting issues. In some cases, both parents have a history of violence and there must be a comparative assessment of their parenting capacities.

In the 1990 British Columbia case of *L. (D.L.) v. L. (D.J.)*,[50] the father was awarded custody of the parties' daughter even though the Court found that his conduct towards the mother before the separation was "despicable"; his insistence on bringing numerous sexual partners of both genders to the family home amounted to emotional

47 See *Lawson v. Lawson*, 2006 CarswellOnt 4789, [2006] O.J. No. 3179 (Ont. C.A.).

48 See *Hallett v. Hallett,* 1994 CarswellOnt 1998 (Ont. Prov. Div.); and *Kennedy v. Sinclair*, *supra*, at note 41.

49 See *Boothby v. Boothby*, 1996 CarswellOnt 4734 (Ont. Prov. Div.), where the mother testified that the father was "controlling, demanding and [...] emotionally abusive" towards her during the period that the parties cohabited. He had interim custody after separation, and on occasion thwarted the mother's access visits; the court nevertheless awarded joint custody, with primary residence to the mother.

50 [1990] B.C.J. No. 1283 (B.C.S.C.).

abuse. At the time of separation, the mother agreed that their daughter would remain with the father. One year later, the mother's claim for custody failed. The Court concluded that it would be contrary to the child's best interests to move her from her father's home that was stable, and separate her from her step-siblings and the extended-family members living nearby.

In *Farden v. Farden*,[51] Justice Baynton of the Saskatchewan Court of Queen's Bench found that the father's drinking and his treatment of the mother were significant factors in the breakdown of the marriage. The Court found that some of what the mother alleged was true, but concluded that she exaggerated a great deal and the parties had been mutually abusive. In addition to engaging in physical altercations, the parents called each other hurtful and demeaning names, and screamed and shouted at each other. The children had witnessed some of these incidents. After separation, the mother attempted to block the father's access to the child of the marriage and attempted to turn that child and a half-sibling from a previous relationship against the father. The court-ordered assessment revealed that the children had misgivings about the father's past conduct respecting their mother, but the assessor concluded that the children were not at risk with their father, as he had a genuine affection for them and had expressed no intentions of abusing them. The Court found that the mother had breached the interim access orders and attempted to disrupt the relationship between father and children. The Court awarded custody of the boy to the father. The older child, a girl whom the father had adopted, no longer saw him as a father figure, and her wishes as to contact with him would prevail. The Court awarded costs against the mother for breaching the interim access order.

In the 1993 Ontario case of *McNichols v. McNichols*,[52] the Court accepted that during the marriage the mother had behaved in an erratic and violent fashion towards the father, had deliberately damaged some of the contents of the house, and that the "child [had] been exposed to these outbursts in a totally unacceptable way" (para. 3). The mother had interim custody. The court-appointed assessor recommended that the father have custody. However, the judge chose to rely on the opinion of the mother's doctor, that after the assessment the mother's emotional condition substantially improved and her con-

---

51 1998 CarswellSask 779, 173 Sask. R. 161 (Sask. Q.B.).

52 1993 CarswellOnt 1607, [1993] O.J. No. 1973 (Ont. Prov. Div.), *per* Pedlar Prov. J. See also *McGrath v. Thomsen*, 2000 CarswellBC 2383, 11 R.F.L. (5th) 174 (B.C.C.A.). In *Nichols v. Hayward*, 2004 CarswellBC 1103, 2004 BCSC 669 (B.C.S.C.), custody was awarded to the father; the mother was violent and suffered from mental health problems.

dition was under control by drug treatment. The Court ordered joint custody in which the children were to principally reside with the mother with extensive access to the father.

In the 2006 Ontario case of *Rice v. Abbot*,[53] the parents separated when the child was one year old, after the father assaulted the mother. The child lived in the custody of her mother until the age of seven, with generous access to the father. As a result of the mother's alcoholism and her excessive physical discipline of the child, as well as numerous domestic disputes between the mother and her new partner, at age seven the child protection authorities became involved and the girl went to live with her father, though continuing to have contact with the mother. At the time of trial, the girl was nine years old, and had witnessed numerous domestic disputes between her mother and her mother's partner. Although the mother had committed acts of abuse against her daughter, since losing care of the girl the mother had used the services of a number of organizations and counsellors to assist her with her alcoholism and improve her parenting skills. The judge observed that the mother's history of violence towards the child was a relevant factor under s. 24(4) of the CLRA, and her alcoholism was also a concern. Further a court-appointed social worker had conducted an assessment and recommended that the father be given custody, as he had a warm relationship with the child and she expressed a strong expressed preference to live with him. However, the judge felt that the assessor had given insufficient weight to the father's history of having assaulted both the mother and his current common law partner, and his on-going problems with anger management and poor impulse control. Further, Justice Blishen was impressed by the fact that the mother had abstained from alcohol for the previous two years and by her willingness to participate actively in treatment and counselling. The judge was also concerned about the risk of emotional harm to the child due to the possibility of her again being present if her father were to lose control and either verbally or physically lash out at his current partner. Justice Blishen ordered that the mother have legal custody and primary residence of the child, with specified access to the father and supervision of exchanges. Both parents were required to continue counselling for their problems, and the mother and daughter were ordered to undertake joint therapy.

---

[53] 2006 CarswellOnt 7769 (Ont. S.C.J.).

Access and Domestic Violence

Access can be very problematic for victims of domestic abuse and their children, as the continuing contact with an abusive spouse that results from access can be stressful and create risks. Abusive spouses may use access to try to denigrate the other parent and undermine the children's relationship with a custodial parent, often encouraging the children to behave in destructive or defiant ways when they return home. It must, however, also be appreciated that many children want to see their access parents, even if these parents have abused their partners, in many cases children "may benefit from such contact, as long as safety measures are provided, the contact is not overly extensive, and the abuser is not permitted to cause setbacks in the child's healing process" (Bancroft, 2002, p. 48).

Post-separation access can be used by an abuser to maintain control over, or cause emotional or physical injury to, a former partner. During access an abusive spouse may question the children about what the custodial parent has been doing and try to turn the child into a "spy", causing loyalty conflicts. In some cases, men have told their children during access that they will kill their mothers, causing intense anguish among the children.[54] It is also not uncommon for abusive spouses to berate or assault their former partners when picking up or leaving their children. Such abusive post-separation conduct should be given very significant weight in an application to terminate access.

Although the legislation and case law effectively create a presumption that continued contact between a non-custodial parent and child is in the child's best interests, it is now clearly accepted that in situations where there has been a history of serious domestic violence, contact may not be in the child's best interests and should not be permitted. As stated by Pugsley J.A. of the Nova Scotia Court of Appeal in *Abdo v. Abdo,* where an abusive husband and father was denied access to his three children:[55]

> While contact with each parent will usually promote the balanced development of the child, it is a consideration that must be subordinate to the determination of the best interests of the child. . .
>
> . . . the burden rested on Mrs. Abdo to establish that it was in the best interests of the children to eliminate supervised access (a burden

---

[54] See *Matthews v. Matthews*, 1998 CarswellOnt 1419, [1998] O.J. No. 1424 (Ont. Gen. Div.), *per* Granger J. where the father's threats to the child about the mother and abusive conduct during access visits caused the court to terminate access.

[55] 1993 CarswellNS 52, 50 R.F.L. (3d) 171 (N.S.C.A.), at pp. 181-183 [R.F.L.]; see also *Westhaver v. Howard*, 2007 CarswellNS 545, 47 R.F.L. (6th) 406 (N.S.S.C.).

> that Mrs. Abdo did satisfy); the use of the word *may* in the phrase "supervised access . . . may be harmful . . ." suggests that Mrs. Abdo may not have established on the balance of probabilities that supervised access *would* be harmful. . .
>
> It was not, therefore, necessary for Mrs. Abdo to establish that supervised access would be harmful to the children.

There are a growing number of cases in which access has been denied to an abusive partner. Almost all of these are cases that fit in the category of "coercive controlling violence by a father".[56] They are typically cases of repeated physical violence and emotional abuse by a man, directed at his female partner and sometimes his children; many of these cases also involve some form of post-separation domestic violence. Although in the many of these cases the custodial mother relied on expert testimony to support the application to deny access, there are cases in which access has been denied without such testimony.[57]

One of the first appellate judgments to deny access based on domestic violence concerns was the 1992 Ontario Court of Appeal decision in *M. (B.P.) v. M. (B.L.D.E.)*.[58] The woman had a son from a previous relationship; the parties were married for two years, during which time the wife gave birth to a daughter. The father began to be abusive during the pregnancy, undermining the woman's relationship with her family and having "violent rages"; after the birth, he became increasingly violent and threatened to kill her. In 1985, the woman left out of concern for the safety of herself and the children. After the separation, the father had access to his daughter, while his harassment and threats against the mother escalated. The man often followed the woman around, left her harassing notes, and was verbally abusive to her at the time of access exchange. He sometimes threatened not to return the child after access. Despite this type of conduct, judges in 1986, 1988 and 1989 permitted unsupervised access; during this time the woman moved from Alberta, where the

---

56 For a case where a mother with a history of drug use and threatening behaviour was given access only with the permission of the custodial father, see *McGrath v. Thomsen*, 2000 CarswellBC 2383, 11 R.F.L. (5th) 174 (B.C.C.A.).

57 *Rasalingam v. Rasalingam*, 1991 CarswellOnt 1456, [1991] O.J. No. 1241 (Ont. Prov. Div.); *D. (C.) v. B. (J.)*, [1996] A.Q. No. 181 (Que. S.C.), *Parker v. Hall*, 1996 CarswellOnt 742, [1996] O.J. No. 756 (Ont. Prov. Div.); and *Alexander v. Creary*, 1995 CarswellOnt 434, 14 R.F.L. (4th) 311 (Ont. Prov. Div.). See also *Matheson v. Sabourin*, 1994 CarswellOnt 4692, [1994] O.J. No. 991 (Ont. Prov. Div.), where Hardman Prov. J. cited literature on the effects of having witnessed spousal violence on children, apparently without this literature having been introduced by a witness.

58 1992 CarswellOnt 295, 42 R.F.L. (3d) 349 (Ont. C.A.).

parties were married, to Ontario, to be near her parents. The daughter found the visits with her father stressful. Supervised access was ordered, but the child continued to experience stress related to the visits. Eventually in 1991, access rights were terminated; the decision was affirmed by the Ontario Court of Appeal in 1992. The Court of Appeal characterized the man's post-separation conduct as "incessant and obsessive", creating stress on both the child and mother. While the child continued to tell the assessor that she was not adverse to seeing her father, as long as it was infrequent and supervised, Justice Abella observed that a court should also consider the effects of continued access on the custodial parent, especially when she has been the victim of continued harassment by the father:[59]

> . . . The needs of children and their parents are obviously inextricable, particularly between children and the parent on whom they depend for their day-to-day care . . .
>
> But the central figure in the assessment is the dependent child. . . .
>
> There is no evidence of any bond whatsoever between this child and her father. On the contrary, there is evidence that she was hostile towards him during supervised access visits, withdrawn before and after the visits, had nightmares and some bedwetting. . .
>
> . . . The biological link cannot be permitted to trump the child's welfare and best interest.

Justice Abella rejected the father's application for supervised access. Although Finlayson J.A. dissented and would have permitted supervised access, the majority position of Abella J.A. must be regarded as the dominant judicial view. The courts are now more willing to terminate access and one would hope that a mother and child would not now be expected to live through years of unsupervised access with such an abusive man, as occurred in the late 1980s in *Montgomery*. Although the situations will be rare, there have been cases involving abusive spouses where the courts have refused access to an abusive spouse without any attempt to try access, even on a supervised basis.[60]

Despite the fact that the *Divorce Act* (and provincial legislation) makes clear that the actual test for determining whether there is to be access is the "*best interests* of the child" and that there are real concerns about access in cases where there are serious domestic violence concerns, some judges, lawyers and mediators continue to op-

---

[59] *Ibid.*, at 359-60 [R.F.L.].

[60] *Pereira v. Pereira*, 1995 CarswellBC 1593, [1995] B.C.J. No. 2151 (B.C.S.C.), in which a husband was violent towards his wife during marriage, and after separation even attempted to arrange for her murder.

erate on the presumption that partners, even abusive ones, will have access.[61] Some judges base this presumption on the notion that there is a "right" to access, but most judges consider that this presumption promotes the "best interests of the child". The case law continues to reflect conflicting judicial attitudes towards access in cases where there are domestic violence concerns, as illustrated by the contrasting approaches taken in two 2001 British Columbia decisions dealing with interim relief concerning access.

In *Harari v. Harari*,[62] the judge accepted that the father had "difficulty controlling his temper", and had abused and threatened his wife. He was facing criminal charges as a result of an incident against the wife that occurred after separation and he had breached an undertaking given as a condition of release in the criminal proceeding that he would have no contact with his wife or child. The wife left British Columbia, where the couple had resided together, and went to Ontario with their eighteen month old child to get the support of her family. The judge acknowledged that she "fled" because as she was "terrified" of her husband, finding that there was "ample evidence to support her feelings". Nevertheless, Vickers J. felt that he could not "ignore the principle . . . that the child should have as much contact with each parent as is consistent with the child's best interests" (para. 9). The judge ordered that the mother was to return with the child from Ontario to British Columbia. The judge was "not persuaded that there is a need for supervised access", and allowed the father unsupervised access every second weekend, though making a restraining order against the father and requiring him to arrange access pick-up through a third party.

By way of contrast to the approach of Justice Vickers in *Harari* is the decision of Justice Veale of the Yukon Supreme Court in *Dhillon v. Dhillon,* also a case dealing with an interim relief application by a woman who had been abused by her husband. She had been assaulted by her husband several times in the course of her nine year marriage, some of the assaults in the presence of their young daughter. The husband also subjected her to controlling behavior, such as disconnecting the telephone to isolate his wife. The police were called on a

---

[61] See *Fullarton v. Fullarton*, 1994 CarswellNB 278, 7 R.F.L. (4th) 272 (N.B.Q.B.).

[62] *Supra*, at note 22. See also *H. (H.) v. C. (H.)*, 2002 CarswellAlta 530, 27 R.F.L. (5th) 63 (Alta. Q.B.), *per* Lee J. where a judge awarded supervised access to a father who was convicted of assaulting his wife and father-in-law with a hammer and who had previously been subject to an anger management course as a condition of a s. 810 recognizance, but still awarded supervised access. For other examples of cases where fathers with histories of spousal abuse were awarded unsupervised access, see *Somerset v. Somerset*, 2004 CarswellOnt 2100, [2004] O.J. No. 2177 (Ont. S.C.J.), *per* Pierce J.; and *Kuzmicz v. Kuzmicz,* 2004 CarswellOnt 1991 (Ont. S.C.J.).

couple of occasions, though charges were withdrawn when the woman recanted and resumed cohabitation. Ultimately, the wife and her five year old daughter fled to a shelter. In opposing the woman's application for interim relief, the husband denied that there had been any assaults, but the judge accepted the woman's "version of the events because it was supported by RCMP involvement and medical records." Although expressing a concern about the lack of expert evidence to assist the court in understanding the effect of the abuse on the child, Justice Veale observed:

> . . . when physical or psychological abuse exists between the parents, or between a parent and child, access is not routinely granted and may be denied if it is not considered to be in the best interests of the child . . . the onus is on the parent seeking access to establish . . . that the access is in the child's best interests . . . I am of the view that any spousal abuse, physical or psychological, that has an impact on the spouse or child, is of concern.[63]

The Court ordered supervised access only, stipulating that the supervision was not to be provided by a member of the husband's family, but only by a "trusted non-family member".

It is submitted that the approach of Justice Veale in *Dhillon* is preferable; the Court, in that case, recognized the harm of spousal abuse to children, and placed an onus on the abusive spouse to show that access would be beneficial to the child and to devise a plan that would ensure the safety of the child. In contrast, Justice Vickers in *Harari* appears to have operated on the basis of an assumption that is not consistent with social science research in this field, namely that access of a child to a parent is beneficial to a child, despite a recent history of significant domestic violence

In cases in which abusive spouses were unable to control their temper or understand how their conduct affected their children, custody has been denied and supervised access ordered until that parent's temper was under control.[64] If, however, a parent with a history of domestic violence acknowledges that he has been abusive and takes steps to demonstrate the ability to properly care for his children, unsupervised access may be awarded.

In the 2003 Ontario case of *Hossack v. McNorgan*,[65] the father had been verbally and physically abusive towards the mother during and after their cohabitation. The child had witnessed some of the incidents; after separation, the boy, then aged six, began to verbally

---

[63] *Supra*, at note 23, at 273-74 [R.F.L.].

[64] *Gallant* v. *Tran*, 2005 CarswellPEI 98 (P.E.I.T.D.).

[65] 2003 CarswellOnt 1151, [2003] O.J. No. 1141 (Ont. S.C.J.)

abuse and pinch his mother when he came back from visits, clearly influenced by the father. In the course of the trial, at which the father was seeking joint custody, the father acknowledged "many of his errors in judgment and misbehaviour. . . pointing out that virtually all of it was in the first eight or nine months of the separation" (para. 13), and that he had enrolled in a post-separation parenting course. The mother testified that she did not believe that the father would intentionally harm the boy, and that the boy loved his father. Justice Aston granted the father access on alternate weekends, on certain conditions, such as abstaining from consuming alcohol or drugs, and with supervision of exchanges at the expense of the father.

Abusive Partners and Access Denial

The unhappiness of a custodial parent about access, or her sense of anger or hatred towards the non-custodial parent, do not in themselves justify a termination of access. However, where there is a history of abuse of the custodial parent during, and especially after the end of the period of cohabitation, the fear of the custodial parent may legitimately be an important factor in terminating access. Consideration of threats to the safety of the custodial parent is important in any decision about access; no parent should be placed in a position of danger to facilitate access for an abusive parent.

In *Matheson v. Sabourin*,[66] the parties cohabited for one and a half years during which they had a son. The father physically and verbally abused the mother during the period of cohabitation, and continued to harass and assault her after the separation. In terminating all access Hardman Prov. J. wrote:

> There can be no question that it is dangerous to state as a principle of law that if access causes stress for the custodial parent then it should be terminated. However, it is clear that there are circumstances where the impact on the custodial parent is such that extinguishing access must be considered. . .
>
> . . . No one could put it more clearly than the respondent[mother] did in her evidence: "I'm trying to raise him and you're trying to destroy me and that affects him." (paras. 14-15)

It may be argued that even in this 1994 decision in *Matheson v. Sabourin,* the mother and child were subjected to abuse for far too

---

[66] *Supra*, at note 57. See also *Dixon v. Hinsley*, 2001 CarswellOnt 3243, [2001] O.J. No. 3707, 22 R.F.L. (5th) 55 (Ont. C.J.), *per* Zuker J.; and *M. (Z.) v. M. (S.)*, 1997 CarswellOnt 807, [1997] O.J. No. 1423 (Ont. Gen. Div.), *per* Ferrier J., where access was terminated because of verbal abuse of the child, including prying information from the child during visits.

long before access was terminated. In those situations where domestic violence continues after separation, access should be terminated, or at the very least the exchange of the child should be supervised. A parent with primary responsibility for the care of a child should not be subjected to abuse so that her former partner can continue to enjoy a relationship with the child.

Justice King refused to order access in *Alexander v. Creary*[67] because of the father's violent temper and abusive behaviour towards the mother during their cohabitation. The father had assaulted the mother after a disagreement and had threatened to kill her. After the separation, despite a non-contact order, the father continued to harass the mother. The father held the view that children should be physically punished by hitting when they were disrespectful, and he treated their mother in the same way. The mother expressed concerns that the father would hit the child if she behaved in a manner the father considered disrespectful, that he had taken no steps to deal with his anger, and that he would use the access to maintain contact with the mother. The Court accepted the mother's position that she would be severely stressed and worried if access was ordered, and that this would affect the child's well-being. In dismissing the father's claim for access, the Court stated:

> The animosity between these parties is palpable. What kind of future does this augur for visits? It would be filled with anxiety, accusations and acrimony. Why would one knowingly subject a little child to this? She is very young and should have as much as possible the right to live without such parental conflict.[68]

The 1995 Ontario case of *DiMeco v. DiMeco*[69] also resulted in a termination of access of a father who had engaged in domestic violence. In this case, the parties' marriage was marked by violence exacerbated by the husband's alcohol addiction. He frequently exhibited episodes of rage and threatening behaviour and was physically abusive towards his wife. Although the physical assaults on his wife stopped after their two children were born, the father continued to create an atmosphere of fear in the home by his violent behaviour. He threw objects, punched walls, and threatened to kill the mother, the children and himself, all in the presence of the children. The children observed his frequent and violent episodes of behaviour. He killed two of the family pets, one by beating it to death and one in the

---

67 1995 CarswellOnt 434, 14 R.F.L. (4th) 311 (Ont. Prov. Div.).

68 *Ibid.*, at p. 318 [R.F.L.].

69 1995 CarswellOnt 2199, [1995] O.J. No. 3650 (Ont. Gen. Div.).

presence of the older child. The mother finally separated from him when their son was almost hit during one of the father's rages.

The father denied all of the allegations made by the mother. At the interim stage, the father was granted supervised access, but he misused the visits and breached the policies of the access centre. His harassing and threatening behaviour continued. The children told the court-appointed assessor that they were terrified of their father and did not want to see him. Justice Beckett found the father's evidence unreliable, and concluded that access would not be in the children's best interests. The judge commented:

> The parent is a role model for the child. Children learn their behaviour from their parents. Surely it is in the best interest of every child that he or she learn the values of love, caring, honesty, integrity, understanding, gentleness to others, and should be shielded from violence and dishonesty. In this case it is difficult to see what positive values could arise for these children by visiting with their father. On the other hand, it is not difficult to see many negative values and undesirable traits that he may impart to these children.[70]

The 2000 Ontario case of *Pavao v. Pavao*[71] also resulted in the denial of access to an abusive father and a restraining order was issued against him. The father had been convicted of assaulting the mother, and the judge accepted that he became angry and physically abusive toward the mother after he had been drinking. Justice Dunn noted that, although their father did not directly physically hurt the children, they were very aware of his abuse of their mother; in one instance, one of the children had telephoned 911 when his father was hitting his mother. At trial, the father was unable to offer any evidence that he had followed recommendations made regarding treatment for his mental health problems and alcohol abuse, problems that had led to violence in the home in the past. Justice Dunn concluded that "what these children saw and heard their father say and do to their mother was so horrific that they cannot countenance the risk of further harm to their mother or themselves by being in contact with their father" (para. 66). Although access was terminated, the judge ordered that the mother should give the children any presents or letters sent by the father and advise him "forthwith in writing if either child requests contact with him". This type of order sends an appropriate message to the mother, that she should respect the wishes that the children may in the future express about their father.

---

70 *Ibid.* at para. 36.

71 2000 CarswellOnt 1002, [2000] O.J. No. 1010 (Ont. C.J.).

While the wishes of a child are not determinative, they are an important consideration in dealing with access issues, especially in those cases involving a battering husband. When there has been a significant history of domestic violence and the children have become fearful of their father, expressing a desire not to see him, this should be a very persuasive factor in denying access.[72] In some recent cases, judges have recognized that if there is significant history of domestic violence that causes a mother and child to fear the non-custodial father, this may justify terminating access, even if there is no clear evidence that the abuse will reoccur in the future.[73] In some measure, the fear of the children may reflect the fears of the mother or may be a form of "alliance" of the child with the custodial parent to avoid a "loyalty conflict". When a child is without affection for the non-custodial parent and has legitimate fears, it would be very upsetting to a child and undermine the child's sense of trust to order access. These types of orders are only appropriate where the woman has "legitimate fears" based on acts of violence, particularly where the abuser has not taken meaningful steps to acknowledge his abusive conduct and deal with it, for example by taking an anger management course or having counselling.

Conversely, if the court concludes that the mother's sentiments towards the father are based more on feelings of anger or resentment at the end of the relationship than on reasonable fears, denial of access based on a child's stated preferences would be less appropriate, and would encourage manipulative and alienating behavior in high emotional conflict divorces.[74]

---

[72] See *Rasalingam v. Rasalingam*, supra, at note 57: access denied to father with history of violence towards mother, until children and their mother consent. See also *Roach v. Kelly*, 2003 CarswellOnt 5037, 49 R.F.L. (5th) 177 (Ont. S.C.J.), where Steinberg J. denied access to an abusive husband, writing:

> Parents [...] have a duty to their children to treat each other with courtesy, respect and to the best of their ability, work towards developing a consistent, positive, secure, nurturing lifestyle for their charges. Where one parent has the major custodial responsibilities, the non-custodial parent has the difficult tasks of supporting the custodial parent and to work with [...] her so that the child is not put in the position of being caught in the middle of physical arguments or other disputes, being forced to chose between parents, or having to adjust to radically different approaches to parenting.

[73] *Roda v. Roda*, *supra*, at note 41, *per* Sachs J.; *Pavao v. Pavao*, *supra*, at note 36, *per* Dunn J.

[74] See *Sekhri v. Mahli*, 1993 CarswellSask 368, [1994] 1 W.W.R. 170, 112 Sask. R. 253 (Sask. Q.B.), where Klebuc J. accepted that there had been at least one assault by the father, but concluded that the mother "grossly exaggerated [...] in some instances, on the verge of being untruthful" allegations of physical and verbal abuse towards her by the father during their nine years of cohabitation in marriage. An assessor concluded that the father was "incapable of significant violence", but rec-

A child's continued desire to have contact with a parent with a history of domestic violence is likely to influence a court to permit access. While denial of access is sometimes necessary, despite the expressed wishes of the child, when a parent has been abusive, in particular toward the child, it should be appreciated that a child will often experience a sense of loss if access is denied or may come to inappropriately idealize the absent parent.[75] In some cases in which a child wishes to have contact with a parent with a history of domestic violence, it may be appropriate to order supervision of the exchange of the child.

If access has been terminated due to concerns about domestic violence and its effect on a child, in order to resume access, the parent with a history of abuse should bear the onus of demonstrating that he recognizes the effect that his conduct had on the children, has taken significant steps to change his behavior and that it will be in the interests of his children to see him.[76] Evidence that it may help the father's psychological state or meet his needs should not be persuasive in any access application, especially an application to reinstate access terminated for abuse. Parents who have lost access rights for their abusive conduct (almost all fathers) generally have very significant histories of abuse and it is thus not surprising that, at least in the reported case law, that these men have rarely succeeded in persuading a court to reinstate access.

Although the case law now makes clear that a judge should deny access if it creates risks for a child *or* custodial parent, there is a concern that too often victims of abuse may still be agreeing to arrangements that may endanger themselves or their children. In the absence of clear evidence of child abuse, many lawyers (in negotiations), judges (in pre-hearing settlement conferences) and mediators (in mediation) tend to pressure victims of spousal abuse into agreeing to ongoing access to a child. As a result of financial and psychological pressures to settle cases, abuse victims may feel pressure to settle

---

ognized that the daughter was fearful of her father due to the mother's influence over the six years since the parents separated. The daughter came to believe that the father would kill her, though there was no evidence to support this fear. Recognizing the fears of the mother and daughter, however unfounded, the court ordered a process of initially supervised access, with a psychiatric assessment of the father and counselling for the mother and daughter.

75 Freeman (1998), at 100.

76 *Baker v. Zwicker*, 2000 CarswellNS 376, 189 N.S.R. (2d) 113, 590 A.P.R. 113 (N.S. Fam. Ct.), *per* Daley J.; *W. (G.A.) v. W. (E.L.G.)*, 2000 CarswellOnt 4268 (Ont. S.C.J.), *per* Dunn J; and *Weiten v. Adair*, 21 2001 CarswellMan 386, 21 R.F.L. (5th) 239 (Man. C.A.). See also Gordon (2004) for a very helpful paper on supervised access in domestic violence cases.

even if they have ongoing concerns about inadequate care, possible child abuse or high risk behavior by the non-custodial parent during access visit (Neilson, 2004).

Supervised Access

Supervised access may be appropriate if there is a reasonable apprehension of a threat to the safety of a child during a visit with a parent, or if the child is afraid of or refusing to visit a parent.[77] Some form of supervised access may be especially appropriate on an interim basis when there are serious allegations and a significant risk of harm to a child, but there is a dispute about whether abuse occurred.

A supervisor can be a trained professional, a volunteer or a relative (i.e., member of father's family chosen by mother).[78] It is important that the supervisor not be an inappropriate person, in particular someone who may be controlled by the abuser and who may not actually protect the child. Not infrequently an abusive parent will suggest that his parents supervise visitation; this can be appropriate, but the grandparents may themselves have a history of being abusive or have anger issues, and their appropriateness as supervisors should be carefully explored. In a number of localities supervised access projects have been established to provide supervision of visits by trained staff. These are valuable services that provide both supervisors and a suitable place for visits; some of these programs are government subsidized.

While the legal precedents indicate that access should only be ordered if it will actually benefit a child, there may be a tendency for some judges to order supervised access as a "compromise" (or some might say a "cop out"), rather than make the hard decision of terminating all access. Given its intrusive, expensive and artificial nature, supervised access should not be seen as a permanent arrangement

---

[77] In Ontario, best practice guidelines are being established for cases in which domestic violence and child sexual abuse are referred to supervised access centres. Personal communication with Judy Newman (program manager, Ministry of Attorney General) on September 12, 2007. For a review of services regarding supervised access across Canada, the reader is encouraged to see the Department of Justice website, which discusses these services and availability: http://www.justice.gc.ca/eng/pi/pad-rpad/rep-rap/chart/ccac_c1e.html, updated, June, 2008. See *Zahr v. Zahr*, 1994 CarswellAlta 248, 24 Alta. L.R. (3d) 274 (Alta. Q.B.), *per* Hunt J. where the court ordered supervised access for a 13 year old boys' visits with his father because of his past threats to take the boy to Lebanon and because the son had witnessed acts of violence by the father against the mother. In addition, the child had not seen the father for two years.

[78] See *W. (K.H.) v. W. (S.M.)*, 1995 CarswellNS 336, [1995] N.S.J. No. 471 (N.S. Fam. Ct.).

for cases where there are significant continuing concerns about leaving a child alone with a parent. Rather, supervised visits should be as a "temporary measure . . . to help resolve a parental impasse over access."[79] Preferably, during the period of supervised access, the abuser will be taking steps, such as participation in counselling, that will reduce the risk to the child and permit unsupervised access at some future time, or an investigation into the validity of any allegations will be completed (Gordon, 2004).[80]

Some parents have such a high potential for unpredictable or uncontrollable violence or abuse towards the children, that a court should not order supervised access. There may also be a concern about subtle non-physical threats or psychological abuse that can occur during even supervised access and this may be a basis for rejecting this option, while long term supervision is not usually seen as viable or in a child's best interest.[81] Ultimately, even if there is no immediate risk to the child, a court should deny any access if it is not satisfied that the child will receive some benefit from visits.

Some agencies or professionals who supervise visits make records of the interactions and will be able to provide an assessor or the court with information about the quality of parent-child interaction during a visit. In some cases there will be sufficient evidence of hostility or stress on the part of the child during supervised access to obtain an order terminating all access. Although the *opinions* of an access supervisor will only be admissible if that person qualified as an expert to express an opinion about parent-child relationships (an unlikely event),[82] *factual observations* about a child crying or appearing upset and about parental conduct may be admissible even if the supervisor is not qualified as an expert witness. Such evidence may play a significant role in the ultimate decision whether to terminate access.[83]

Exchange Supervision

In high conflict situations, the process of exchange of the child has the potential for violence between the parents. Even without the risk of violence, parental shouting matches or displays of anger at the

---

[79] Weisman (1992), at p. 74; quoted with approval by Abella J.A. in *M. (B.P.) v. M. (B.L.D.E.)*, *supra*, at note 58, at 360 [R.F.L.].

[80] See *W. (K.H.) v. W. (S.M.)*, *supra*, at note 78; and *F. (E.) v. S. (J.S.)*, 1995 CarswellAlta 426, 17 R.F.L. (4th) 283 (Alta. C.A.). The failure to comply with terms of supervised access, such as obtaining counselling for anger management, may result in the termination of even supervised access: *D. (C.) v. B. (J.)*, *supra*, at note 57.

[81] *Abdo v. Abdo*, *supra*, at note 55.

[82] *M. (B.P.) v. M. (B.L.D.E.)*, *supra*, at note 58, at p. 360 [R.F.L.].

[83] *Pavao v. Pavao*, *supra*, at note 36: logs of access supervisor admitted.

time of exchange can be very distressing to the child. In such cases, it may be appropriate to have supervision of the transition. Even if it is the parent with the history of domestic violence who is awarded custody, the exercise of access rights by the other parent may be an occasion for continuing the abuse, intimidation or control, in which case a court order may be required to supervise the exchange of the child or otherwise prevent harassment.[84]

Supervision may be especially appropriate during an initial period after separation when the risk of recurrence of violence may be higher. Exchange supervision is less costly, intrusive and restrictive than access supervision, but should only be contemplated if the there is no significant risk of direct harm to the children.

An example of a cases where supervised exchanges were appropriate is provided by the 1994 New Brunswick case of *Fullarton v. Fullarton*.[85] The parents separated after five years of marriage, during which the husband had assaulted the wife many times, including breaking her jaw and holding a knife to her throat. The three children witnessed many of these assaults. After several years of access that apparently occurred without incident, the man assaulted the mother when she came to his residence to get the children at the end of an access visit. While even the father acknowledged that the violent nature of his relationship with his wife had an adverse effect on the children, the mother accepted that he did not pose a direct threat to the children when they were in his care. Citing the *Divorce Act*, s. 16(10) the judge felt that the children had a "right" to access to their father (though there was no evidence in the judgment about their views). The judge concluded that any "risk of harm to the children can . . . be substantially eliminated if the parties have no contact with each other" (para. 17). Accordingly, the Court ordered that arrangements should be made that a third person acceptable to both parents pick up and return the children, with the judge to select someone if the parents could not agree. The father was also to abstain from consuming drugs or alcohol during access and 24 hours prior, and to "refrain from any displays of anger, violence or threats thereof in the presence of the children." If there had not been several years of access with only the one assaultive incident, termination of access would clearly have been more appropriate given the father's history of violence towards the mother, and its negative effects on the children.

---

84 *Brown v. Brown*, 1996 CarswellOnt 2288, 23 R.F.L. (4th) 23 (Ont. Gen. Div.).

85 1994 CarswellNB 278, 7 R.F.L. (4th) 272 (N.B.Q.B.); see also *Hossack v. McNorgan*, *supra*, at note 65, *per* Aston J.

Where supervised visitation programs exist, they can also provide supervision for an exchange.[86] Relatives like grandparents may also be appropriate for supervision of an exchange, or for taking the children from one home to the other. Having an exchange or transition at school or daycare may be the most appropriate and natural way to avoid having the parents in direct contact, if this is possible and there is overnight contact.[87]

In some cases judges have ordered that the access exchange occur outside a police station, to limit any threat of violence or outbursts of anger at the time of exchange. Although this may be a last resort, these locations may be frightening for a child as well as inconvenient. A public place, like a fast food restaurant, is a less intrusive public place for exchanges, though also less secure.

Judicial Control Over Abusive Partners—What are the Limits of the Law?

One of the challenges that judges face when dealing with high conflict cases, especially those where there are domestic violence issues, is determining how much they should try to regulate the conduct of parents to promote the best interests of a child. The legal power to make an order regulating parental conduct derives from the responsibility for placing conditions on the exercise of custody or access. In cases where there are concerns about violence, an attempt to control parental conduct can also be made as part of a restraining order. In dealing with this challenge, there may be issues related to judicial expertise, judicial knowledge about the individual parents and children before the court, and the enforceability of any order made by the court. If there is a threat of further domestic violence or child abuse, there may also be safety issues.

Parents in high conflict cases need structure and direction from the court. In a high conflict situation, it is not appropriate for a court to simply make an order for "reasonable access", as the parents are unlikely to agree what this means. Even in high conflict cases it is often preferable for the parties to work out a clear, detailed arrangement for access and care of the children, with the assistance of an assessor, their lawyers or a mediator rather than having an arrangement imposed by a judge. However, when this is not possible (or suitable professionals are not involved), a judge may have to impose an arrangement, making a detailed order to govern visitation and

---

[86] See *Orszak v. Orszak* , 2000 CarswellOnt 1574, [2000] O.J. No. 1606 (Ont. S.C.J.).

[87] See *Fang v. Fang*, 2004 CarswellOnt 896 (Ont. S.C.J.).

communication between parents and child.[88] Further, even if an arrangement is made on consent in high conflict cases, it is often useful to incorporate it into an order to ensure compliance and enable better enforcement. If there is a threat of future violence, it may be appropriate that there be no visitation.

Some judges will make very detailed orders about communications between parents concerning the child. For example, a judge may require that the parents only communicate about the child in a written notebook that is exchanged when access occurs, or by email. In some cases this can be a useful way of helping estranged parents to (re)learn how to communicate in a clear and non-abusive fashion, but in other cases the written communication can itself become problematic or abusive.

It is not uncommon for judges to order that a parent with a history of abusive conduct attend counselling or take an anger management course as a condition of exercising access. Imposing a requirement of counselling should not be seen as a solution to all problems of abuse, since individuals who participate in counselling or therapy may not fully engage (or may not participate at all), or may have deeply rooted problems that will not be resolved by participation in a relatively short course of treatment.[89] However, if suitable therapists or programs are available, this can be a useful condition for cases where there are anger management or communication problems, *provided* that there are not significant safety concerns *and* the abuser indicates a willingness to engage in counselling.

In *Aguilera v. Reid*,[90] Rogers J. ordered that a violent husband would only have supervised access for two hours, twice a month, but offered some suggestions for the type of actions that he would have to undertake to get unsupervised access at some future time. Justice Rogers suggested that the husband should undergo counselling for his drug and alcohol abuse, see a psychologist to deal with his issues of anger and violence and eventually obtain a report from that professional about his progress. The judge commented:

> The court feels the respondent ought to have some guidance as to what would advance his claim. This judicial officer cannot predict the future but suggests to the respondent that he ought to demonstrate he is capable of change. . .

---

[88] See *Orszak v. Orszak*, *supra*, at note 86, *per* Himel J.

[89] *W. (D.J.A.) v. T. (G.D.)*, 2000 CarswellSask 578, [2000] S.J. No. 594 (Sask. Q.B.), *per* Kraus J: expert concludes that abusive conduct cannot be resolved in a one day or five day course

[90] 2006 CarswellOnt 1227, [2006] O.J. No. 810 (Ont. S.C.J.).

The court shall not make these suggestions terms of any order. (paras. 39-42)

It is common for judges to make orders that a parent not consume drugs or alcohol during access visits. This type of order may well be appropriate. If the non-custodial parent appears for an access visit and is intoxicated, the custodial parent will then be justified in denying access. Indeed, even in the absence of such an explicit term, a custodial parent would have the right (and indeed the duty) not to give over the care of a child to the other parent if they appear intoxicated. The situation becomes much more problematic, however, if the use of drugs or alcohol occurs during the visit. Is the child to be expected to "report" on the non-custodial parent? How should the court assess the credibility of the custodial parent's statements about the child's report? Should the child be called as a witness on an application for contempt (by either parent), or on an application to terminate or suspend access?

In *Dhaliwal v. Dhaliwal*[91] the husband was physically and verbally abusive to his wife, often in the presence of his children, and abusive of the eldest daughter. The family was a part of the Sikh community in Canada; the husband frequently used a Punjabi term to verbally abuse his wife which was "extremely degrading and offensive and which signified a woman who made herself available for sexual relations with anyone who asked. This term, somewhat erroneously translated in some of these proceedings as 'prostitute', is said to have serious repercussions on a woman's reputation, social status and acceptability in the Sikh community" (para. 11). The woman suffered depression and anxiety, exacerbated by her loss of status within the Sikh community. Justice Métivier awarded custody to the woman (calling the man's custody application "frivolous") and awarded her a $10,000 damage judgment in tort. As a condition of access the father was ordered to use his "best efforts to ensure that all people in contact with the children say nothing bad about their mother." This type of order sends a clear and appropriate message to the father, even though enforcement may be very problematic.

In many cases of moderately high conflict, it may be useful for a judge to try to exhort parents towards "good behavior" and appeal to their "better natures", even though the judge is aware that the order is effectively unenforceable. The judge need not (and should not) tell the parties that the order is "effectively unenforceable", as the "magic" of such an order is that many parents will make good faith efforts to comply. This type of order may be especially appropriate if there is a

---

91 1997 CarswellOnt 5774, [1997] O.J. No. 5964 (Ont. Gen. Div.).

lack of resources for mediation, but the parents seem like they will respond to judicial exhortations towards good behavior.

Ultimately, judges, other professionals in the justice system, and parents need to recognize that the law is a blunt instrument and that judicial wisdom and social resources are limited. In high conflict situations and cases where there are significant issues of physical safety, it is submitted that judges should focus on making orders that are clear, can be enforced, and that reduce the risk of injury and opportunities for further argument. Even then, enforcement issues, whether by contempt application or variation of custody or access, can be highly problematic.

In some cases, even if access is terminated, an abusive parent will attempt to use the legal system to harass a former partner, bringing repeated applications to vary to allow access to resume. In such cases, it may be appropriate to impose cost sanctions, making any further applications conditional on the prior costs order being paid. It may also be appropriate to impose pre-conditions on any future applications of the abusive spouse, such as, that he produce evidence about his criminal record and medical or psychological treatment.[92] If there are concerns about use of the justice system to harass a parent, every effort should be made to ensure that one judge will continue to handle the case at each application or appearance, so that the court can be more fully aware of the manipulative and abusive aspects of the relationship.

Concluding Remarks

Researchers agree that children who are exposed to domestic violence are harmed emotionally, and that their behaviour and adjustment may be affected in significant ways, both in the short and long term. They are also at increased risk of direct maltreatment and abuse. The available research, however, reveals a significant variability in children's experiences and the impact of these on a child.[93] Therefore, a child custody assessor always needs to screen for domestic violence, even if the referral question does not specifically address the issue or if the parents have not alleged violence of any kind. When domestic violence concerns are present, an assessor should conduct a specialized assessment that specifically addresses domestic violence concerns, taking the results into account when developing parenting

---

92 See *Roach v. Kelly, supra*, at note 72.

93 Jeffrey L. Edleson, (2004). Should childhood exposure to adult domestic violence be defined as maltreatment under the law? In P.G. Jaffe, L.L. Baker and A. Cunningham (Eds.) *Protecting Children from Domestic Violence: Strategies for community intervention.* (pp. 8-29). New York: NY: Guilford Press.

plan recommendations that are in the best interests of a particular child and family.

It is imperative that custody assessors follow appropriate professional guidelines (i.e., Association of Family and Conciliation Courts, American Psychological Association, Canadian Psychological Association, Ethical Guidelines for Psychological Practice Related to Child Custody and Access) when assessing for domestic violence, including their obtaining specialized training. Further, at least initially, assessors should obtain supervision followed by regular peer consultation for these extremely challenging cases. Even the most seasoned child custody assessor needs to be vigilant regarding this specialized area, given the complexities of the family dynamics in cases of domestic violence. Assessing the allegations and risk, and providing differentiated recommendations requires specialized skill and knowledge above and beyond the knowledge base necessary for conducting a child custody assessment. We cannot state strongly enough that all allegations of domestic violence must be investigated, whether or not there is corroborating evidence: a child's life could be at risk.

We support a mandatory training requirement found in other jurisdictions, such as California, for doing assessments. In Ontario, the *Arbitration Act* sets out that in conducting family arbitration, an arbitrator is required to have specified training approved by the Attorney General, including 14 hours of screening for domestic violence and power imbalance. Notwithstanding the many issues raised about confidentiality and the practical limitations of the legislation, this is the first time that domestic violence has been given legislative attention in the *Arbitration Act*. Many members of the judiciary have training relevant to domestic violence and many acquire relevant knowledge through continuing education. Such training and ongoing education are essential for all judges if they are to effectively decide cases in which there are allegations of domestic violence.

In addition, there is need for a coordinated response between mental health professionals (assessors and therapists), lawyers, and judges, to better assist children and their families through the post-separation experience when issues of domestic violence arise. We strongly encourage the courts to take a case-management approach while acting as the final arbiter, monitoring cases as they move through the legal system with the assistance of mental health professionals. To accomplish this goal effectively, the necessary resources (i.e., supervised access facilities, access to mental health professionals) need to be known to the court and available to the family. There must also be a more restrictive approach to the principle of "maximum contact" in s. 16(10) of the *Divorce Act*; in domestic violence cases it is often appropriate to have less contact with a parent with a history of familial violence than in other cases.

All justice system professionals need to be cognizant that a one-size-fits-all approach to domestic violence does not produce decisions that are in a child's best interests. They must ensure that the very real differences amongst families are taken into account. With the inclusion of domestic violence as a factor in determining the best interests of the child in a growing number of the provincial child custody and access statutes, it is hoped that other provinces will follow suit, and that policy-makers will provide adequate resources for families and the courts.

In this chapter we explored various assessment protocols used in cases where domestic violence is an issue and reviewed case law illustrating the issues that judges face in dealing with these cases. In the next chapter, we address child sexual abuse allegations made in the context of child custody and access disputes. Similar to this chapter, we discuss the problems with definitions, the dynamics of these cases, and concerns about false allegations, as well as review legal trends. There are important similarities in cases where child abuse and domestic violence allegations are made, as both raise issues of exploitation of an intimate relationship of trust, but there are also some critical differences.

Chapter 5

Sexual Abuse Allegations in Child Custody Disputes

Following a thorough assessment, the clinician may reach one of three conclusions: that the sexual abuse has probably occurred, has probably not occurred, or is unsure. A strong caution is given against becoming entangled in an endless process of trying to find out whether the allegations are true or false. Whatever conclusions are reached are but one factor in the recommendation regarding custody and/or access. Ultimately the recommendation will be made according to the best interests of the child, taking into account the child's relationship and attachments, as well as the sexual abuse allegations.

George A. Awad (1987)[1]

Child sexual abuse allegations are not an uncommon feature of high conflict separations, and create special challenges for the family justice system, as the emotional tension, bitterness and complexity of a case is invariably heightened. It is important for assessors and family lawyers to understand issues related to such allegations, although in Canada, the primary responsibility for the investigation of the validity of allegations of child sexual abuse usually rests with child protection agencies, and in some cases the police. Typically it is only *after* the allegation has been investigated and has been substantiated or not by the child protection process that a child custody assessor becomes involved in making parenting recommendations post separation. However, it is not unusual that *during* a child custody assessment an allegation of child sexual abuse is made. In these latter situations, child sexual abuse allegations *must* always be taken seriously and reported to the appropriate child protection agency for an investigation.[2] Further, there are cases in which the parties or even

---

1 Awad, G., A. (1987). The assessment of custody and access disputes in cases of sexual abuse allegations. *Canadian Journal of Psychiatry, 32,* p. 539.

2 All mental health professionals are obligated by their Colleges and child welfare legislation to report any child who is in need of protection. In Ontario, Section 37(2) of the *Child and Family Services Act*, R.S.O. 1990, c. C.11 outlines when a child is in need of protection. Mental health professionals should consult with their Colleges and appropriate legislation in each province. The legislation can be found on the legal website at: www.canlii.org.

a child protection agency may ask an assessor for an opinion about the validity of a sexual abuse allegation.[3]

Determining the validity of an allegation of child sexual abuse may be only one factor in making post-separation best interests determinations but, once the allegation is made—it may dominate other issues. If an allegation that a parent has sexually abused a child is founded, it raises serious concerns about the person's capacity to parent. Yet, even if a parent has sexually abused their child, that parent-child relationship will not necessarily be severed and may have to be managed by the family justice system. If the allegation is unfounded, it can be traumatic and challenging for the child's relationship with the parent who has been falsely alleged to have been a perpetrator of abuse, as the child may come to believe in the veracity of a false allegation.

Bala, Mitnick, Trocmé and Houston (2007b) conclude that, "a significant proportion of allegations of child sexual abuse made in the context of parental separation are unfounded" (p.27), though even in this context all allegations of abuse must be taken seriously, and there are many founded allegations as well. Unfounded allegations of abuse following separation can occur for a number of reasons. For example, the family is already experiencing a highly conflictual separation and one parent wishes to exact revenge on the other. In some cases, unfounded allegations may reflect a disturbance in personality functioning or a misunderstanding. (Bala *et al.*, 2007b; Bernet, 2006; Bow, Fancella, Quinnell, Zaroff & Assemany, 2002; Gardner, 1992b; Johnston, Lee, Olesen & Walters, 2005; Tonmyr, De Marco, Hovestad & Hubka, 2004). Often unfounded allegations are a result of miscommunication, misunderstandings, and inappropriate questioning. The "honest mistake" is more common than the "deliberate lie" in a situation where there are high levels of mistrust and suspicion.

Allegations of child sexual abuse present a significant clinical challenge to even the most seasoned assessor. This is because young children are more often involved, there is usually no conclusive forensic evidence, and there are no valid psychological tests or profiles that can prove or disprove whether the accuser, the accused, or the child is telling the truth about the allegation (Bala *et al.*, 2007b; Bernet, 2006; Boat & Forman, 2008; Faller, 2007; Sachsenmaier, 2005; Weissman, 1991). Further difficulty arises since most acts of sexual exploitation do not involve penetration, but fondling or touching. Not only

[3] The reader should consult with their professional regulatory College before they conduct an assessment of the family regarding sexual abuse allegations and provide an opinion, because different professional Colleges may have different interpretations of the role of the assessor in these specialized circumstances.

is there no forensic evidence, but, there must be a determination of whether the touching of a young child was innocent (i.e., washing the child's genitals) or sexual, and the child, even if accurately reporting the incidents, may not be able to tell the difference. Frequently assessors, and ultimately the courts, must deal with cases where there is a degree of uncertainty about whether the allegations are true or false, and must formulate parenting plans that promote a child's best interests while ensuring safety for the child.

It is incumbent upon all mental health professionals who undertake child custody assessments that involve child sexual abuse allegations to be aware of the ever-increasing body of social science and research literature on allegations of child sexual abuse in the context of parental separation (see, for example, Ackerman, 2006; Bernet, 2006; Boat & Forman, 2008; Bala *et al.*, 2007b; Bow, Quinnell, Zaroff & Assemany, 2002; Carnes, 2000; Faller, 1991, 2007; Friedrich, Gully & Trane, 2005; Gardner, 1995; Gould & Martindale, 2007; Hewitt, 1999; Kuehnle & Kirkpatrick, 2005; Oates, Jones, Denson, Sirotnak, Gary & Krugman, 2000), and how best to make recommendations in these specialized circumstances. In addition to being familiar with the guidelines and standards of practice relevant to their discipline and to child custody assessments, the assessor should also be familiar with standards and guidelines relevant specifically to the assessment of sexual abuse.[4]

In this chapter we explore, specifically: (1) the definition of child sexual abuse; (2) the dynamics of child sexual abuse allegations post separation and/or divorce and the role of child protection and the police; (3) the prevalence, validity, and credibility of the allegations during a child custody dispute; (4) clinical and legal considerations for child custody assessors; and (5) the role of assessors and the role of the court.

Definition of Child Sexual Abuse

One of the difficulties with assessing sexual abuse allegations lies in the lack of consensus between professionals regarding an appropriate or accurate definition of child sexual abuse. Although there is

---

[4] See Guidelines for the Clinical Evaluation of Child and Adolescent Sexual Abuse (American Academy of Child and Adolescent Psychiatry, 1988), Guidelines for Psychological Evaluation of Suspected Sexual Abuse in Young Children (1990), Guidelines for Psychological Evaluations in Child Protection Matters (American Psychological Association, 1998), Practice Parameters for the Forensic Evaluation of Children and Adolescents Who May Have Been Physically or Sexually Abused (American Academy of Child and Adolescent Psychiatry (AACAP, 1997), and Guidelines for Psychosocial Evaluation of Suspected Sexual Abuse in Young Children (American Professional Society on the Abuse of Children, 1990).

agreement about certain acts, such as intercourse with one's child, as clearly being acts of sexual abuse, in many situations it is less clear. When, for example, if ever, is it sexually abusive to shower with a child of the opposite gender? Further, there are other definitional issues, for example, when trying to characterize sexual abuse as "moderate" or "severe", and controversy over whether to chartacterize child sexual abuse as a "syndrome".

Viewing it from a social science perspective, Finkelhor (1987) states that child sexual abuse is "most commonly used in reference to sexual activity involving a child that has at least one or two characteristics: (1) it occurs within a relationship where it is deemed exploitive by virtue of an age difference or caretaking relationship that exists with the child; and (2) it occurs as a result of threat or force" (p. 233).[5] Gardner (1995) also reports that there is no good definition of sexual abuse, but that the term refers rather to a continuum, from the most minimal form of sexual contact to the most severe. Along the spectrum of sexual abuse, the impact on the child victim can be traumatic, irrespective of whether the abuse was a one-time occurrence or repeated over time. The effect of abuse is not solely dependent on the nature or frequency of the acts, and may not be reflected in the clinical words that are used to describe the acts (i.e., severe) (Haugaard, 2000).

Another compounding difficulty in defining sexual abuse arises from the previous work of Summit's (1983) description of the potential effects of sexual exploitation on children, also known as "Child Sexual Abuse Accommodation Syndrome". Summit (1983) identified five symptoms and behaviours suggested as occurring together in a "syndrome" in children who have been sexually exploited in a familial context: secrecy; helplessness; accommodation; delayed convincing disclosure; and retraction. In commenting on the "syndrome" identified by Summit (1983), Kuehnle (1998) observed that there has been no research to empirically establish how often some or all of the symptoms and behaviours occur among sexually abused children, and hence the "syndrome" should be considered with caution. Moreover, she asserts that when sexual abuse is conceptualized as a discrete clinical syndrome, the clinician can fall into traps similar to those that can occur while conducting a child custody assessment—that is, making inappropriate inferences based on the information received as that may be subject to distortions due to confirmatory bias, or

[5] Also see Finkelhor, D. (1994). Current information on the scope and nature of child sexual abuse. In *Future of Children. 4(2),* 31-54, for an excellent chapter on the difficulties with defining sexual abuse and the scope of the problem.

believing that a sexually abused child fits into a homogenous group (Dammeyer, 1998; Kuehnle, 1998).

In a joint submission by a group of experts gathered at a conference in Sweden in 1993 to discuss child sexual abuse, Lamb (1994) wrote that there is no specific behavioural syndrome that characterizes the victims of child sexual abuse and, in fact, a broad range of behaviours appears with widely varying side effects on the victim. In Dammeyer's (1998) subsequent review of the literature, he too, concludes that no specific syndrome exists among child sexual abuse victims. He adds that many sexually abused children do not show identifiable symptoms, and that many non-abused children show behaviours that can be indicative of abuse.

Gould and Martindale (2007) also caution assessors and investigators to be mindful of how sexual abuse is identified, advising of the need to explore the perspective of the referring source (i.e., when and by whom was the referral made) and the meaning of the behaviour that is being described as sexual abuse. In addition, they note the need to describe, as well as operationalize, the specific behaviours alleged to have occurred, as well as consider any conduct that may be symptomatic of sexual abuse. Kuehnle (1996) aptly asserts that while it is important to note when a child exhibits an unusual preoccupation with sexual acts or fears a particular person, professionals must still ask what the meaning of this information and behavior is *before* formulating any conclusions. We would add that given that these matters often go before the courts, the mental health professional should also be aware of the legal perspective and of the evidentiary requirements of the particular court process in order to assist the court in decision-making. This is not an easy endeavour, either for the professional investigating the allegations or for the judge ultimately making a decision with respect to the custody of or access to a child.

The Dynamics of Post-Separation Child Sexual Abuse Allegations and the Role of Child Protection Services and the Police

The Context

Allegations of child sexual abuse made within the context of parental separation often occur in high conflict cases where there is an atmosphere of mutual blame, hostility, and recriminations (Johnston *et al.*, 2005). While some advocates (i.e., mental health professionals and fathers rights groups) have embraced the notion that sexual abuse allegations are almost always false and that "malicious mothers" are behind these allegations (Gardner, 1992; Turkat, 1999), many allegations made after the separation are founded (Bala *et al.*, 2007b). Further, a significant number of unfounded post-separation allegations of sexual abuse are made by fathers, most often against the mother's new partner.

Faller (1991) identified four family dynamics related to allegations of sexual abuse pre- and post-separation. These are: (1) the mother finds out about the sexual abuse and separates from her partner as a result of this discovery; (2) the abuse has been longstanding, but only comes to light during or after the separation; (3) the abuse is precipitated by the separation; and (4) the allegation is false. She suggested that the largest proportion of sexual abuse cases are ones where the abuse begins after the separation, followed by those in which the separation is triggered by the discovery of the abuse. Freidrich (2005) believes that while some parents involved in these cases may be paedophiles (i.e., individuals with a sexual preference for children), perhaps with their paedophilia repressed during the marriage, most of the cases do not involve paedophiles but rather are situational in nature.

Bernet (2006) identifies five additional dynamics to those raised by Faller (1991) that can arise when an unfounded allegation of child sexual abuse is alleged in the context of parental separation. These are: (1) an anxious parent misinterprets the child's behavior or physical condition; (2) the accusing parent is delusional; (3) the accusing parent blatantly brainwashes and intimidates the child or provides subtle but sophisticated suggestions to the child, as found in some types of alienation cases; (4) accidental indoctrination where the parent is overly anxious and protective; and (5) cases of parent alienation.[6]

False and Unproven Allegations of Abuse after Parents Separate

A significant proportion of allegations of abuse made following parental separation are not proven in court. In some of these cases, the allegations are in fact true, but the accusing parent, who bears the burden of proof, is unable to satisfy the court that the abuse occurred. As we noted, it may be difficult to prove abuse, as there is frequently no physical evidence of abuse, and children, especially young children, may have great difficulty in communicating a coherent and consistent story. There are, however, also a significant number of cases in which the allegations of abuse are not just unproven, but are actually untrue. While in some cases of unfounded allegations

[6] We explore alienation more fully in Chapters 6 and 7.

there may be a deliberate effort to deceive, more commonly the parent who brings forward the unfounded allegation of abuse following separation has an honest belief in the claim. Leonoff and Montague (1996) state:

> . . . [unfounded] accusations are most often multi-causal and are rarely simply the conniving manipulation of a competitive parent who wishes to win at all cost. There is a gradient between the parent who consciously deceives and the one who is deluded in belief and whose accusations are built of several elements: personal history projected onto the present relationship; shock and betrayal turned into malevolent mistrust of the other; aggression and hatred; fears based on regressed violent behaviour at the termination of the marriage; comments made in emotional turmoil; suggestibility enhanced by outsiders who are keen to find sexual abuse in men; wishes to denigrate, humiliate and punish the ex-spouse; distortion in thought processes in mentally vulnerable parents who view their overreactions as protectiveness; and finally, a fervent desire to win a custody case and be rid of that person forever (p. 357).

Kathy Kuehnle (1996) stated: "We presently have some understanding of the potentially devastating psychological effects of child sexual abuse; however, we know very little about the psychological damage that may be caused to a child who grows up falsely believing he or she has been sexually abused by a loved parent."[7]

A child who has been repeatedly questioned by a parent with preconceptions or biases may be quite suggestible. Repeated questioning by a trusted adult can alter the memory of a child, especially a young child, to resemble the beliefs of the questioner. Because of repeated, and both leading questions and misleading suggestions from a parent, a child may come to believe that he or she was abused and create descriptions of events that did not occur (Ceci & Bruck, 1995).

Another complicating factor arises in cases where a child has in fact been abused, but the offender has been misidentified. Misidentification may, for example, result in a father with visitation rights being identified as the perpetrator when it is actually the mother's new partner who is abusing the child. This may be an especially challenging situation to assess, since the child may exhibit genuine symptoms of abuse, but the alleged perpetrator is innocent.

---

[7] Kuehnle, K. (1996). *Assessing Allegations of Child Sexual Abuse.* Professional Resource Press, Sarasota, Florida, p. 294.

Studies on the Incidence of Founded and False Allegations

Some of the research on the incidence of founded and false allegations in these types of cases is problematic. A number of early studies had small or biased samples. Further, the nature of different studies is important, and may explain some of the apparent discrepancies in the research. Studies that consider all reports of abuse in a particular jurisdiction tend to have lower rates of intentionally false cases. Studies that report on clinical samples of high conflict parental separation cases involving allegations of sexual abuse in the family court system generally have higher rates of uncertain and deliberately false outcomes than jurisdiction-wide studies.

While there is understandably some variation in the results of studies that have different methodologies and are studying different populations, there is also significant consistency in the research. Among the high conflict cases that go to trial in family court, a relatively large number are likely to involve some type of allegation of familial abuse, most commonly spousal violence, though not infrequently child abuse or neglect (Moloney, Smyth, Weston, Richardson, Qu & Gray, 2007). Separated fathers and mothers seem about equally likely to make unfounded allegations, though mothers are more likely to make unfounded allegations of child sexual abuse, and fathers more likely to falsely claim that mothers are neglecting their children (Johnston *et al.*, 2005). Although the rate of unfounded allegations of child sexual abuse in the context of parental separation is relatively high, with less than half being substantiated, a significant portion of these allegations are founded and such allegations must never be dismissed without careful investigation (Bala *et al.*, 2007b). Further, even where the allegation is unfounded, the incidence of deliberate lying is relatively low. Most unfounded allegations are a product of miscommunication or misunderstanding, which may be exacerbated by hostility surrounding parental separation.

Child Protection Agency Involvement

As we noted earlier, when a parent believes that their child has been abused, a child protection agency is likely to become involved in the case. Sometimes the accusing parent contacts the agency directly, or the parent may first contact a doctor or mental health professional, who may then be obliged under child abuse laws to report a *suspected* case of abuse. When a child protection agency begins an investigation of suspected abuse, the agency will take steps to ensure the immediate safety of the child. If, for example, the allegation is against a non-custodial parent, the agency may go to court under child protection legislation to suspend visitation by the suspected abuser, but more typically the agency will "request" a "voluntary" suspension or supervision of visits, with the threat of going to court if there is no agreement.

If the agency does not make a child protection application, the agency workers may still testify in the family law case, or may be asked to supervise visits by the alleged abuser. There are also cases in which the agency decides to commence child protection proceedings, such as if the accusing parent does not pursue family law proceedings, perhaps for financial reasons. Alternatively, if the evidence of abuse is relatively weak, or if the allegations of abuse are less serious, the agency may decide after the investigation that no further action on its part is warranted, though the accusing parent may still proceed with the family law case.

Criminal Prosecution of the Alleged Abuser

In some cases, the accusing parent may contact the police directly to report an abuse allegation, though more commonly the police are contacted by child protection workers involved in the case. If the agency believes there is a serious abuse allegation, they will usually inform the police and a joint investigation may be conducted. In some cases, there may be considerable delay between the initial disclosure of abuse and the police being informed, complicating the police investigation. Given the nature of criminal law, it is only when there is strong evidence of abuse that criminal charges will be laid. It is relatively uncommon for criminal and civil proceedings to be conducted simultaneously in these types of cases, though this does occur.

It is much more difficult to prove abuse in a criminal proceeding than in the civil context. For a criminal conviction, there must be proof beyond a reasonable doubt, while a civil case only requires proof on the "balance of probabilities" (or "preponderance of evidence"). Further, the criminal rules of evidence may result in the exclusion of evidence in a criminal proceeding that is admissible in civil child protection or family law proceedings.

If criminal charges are laid, they will tend to "dominate" any family law proceedings, at least until the criminal charges are resolved. A usual condition of the release of the accused in the community, pending a criminal trial, is the denial of contact with the alleged victim. In some cases, the criminal court judge will release the accused on bail with a condition that there is to be contact with the child only if permitted by an order of the family law judge.

While a criminal conviction for child abuse will often result in the termination of visitation, even if there is a conviction, a judge in a family law case must still consider whether it is in the "best interests" of a child to continue or resume contact. Children who have been sexually or physically abused by a parent will often feel an attachment to that parent, despite the abuse. A family court may allow visitation by a convicted abuser if it is satisfied that this is in the child's best interests. If the prosecution withdraws the criminal charges or the alleged abuser is acquitted in criminal court, there may be a tendency for parents or others involved in the case to accept this criminal finding for civil purposes as well. However, the issues and standard of proof are different in the two courts, and the family proceedings may well continue despite a dismissal of the charges in criminal court.

Unfounded Allegations: Misunderstanding, Fabrication or Mental Disturbance?

As we noted, there is a range of circumstances that may lead a parent to make unfounded allegations of abuse in the context of parental separation. These include:

- allegations that are genuinely believed, but mistaken, often due to some misinterpretation of behaviours and situations;
- allegations that are made knowingly with the intent to seek revenge or manipulate the course of litigation; or
- allegations that are genuinely believed, but false, as a result of an emotional disturbance or mental illness of the accusing parent.

It may be difficult to determine which of these factors, or what combination of factors, resulted in an unfounded allegation being made. In the majority of cases involving unfounded allegations of abuse, the accusing parent has an honest but erroneous belief that the child has suffered some form of abuse. For example, the allegation may arise from a custodial parent's misinterpretation of a young child's answers to questions posed after a visit. The custodial parent may ask about red genitalia, and the child, with limited vocabulary, may describe innocent and appropriate touching, for example for the purpose of washing, but the acts may be misinterpreted as abusive. An unfounded allegation may also arise from a misunderstanding about innocent conduct, such as parental nudity or bathing with a young child. A young child, for example, commonly has considerable interest in the sexual organs of the opposite sex parent, and may want to touch them. In a non-divorced family, this type of touching is quickly and appropriately dealt with, but in a situation of mistrust, and a custody or access dispute, a child's description of acts with one parent may be misunderstood by the other parent and result in a child protection investigation or litigation.

Parents who are questioning their children about what occurs during visits may also misinterpret children's behaviour as distress. Children are often emotionally distressed after parental separation, and may have such symptoms as bet wetting or nightmares. If there is high parental conflict, the change of care that occurs with visits may be disturbing to the child. One parent may misinterpret generalized anxiety about visitation as fear of the other parent as opposed to distress associated with the level of conflict between the parents and about the associated changes in routine (Kuehnle & Kirkpatrick, 2005).

Prevalence, Validity and Credibility of Sexual Abuse Allegations

Kuehnle and Kirkpatrick (2005) believe that the conclusions drawn about child sexual abuse and the prevalence of it arises from a number of myths that have surrounded the identification and reporting of sexual abuse allegations. They suggested that these *myths* include the following:

(1) there are reliable estimates on the rate of child sexual abuse existing in the United States and around the world;

(2) only a minority of children avoid disclosure of their sexual abuse;

(3) coercion/threats and fear of harm decrease the likelihood of disclosure of sexual abuse;

(4) a substantial number of child sexual abuse victims recant after making a disclosure;

(5) reliable estimates exist on the numbers of litigated complex child custody cases that also have child sexual abuse allegations;

(6) there are reliable estimates on the numbers of false child sexual abuse claims in litigated complex child custody matters; and

(7) forensic evaluators are competent at identifying false child sexual abuse claims.

They caution mental health professionals to canvass carefully their own beliefs and knowledge base when undertaking a child sexual abuse assessments or custody assessments involving allegations of sexual abuse.

Hovestad, Tonmyr, Hubka and De Marco (2005) suggest that the prevalence and nature of sexual abuse is often misunderstood for a variety of reasons. They argue that sexual abuse may be misperceived to be the most common form of child maltreatment, given the publicity of scandals amongst the clergy in both Canada and the United States. Finkelhor (2003), a child maltreatment expert, states of the many incidents of sexual abuse by the clergy disclosed in the US: "The scandal continued and exacerbated the elevation of the problem of sexual abuse above all other forms of child maltreatment. . . [T]here were many times in the course of this crisis when child abuse was actually used as a synonym for sexual abuse" (p. 1226).

Complicating the matter of differentiating child sexual abuse from other forms of maltreatment is the nature and number of false or unproven allegations of sexual abuse that arise in cases after separation and/or divorce. London, Bruck, Ceci and Shuman (2005) report that estimating the prevalence of child sexual abuse allegations is confounded by several factors, including the following:

(1) the present estimates of child sexual abuse are based primarily on reports received and validated by child protection agencies;

(2) the figures do not reflect the number of unreported cases or the number of cases that are reported to other professionals (i.e., the police, mental health therapists, etc); and

(3) there is little, if any, definitive medical or physical evidence to conclude that sexual abuse took place.

As a result of these limitations, mental health professionals and legal decision-makers must often rely on children's statements, which are similarly difficult to assess. In addition, in most cases there is no clear physical evidence to substantiate allegations of sexual abuse. This is especially true with younger children as we stated earlier, who may have difficulties expressing themselves in a coherent and consistent manner; as a result, their stories may be discounted, disbelieved or misinterpreted. Investigations into sexual abuse allegations are especially difficult, as the alleged abuser may have had legitimate reasons for touching the child; determining whether the touching was sexual in nature requires an assessment of not only opportunity but also of intent.

Overview of Prevalence Studies

In this section, we review both Canadian and American social science and legal studies conducted to date, with a view to understanding the difficulties in estimating the prevalence of sexual abuse allegations in post-separation families. By reviewing the studies, we hope to illuminate two important issues:

(1) how research literature over the past few decades has become clearer and more sophisticated in differentiating various forms of child maltreatment (i.e., physical, emotional, and verbal abuse) as distinguished from child sexual abuse, in turn, this provides not only better reporting of data, but also allows for a differentiation of intervention approaches; and

(2) the difficulty of substantiating child sexual abuse allegations in the midst of custody and access disputes, as the child is often young, susceptible to suggestibility and experiencing problems with memory, and given that parents involved in the traditional adversarial process experience heightened emotions and demonstrate polarized behaviour (Kuehnle & Kirkpatrick, 2005; Bala *et al.*, 2007b; London *et al.*, 2005).[8]

Studies in the United States

In the United States, of the studies that explored this issue to date, the rate of false allegations of sexual abuse varied between 14 and 55 per cent.

Two of the early studies were based on small clinical samples and found relatively high rates of false allegations. In the first reported study of false allegations, Benedek and Schetky (1985) reported on 18 cases of alleged incest that were reported post-separation (14 cases in the context of an on-going custody dispute), concluding that 10 (55 per cent) of the cases were false. Similarly, Green (1986) reported that four (36 per cent) out of 11 cases of alleged child sexual abuse in the context of on-going child custody dispute were false, and concluded that false allegations in this situation were a significant concern.

Thoennes and Tjaden (1990) also examined the prevalence and patterns of sexual abuse allegations in post-separation families. In this study, the researchers wanted to examine whether or not mothers made false allegations against fathers more often during custody and access disputes. Data was collected from court evaluators and child

[8] See Crossman, Powell, Principe and Ceci (2002) for a good review of the issues related to memory in children's testimony in child custody cases. Also see Ceci and Bruck (1998); Emery and Haugaard (1998); and Faller (2007) on issues related to suggestibility and coaching. For studies on accuracy and consistency of children's reports of physical and sexual abuse, see Ghetti, Goodman, Eisen, Qin and Davis (2002); Orbach and Lamb (1999); Lamb, Sternberg, Esplin, Hershkowitz and Orbach (1997); Poole and Lamb (1998); and Saywitz and Goodman (1996).

protection workers in 12 cities across the United States. The participants were asked to document demographic and specific allegation information for all cases involving sexual abuse allegations within the sample. Of the 9,000 cases involving a custody dispute, less than two per cent (n=165) involved allegations of sexual abuse. In the 129 cases for which they were able to obtain assessment data from a custody evaluator, child protection worker or both, Thoennes and Tjaden found that: (a) sexual abuse was believed to have occurred by the clinician in half of the cases; (b) no abuse was thought to have occurred in one third of the cases; and (c) 17 per cent of the remaining cases were considered indeterminate. Their research is important for two reasons. First, they found there was "no evidence to support the belief that these cases typically involved mothers falsely accusing fathers to gain or maintain custody of the children" (p. 161). Secondly, they concluded, "our findings on validity determinations do not support conclusions drawn from previous clinical assessments which suggest that false sexual abuse allegations are disproportionately high in custody and visitation disputes" (p. 161).

Faller (1991) examined 136 cases involving post-separation allegation of child sexual abuse, referred to a child abuse clinic by child welfare agencies, courts, community agencies and parents. Of the 120 cases included in her analysis, 75 per cent (n=89) were reported as confirmed cases of sexual abuse. McIntosh and Prinz (1993) reviewed the family court files opened over the course of a year in one South Carolina county to determine the extent of sexual abuse allegations in child custody disputes. They found that 85 of the 603 divorce cases they examined involved a custody and access dispute. Only three (3 per cent) of these disputed custody and access cases involved allegations of sexual abuse. However, they also found two cases of allegations of sexual abuse in uncontested cases. Unlike the study of Thoennes and Tjaden (1990), this latter study did not report on the prevalence of confirmed and unconfirmed cases.

Faller and DeVoe (1995) reviewed a sample of 215 cases, drawn from a university-based clinic over a period of 15 years, in which sexual abuse allegations were involved in a divorce matter. Based on the clinical judgment of the multidisciplinary team, they found that alleged abuse was substantiated in 73 per cent of the cases, 20 per cent were deemed unlikely, and 7 per cent were classified as uncertain. In contrast, in the same 215 cases, the court substantiated abuse in 35 per cent of the cases, did not substantiate them in 44 per cent of the cases, made no mention of the alleged abuse in 14 per cent of the cases, and was unclear in 7 per cent of the cases. Faller and DeVoe (1995) also examined the relationship of divorce to sexual abuse allegations. They found that: (1) in 14 per cent of the cases the abuse occurred prior to divorce; (2) in 25 per cent divorce preceded discovery of a pre-existing abuse; (3) in 27 per cent marital dissolution preceded the sexual abuse; (4) in 13 per cent the allegations were unrelated to parental separation; and (5) in 4 per cent children made false allegations.

While the social science research is becoming more sophisticated in differentiating sexual abuse allegations from other forms of maltreatment in post-separation cases, McGleughlin, Meyer and Baker (1999) caution that empirical research on the incidence of true and false allegations in post-separation cases has generally been characterized by small and biased samples. Additionally, they caution that in some studies there are significant flaws in the method of grouping cases. For example, unsubstantiated cases are often grouped together, regardless of whether they are based on a parent's honest belief or suspicion, which turns out to be unproven; a child's inability to provide clear disclosure; or a deliberately false or fictitious allegation. They argue that the lack of differentiation of cases inflates the prevalence of "false allegations". Moloney *et al.* (2007) aptly note that during the early 1990s, research in child sexual abuse was not as fully developed, and allegations determined unlikely were perceived as being false, thereby excluding possible false negatives.

Johnston, Lee, Olesen and Walters (2005) reported on 120 high-conflict custody and access cases for which assessments were ordered. They found that allegations of child maltreatment (i.e., neglect, physical, verbal, emotional, or sexual abuse) or spousal violence were made in 77 per cent of the cases. Allegations of sexual abuse were made against mothers in six per cent of the cases and against fathers in 23 per cent of the cases. Clinicians conducting the assessments concluded that against fathers, 26 per cent of the sexual abuse allegations were substantiated; 34 per cent of the child abuse or neglect allegations were substantiated; and 67 per cent of the spousal violence allegations were substantiated. Interestingly, the rates of substantiation of all types of allegations made by mothers against fathers (51 per cent) in this study were almost equal to the rates of allegations by fathers against mothers.

Studies in Canada

Bala and Schuman (1999) identified Canadian family law judgments that involved sexual and physical abuse allegations in the context of parental separation over a ten-year period. Of the 196 cases reviewed, in 46 (23 per cent of all cases) there was a judicial finding that on the balance of probabilities, abuse had indeed occurred. Additionally, the authors found 89 cases in which a judge made a finding that the allegations were unfounded, and 61 in which there was evidence of abuse, but not finding that abuse had occurred. The authors also found that of these 150 cases (n=45), abuse was not proven on a balance of probabilities, in 30 per cent of them where the allegations were in fact found by the judge to be intentionally false.

The Canadian Incidence Study of Reported Child Abuse and Neglect (CIS) (1998) was the first national study documenting rates of false allegations of abuse and neglect investigated by child welfare services in Canada. Data on child and family background, alleged perpetrator characteristics, severity and types of maltreatment, types of service, and outcomes of investigations were collected from child welfare workers at selected agencies over a three month period in 1998. Overall, sexual abuse allegations accounted for 11 per cent of the cases, physical abuse for 31 per cent, neglect for 40 per cent, and emotional maltreatment for 19 per cent of the investigations. Trocmé and Bala (2005) reported on data from the 1998 study and found that one-third of maltreatment investigations (involving all forms of abuse) were unsubstantiated and four per cent of the allegations were considered by the child welfare worker who investigated the case to be intentionally fabricated. Within the sub-sample of cases in which there was a custody and access dispute, the rate of intentionally reporting false allegations was higher (12 per cent)—three times the overall rate of false allegations. Trocmé and Bala (2005) also found that neglect was the most common form of intentionally fabricated maltreatment. Further, of these intentionally fabricated false allegations of maltreatment, children were least likely to fabricate reports of abuse or neglect, with parents the most common source of fabricated allegations of abuse in the context of separation cases.

Bala, Mitnick, Trocmé and Houston (2007) reported on a second wave of data analysis on false allegations of child abuse gathered from the 2003 CIS.[9] When sexual abuse was alleged as the primary form of maltreatment (n=655), 26 per cent of the allegations were substantiated, 15 per cent were suspected, and 54 per cent were considered unsubstantiated but made in good faith. They also found that about five per cent of all the sexual abuse allegations were considered by the investigating worker to be intentionally false, while the rate of intentionally false allegations of neglect against a parent, at seven per cent, was higher. If there was a custody and access dispute at the

[9] See Trocmé and Bala (2005) for a description of the data collected nationally, including the methodology of the CIS-98 data. See the Centre of Excellence for Child Welfare (CECW) website at: www.cecw-cepb.ca for a complete listing of all of the results of the data gathering regarding all forms of child maltreatment across Canada, except for Quebec.

time the report was made (n=1,136), they found, the rate of intentionally making false allegations was higher, sitting at 14 per cent of the sample. In the cases in which intentionally false allegations of child sexual abuse (n=28), were made, Bala *et al.* (2007b) found that custodial parents were more likely to make false allegations of sexual abuse than were non-custodial parents. Children (usually adolescents) made only four per cent of the intentionally false allegations of sexual abuse against a parent or guardian.

Bala, Mitnick, Trocmé and Houston (2007b) also found that of the allegations of sexual abuse made during an ongoing custody and access dispute (n=69), 44 per cent were reported by custodial parents, 10 per cent by non-custodial parents (usually fathers against a mother's new partner), and 29 per cent by professionals involved with the family. Further, the sexual abuse allegations made during parental separation were substantiated in 11 per cent of the cases, while 34 per cent were suspected, 36 per cent were unsubstantiated but made in good faith, and 18 per cent were considered intentionally false.

Summary of Studies

As stated by Kuehnle and Kirkpatrick (2005):

> It is difficult, if not impossible, to prove an indisputable negative (i.e., a particular child was never sexually abused). Because the custody evaluator does not have access to accurate base rates of true and false allegations of child sexual abuse occurring in the litigating child custody population, the forensic evaluator should assume an allegation of child sexual abuse is as likely to be true as not true (p. 10).

We can conclude the following:

(1) Contrary to popular opinion that sexual abuse allegations are often raised in child custody disputes, the studies reviewed indicate that only a relatively small portion of all litigated custody cases raise sexual abuse allegations;

(2) A significant proportion of the child sexual abuse allegations made in the context of parental separation are unfounded;

(3) While some of the unfounded allegations of child sexual abuse made in the context of parental separation are made maliciously or in an attempt by one parent to gain an advantage in a custody dispute, a majority of the unfounded allegations are made in good faith but reflect misunderstandings or miscommunication in an often highly charged emotional atmos-

phere. Some of the unfounded allegations reflect emotional disturbance or personality disorders;

(4) A relatively large number of referrals to child welfare agencies involve a post-separation allegation of some type of abuse (i.e., physical, sexual, or emotional abuse); each report requires a careful investigation;

(5) Mothers make more substantiated allegations of violence, child sexual abuse and substance abuse, against fathers than fathers make against mothers;

(6) Fathers tend to make more allegations of psychological problems and child neglect against mothers than any other type of allegation; and

(7) Developing, implementing and monitoring a systematic review of data across large and representative samples using the same definitions is essential if there is to be an improvement in understanding these complex cases and providing appropriate interventions when sexual abuse allegations are raised in the context of a custody and access dispute.

Clinical and Legal Considerations for Child Custody Assessors

As Kuehnle and Kirkpatrick (2005) observe, the primary responsibility for confirmation or disconfirmation of sexual abuse rests with child welfare agencies and the courts, but in cases where these allegations are made, the assessor should also make recommendations that focus on the needs and safety of the child. This requires a risk/benefit analysis of whether or not contact is warranted between a child and a parent who has sexually abused that child. Therefore, parenting plan recommendations need to consider the nature of the abuse and the extent to which the perpetrator has in fact acknowledged that the sexual abuse took place and what, if any, treatment should be provided to the offender and to the child. Further, it is critical to evaluate the extent to which the offender has meaningfully engaged in any treatment provided and utilized it towards successful rehabilitation (Jaffe, Crooks & Bala, 2005).

There are Canadian judgments which have accepted that, in principle, the courts should attempt to resolve the validity of an allegation of sexual abuse as quickly as possible; otherwise, the relationship between parent and child will be negatively impacted.[10] In practice,

[10] See *Stuart v. Stuart*, 1985 CarswellOnt 1863 (Ont. S.C.); *Thomas v. Thomas*, 1986 CarswellNfld 139, 60 Nfld. & P.E.I.R. 271, 181 A.P.R. 271 (Nfld. U.F.C.).

however, it may take many months and sometimes years for these cases to be resolved in the family courts. Generally, when such an allegation is ruled to be unfounded, the courts believe that a parent's access should be restored, notwithstanding the fact that the parent-child relationship may have been damaged during the investigation.[11] There are, however, some cases in which the courts have held that despite the allegation being unfounded, it is in the child's best interests to supervise or even suspend contact as a result of the child's staunch yet false belief that the parent had actually abused them. In such cases, it is possible that continued contact would be emotionally harmful to the child.[12] Further, there are cases where access should be granted even though allegations of sexual abuse have been substantiated, as it is in the best interests of the child to have contact with the abusive parent, and there is no risk of any reoccurrence of abuse.[13]

More often than not, recommendations are made in these cases with no provision for monitoring or ongoing evaluation as to how the needs of the child are being met—or not—by each of his or her parents. Johnston (2006) strongly recommends that when domestic violence has been substantiated, case coordination is necessary between the justice system and any other programs in which the offender is involved. This type of co-ordinated case management is equally necessary when sexual abuse has occurred. In cases involving substantiated child sexual abuse allegations, if continuing contact is to be recommended, the assessor should also provide recommendations for a co-ordinated plan implemented under judicial control that will typically include therapy for the child, treatment for the offender and supervision of their contact.

Impact of Unfounded Sexual Abuse Allegations on Children

The negative impact of sexual abuse on children, while different for different children based on age, gender and stage of emotional and cognitive development, is well documented in the literature (Briere & Elliot, 1994; Conte & Berliner, 1988; Duncan, 2004; Finklehor &

[11] See *S. (G.M.) v. S. (D.B.),* 1999 CarswellNfld 286, 181 Nfld. & P.E.I.R. 304, 550 A.P.R. 304 (Nfld. U.F.C.).

[12] See *S. (P.A.) v. S. (L.A.)*, 1987 CarswellMan 261, 47 Man. R. (2d) 161 (Man. Q.B.); *Willis v. Willis*, (October 14, 1987), Houghton J. (B.C.S.C.); *M. (N.L.) v. M. (R.B.)*, 1986 CarswellBC 892 (B.C.S.C.); subsequent proceedings (October 28, 1987), Lamperson J. (B.C.S.C.).

[13] See *K. (J.D.) v. K. (S.A.)*, 1989 CarswellBC 403, 20 R.F.L. (3d) 372 (B.C.S.C.); *R. v. R.* (April 9, 1991), Doc. No. A892673 (B.C.S.C.).

Browne, 1988; Nash, Hulsey, Sexton, Harralson & Lambert, 1993; Paolucci, Genuis & Vilato, 2001; Putnam, 2003). The negative impact of living in an environment where false allegations of abuse are repeated and remain unfounded have also been documented in the literature, though much less extensively (Bala *et al.*, 2007; Gardner, 1992a, 1992b). As Hickman and Reynolds (1994) and Kuehnle (2003) aptly note, although we do not have empirical data to document the negative effects on children when sexual abuse allegations are unfounded, we can extrapolate the effects from children who are tramautized by divorce (McGeughlin, Meyer & Baker, 1999). Gardner (1992a) explored the traumatic effects of sexual abuse evaluation (assessments) for both abused and non-abused children. He concluded that repeated investigations by child welfare authorities, police, therapists, assessors, and parents can cause significant psychological trauma for both groups of children. Repeated investigations of sexual abuse, which can occur in false allegation cases, erode the relationship of the child and accused parent, and can lead to post-traumatic stress disorder and attachment problems in the parent-child relationship. Further, if there are repeated unfounded allegations, the accusing parent will generally be paranoid, delusional or suffering from a personality disorder that severely limits their insights; leaving a child in the care of such a parent can have serious deleterious consequences for children.

As we discuss in the chapters on domestic violence and alienation, a child being deprived of a relationship with a parent who has been falsely accused only further victimizes a child.[14] It is important for an assessor to understand the implications of the allegations both for a child who has been sexually abused, as well as for a child who has not. It is equally important for an assessor to understand the legal and psychological consequences that can happen not just to the child being deprived of a parent-child relationship, but also for a healthy falsely-accused parent who has to respond to these allegations as a result of the other parent's unhealthy personality.

In Chapters 6 and 7, we discuss at length the severe trauma that occurs to these children who had been deprived of a parent-child relationship when false accusations or alienation arise during child custody disputes (Johnston & Roseby, 1997; Rand, 1993).

---

14 See Hickman and Reynolds (1994), "Effects of False Allegations of Sexual Abuse on Children and Families" in Threatt, B. (Ed.) (1994). Evaluating children's allegations of sexual assault. Austin, TX; also see, Gardner, R. (1992, 1994).

Options For Parenting Plan Recommendations

Any conclusions or opinions regarding the veracity of the sexual abuse allegations and the basis for these, including the degree of certainty, should be clearly stated in the assessor's report. The report, then, will include a discussion of the obtained information from other sources and the results of the assessment process (i.e., from interviews, observations, psychological testing, personal and professional third-party reports, etc.) that are consistent *and* inconsistent with both a true *and* false allegation.

When Child Sexual Abuse Has Been Substantiated

If sexual abuse has been substantiated, for example by child protection investigators, it is very likely that sole custody will be recommended to the non-abusing parent. With respect to parenting time, there are several options available to the assessor and, ultimately, to the court. These include, but are not limited to:

(a) no contact between the child and the offender;

(b) supervised access[15] in combination with treatment as appropriate for the family members in various combinations, jointly and individually;

(c) therapeutic supervised access[16] with a therapist who works with the child, the offender, and the custodial parent together to restore the relationship between the child and the abusive parent; or

(d) unsupervised access is rarely appropriate, but may be considered for some cases, taking into account the time since the incident, the child's adjustment and relationship with the abusive parent, the abusive parent's attendance and engage-

---

15 In Ontario, there are 74 supervised access site locations across the province operated by community-based, non-profit charitable organizations who have transfer payment agreements with the Supervised Access Program, Family Justice Services Division (MAG). Each centre has its own board of directors and is independent of the others. Each centre has a local manager who is paid and reports to the board of directors. The majority of staff members who supervise access visits between children and their non-custodial parents are usually volunteers who are not required to have any specific professional qualifications. In 2007, the Ministry provided best practice guidelines on domestic violence and child maltreatment; however, there is no uniform practice across the province regarding children and supervised access.

16 A form of supervision by a mental health therapist (i.e., social worker, psychologist, or psychiatrist) with the goal of treating *the child and the offender*, which requires a highly skilled clinician.

ment with treatment, the absence of risk to the child, and court monitoring.

The recommendations will be affected by such factors as the age of the child, the nature of the abuse, the child's response to the abuse and the abuser's willingness to accept responsibility and participate meaningfully in treatment. When making recommendations in cases of substantiated allegations, assessors must be knowledgeable of the resources in their community and the practicality of the recommendations. For example, while supervised access may seem a viable option to keep a child safe, the child can still experience emotional abuse under such circumstances, because supervised access is limited to observation of parent and child. There is little, if any, therapeutic intervention; the role of the supervisor is to monitor and provide notes if requested (Stern & Oehme, 2002). In the final analysis, the child's safety (physical and emotional) must be paramount in any recommendation to the court.

Kuehnle and Kirkpatrick (2005) suggest that parent only treatment and parent/child treatment, when combined, have been shown to be the most effective strategies in decreasing a child's internalized behaviours that may be the result of the abuse (i.e., anxiety, distress, physical upset). They also suggest that psycho-educational interventions are effective when a sexually abused child exhibits fewer internalized and externalized problems.

When Child Sexual Abuse Has Not Been Substantiated

These cases are often very challenging for the mental health clinician. As discussed above, situations involving unsubstantiated allegations are varied. It is important for the assessor's report to provide an explanation for how these false allegations may have came about.

In some cases, taking all of the information obtained into account, the assessor may conclude that the alleged abuse did not occur (or is unlikely to have occurred), but the making of the allegation was the result of an honest mistake due to misinterpretations or over-interpretations of the child's or other parent's behaviour. In other cases, the assessor may conclude that the abuse is not only unsubstantiated, but also that the allegations were knowingly fabricated to seek revenge or gain tactical advantage, and more generally part of an alienation process. In yet other situations, the assessor may conclude that the abuse is unsubstantiated but genuinely believed by the accusing parent as a result of that parent's paranoia, mental illness or distorted perceptions, which may or may not be part of an alienation process. We discuss alienation more fully in Chapters 6 and 7.

Each of these different scenarios of unsubstantiated allegations warrants a different set of recommendations. While the lack of substantiation of the allegations does not necessarily mean the abuse did not occur, this needs to be balanced with the child's need to have a meaningful relationship with both parents, unless of course there is a good reason and some evidence that this should not occur.

Regardless of the allegations being substantiated or unsubstantiated, the child's emotional and physical safety must remain a priority given the long-term effects previously outlined. Therefore, if the allegations are regarded as unfounded, the parenting plan recommendations must still take into account the extent to which the child believes the abuse occurred, the custodial parent's willingness and ability to support the child's relationship with the other parent, and the accused parent's sensitivity to the child's predicament.

The recommendations in unsubstantiated allegation cases are likely to include several gradual steps, beginning with a therapeutic reintegration process. Therapeutic reintegration occurs when a therapist meets with both parents and child to restore the child's relationship with the accused parent and address issues evident in the child's relationship with the accusing parent, such as lack of adequate boundaries, dependency and parents' fixed behaviour. While therapeutic reintegration is similar to therapeutic supervised access (one option in substantiated cases), in unsubstantial cases supervision *per se* is not the objective, and the recommendation should not be referred to as "supervised" and should not occur in a supervised access center. Doing so will only reinforce the child's fear and that the visiting parent is "bad" or dangerous. Also, if the child refuses contact with the parent, the access center is unlikely to force or even strongly encourage the child to see that parent.

If a child has been estranged from one parent as a result of a false allegation, the assessor may need to develop a parenting plan that involves gradual reunification of the child with the parent. This reunification typically involves therapy with the entire family in various combinations. In many cases, unsupervised access will be appropriate, although if the child is afraid of the parent, it may be necessary to work towards this in a gradual way. Recommendations should be based on a gradually increasing parenting time schedule that is court-ordered to allow for a review and re-evaluation of the effects on the parent-child relationship. In the final analysis, whether the allegations are substantiated or unsubstantiated, the recommendations must be based on a child-focused approach in order to address the fears and anxieties of the child, and the capacities of each parent.

In addition, and most importantly, the reintegration therapy needs to be accompanied by the court's ongoing monitoring to ensure adequate implementation of the intervention given that malicious accusing parents often sabotage the attempts to reintegrate their children with the falsely accused parent. Further, the court's involvement will be important to subsequent decisions regarding any next steps, including the implementation of parenting time apart from the therapeutic access.

Options for custody will include sole custody or joint custody to the falsely accused parent, in an effort to preserve that parent's relationship and involvement with the child and counteract any compromised parenting and poor judgment evident in the accusing parent. This will also send a strong and important message to the accusing parent.

If the assessor is unable to provide an opinion as to the veracity of the allegations, the report should state this and indicate why. In this scenario, the parenting plan recommendations will need to carefully balance concerns about maintaining the safety of the child, repairing and sustaining the child's relationship with the accused parent, and protecting the child from the ill-effects of compromised parenting by a delusional parent, who may be suffering from a mental illness.

Later in this chapter, we discuss the court's approach to the different scenarios and parenting plan options, and its management of the uncertainty present in cases involving unsubstantiated allegations. In Chapter 7, we elaborate more fully on various options or remedies for the assessor and the court in alienation cases, some of which also involve unsubstantiated allegations of child abuse.

The Role of Assessors and Admissibility of Expert Testimony

In most family law cases where allegations of abuse are made, there are likely to be a number of professionals involved, such as custody assessors, therapists, other mental health professionals, police, and child welfare investigators. All of these professionals play an important role in the resolution of family law cases where abuse allegations are made.

One of the difficulties in this area is that some of the assessors, investigators and other "experts" who are involved in these cases lack the objectivity, experience, skills and knowledge to deal effectively with this particular type of child abuse case (Behnke & Connell, 2005).[17] Many of the behavioral patterns that may be consistent with

---

[17] Assessors who provide parenting recommendations in cases involving alleged child sexual abuse should review the assessment protocols and work of Bernet (2006);

a child having been sexually abused by a parent may also be consistent with a child suffering from the effects of a high conflict parental separation. There is research which suggests that mental health professionals have considerable difficulty in reliably assessing whether young children have been sexually abused based solely on observing an interview of a child's "disclosure" (Herman, 2005).

In practice, once the investigators and other experts have assessed the validity of an allegation, many cases are resolved without a family law trial. An accusing parent, who is not emotionally disturbed or suffering from a personality disorder, is unlikely to pursue a matter to trial if all of the "expert" evidence supports the position of the other party. In cases where the initial allegation is a result of an honest mistake, the accusing parent may be relieved that investigators or assessors have all agreed that the allegation is unfounded and the child has not been harmed; such cases are less likely to be pursued in court.

Cases are most likely to proceed for a family law trial if there are competing opinions among the various mental health professionals and investigators, if one parent seems especially hostile, or if a parent is emotionally unbalanced and is disregarding the expert opinions. There is an understandable judicial preference for the opinions of professionals who are state employees, like child protection workers, or assessors appointed by the court; these professionals are perceived to be "independent" of the parties. While a therapist or mental health professional retained by one party may provide valuable testimony, there is a concern that such an expert may be biased to the extent that he or she lacks access to all of the parties and consequently can

---

Bow, Quinnell, Zaroff and Assemany (2002); Gardner (1995); Kuehnle and Kirkpatrick (2005); Kirkpatrick (cited in Gould (2006), *Conducting scientifically crafted child custody evaluations (second edition),* (pages 206-209); and Ney (1995). As Kuehnle and Kirkpatrick (2005) note, while there are many useful testing instruments to assist the mental health professional in the work of child custody and access assessments, there is no standardized instrument that reliably distinguishes a sexually abused child from a non-sexually abused child. For useful resources on interviewing protocols with children and adults, see Hewitt (1999); Kuehnle (1996); Ney (1995); and Poole and Lamb (1998). In addition, for a review of some inventories and measures used with parents and children in assessing trauma, see Straus (CTS: 1979); Straus, Hamby and Warren (CTS2: 2003); Danger Assessment Scale (DAS: Campbell, 1995); The Index of Psychological Abuse (Sullivan, Parisian & Davidson, 1991); Trauma Symptom Inventory (TSI: Briere, 1995) for adults; Trauma Symptom Checklist for Children (TSCC: Briere, 1996); and Friedrich (1997, 2002). Any inventory, interviewing protocol or psychological test relied on in making child custody recommendations should include the strengths and limitations of these tests and inventories. Also see Birnbaum, Fidler and Kavassalis (2008) and Gould and Martindale (2007) for additional tests and measures that discuss further the strengths and limitations of projective testing in child custody and access assessments.

only provide an incomplete assessment. As well, there may be a concern that the expert was selected because of known predispositions (Behnke & Connell, 2005).

Cases most likely to be litigated are ones where there are divergent expert opinions about whether abuse occurred and the judge must decide which expert opinion to follow. In some cases it may be relatively easy for one party to demonstrate that the opinion of one "expert" should be discounted. For example, an opinion may be of little value if the investigator or assessor lacks expertise concerning the special issues that arise with child sexual abuse allegations in the context of parental separation. In some cases an officially "independent" investigator, such as a child protection worker, may become "allied" with one parent (often the accusing parent who is usually the first parent to contact the investigator). A biased investigator may, for example, behave in an unfair or unprofessional manner with the other parent (often the accused parent). In this situation, the evidence of an investigator is likely to be discounted.

In some cases, a parent retains an expert to review and comment on a previous court ordered assessment or child protection investigation in order to persuade the court to reject the opinions and recommendations.[18] Litigation involving allegations of abuse is often very expensive and many parents lack the resources to retain experts. If court appointed assessors or government paid investigators lack skill, or are biased, this may be seriously and perhaps irreversibly prejudicial to the parent and child whose case has been improperly assessed. The solution to this problem, however, is not to exclude expert evidence when it is available, but rather to allow such evidence to be challenged by cross-examination or by adducing other evidence, and then allowing the judge to make the best possible decision in light of the evidence presented.

In some cases, a therapist, counsellor or other professional, such as a shelter worker,[19] has a critical role in the case of a false allegation

---

[18] *T. (M.) v. T. (J.)*, 1993 CarswellOnt 3941, [1993] O.J. No. 3379 (Ont. Prov. Div.), *per* Hatton Prov. J.

[19] See Donna Laframboise, "One-stop divorce shops", *National Post*, Nov. 21, 1998. Ms Louise Malenfant, of the Parents Helping Parents advocacy group, reported that over a four year period she had been an advocate for 62 individuals in Manitoba who had been falsely accused of child sexual abuse in divorce proceedings. In one third of those cases women's shelters were involved. Ms. Malenfant claimed that shelter workers gave children sessions "educating" them about sexual abuse. The workers then followed this up with suggestive questioning that resulted in false allegations. As a result of the efforts of this advocacy group and litigation by wrongly accused parents, Manitoba changed the way that it deals with child protection cases involving allegations of abuse.

of child abuse. A professional may, for example, lead a parent to misinterpret statements or behaviour of the child. In some of these cases there is professionally inappropriate behaviour and obvious bias, while in other cases the problems arise because professionals are acting outside the scope of their area of expertise. The problematic role of a parent's therapist may be an example of concerning behaviour if that professional comes to court and testifies about the child's condition. Less obvious, but also problematic, are cases in which a therapist may be inappropriately encouraging a parent to make an unfounded allegation.[20]

In *K. (M.) v. M. (P.)*[21] the mother alleged that the father had sexually abused their six year old daughter. Child protection, police and experienced medical investigators all concluded that the allegations were unfounded, that the child's "disclosures were a result of the mother's manipulation and suggestions to the child". However, two mental health professionals testified to support the mother's allegations. Both had been involved in a therapeutic relationship with the mother. One had been the mother's therapist for over two years. Neither therapist had interviewed the child or the father. They nevertheless came to court to critique the work of the independent assessors and investigators, and to express their "professional opinion" that the mother did not "consciously or unconsciously" suggest anything to the child. In rejecting their evidence, Madame Justice Janet Wilson commented:

> Therapeutic counselling and providing objective expert opinion are two very different professional functions. . . therapeutic contact [with a parent] may make it very difficult for an expert to provide a neutral balanced assessment of a situation. Unless the expert evidence relates to the course of counselling itself, it . . . may not be very useful. (para. 127)

---

20 See Birnbaum, Fidler and Kavassalis (2008) in Chapter Five where the authors discuss dual roles and ethical practice dilemmas for clinicians and how to avoid them.

21 1996 CarswellOnt 3353, [1996] O.J. No. 3212 (Ont. Gen. Div.). See also *C. (B.A.) v. C. (D.L.)*, 48 R.F.L. (5th) 15, 2003 BCCA 672, 2003 CarswellBC 3143 (B.C. C.A.), where the Court was satisfied "beyond a reasonable doubt" that the sexual abuse allegations were unfounded, rejecting the opinion of a general practitioner to whom the children were taken, finding that that the doctor had "become an 'advocate' for the mother's views".

How Courts Evaluate the Evidence and Decide on How to Manage Child Sexual Abuse Allegations

Factors Considered by the Court

Justice Robertson of the Ontario Superior Court, in the 1998 case of *G. (J.A.) v. R. (R.J.)*,[22] outlined a summary of the factors for assessing allegations of sexual abuse in custody and access matters before the Court. She stated:

> While there is no formula to determine probability, the process must be more than intuitive. In evaluating the evidence and determining best interest, the court must filter the circumstances, facts, and expert opinion and assess the credibility of witnesses before reaching a conclusion. In weighing the evidence, I considered the following:
>
> 1) What were the circumstances of disclosure—to whom and where?
> 2) Did the disclosure or evidence of alleged abuse come from any disinterested witnesses?
> 3) Were the statements made by the child spontaneous?
> 4) Did the questions asked of the child suggest an answer?
> 5) Did the child's statement provide context such as a time frame or positioning of the parties?
> 6) Was there progression in the story about events?
> 7) How did the child behave before and after disclosure?
> 8) Is there physical evidence that would be available by medical examination? If so, and no medical report has been filed, is there a sufficient explanation for its lack?
> 9) Was there opportunity?
> 10) What investigative or court action was taken by the parent alleging abuse?
> 11) Who provided background information to the experts and investigators, and is it accurate, complete and consistent with both parties' recollections?
> 12) Was there other evidence supporting the allegations of sexual abuse?
> 13) Was the custodial parent cooperative regarding access, or was access resisted on other grounds prior to the allegations and after disclosure?

---

22 1998 CarswellOnt 1487, [1998] O.J. No. 1415 (Ont. Gen. Div.).

14) Was there harmony between the evidence of one witness and another, and between the evidence of the experts?

15) Was there consistency over time of the child's disclosure?

16) Did the child use wording in statements which appeared to be prompted, rehearsed or memorized?

17) Was the language used by the child consistent and commensurate with the child's language skills?

18) Was the information given by the child beyond age-appropriate knowledge?

19) What was the comfort level of the child to deal with the subject matter, in particular with respect to the offering of detail?

20) Did the child exhibit sexualized behaviour?

21) Was there evidence of pre-existing inappropriate sexual behaviour by the alleged perpetrator?

22) Was a treatment plan put forth by either parent?

23) Was the child coached or prompted?

24) Did the evidence of the expert witnesses, as accepted by a trial judge, support the allegations of sexual abuse?[23]

Family law disputes involving allegations of sexual abuse are among the most challenging for lawyers and the judiciary. Each case is decided on its own merits with the evidence being weighed by the presiding judge using the civil standard—that is, on a balance of probabilities. This must be contrasted with the burden of proof in criminal cases, in which the Crown must prove its case beyond a reasonable doubt. If there is a conviction in criminal court, this will generally be admissible and establish that the abuse occurred for both criminal and family proceedings. If there has not been a conviction in criminal court, the burden of proof in family court in a custody case involving child sexual abuse lies instead on the party making the allegations, who has the onus of proving the charges on a balance of probabilities. Of course, the best interests of the child are paramount, irrespective of the nature of the allegations.

The court deciding issues of custody and access between parents may not be the first judicial venue that parties encounter in cases where sexual abuse has been substantiated. For many families, it may be one of many courts, in different proceedings, that will deal with the allegations.

---

[23] *Ibid.*, at para. 17.

Parental conduct is only a relevant consideration in determining issues of custody or access to a child if it relates to a person's ability to act as a parent. Many of the provincial statutes that deal with issues of custody and access contain provisions that specifically recognize, amongst other things, that abuse or violence committed by one or both parties to a child is of particular importance in determining a person's suitability to parent the child who is the subject of a family law proceeding.

Once an allegation of sexual abuse has been proven on a balance of probabilities, the court is likely to do one of two things: deny the offending parent any access to the child; or grant supervised access only. There have been instances, however, when unsupervised access was granted even though the allegations of sexual abuse were confirmed.[24]

There are relatively few reported decisions that involve substantiated allegations of child sexual abuse made by one parent against the other in the context of a custody and access dispute. One reason for this is that many of the cases in which the allegations are substantiated settle before trial. Additionally, in cases of substantiated sexual abuse, child protection agencies may be involved, and the litigation becomes child welfare litigation rather than a custody and access dispute.

When Sexual Abuse Allegations are Substantiated in Court

Access Denied

In *W. (T.L.D.) v. W. (B.J.)*,[25] the mother had two children from her former marriage in her care when the parties started living together; the couple then had one child of their own. The father pled guilty to criminal charges for the sexual assault of the eldest daughter. He sought interim access to the youngest daughter, whom he had not seen for over a year. The Court found that the three children were closely bonded to each other and that access to the youngest child would upset the older children, particularly the one who had been abused. The Court found that this would promote strife in the family and that such disruption would not be in the youngest child's interests. Accordingly, access was denied to all of the children.

In *M. (Z.) v. M. (S.)*,[26] access difficulties began because of the father's emotionally abusive conduct. He harboured deep anger and

---

[24] See *L. (D.L.) v. L. (E.M.)*, 1994 CarswellOnt 2154 (Ont. Gen. Div.).

[25] 2001 CarswellBC 2366, 2001 BCSC 1500 (B.C. Master).

[26] 1997 CarswellOnt 807, [1997] O.J. No. 1423 (Ont. Gen. Div.).

resentment towards the mother, and on numerous occasions would denigrate her and call her names in the child's presence. The child's daycare teachers noticed that the child had changed from a happy, confident, outgoing child to a sad, clingy and unhappy child. Furthermore, the child made consistent statements disclosing sexual abuse by her father to her mother, teachers, the Children's Aid Society (CAS), a police officer, and an expert in child abuse investigations and assessments. As a result, access was suspended and there was no further contact for almost two years. The father commenced a petition for divorce, which included a claim of relief for custody or joint custody of the child. The Court denied access. The mother, on a balance of probabilities, had established the allegation that the father had sexually assaulted the child. In addition, it was felt that the father's utter contempt for the mother would be carried through to the child if access was permitted, and the child would therefore continue to be in turmoil. On that ground alone, access could have been denied.

In the Nova Scotia case of *Neill v. Best*,[27] the Court adopted the best interests test in denying a father access to his child. In this case, the child was conceived during a brief relationship between the parties, and the mother had left Ontario for Nova Scotia before the child was born. The father applied for custody and the mother sought an order denying him contact. He had been convicted of sexually assaulting the daughter of his girlfriend over a period of a few years, and lacked remorse about the effects of the assaults upon the child involved. In determining that access should be denied, the Court considered that in his testimony the father had not presented any concrete ways in which he could benefit his child's life. In addition, the mother had proven, on the balance of probabilities that the child's welfare was best served by denying access. The Court was not prepared to "experiment" with the uncertainty of the potential risk to the child through access.

In the Ontario case of *Shouldice v. Dorsey*,[28] a father had been convicted of the sexual assault of two girls under the age of 14 and indecent assault of a 13-year-old girl. He sought access to his five-year-old son, whom he had not seen in over two years. The boy's mother no longer had any contact with the father, and the son's last contact with him had been a phone call nine months before the hearing. The father was not pursuing counselling and had unresolved problems with alcohol addiction. The Court held that the father had failed to show that granting access would benefit the child. The boy

27 1995 CarswellNS 163, 18 R.F.L. (4th) 440 (N.S. Fam. Ct.).

28 2003 CarswellOnt 5356, [2003] O.J. No. 5416 (Ont. S.C.J.).

was enjoying a stable home life and it would not be in his best interests to disturb that by granting the father access.

In Nova Scotia case of *H. (E.A.) v. G. (T.D.)*,[29] the mother appealed the dismissal of her application to terminate the father's access. The child consistently told her mother, doctors, and social workers about incidents of inappropriate sexual contact by the father during access visits. The father admitted that the child was spanked on every access visit. Medical evidence supported the child's report that the father had inserted something up the child's anus on more than one occasion. A child abuse specialist who assessed the child recommended that the father's access be terminated. However, at trial, the child testified that the father had never abused her sexually and that her previous allegations were only dreams. The Nova Scotia Court of Appeal subsequently found that the trial judge had erred in concluding that the spanking, which included injury to the child's anus, did not constitute a violation of the child's sexual integrity. Furthermore, it ruled that the trial judge had erred in disregarding material evidence without reason. Amongst other oversights, he did not take into account the strong recommendations against access made by the child abuse specialist. He also limited his focus to physical and sexual abuse, and failed to take into account the emotional effect of the father's actions on the child and the father's blatant disregard for the child's best interests in administering such abusive discipline. Access to the father was terminated.

Supervised Access

In the Alberta case of *K. (R.M.) v. H. (L.W.)*,[30] a father sought supervised access to his daughter. For a period of two and a half years before the hearing, the father had seen his daughter on a regular basis. His visits were terminated after it was discovered that he may have been sexually abusing the daughter, who was aged three at the time. The father suffered from chronic depression; he testified that he did not recall touching the child inappropriately, but did not dispute her disclosures. He was receiving counselling and attending Alcoholic Anonymous. A therapist with expertise in counselling sexual abuse victims testified that the child was coping well and that although she missed her father, she was afraid to see him. In the Court's view, it was in the child's best interests to have an opportunity to reconcile with her father and to have the potential for a healthy relationship with him. Accordingly, the Court ordered highly struc-

---

29 1995 CarswellNS 264, 18 R.F.L. (4th) 21 (N.S.C.A.).

30 2000 CarswellAlta 1086, 2000 ABPC 152 (Alta.Prov.Ct).

tured, supervised access to be introduced gradually, starting with a joint therapy session after which the therapist would provide an opinion as to whether or not it would benefit the child to continue the attempt at reconciliation.

In the Ontario case of *E. (D.) v. L. (O.)*,[31] a father had initially sought access to his son, aged 6, and two step-daughters, aged 12 and 14 years. The man had previously been charged with and acquitted of the indecent assault of another stepdaughter more than 10 years previously. One stepdaughter had testified at the previous criminal trial that the man had sexually abused her once or twice a week when she was between the ages of five to twelve. Although he was acquitted of the specific charges, the criminal court judge had found beyond a reasonable doubt that the man had sexually assaulted one of the the girls, though not in the manner alleged in the criminal charges, and further that the father's wrestling with the girl and putting his tongue in her ears showed an utter lack of respect for the child. Based on a social worker's report and the reasons for judgment in the prior criminal trial involving the father, the mother brought a motion to change access to restricted supervised only. The social worker's report dealing with the two stepchildren in the case at hand raised further concerns. The report also indicated that a doctor had found teeth marks on the penis of the father's six-month-old biological son. As well, one of the stepdaughters insisted that for years, on a regular basis and for no apparent reason, the father had spanked her on her bare buttocks when she came home from school. The Court granted the mother's motion, and the father was not allowed any unsupervised contact with any of the children.

In *H. (D.A.) v. M. (T.A.) (sub.nom. Heinecke v. Martin)*,[32] the Court ordered access, albeit supervised, despite evidence that the father had sexually abused the children while they had been in his custody and that he had an alcohol problem. The Court concluded that he was actually more skilled as a parent than the mother. The children also expressed a desire to visit with their father. Accordingly, the father was granted access, to be supervised by the Children's Aid Society.

When Sexual Abuse Allegations are not Substantiated in Court

In *M. (L.J.) v. M. (K.A.)*,[33] the appellate court upheld a trial judge's decision reinstating a father's access to his daughter, concluding that

[31] 1996 CarswellOnt 3408, [1996] O.J. No. 3136 (Ont. Prov. Div.), *per* Renaud Prov. J.
[32] (December 6, 1985), Doc. 13866/84 (Ont. Dist. Ct.).
[33] 2002 CarswellNS 36, 2002 NSCA 19, 201 N.S.R. (2d) 55, 629 A.P.R. 55 (N.S.C.A.)

there had been no improper sexual conduct by the father. The father had been denied access for over three and a half years because the mother alleged that he had sexually abused the daughter. Although many assessments had been conducted, the Court concluded that they were flawed because the assessors had prepared them with an assumption that the father had committed the abuse. There had not been any investigation to rule out other possible sources of the child's sexual knowledge, and the Court was not satisfied that the father had sexually abused his daughter. Given the father's lengthy absence from the child's life, the Court ordered that access be gradually introduced under the supervision of an appropriate therapist.

In *L. (S.A.) v. L. (P.J.)*,[34] there was a concern because of the father's "proclivities" to "sexually exploit" adult women. An assessment was ordered pursuant to s.30 of the *Children's Law Reform Act*. The assessors were to focus upon the nature and appropriateness of contact between a father and his son. The recommendation of the assessors was that the father's access has to be exercised in the presence of the mother's parents or some other close relative, with no overnight access. Their report shared the concern of the mother that there was a high risk that the child might be used as a "prop" for the father's sexually exploitative conduct towards adult women. In contrast, a doctor's report indicated that the father's sexual behaviour posed no threat to children. The Court concluded that joint custody was a practical impossibility in the circumstances of the case; the children were thriving in their mother's care and that it was not in their best interests for her to feel insecure in her position. However, with respect to access, the assessment report did not offer any compelling reason as to why it should be supervised. The Court concluded that it was not appropriate that supervised access "be used as a means to punish" the father "for anti-social behaviour or to coerce him into therapy" as there was no demonstrated risk to the children. The Court concluded that the mother should be awarded custody of both children and the father was granted alternate weekend access with no restrictions.

In *R. (L.) v. S. (M.)*,[35] the mother claimed that the father had sexually molested their daughter when she was one month old and touched her sexually when she was four years old. The Court, finding that the father had not sexually molested or touched the daughter, further noted that he had not missed any of his more than 90 supervised access visits which occurred while the case was under investi-

---

aff'g. 2001 CarswellNS 122, 2001 NSSF 16, 193 N.S.R. (2d) 66, 602 A.P.R. 66, [2001] N.S.J. No. 118 (N.S.S.C.).

34 1996 CarswellOnt 3442 (Ont. Gen. Div.).

35 1996 CarswellBC 1649 (B.C.S.C.).

gation and that he had a good relationship with the child. Access was expanded to one continuous, unsupervised, eight-hour period each week.

The Manitoba Court of Queen's Bench dealt with allegations of sexual abuse in *M. (H.D.) v. M. (E.H.)*.[36] The mother suspected sexual abuse by the father, and the previously ordered supervised access was suspended pending an investigation. The father passed a polygraph test and the supervised access resumed. The mother again made sexual abuse allegations against him. The father passed another polygraph test and the child welfare agency recommended resumption of supervised access. The mother unsuccessfully applied to terminate the father's access. The father's application for unsupervised access was allowed, as the allegations against him were unsubstantiated and the children were found not to be in need of protection from him. The Court determined that unsupervised visits would be in the childrens' best interests.

Making an Unfounded Allegation—Effect on Family Law Decisions

Some lawyers and advocates for women worry that the courts may "punish" accusers if an allegation of abuse is made which the judge does not accept.[37] Of particular concern is that a custodial mother may lose custody if she makes an allegation of abuse in good faith against an access father which is not proven in court. There are some reported cases where judges have suggested that a custodial parent who makes an unfounded allegation is by that very act harming the child and should therefore lose custody. For example, in one Ontario case the judge commented:

> It is also my opinion that if the allegations of abuse are determined to have been unfounded, then the raising of these allegations by the accuser parent are in themselves the ultimate abuse by that parent against the child, for it spoils or at least shadows, the future relationship that child has with the now proven innocent parent.[38]

There is an understandable concern that this type of judicial response may discourage parents from bringing forward valid concerns of abuse for fear that they might not be able to prove them, and that parents who make true allegations which are not proven in court

---

36 1995 CarswellMan 62, 99 Man. R. (2d) 239 (Man. Q.B.).

37 See Law Society of British Columbia Gender Bias Committee (1992), Vol. II: 5-49; and Neustein and Leshner (2005).

38 *Flannigan v. Murphy*, 1985 CarswellOnt 1923 (Ont. S.C.), *per* Cork M.

may be unfairly punished for bringing these allegations to the attention of the authorities. While these are legitimate concerns, it would appear that most judges take a sensitive and contextual approach to cases where there are abuse allegations that are not proven. Where an allegation of abuse is rejected by a judge, the most common response is to then proceed to a "best interests" assessment. That assessment considers the accuser's motive in making the allegation, the reaction of the children to the allegation, and whether the accuser can maintain a positive relationship with the child and the other parent.

In the majority of reported cases where a judge finds an abuse allegation by a custodial parent to be unfounded, the accusing parent continues to have custody.[39] Although in some of these cases the judge warns the accuser that if she persists in making unfounded allegations of abuse, custody might be varied. Indeed, even in a case like the Manitoba decision in *Plesh v. Plesh* where the trial judge concluded that the mother's motive in making a false allegation of child sexual abuse against the father was "revenge, pure and simple", and that the child was the "real loser", the Court did not vary custody but simply restored the father's access which had been suspended during the investigation.[40]

Those cases in which a judge is likely to reverse custody (or terminate access if the allegation was made by an access parent) are ones where the accuser appears to be suffering from an emotional disturbance or personality disorder that contributes to the making of the allegation, or appears to be so hostile towards the wrongfully accused parent that the children would suffer if the accusing parent continued to have custody. We discuss this further in Chapters 6 and 7 on alienation.

An example of a case where the accusing parent lost custody is the Ontario decision of *R. (J.) v. A. (J.)*.[41] Following separation and the establishment of a joint custody regime for a young girl, the mother repeatedly made allegations of physical and sexual abuse against the father. She made the allegations to doctors, who could find no evidence of abuse. The doctors began to have concerns about the effect on the child of relatively intrusive medical examinations and about the mother's open discussion of her allegations in the presence of the child. Assessors from the Family Court Clinic expressed

---

[39] See *H. (D.W.) v. S. (D.I.)*, 1997 CarswellOnt 3264, [1997] O.J. No. 3074 (Ont. Gen. Div.); *M. (S.A.J.) v. M. (D.D.)*, 1998 CarswellMan 178, 40 R.F.L. (4th) 95 (Man. Q.B.).

[40] 1992 CarswellMan 44, 41 R.F.L. (3d) 102 (Man. Q.B.), *per* Carr J.

[41] 1994 CarswellOnt 4691, [1994] O.J. No. 806 (Ont. Prov. Div.), *per* Pedlar J.

similar concerns and concluded that the father was more "child-focussed and more likely to promote a positive relationship with both parents" (para. 7). Counsel for the child expressed "great concern about the insight of a parent who would continually expose her own child to these false allegations and not be apparently aware of the risk to the child" (para. 10). The judge terminated the mother's custody and awarded custody to the father, with reasonable access to the mother.

In its 2004 judgment in *B. (S.L.) v. A. (G.)* the Alberta Court of Appeal upheld the decision of the trial judge to transfer custody of a six-year old boy from the father to the mother, after having concluded that the father intentionally convinced the child to make false allegations of sexual abuse against his half-sister. The Court concluded that the father's conduct constituted a "grave breach of parental responsibilities", remarking:

> We recognize that each case is fact dependant and it is not a general rule that false allegations of sexual misconduct precludes the parent advancing those allegations from acting as a custodial parent. Allegations may range from what is relatively minor inappropriate tickling and physical "play" to serious sexual assaults. Moreover, there are situations where the parent making the false allegation does not involve the child in his or her scheme. In such situations the harm to the child is not as obvious or reprehensible.[42]

In some cases the non-custodial parent makes repeated unfounded allegations that result in intrusive assessments and investigations. These parents cause real harm to their children and demonstrate an insensitivity to the interests of the children, as well as a manipulative personality. In such cases a judge may well suspend access rights of the accusing parent.[43]

In cases in which there are repeated false allegations of abuse, child protection workers may become concerned that the children are being emotionally abused by the false allegations and subsequent investigations. These situations are always high conflict parental separation cases, in which parents are having difficulty giving pri-

---

[42] 2004 CarswellAlta 1514, 9 R.F.L. (6th) 35, 2004 ABCA 366 (Alta. C.A.), at para. 14.

[43] See *Jeanson v. Gonzalez (Watts)*, 1993 CarswellOnt 1803, [1993] O.J. No. 3269 (Ont. Gen. Div.), where MacLeod J. terminated access to a mother who repeatedly made false allegations of sexual abuse against the two fathers of her two daughters, each of whom had custody. In *L. (J.K.) v. H. (J.S.)*, 1997 CarswellOnt 1400, [1997] O.J. No. 1305, 26 O.T.C. 399 (Ont. Gen. Div.) and *T. (C.L.) v. P. (E.)*, 1997 CarswellAlta 1190, [1997] A.J. No. 739, 214 A.R. 161 (Alta. Q.B.), repeated unfounded allegations of abuse were made against the custodial mother and the accusing parties (the father and grandparents respectively) lost access rights.

ority to the needs of the children. It may be necessary for the children to be taken into child protection agency custody, or placed in parental care subject to agency supervision.[44]

In general, judges do not appear to be reducing the parental rights of those who make "honest mistakes" that result in allegations that are ultimately not proven in court, provided their continued involvement with their children does not pose a risk to the welfare of the child. On the other hand, the court will consider whether the accusing parent appears to be mentally unstable or deliberately undermining the relationship of the child to the other parent.

Managing the Uncertain Outcome

No matter how careful the investigation and assessment, there will be cases in which judges, professionals and parents will have to accept that there are *reasonable suspicions of abuse, but not sufficient proof to convince a court* that abuse has occurred. Learning to live with uncertainty may be a very challenging dimension of some of these cases.[45]

It is often possible to take steps to protect the child against the *possibility* of further abuse without completely terminating contact with a *suspected* abuser. This may be done, at least for a time, through supervision of access, first in a neutral setting and perhaps eventually in the home, provided that the supervisor is a person committed to the welfare of the child.[46]

In some cases concerns about physical or even sexual abuse may be a result of inappropriate parenting as opposed to a desire to exploit a child; in such cases the court may order counselling or education of the parent if appropriate.[47]

---

44 See *S. (D.), Re*, 2001 CarswellOnt 733, [2001] O.J. No. 626, 14 R.F.L. (5th) 414 (Ont. S.C.J.), additional reasons 2001 CarswellOnt 1243, [2001] O.J. No. 1274 (Ont. S.C.J.), *per* Linhares de Sousa J. (The mother suffered from mental illness after separation. The custodial father made repeated unfounded allegations that the mother physically and sexually abused the children during access visits. The police, child protection workers and the assessor concluded the allegations were unfounded. A child protection application commenced based on emotional abuse. After a period in foster care, the three children were placed in the care of the mother under agency supervision and one child in the care of the father under agency supervision.)

45 For further discussion, see Hewitt (1999)

46 See *S. (E.) v. M. (D.)*, 1996 CarswellNfld 278, 143 Nfld. & P.E.I.R. 192, 448 A.P.R. 192, [1996] N.J. No. 216 (Nfld. U.F.C.), where the Court was concerned that there was a "significant possibility" that the father had sexually abused the child during access visits, and allowed supervised access at the father's home.

47 *Children's Aid Society of Waterloo (Regional Municipality) v. B. (D.)*, 1991 CarswellOnt 1360, [1991] O.J. No. 2398 (Ont. Prov. Div.) was a child protection case

A long term plan to ensure the safety of the child may include therapy by a skilled neutral professional, who can both provide support for the child after the stresses of litigation and monitor for possible abuse.[48] In some cases educating the child about inappropriate touching and the need to report it is useful, though it must be recognized that in some cases the children may be too young or otherwise unable to protect themselves.

There are also cases in which the judge determines that the allegation of abuse is unfounded and the accusing parent, who is unwilling to accept that conclusion, "goes underground" rather than expose the child to the prospect of further abuse. Occasionally the abducting parent may be correct and the judge was indeed wrong to have concluded that abuse did not occur.[49] However, in most cases the abducting parent is the one who is wrong.[50] The abducting parent may be suffering from some form of personality disorder, perhaps a consequence of his/her own history of having been abused.

---

involving allegations of sexual abuse against a father who was separated from the mother of their two girls. Robson Prov. J. was ultimately not satisfied, on the civil standard of proof, that abuse had occurred, but he was sufficiently concerned to take steps to try to protect against the possibility of future abuse. He concluded that there was a "substantial risk of sexual abuse occurring" during visits, and ordered that the father should take a parenting course as well as a course on the effects of child abuse on children as a condition of his visitation with the children.

The allegations arose following a mother's report of complaints by her six-year old daughter about the father touching her vulva, while he was bathing her during an access visit. The mother initially reported her concerns to a doctor, and then to the Children's Aid Society and the police. The decision in *Children's Aid Society of Waterloo (Regional Municipality) v. B. (D.)* reflects a judicial effort to deal with uncertainty about an abuse allegation without unduly jeopardizing the welfare of children. In part, the decision also may reflect a response to what the judge referred to as "inexcusable" record keeping and "bias" by the Children's Aid Society worker responsible for investigating the allegations. The judgment emphasized the need for investigators in these cases to maintain the appearance of objectivity and fairness.

48 See *N. (D.) v. K. (B.)*, 1999 CarswellOnt 1334, 48 R.F.L. (4th) 400 (Ont. S.C.J.), *per* Métivier J.

49 See *R. (D.) v. K. (A.A.)*, 2006 CarswellAlta 515, 63 Alta. L.R. (4th) 249 (Alta. Q.B.), where a Canadian court accepted that the mother was justified in taking her child from France to Canada because of the failure of the French justice system to protect the child from sexual abuse by the father. In one infamous American case, the mother, Elizabeth Morgan, was jailed for contempt of court for refusing to allow an abusive father to visit her daughter. Only later was it established that the judge was wrong to conclude that the father was not sexually abusing his daughter during access visits. A network of American feminists—the "Underground Railroad" helps women and children to "disappear"; see Fahn (1991), at 194-197.

50 See *C. (D.M.) v. W. (D.L.)*, 2001 CarswellBC 860, 2001 BCCA 285, 155 B.C.A.C. 235, 254 W.A.C. 235, 15 R.F.L. (5th) 35 (B.C.C.A.); *A. (J.E.) v. M. (C.L.)*, 2002 CarswellNS 425, [2002] N.S.J. No. 446, 33 R.F.L. (5th) 1, (N.S.C.A.).

Conclusion

As demonstrated in this chapter, child sexual abuse allegations in the context of child custody disputes can be extremely challenging. The investigation and assessment of these allegations requires a high degree of skill, competence, and experience in family law-related matters as well as knowledge of and experience with child custody assessments in general. We do not purport to have answered all the questions that arise in complex child custody disputes involving allegations of sexual abuse. We have highlighted the range of the issues that need to be addressed in the investigation and assessment of these allegations—both founded and unfounded. We strongly caution our mental health colleagues working in this area to seek out as much information as possible to substantiate sexual abuse allegations, and further, to test rival hypotheses before arriving at any conclusions regarding the veracity of the allegations.

There are no easy answers and these cases are difficult for everyone. Sifting through substantiated cases that include a criminal conviction and physical evidence, or those that involve unsubstantiated cases lacking physical evidence and credibility, obtaining corroborating evidence from personal or professional sources is extremely challenging. Better coordination between the various courts (i.e., family, child welfare and criminal) and the mental health community, such as child protection workers and police who investigate, individual and family therapists who provide treatment, and assessors who provide parenting plan recommendations will assist us to better meet the needs of these children and their families.

Chapter 6

Understanding Child Alienation and Its Impact on Families

Divorce is one of life's most painful passages. . . We can understand and empathize with the spouse who feels wronged and wants revenge, or the spouse who is overwhelmed with anxiety at the thought of losing the children, or the spouse who prefers to forget that the marriage ever was. But using the children to get revenge, to cope with anxiety, to erase the past, is unacceptable. Parents must hold themselves to a higher standard. They must have the courage to face what they are doing to their children. They must honor their mission to safeguard their children's welfare, even when the darkest feelings beckon them to dim their awareness of their betrayal of their children. . . .Children deserve no less.

Richard Warshak (2001)[1]

Children from separated and divorced families who vigorously resist or refuse contact with one parent frequently are referred for child custody assessments. Like those involving allegations of domestic violence and child maltreatment, such cases are among the most difficult to handle for both legal and mental health professionals. As discussed in previous chapters, both parents in high conflict families disputing custody and access commonly make multiple allegations of domestic violence and child maltreatment. The alleged perpetrator frequently makes counterclaims of brainwashing or alienation against the parent making the abuse allegations (Johnston, 2006).

There is significant debate in the mental health and legal literature about the conceptualization and etiology of parent-child contact problems, and about the most appropriate mental health interventions and judicial remedies relating to them. Although most authors agree that the phenomenon exists, finding an appropriate name for the problem is also a subject of debate. It is referred to variously as: "parental alienation syndrome" ("PAS") (Burrill, 2006b; Gardner, 1985); the "alienated child" or "child alienation" (Kelly & Johnston, 2001); "pathological alignments" and "visitation refusal" (Johnston,

[1] Warshak, R.A. (2001). *Divorce Poison; Protecting the Parent-Child Bond from a Vindictive Ex*, pp. 22-23.

1993; Johnston & Campbell, 1988; Wallerstein & Kelly, 1980); "parental alienation" (Baker, 2005a; Darnell, 1998; Garrity & Baris, 1994); "visitation interference" and "divorce-related malicious mother syndrome" (Turkat, 1999); "pathological alienation" (Warshak, 2003a); "threatened mother syndrome" (Klass & Klass, 2005); the "toxic parent" (Cartwright, 1993); and as a subtype of "disorders of created reality" (Shopper, 2005).[2]

The literature is replete, dating back to the mid-1980s, with theoretical discussions, analyses and debate relating to this phenomenon (Bruch, 2001a; Gardner, 1985, 1992a, 1999d, 2001a, 2001b; Cartwright, 1993; Darnell, 1998; Johnston, 1993; Kelly & Johnston, 2001; Johnston, Walters & Friedlander, 2001; Lee & Olesen, 2001; Lund, 1995; Rand, 1997a, 1997b; Sullivan & Kelly, 2001; Ward & Harvey, 1993; Warshak, 2001a, 2003a). Recently there has been a renewed interest in the debate (Baker, 2006, 2007; Bala, Fidler, Goldberg & Houston, 2007a; Bond, 2007; Burrill, 2006b; Drozd & Olesen, 2004; Ellis, 2007; Emery, 2005; Gardner, 2004; Gardner, Sauber, & Lorandos, 2006[3]; Johnston & Kelly, 2004a, 2004b; Walker, Brantley, & Rigsbee, 2004a, 2004b; Warshak, 2000a, 2006; Vassiliou & Cartwright, 2001; Williams, 1990).

File reviews, case studies and research on non-randomly assigned samples have been reported over the last few decades (Baker, 2005a, 2005b, 2006; Burrill, 2006a; Clawar & Rivlin, 1991; Gardner, 2001b; Dunne & Hedrick, 1994; Johnston, 1993; Johnston & Campbell, 1988; Kopetski, 1998a, 1998b; Kopetski, Rand & Rand, 2006; Lampel, 1986, 1996; Rand, 1997a, 1997b; Rand, Rand & Kopetski, 2005; Racusin & Copans, 1994; Wallerstein & Kelly, 1980). An exploratory research project by Janet Johnston and her colleagues resulted in nine papers (Kelly & Johnston, 2001; Johnston, 2003; Johnston, Lee, Olesen, & Walters, 2005; Johnston, Walters & Olesen, 2005a, 2005b, 2005c; Lee & Olesen, 2001; Sullivan & Kelly, 2001; Johnston, Walters, & Friedlander, 2001). We return to a discussion of these various findings later in this chapter.

In this chapter, we review the prevalence, definition, and causes differentiating various parent-child contact problems. In addition, we summarize the characteristics and psychopathology in alienating

---

[2] "Disorders of a created reality" refer to situations in which a person's own autonomous sense of reality testing and reality appreciation are devalued and/or overwhelmed and replaced by a different reaction through the actions of another.

[3] This is an edited book with 34 chapters addressing concepts, clinical considerations, and legal issues relating to alienation. Several chapters include overviews of how alienation has been addressed by both the legal and mental health systems in various countries (i.e., Australia, Germany, Israel, the United Kingdom, and the United States).

parents, and provide an overview of the impact of alienation on children and adults who were alienated as children. In the next chapter, we focus on conducting assessments when alienation is alleged, elaborate on protocols useful for differentiating various types of parent-child contact problems, discuss clinical remedies and the role of the courts, and provide an overview of possible legal remedies, illustrating these with examples of case law.

Prevalence of Alienation

Most children involved in separation and divorce experience some degree of pain and loyalty conflict (Kelly & Emery, 2003). Even in high conflict separations, where it is common for each parent to express negative sentiments about the other parent to the child, most children continue to long for and seek contact with both parents (Wallerstein & Kelly, 1980; Hetherington, Cox, & Cox, 1985; Johnston, Walters & Olesen, 2005b; Warshak & Santrock, 1983). Writers note that even abused children are likely to want to maintain a relationship with their abusive parents. Only a minority, between 11 and 15 per cent of children from community samples of divorcing families, have been found to reject or resist contact with one parent while remaining aligned with the other parent (Johnston, 1993, 2003; Johnston, Walters & Olesen, 2005b; Racusin & Copans, 1994; Wallerstein & Kelly, 1980). Estimates of alienation are higher in custody-disputing samples, with some studies reporting about 20 per cent (Kopetski, 1998a, 1998b; Johnston, 1993, 2003; Johnston, Walters & Olesen, 2005c), and others reporting that as many as 40 per cent of children exhibit alignment with one parent (Johnston & Campbell, 1988; Lampel, 1996). In one study of highly-conflicted custody disputing families conducted by Johnston and her colleagues, about one-fifth (20 to 27 per cent) of children had alienation issues, but only about six per cent were found to reject a parent severely.

Amy Baker conducted a qualitative retrospective study of 40 adults from both divorced and non-divorced families who, as children, had experienced alienation from one parent (2005a, 2005b, 2007). Confirming previously reported qualitative case studies and clinical observations (Kopetski, 1998a; Shopper, 2005; Turkat, 1994), Baker found that although alienation was most common in litigating families, it was also a phenomenon in both non-litigating divorced and non-divorced families.

Research consistently indicates that boys and girls experience alienation about equally, but that adolescents are more likely to become alienated from a parent (Kelly & Johnston, 2001) than are younger children. The earlier studies reported that fathers were more likely to be the rejected parents (Gardner, 1985, 1987; Wallerstein & Kelly, 1980). While a number of recent studies (and more cases overall) report that mothers and fathers are being rejected by their children in about equal proportions (Berns, 2001; Gardner, 2002a), some recent studies report that it is still more common for children to reject their fathers (Johnston, Walters & Olesen, 2005c; Kopetski, Rand & Rand, 2006).

Definitions, Conceptualizations and Causes

Becoming alienated from one parent because of the other parent's influence is not a new phenomenon. In 1949, psychoanalyst Wilhelm Reich wrote in his book, *Character Analysis*, that certain personality types amongst divorced parents defend themselves from narcissist injury by fighting for custody of the child and defaming the partner in an effort to rob the other parent of the pleasure of the child. Wallerstein and Kelly (1980) referred to a parent's manipulation of a child in a custody battle as an "unholy alliance between a narcissistically enraged parent and a particularly vulnerable older child or adolescent, who together waged battle in efforts to hurt and punish the other parent." Ten years later, Wallerstein and Blakeslee (1989) used the term "Medea syndrome" to describe a parent who seeks revenge on a former spouse by destroying the child's relationship with that parent. Others have described this as "pathological alignments", "visitation refusal" (Johnston, 1993; Johnston & Campbell, 1988) and "pathological alienation" (Warshak, 2001a, 2003a). Johnston and Roseby (1997) note that these "unholy alliances" are a later manifestation of a failed separation-individuation process in vulnerable children exposed to dysfunctional family relationships during their early years.

Garbarino and Stott (1992) noted that psychological maltreatment is more likely to occur in families facing stressful circumstances such as marital conflict and divorce. A pattern of adult behaviour that sabotages the child's normal development of self and social competence is noted. They identified five types of maltreatment, later adapted by Deirdre and Randy Rand (1979b) for Parental Alienation Syndrome: rejecting; terrorizing; ignoring; isolating; and corrupting.

Richard Gardner and PAS

In 1985, based on his many years of clinical experience as a psychiatrist working with children and families, the late Richard Gardner introduced the term "parental alienation syndrome" (PAS), a form of emotional child abuse almost exclusively seen in separated and divorced families engaged in custody disputes.

Gardner (1985) and others (Kopetski, 1991, 1998a; Rand, 1997a) have theorized that PAS became more prevalent in the last quarter of the twentieth century as a result of two legal developments. One was the replacement of the tender years presumption, which had guaranteed that most children remained in their mother's custody. The other was the increasing popularity of joint custody, which emerged during the 1980s and changed the previous pattern for custody determination in the courts: that in the event of separation the mother was nearly certain to have custody of the children and that father had a relatively narrow set of visitation rights. Gardner argued that these two developments caused many mothers to feel threatened and, in turn, motivated to do whatever was necessary to prevent losing their children.

In his first publication on this subject in 1985, Gardner defined PAS:

> The parental alienation syndrome (PAS) is a disorder that arises primarily in the context of child custody disputes. Its primary manifestation is the child's campaign of denigration against a parent, a campaign that has no justification. It results from the *combination* of a programming (brainwashing) parent's indoctrination and the child's own contribution to the vilification of the target parent. When true parental abuse and/or neglect are present, the child's animosity may be unjustified, and so the parental alienation syndrome explanation for the child's hostility is not applicable. (p. 61)

In the same article, Gardner placed particular emphasis on three contributing factors: "parental 'brainwashing', situational factors, and the child's own contributions".

Expanding upon Gardner's writings, Warshak (2001a) identified the following three components that must be present for a bona fide diagnosis of PAS:

(1) a persistent, and not occasional, rejection or denigration of a parent that reaches the level of a campaign;

(2) an unjustified (unreasonable) or irrational rejection by the child; and

(3) rejection by a child that is a *partial* result of the alienating parent's influence.

Table 8 lists the eight primary symptoms (diagnostic criteria) identified by Gardner (1992a) and manifested by the child. Additional considerations noted by Gardner include behaviour during transitions and visits, bonding with the alienating parent, and the nature of the bonding with the rejected parent before the alienation. Gardner noted that PAS is determined by the extent to which the efforts of the alienating parent have been successfully manifested in the *child*, and not by the parent's efforts alone. These eight symptoms are likely to appear in moderate and severe cases of PAS, while some but, not all of them, are likely to occur in the mild form.

Table 8: Primary Symptoms Manifested by Child Identified by Gardner (1998a)

1. Campaign of denigration
2. Weak, frivolous or absurd rationalizations for the deprecation
3. Lack of ambivalence
4. The "independent thinker" phenomenon (child claims these are their own, and not the alienating parent's beliefs)
5. Reflexive support of the alienating parent in the parental conflict
6. Absence of guilt over cruelty to or exploitation of the alienated parent
7. Presence of borrowed scenarios
8. Spread of anxiety to extended family and friends of the alienated parent

Table 9 lists factors relevant to the assessment of the alienating parent's behaviour.

Table 9: Primary Factors Manifest by Alienating Parent—Gardner (1998a)

1. Presence of severe psychopathology prior to separation
2. Frequency of programming thoughts
3. Frequency of programming verbalizations
4. Frequency of exclusionary manoeuvres
5. Frequency of complaints to police and child protection services
6. Litigiousness
7. Episodes of hysteria
8. Frequency of violation of court orders
9. Success in manipulating the legal system to enhance the programming
10. Risk of intensification of programming if granted primary custody

Gardner was the first to propose this type of parent-child contact problem as a "syndrome" that should be treated as a childhood psychiatric disorder and classified in the *Diagnostic and Statistical Manual of Mental Disorders* (DSM). While some mental health professionals support the validity of such a diagnosis (Brody, 2006b; Burrill, 2006b; Katz, 2004; Kopetski, 2006; Leving, 2006; Lorandos, 2006;

Rand, 1997a, 1997b; Rand, Rand & Kopetski, 2005; Walsh & Bone, 1997), others argue that PAS is not valid clinically or from an evidentiary perspective (Bruch, 2001a; Emery, 2005; Faller, 1997; Johnston & Kelly, 2004b; Walker, Brantley, & Rigsbee, 2004b; Williams, 2001; Zirogiannis, 2001).[4]

Gould and Martindale (2007) provide a good summary of Myers's critique of "syndrome" evidence and apply this to PAS. They explain that Myers (1993) makes an important distinction between a "disease" and a "syndrome": "The relationship between symptoms and etiology is clear with many diseases but varies much more with syndromes. Syndromes are on a continuum of certainty, with some having greater certainty as to their causes than others" (p. 238). Gould and Martindale further state that "Myers uses the term nondiagnostic syndrome to refer to a syndrome that does not fall within the traditional meaning of the word and that does not have a particular etiology" (p. 329). PAS, then, may be an example of a nondiagnostic syndrome.

Other Opinions

Notwithstanding the debate regarding whether or not this parent-child contact problem is a syndrome or warrants a psychiatric diagnosis—that it is abnormal—few would disagree, as noted earlier, that the problem exists.[5] Gardner's views are supported by many

---

[4] Criticisms include the observation that PAS is not included in the latest edition of the *Diagnostic and Statistical Manual of Mental Disorders, Fourth Edition* (DSM-IV). In response, Gardner (2002b, 2004) notes that no submissions were ever made for PAS to be included in DSM-IV; the current version, and thus the committees did not have occasion to reject it. He adds that in the 1980s, when he began noticing and writing about PAS, it would have been premature for PAS to have been considered for DSM-IV since there were too few articles in the literature to warrant a submission for inclusion to the committees that started meeting in the early 1990s. He further cites the stringent criteria for inclusion in the diagnostic manual, noting by way of example that although Tourette's was first described as a syndrome in 1885, it was not included as a disorder in the DSM until 1980. Similarly, although Asperger's Syndrome was first described in 1957, it took 37 years for it to be included in DSM. Previously, Gardner noted that the committees for DSM-V are likely to consider a submission for inclusion given that there are well over 100 articles on PAS, including 18 by Gardner in peer-review journals, 66 by others, and 51 on the phenomena of pathological alienation (list available from www.rgardner.com and www.warshak.com. Warshak (2006) adds, however, that the DSM-IV specifically cautions against its use in forensic settings. He further argues that assessors do not need to use the term "parental alienation syndrome" in reports and testimony; instead, they should include statements made by parents and children and descriptions of family dynamics and behaviours (Warshak, 2001a).

[5] Although they agree that children can reject and denigrate one parent, even irrationally, a minority of writers maintain that this reaction is not abnormal, does not

(Burrill, 2006a, 2006b; Clawar & Rivlin, 1991; Dunne & Henrick, 1994; Kopetski, 1998a, 1998b, 2006; Lorandos, 2006; Lowenstein, 2006; Rand, 1997a, 1997b; Rand, Rand, & Kopetski, 2005; Warshak, 2001a, 2002, 2003a, 2006), while criticized, to one extent or another, by others (Bruch, 2001a; Emery, 2005; Johnston & Kelly, 2004a, 2004b; Katz, 2004; Lee & Olesen, 2001; Walker, Brantley, & Rigsbee, 2004a, 2004b; Williams, 2001). Some of the criticisms appear to be due to misunderstandings of Gardner's writings. A careful review of the extensive literature indicates that, with the exception of two or three writers who reject Gardner's views outright, there is more agreement amongst experienced professionals than there is disagreement.

The strategies and processes exhibited by alienating parents, along with the primary symptoms exhibited by their children and the behaviour of rejected parents, have been observed by many judges, lawyers, child custody assessors, therapists, mediators, parenting coordinators, and researchers (Baker, 2005a, 2006; Burrill, 2006a; Clawar & Rivilin, 1991; Ellis, 2007; Garber, 2007; Gardner, 1999d; Gould, 2006; Johnston, 1993, 2003, 2005b, 2006; Johnston & Campbell, 1988; Lampel, 1996, 2002; Lee & Olesen, 2001; Lowenstein, 1998, 2005b, 2005c; Lund, 1995; Kopetski, 1998a, 1998b; Rand, 1997a, 1997b; Racusin & Copans, 1994; Stahl, 1994, 1999; Stoltz & Ney, 2002; Turkat, 1994, 1999; Waldron & Joanes, 1996; Wallerstein & Kelly, 1980; Walsh & Bone, 1997; Ward & Harvey, 1993; Warshak, 2000a, 2002). While there are variations in how different professionals and researchers describe and analyse the phenomenon, there is a broad consensus that in high conflict separation some children do become alienated—unreasonably rejecting a parent—and a proper understanding of these cases requires an assessment of both parents and the child.

Table 10, adapted from the work of Baker (2005a), lists five types of strategies alienating parents use to turn children against their other parent (some or all may be used), with levels of severity and explicitness ranging within each of these categories.

---

require mental health or legal intervention, and is likely to improve spontaneously (Bruch, 2001a; Faller, 1997)—a point we return to later.

Table 10: Processes and Strategies Used by Alienating Parents—Adapted from Baker (2005a)

1. Badmouthing the other parent's qualities, parenting, and involvement with child; may or may not include allegations of abusive behaviour (reduces parent's importance to the child).
2. Other parent sometimes portrayed as dangerous, i.e., harmful, angry, mean (instills fear and rejection of the other parent, fosters dependency on and need for protection from alienating parent).
3. Other parent portrayed as having abandoned the child, as not loving or caring for the child (creates hurt, resentment, emotional distance, fosters dependency on the alienating parent).
4. Withdrawal of love: love of alienating parent is conditional upon the child's not showing positive feelings or desire for the other parent (fosters child's insecurity, dependency, need to please the alienating parent, and feeds the parent's narcissism).
5. Minimizing actual and symbolic contact with the other parent (eradicating the other parent from child's life and awareness).

Douglas Darnell (1997, 1998) differentiates PAS from Parental Alienation ("PA"), noting that PAS focuses on the child's behaviour while PA, his preferred term, focuses on the alienating parent's behaviour. He maintains that the conscious *or* unconscious behaviour of the parent may not necessarily evoke rejecting behaviour in the child. Darnell identifies three types of alienators, which we summarize in Table 11.

Table 11: Darnell's Three Types of Alienators—Adapted From Darnell (1998)

1. *Naïve alienators* are passive about the relationship with the other parent and occasionally say or do something to alienate or reinforce alienation.
2. *Active alienators* know that what they are doing is wrong but, in an effort to cope with hurt and anger, alienate as a result of emotional vulnerability or poor impulse control.
3. *Obsessed alienators* feel justified; these parents want to destroy the target parent and the child's relationship with that parent, rarely showing self-control or insight.

Writing independently, apparently without knowledge of the concurrent work of Gardner and Darnell, Leona Kopetski (1991, 1998a, 1998b), a custody evaluator in Colorado, reported clinical observations based on a qualitative file review of 600 court-referred cases between 1975 and 1990.[6] Of the 413 cases involving a court-ordered custody evaluation, Kopetski (1998b) identified 84 as having what appeared to her to be a "phobic reaction" to one parent. Kopetski observed that the parent causing this reaction could be acting consciously or unconsciously, but often suffered from a personality disorder with various social-legal factors contributing to the problem—a psychosocial pathology. Although Kopetski did not use the term "alienation", she identified the same cluster of symptoms as Gardner.

In another published study, sponsored by the American Bar Association, that tracked 700 separating and divorcing families over 12 years, Clawar and Rivlin (1991)[7] wrote about programmed and brainwashed children.[8] Multiple sources were analyzed, including court records, reports from forensic assessors and therapists, and direct observations of and interviews with children, parents, lawyers, relatives, family friends, mental health professionals, and collateral sources. In addition to relying on the literature indicating the negative effects of parental conflict on children, these researchers drew upon long-standing academic (but not clinical) research relating to social psychology and social influence—including persuasion, attitude change, indoctrination and brainwashing, modelling and ways in which those in authority can influence beliefs, attitudes and memory and, in particular, children's suggestibility—to explain how one parent can influence a child to reject the other parent.[9]

Noting the power imbalance between a parent and a child, Clawar and Rivlin (1991) identified eight stages of programming/brainwashing that culminate in severe PAS. Notwithstanding their large sample of 700 families, these results are descriptive and derived from qualitative and clinical studies. The authors do not provide details on the procedures used or the method of analyzing the data, making it difficult to evaluate their findings. More recently, in a qualitative

---

[6] Kopetski describes a team model for conducting child custody assessments. The results were first reported in 1991 at the Fifteenth Annual Child Custody Conference in Keystone, Colorado (Kopetski, 1991). Due to illness, the author's work was not completed. More recently, descriptive statistics on the 84 cases of PAS were published (Kopetski, Rand & Rand, 2006). Rand, Rand and Kopetski (2005) provide a follow-up of these families.

[7] See a detailed summary of their work in Rand (1997a).

[8] This publication was commissioned in the late 1970s out of a rising concern about parents' attempts to influence the outcome of custody disputes by programming their children.

[9] See Ceci and Bruck (1993, 1995) for excellent reviews of the suggestibility literature as it pertains to children. Warshak (2006) cites references relating to how negative opinions can become entrenched and resistant to change, especially when publicly expressed, supporting his view that caution should be exercised when evaluating children's preferences and assigning weight to their testimony (2003b).

study that used Gardner's criteria, Dunne and Hedrick (2004) differentiated 16 cases of severe PAS from other forms of divorce-related disturbance.

Malicious and False Allegations of Child Maltreatment

Gardner was the first to assert that PAS *may* involve malicious and false *sexual* abuse allegations, usually against the father (Gardner, 1987, 1992b).[10] This particular subtype of PAS has been written about by others and referred to variously as: "sexual abuse allegations in divorce syndrome" (SAID) (Blush & Ross, 1987); "divorce-related malicious mother syndrome" (Turkat, 1994); "Munchausen syndrome by proxy-contemporary type" (Rand, 1993; Rand, 1997a, 1997b);[11] and "threatened mother syndrome" (Klass & Klass, 2005). False allegations may involve a paranoid psychosis or delusional disorder focused on the rejected parent in which the child becomes embroiled, creating a folie à deux that results from a failure in separation-individuation.[12]

Allegations of domestic violence and all forms of child maltreatment are frequently advanced by custody litigants (Johnston *et al.*, 2005), specifically in the context of parent-child contact problems (Bala & Schuman, 1999; Bala, Mitnick, Trocmé & Houston, 2007b). As we discuss further in Chapters 5 and 7, an important distinction needs to be made between a false allegation, which may be unsubstantiated but truly believed (an honest mistake) by the parent making the report, and a fabricated allegation that is known to be untrue and is a deliberate and malicious attempt on the part of the alleging parent to keep the child from the other parent. In some cases, a personality disorder or emotional disturbance of the accusing parent may contribute to the making of an unfounded report.

While Gardner initially reported a much higher percentage, he later stated that malicious and false allegations of sexual abuse occurred in 10 to 20 per cent of the cases he had seen; these were identified as exhibiting severe PAS (Gardner, 1998c).[13] Gardner notes

---

10 Rand (1997a) notes the rise in false allegations of sexual abuse in the late 1970s and 1980s, at least in part as a result of widespread (but erroneous) professional belief that children do not lie about sexual abuse.

11 Rand (1993) defines contemporary-type Munchausen syndrome by proxy as occurring "when a parent fabricates an abuse scenario for the child and welcomes or actively seeks out repeated abuse interviews of the child by police, social workers and therapists."

12 Shopper notes that in addition to occurring in false allegations of sexual abuse and PAS, "disorders of a created reality" occur in *folie à deux*, cults, Munchausen syndrome by proxy, and mass hysteria.

13 In this second edition, Gardner provides further elaboration on the differential diagnosis of PAS from *bona fide* abuse and/or neglect.

that PAS-indoctrinating fathers sometimes accuse the mother's new male partner or stepfather of sexual abuse. More recently, Kopetski, Rand and Rand (2006) reported that false allegations of child maltreatment occurred in 54 per cent of the cases they reviewed, with neglect alleged primarily by alienating fathers and sexual abuse alleged primarily by alienating mothers.

Relying on a clinical sample of 120 families, Johnston *et al.* (2005) found that allegations of maltreatment and spousal abuse were advanced in 77 per cent of the families disputing custody and access to children who had been sent for an evaluation (assessment), this representing a subset of separating and divorcing families; mothers alleged sexual abuse by fathers in 23 per cent of these cases, and fathers alleged sexual abuse by mothers in six per cent of the cases. Based on the clinicians' assessments, 26 per cent of the sexual abuse allegations made against fathers were substantiated, leaving 74 per cent unsubstantiated. It remains unclear, however, what percentage of these allegations were false but truly believed, or intentionally false.

Many child sexual abuse allegations made in the context of parental separation remain unfounded, most are truly believed by the accusing parent, and a minority are intentionally false. While there may be disagreement regarding the actual incidence of intentionally false allegations in custody and access disputes, and which parent is more likely to make such claims, few would disagree that involving children in false allegations is a form of child abuse itself, even if the allegation is made by a vulnerable, disturbed parent who truly believes the abuse occurred or is occurring. Even if the report is unfounded, children will often be influenced by the accusing parent to believe the allegation (Bala, Mitnick, Trocmé & Houston, 2007b). These children are frequently exposed to repeated and intrusive physical examination and interviewing. While their relationship with the accused parent can be damaged, their relationship with the alienating parent is often compromised and unhealthy as well. Just as assessors must approach their work with the view that abuse may have occurred, they must also consider the alternative, that abuse did not occur. Still, although rates of unfounded allegations of abuse and neglect are relatively high in parental separation, a significant portion of such allegations are founded. We will discuss additional considerations for the assessor and the legal system in cases where there are allegations of child abuse in the next chapter.

Criticisms of Gardner and PAS

In addition to the previously discussed debate as to whether or not PAS is an actual syndrome and a clinical diagnosis, criticism of the work of Gardner revolves around what is believed to be his heavy focus on the role of the alienating parent. Further criticism focuses on his recommendations for a change of custody to the rejected parent in some moderate and in all severe cases, which he suggested comprise a minority of about 10 to 20 per cent of the cases (Bruch, 2001a, 2001b; Faller, 1997; Kelly & Johnston, 2001; Kerr & Jaffe, 1998; Walker, Brantley, & Rigsbee, 2004a, 2004b; Williams, 2001). In addition, some have criticized his recommendations for enforced visitation and punitive measures such as fines and imprisonment for the alienating parent and even, in more extreme cases, for placing the alienated adolescent in a juvenile detention facility. Noting the lack of empirical data, these critics focus on what they perceive to be Gardner's overemphasis on and blame of alienating parents, who at the time of his research were predominantly mothers, whom he characterized as bitter, vengeful and malicious, to the point of advancing false allegations of abuse against their spouses. However, Gardner later wrote, as did others, that the gender difference is no longer as evident, with fathers also alienating children from their mothers (Gardner, 1998c).

Critics maintain that in overemphasizing the role of the alienating parent, Gardner overlooked the complexities involved when a child becomes alienated from one parent, including factors associated with: (a) the child (i.e., age and temperament); (b) normal childhood development (i.e., separation anxiety, age and gender affinities and preferences); (c) the behaviour of the rejected parent; (d) normal and expected reactions to parental separation and divorce; and (e) the impact of significant parental conflict associated with the adversarial system (Bruch, 2001a, 2001b; Kelly & Johnston, 2001; Walker, Brantley & Rigsbee, 2004a).

In addition, critics of PAS note that in response to allegations of abuse against them, male perpetrators advance counter-allegations of PAS as a smokescreen for their own violent and abusive behaviour (Johnston & Kelly, 2004a; Walker Brantley, & Rigsbee, 2004b). Critics charge that this often results in the courts awarding custody to abusive fathers when in fact the battered mothers were justifiably protecting, and not alienating, their children from their fathers. These writers appear to be arguing that if PAS were not accepted in the courts, such counter-allegations against victim mothers would not be as frequent and would not carry as much weight. Some advocates of victims of domestic violence assert that there is absolutely no evidence to support the claim that mothers are falsely accusing fathers of domestic or child abuse (Bruch, 2001a). They caution that Gardner's theory, which has been conveniently adopted by many fathers' rights advocates, is yet another manifestation of mother- and victim-blaming.[14] Domestic violence advocates note that a child's rejection of an abusive father is to be expected and is in fact a healthy response to both direct and indirect exposure to domestic violence (Kerr & Jaffe, 1998) and/or to child neglect and abuse (Bruch, 2001a, 2001b; Faller, 1997).

Clarifying and expanding his views, Gardner and his supporters maintain that criticism of his work is unfounded in many respects. In his reply commentary to Kelly and Johnston (2001), he states that throughout his scholarly publications, including not only those on PAS but those written long before, he has emphasized that a family-systems perspective is needed to understand all childhood disorders, including PAS (Gardner, 2004). He maintains that his writings (1992b, 1998c, 1999a, 199b, 1999c), including his first publication on the topic in 1985, routinely differentiated PAS from other forms of alienation resulting from child abuse, neglect, abandonment, and rebellion. Moreover, he notes that he introduced the concept of PAS because of the need to differentiate it from other types of parent-child and contact problems about which he had written previously. In his reply commentary, Gardner reiterated his original 1985 definition: "[PAS]. . .results from a *combination* of a programming (brainwashing) parent's indoctrination and the child's own vilification of the target parent." In the second edition of his book, *The Parental Alienation Syndrome* (1998c), he writes:

> Unfortunately, the term 'P.A.S.' is sometimes used to refer to the animosity that a child may harbor against a parent who has actually abused the child . . . the term 'P.A.S.' has been used to apply to the major categories of parental abuse, namely, physical, sexual, and emotional. Such application indicates a misunderstanding of the P.A.S. The 'P.A.S.' term is applicable only when the targeted parent has not exhibited anything close to the degree of alienating behavior that might warrant the campaign of denigration exhibited by the child. Rather, in typical cases, the parent would be considered by most examiners to have provided normal, loving parenting or, at worst, exhibited minimal impairments in parenting capacity. It is the *exaggeration* of minor weaknesses and deficiencies that is the hallmark of the P.A.S. When bona fide abuse does exist, then the child's responding hostility is warranted and the P.A.S. diagnosis is not applicable. (p. 74)

Gardner's clarification explicitly describes different causes for and types of alienation. The term parental alienation or alienation is non-specific, while PAS is differentiated as *one subtype* of alienation

---

[14] There are also groups headed by mothers advocating greater awareness of PAS. See http://www.noncustodialmoms.com/PAS%20Page.htm.

where brainwashing by the alienating parent is the primary etiologic component. He states that when there is no brainwashing and no irrational or unjustified rejection, there is no PAS, although the child may indeed be alienated for other justifiable reasons, such as a response to abuse or neglect (Gardner, 1999b). He maintains that by calling the problem child alienation or parental alienation, and in effect not differentiating it as a syndrome, the critics are adding further to the confusion relating to etiology, the very problem they are criticizing.[15] Moreover, contrary to allegations that PAS further victimizes women, Gardner (2001a, 2002a, 2004) maintains that it is the lack of acceptance of PAS that harms the many women who have been alienated from their children. More specifically, acknowledging that parental alienation (or alienation) exists, but claiming it is not due to the alleged alienator's behaviour but rather to the rejected parent's behaviour, is less likely when there is a specific designation (PAS), rather than the more generic term parental alienation, in which either parent can be responsible (Gardner, 2006).

Kelly and Johnston's Reformulated Model

In response to Gardner's writings, and based on their many years of clinical experience and research on separation and divorce (Johnston, 1993; Johnston & Roseby, 1997; Kelly & Johnston, 2001)[16] provided a reformulated, systems-based[17], multi-factor model to explain why some children resist visitation or reject a parent and remain aligned with the other parent. Table 12 summarizes these multiple factors.

---

15 Although it has not been recognized in every state or in every case, PAS has been recognized in decisions in at least 22 states of the United States and eight Canadian provinces, as well as in Australia, Germany, Great Britain, Israel, and Switzerland (Gardner, 2006). For further elaboration of the various perspectives on pathological alienation as a syndrome, see Bruch (2001a, 2001b); Emery (2005); Gardner (2001c, 2002b, 2004); Kelly and Johnston (2004b); Kopetski (2006); Leving (2006); Lorandos (2006a); Walker, Brantley, and Rigsbee (2004a); Warshak (2001a, 2003a); Williams (2001); and Zirogiannis (2001).

16 See Gardner's commentary (2004) and Johnston and Kelly's rejoinder (2004b).

17 Systems refers to the intrapsychic (within the individual), the interaction between and amongst family members, and to the external sources, like extended family, lawyers, and the broader community like church, school and extracurricular.

Table 12:
Reformulated Conceptualization of Multiple Factors Relating to Child Alienation—Kelly and Johnston (2001)

1. The alienating behaviour of the aligned parent.
2. The rejected parent's inept parenting and counter-rejecting behaviour (before or after rejection).
3. Domestic violence/abuse and child abuse/neglect.
4. Chronic litigation that typically includes "tribal warfare" (involvement of family, friends, new partners, spouses).
5. Sibling dynamics and pressures
6. A vulnerable child (dependent, anxious, fearful, emotionally troubled, and with poor coping and reality testing)
7. Developmental factors (i.e., age-appropriate separation anxiety, response to conflict consistent with the cognitive development of children aged 8 to 15)

Clinical observations indicate that while many parents embroiled in high conflict access and custody disputes engage in undermining and indoctrinating behaviours, only some of their children become alienated (Johnston, 1993). Thus, in this model the behaviour of the alienating parent is one of many interacting factors, and not necessarily the primary component in understanding the parent-child relationship problem. Kelly and Johnston (2001) proposed that the term "alienated child" is preferable to "parental alienation" because the former focuses on the child and is less blaming of the parent. They define an alienated child as one who "freely and persistently expresses unreasonable negative feelings and beliefs (such as anger, hatred, rejection, and/or fear) toward a parent that are disproportionate to their actual experience of that parent" (p. 251).

Differentiating Types of Parent-Child Contact Problems

In the reformulated model of Kelly and Johnston, then, the behaviour of an alienating parent is an important factor, although they note that child alienation can occur in the absence of an alienating parent. Interestingly, by elucidating the complexity of the contributing factors, and thereby broadening Gardner's concept, the reformulated model requires the various types of rejection of a parent to be differentiated based on the reasonableness of the child's resistance and/or refusal to see the parent (i.e., stage of development, response to the parental separation and/or high conflict, rational and justified due to abuse or violence, irrational and unjustified and due to alienation, etc.) (Garber, 2007; Gardner, 2002b; Warshak, 2000a, 2001a).

Warshak (2003a, 2006) suggests that the term "pathological alienation" may bridge the evident differences in the literature. He defines a pathological alienation as "a disturbance in which children, usually in the context of sharing a parent's negative attitudes, suffer unreasonable aversion to a person or persons with whom they formerly enjoyed normal relations or with whom they would normally develop affectionate relations" (2006, p. 361). This definition considers the role of the child and identifies explicitly the role of the alienating parent who is a necessary component of the problem. Warshak's definition further identifies two critical aspects for proper diagnosis: (a) a *change* from a previously good relationship; and (b) the possibility that the aversion may also be *applied to others* (such as other family members), and not only to the parents.

Consistent with the work of Gardner (1992a) and others (Warshak, 2002, 2002b), Kelly and Johnston's reformulated model notes the need to differentiate the truly alienated child, consequent to a parent's brainwashing or indoctrination, from the child who resists or refuses contact with a parent for reasons not primarily due to an alienating parent's overt or covert campaign against the other parent. The reformulated model elaborates this need by conceptualizing parent-child relationships on a continuum, with positive relationships at one end and troubled or alienated relationships at the other. They suggest that this continuum be used as a tool to understand the complexity of parent-child relationships, assisting in the differentiation of various types and causes of alienation.

At the healthiest end of the continuum, the child whose parents are separated or divorced has positive relationships with both parents and wants to spend significant time with each. Next, and still towards the positive end of the continuum, the child prefers contact with both parents, although there may be an *affinity* toward one parent because of temperament, gender, age, familiarity, greater time spent with that parent, or shared interests. For example, a toddler may experience normal separation anxiety or a preference for the parent of the opposite gender, while an older child may prefer the parent of the same gender. A four-year-old girl may only have eyes for her daddy; at 12, however, she may prefer and even insist on her mother's companionship for certain activities, desires and needs. Similarly, a three-year-old boy may demonstrate a preference for his mother, especially when he is ill, and then at 11 choose to spend more time with his father, with whom he shares a love of hockey. This normal and developmentally expected ebb and flow of preferences (affinity) and gender identification occurs in both divorced and non-divorced families, and is not the result of a pathological alienation process. When it occurs in divorcing families, however, affinities and gender identifications can be a concern to the preferred parent and a threat to the non-preferred parent, who incorrectly concludes that the other parent is trying to alienate the child.

Moving along the continuum, the child, while still having some ambivalence towards the non-preferred parent, may exhibit a stronger preference for one parent, creating what is referred to as an *alliance*. An alliance may occur before or during separation because of the non-preferred parent's minimal involvement in parenting, inexperience or inept parenting, although these shortcomings do *not* reach the level of abuse. In addition, there may be divorce-specific reasons for such an alliance, such as when a child who has the ability to form moral judgments becomes angry at the parent who leaves the family or forms a new relationship, which may explain the child's reticence or temporary refusal to spend time with the parent (Warshak, 2000a). Remaining estranged from a parent who has disappointed a child, notwithstanding the parent's efforts to repair matters, may be an indication that the child is refusing to risk trust and the chance of being vulnerable again (Bernstein, 2007).

Further along the continuum, an *alignment* may arise in response to parental hostility and the child's subsequent loyalty conflict, this sometimes also predates the parents' separation. As children mature cognitively, they move from egocentric and concrete reasoning to a position where they can entertain the perspective of others. While children can consider the perspective of the parent they are with at the time, they are unable, at least initially, to consider discrepant perspectives simultaneously. Accordingly, loyalty conflicts initially manifest with a child's demonstrating a shifting allegiance (Johnston & Roseby, 1997). As children mature cognitively, they acquire the capacity for reflexive thought ("I know that you know that I know") and can then partially begin to retain more than one perspective at a time. When a child experiences contradictory parental perspectives, cognitive dissonance and true loyalty conflicts emerge. The situation's complexity, including the incompatibility of the parents' perspectives, induces distress and anxiety in the child, who now wonders which parent is telling the truth, asking: If *this* is true, how can *that* be true?

In the face of negative and contradictory information, the child, who identifies with parts of each parent, begins to feel self-doubt about his or her own worth, and questions one parent's love. To cope with the contradictory information, distress and confusion, the child moves from a shifting allegiance to alignment with one parent, accompanied by either a resistance or refusal to spend time with the other parent. To rationalize this behaviour, the child tends to see the situation in all or nothing terms, believing that one parent is all or mostly good while the other is all or mostly bad. This "reasoning" can become fixed and inflexible.

At the extreme end of the continuum, the child rejects one parent without ambivalence while having a strong alignment with the other parent. In some cases, this reaction may be a *pathological alienation* resulting primarily from indoctrination, psychological manipulation and control by the alienating parent. These efforts on the part of the parent can be conscious, malicious and direct, or more unconscious, manipulative and indirect. It is not uncommon for family and friends of the alienating parent to exert control and manipulation as well. Sometimes the alienating parent is a perpetrator of abuse, who through a process of identification with the aggressor, in such situations, alienates the child from the victim parent (Drozd, Kuehnle & Walker, 2004; Drozd & Olesen, 2004; Johnston Walters & Olesen, 2005b).

In other cases, the child's resistance or refusal to visit may result from the trauma of witnessing domestic violence or from physical abuse, sexual abuse, or significant emotional abuse or neglect on the part of the rejected parent. These children may exhibit symptoms of post-traumatic stress disorder rather than those of parental alienation. Differentiating this reaction from alienation, writers refer to the child's having a *realistic estrangement*. In these situations, reacting with anger, fear or a need to retaliate, the aligned parent may attempt to protect the child from abuse. This protective parenting often resembles alienating behaviour, and in some instances may be disproportionate to the circumstances and even counterproductive. Further elaboration on the impact of alienation on children and ways to thoroughly assess and differentiate its various forms follows later in this and the next chapter.

Building on the reformulated model, Drozd and Olesen (2004) identify 10 types of parent-child relationships, four of which are considered non-pathological and six pathological. The four non-pathological parent-child relationships include: (1) equal relationships; (2) affinity in non-abusive families; (3) alignment in non-abusive families; and (4) protective parenting in abusive families, which often looks like alienating behaviour. The six pathological parent-child relationships comprise: (1) identification with the aggressor; (2) estrangement in response to abandonment or poor parenting; (3) estrangement in response to abuse in the family; (4) alienation from either parent in non-abusive families; (5) alienation from an abusive parent when abuse has been substantiated; and (6) alienation from a victim mother in families where there has been substantiated abuse.

Garber (2004) discusses parental alienation in the context of the development of attachment. He provides a useful hierarchical decision tree (2007) for conceptualizing and assessing what he terms visitation, resistance and refusal ("VRR").

Preliminary Research Findings

Janet Johnston and her colleagues (2005b) attempted to test out the various conceptualizations and etiological theories in two empirical studies. Data were collected on two samples, one including 215 and the other 125 children under the age of 13. All the families involved were disputing custody, with some referred for custody evaluations and others referred for confidential counselling. The researchers identified four competing hypotheses, listed in Table 13, to explain child alignments, estrangements and rejections, separate and apart from developmentally expected alliances, such as age-appropriate separation anxiety and latency-age gender affinity. The Family Structure/Child Vulnerability Perspective, derived from family systems theory and family therapy (Minuchin, 1974), relates to the breakdown of the parental unit and the concomitant over reliance by one parent on a child. Similarly, the child development literature refers to the overburdened or "parentified" child (Barber, 2002; Chase, (1999).

Table 13:
Hypotheses to Explain Child Alignments and Rejections—Johnston *et al.* (2005b)

1. *PAS Perspective*: Primarily malicious brainwashing by an alienating parent of an innocent, rejected parent.
2. *Family Abuse / Violence Perspective*: Realistic estrangement due to substantiated child abuse or domestic violence.
3. *Family Structure / Child Vulnerability Perspec*tive: Parent-child boundary diffusion, enmeshment, role reversal.
4. *Multi-factor Systems-Based Perspective*: Real abuse or poor parenting by rejected parent, plus anger or role reversal of the aligned (custodial) parent.

Johnston and her colleagues emphasize that their findings are preliminary and based on exploratory studies, and that since the groups were not randomly assigned, the results may not be representative of other custody-disputing families. Their research employed newly developed clinical scales that raters then applied to detailed case records from data originally collected between 1981 and 1991. The analyses from these correlational studies were concurrent, and accordingly we cannot know which factors preceded and which followed each child's rejection of the parent. In addition, data are needed from contemporary samples reflecting more recent legal and social changes.

Consistent with the existing literature, the results indicated that most parents from this high-conflict sample exhibited negative behaviours and attitudes about the other parent's parenting, some expressing these opinions more overtly than others. Further, few of the parents exhibited active support of the other parent, such as reassuring the child of the other parent's love, letting the child know he can enjoy his time with the other parent, or encouraging the child to work out any problems directly with the other parent. Despite the evidence of these negative and alienating behaviours, not all children became alienated, a finding the researchers note is supported by previous studies on children's resiliency (Ahrons & Tanner, 2003; Amato, 2001; Emery, 1999c; Hetherington & Kelly, 2002; Kelly & Emery, 2003).

The results indicated that the PAS, Family Abuse/Violence and Family Structure/Child Vulnerability perspectives alone were insufficient to explain why some children rejected one parent while aligning with the other. Johnston, Walters and Olesen (2005b) summarized the results:

> Alienating behaviour by an emotionally needy aligned parent (mother or father), who offers the child warm, involved care in return for unquestioned loyalty, together with critical incidents of child abuse and/or lack of warm, involved parenting by a marginalized rejected parent, jointly explain why some children lose their merging sense of self and their capacity for realistic judgment, become psychologically enmeshed and form a pathological alliance with one parent against the other. (p. 15)

More specifically, the PAS and Family Structure/Child Vulnerability perspectives (see Table 13) were strongly correlated, a finding identified and observed frequently by therapists, assessors, and parenting coordinators. In other words, parents whose children were alienated from them also tended (a) to have poor boundaries; (b) to engage in role reversal; (c) to have an inability to separate their own needs from their children's needs; and (d) to over rely on their children for emotional support. In addition, alienating behaviour by a mother, accompanied on her part by high levels of warm and involved parenting, predicted a stronger degree of rejection of a father by a child. Their results replicated earlier studies and clinical observations that older children were more likely to reject a parent than were younger children. They also indicated that a parent's emotional neediness, apart from their hostility towards the former spouse, contributed in part to a child's alignment. However, because the study was correlational, it remains unclear if role reversal and enmeshment are the cause or the outcome of the alienating behaviour. This is indeed an important distinction and one that could be clarified in future research.

Consistent with other researchers, and as previously noted, Johnston and her colleagues reported that allegations of domestic abuse or violence and child abuse (neglect, physical and/or sexual) were common, reaching 77 per cent in their sample of 120 custody-litigating families (Johnston, Lee, Olesen & Walters, 2005). Close to half of the domestic violence allegations were substantiated, with fathers being three times more likely than mothers to be the perpetrators of abuse. These findings are consistent with previous reports of substantiated allegations of domestic violence in custody-disputing families (Shaffer & Bala, 2003). Child abuse was substantiated in only 27 per cent of the families, with mothers and fathers found to be equally as likely to be perpetrators, findings consistent with other reports of substantiation rates ranging from 14 to 55 per cent (Brown, 2003; Shaffer & Bala, 2003; Thoennes & Tjaden, 1990).

The findings reported by Johnston and her colleagues confirmed that some children have good reasons for rejecting one parent. However, these researchers report that domestic violence did not predict a child's rejection of a parent directly. In addition, the results did not support claims of widespread parental alienation (syndrome), frequently advanced by some fathers' rights advocacy groups. Instead, the findings indicate that, as a group, women victims of violence or abuse were no more likely than non-victims to alienate their children from abuse-perpetrating fathers. The results further indicated that a father's violent and abusive behaviour towards the mother predicted his own tendency to exhibit alienating behaviours. These researchers suggested that it would appear that the violence or psychological control exhibited by a father towards the mother prior to separation was reflected in the father's parenting of the children, who in some cases identified with their aggressors (fathers) and rejected their abused mothers.

Impact of Alienation

Psychopathology in Alienating Parents

A significant proportion of high-conflict parents litigating over custody or access issues exhibit psychopathology and personality disorders (Feinberg & Greene, 1997; Friedman, 2004; Johnston, 1993; Siegel & Langford, 1998). Psychological testing indicates that these parents tend to be rigidly defended and moralistic; they tend to perceive themselves to be flawless and virtuous, externalizing responsibility onto others and thereby lacking insight into themselves and the effect they have on others (Bagby, Nicholson, Buis, Radovanovic, & Fidler, 1999; Bathurst, Gottfried & Gottfried, 1997; Siegel, 1996). Examining alienation, in particular using the MMPI-2, Siegel and Langford (1998) found that alienating parents participating in a custody evaluation were significantly more defensive on two validity indicators—scales F and K—than both the normative sample of non-custody litigants and a group of custody-evaluation participants not identified as alienators. Other clinical observations and test results indicate that favoured-parents, in comparison with rejected-parents, have more substance abuse and psychological disturbance, including histrionic, paranoid, and narcissistic personality disorders or characteristics, psychosis and suicidal behaviour (Baker, 2006; Clawar & Rivlin, 1991; Gardner, 1992b; Hoppe & Kenney, 1994; Kopteski, 1998a, 1998b; Johnston & Campbell, 1988; Johnston, Walters & Olesen, 2005a; Lampel, 1996; Siegel & Langford, 1998; Rand, 1997a; Racusin & Copans, 1994; Turkat, 1994, 1999; Warshak, 2001b).

More recently, Johnston and her colleagues compared the Rorschach protocols of parents, some of whom were alienating, participating in custody evaluations with data from two current non-patient samples (Johnston, Walters & Olesen, 2005a). They found that custody litigants were significantly different from the non-patient samples on numerous dependent variables, most notably their lack of resilience to separation and their experiences of loss. Clinical judgments of parenting behaviours, such as alienating co-parenting, parent-child role reversal, lack of warm and involved parenting, and child abuse, were tested to see if these could be validated by the parents' responses on the Rorschach. Preliminary results suggest that the Rorschach provides indications about a parent's capacity for empathy and ability to cope with stress and conflict, both of which are associated with warm and nurturing parenting (Johnston, Walters & Olesen, 2005a).

Research examining the reports from adults alienated from one parent as children is limited (see for example Baker, 2005b, and von Boch-Galhau & Kodjoe, 2006). In her qualitative retrospective study, Baker (2006) identified three patterns of alienation: (a) narcissistic alienating mothers in divorced families (N=14); (b) narcissistic alienating mothers in non-divorced families (N=8); and (c) abusive/rejecting alienating mothers and fathers (N=16, 3 in non-divorced and 13 in divorced families). For the first two patterns, the adult children described their mothers as self-centred, demanding of attention and admiration, and unable to see their children as separate from themselves. Baker's results are consistent with the reports of the Johnston group and others indicating that lonely and needy mothers often respond to rejection and humiliation by over relying on their children to the point of enmeshment. Consistent with the Family Structure/ Vulnerable Child Perspective developed by Johnston and her colleagues, Baker reports that these mothers are loving, attentive and persuasive; she further posits that the mothers fostered in their children an unhealthy need for the mother's acceptance and approval, much the way cult leaders do with their members (Baker, 2005a, 2006). However, when the children strayed from gratifying their mother's narcissistic needs, they became the recipients of her anger, distance, and disapproval, just as they observed had happened to their fathers. To avoid this rejection, the children colluded with their mother's campaign of denigration and rejected their fathers.

The third pattern described by Baker included mothers and fathers described by their adult children as uniformly cold, abusive and rejecting. Five of these alienators were fathers and 11 were mothers. In half of these families, the rejected parent was an alcoholic in addition to being physically, emotionally, sexually, or verbally abusive. Baker reported that unlike the first two patterns, in which loving warmth, charm, and persuasion were operative, alienation occurred because of the child's fear of the abusive parent. Baker reported that children identified with their aggressors in order to avoid pain and powerlessness, a process consistent with the findings reported by the Johnston group that violent and abusive men tend to be alienators more often than their victim females.

The Effects of Alienation on Children

Understanding the short- and long-term effects of pathological alienation on children is crucial when considering if, when, and how there should be intervention. Although well controlled studies using reliable and valid measures have yet to be conducted, the literature consistently reveals that alienated children are at risk for emotional distress and adjustment difficulties—in some cases at greater risk than children from litigating families who are not alienated (Burrill, 2006a; Cartwright, 1993; Clawar & Rivlin, 1991; Dunne & Hedrick, 1994; Gardner, 1992a, 2006; Garrity & Baris, 1994; Kelly & Johnston, 2001; Kopetski, 1998a, 1998b; Johnston, 2003; Johnston & Roseby, 1997; Lampel, 1996; Lee & Olesen, 2001; Lowenstein, 2006; Lund, 1995; Racusin & Copans, 1994; Rand, 1997a, 1997b; Rand, Rand & Kopetski, 2005; Stahl, 1999; Stoltz & Ney, 2002; Turkat, 1994, 1999; Waldron & Joanes, 1996; Walsh & Bone, 1997; Wallerstein & Blakeslee, 1989; Ward & Harvey, 1993; Warshak, 2001b). Clinical observations, case reviews and qualitative comparative studies uniformly indicate that alienated children may exhibit certain characteristics: (a) poor reality testing; (b) illogical cognitive operations; (c) simplistic and rigid information processing; (d) inaccurate or distorted interpersonal perceptions; (e) self-hatred; (f) low or inflated self-esteem; (g) pseudo-maturity; (h) gender-identity problems; (i) poor differentiation of self (enmeshment); (j) aggression and conduct disorders; (k) disregard for social norms and authority; (l) poor impulse control; (m) emotional constriction, passivity, or dependency; and (n) lack of remorse or guilt.

In their study of 74 children aged five to 12 from litigating families, Johnston, Walters and Olesen (2005c) reported that compared with non-alienated counterparts from custody-litigating families, alienated children have more difficulties with information-processing, coping, self- and other representation, and affective functioning. As predicted, the alienated children were older and more vulnerable, exhibiting emotional/behavioural problems, social incompetence, and an inflated self-confidence. Racusin and Copans (1994) reported that these older alienated children are more likely to be in special-education programs than their non-alienated counterparts are.

Johnston, Walters and Olesen (2005c) explored children's adjustment using two sources of information: parent reports on a standardized behaviour checklist (the Achenbach CBCL), and personality assessment using the Rorschach protocols. Parent reports indicate that alienated children had more emotional and behavioural problems than both their non-alienated counterparts and the normative samples. The Rorschach results, while preliminary, are generally consistent with the previously cited clinical observations and findings related to varied child maladjustments.

The results of Baker's (2007) qualitative retrospective study of adults alienated as children are sobering. Many suffered from low self-esteem, having internalized the negatives of the rejected parent. Self-esteem suffered because the children believed that the alienating parent must also hate the aspects of them that were like the rejected parent. As children, they reasoned that since they were genetically similar to the rejected parent, they too must be bad. In addition, respondents indicated that they had ultimately accepted as true their alienating parent's campaign of assertions that the rejected parent did not love them and had abandoned them. Self-hatred and self-blame resulted from feeling guilty for rejecting the parent and, in some cases, from having abandoned their younger siblings who continued contact when the alienated child did not.

Baker (2005a, 2005b, 2006) reported that 70 per cent of her respondents disclosed suffering significant episodes of depression in their adult lives related to feeling unloved and to extended separations from a parent to whom they had been attached. Feelings of loss were amplified by not being afforded the opportunity to mourn the loss of a rejected parent or to share their sadness with an alienating parent, who touted the lack of contact as positive. Approximately one-third of the sample reported having had serious problems with drugs or alcohol at some point in their adolescent lives, using such substances to cope with painful feelings arising from loss and parental conflict.

Respondents reported that their own experiences and memories did not match the picture painted by their alienating parent, and they consequently experienced self-doubt about their own perceptions and feelings about themselves and others. They had difficulty trusting that anyone would ever love them; two-thirds of them had been divorced once and one quarter more than once. The respondents described former spouses as being similar to their alienating parent in terms of exerting control, lacking empathy, and exhibiting self-focus and narcissism. Consistent with case studies and clinical literature, Baker's respondents reported that they eventually became angry and resentful about being emotionally manipulated and controlled, and that eventually this negatively affected their relationship with the alienating parent. Some of the adult children reported that their alienating parents had experienced conflicted or distant relationships with their own parents, an observation previously reported by Warshak (2001b). Sadly, about half of Baker's sample reported that they had become alienated from their own children. Baker reported that many of the respondents spoke about positive events in their lives in addition to their adversity, suggesting that for some, the pain of divorce was not necessarily equivalent to pervasive maladaptation (Amato, 2001, 2003; Kelly & Emery, 2003; Laumann-Billings & Emery, 2000).

Relevant to the controversy over how much weight to give children's preferences, whether or not we should heed their wishes, and if they mean what they say, Baker reported that most of the adults distinctly recalled *claiming* during childhood that they hated their alienating parent while secretly hoping that the same parent would realize they were not telling the truth. Consistent with the findings of other researchers that 80 per cent of alienated children wanted the brainwashing detected and stopped (Clawar & Rivlin, 1991), Baker found that most of her respondents also secretly longed for the parent to discover that they did not mean what they said. Her results further indicated that for more than half of those alienated, their relationships remained severed for more than 22 years, while for all of them the alienation had lasted at least six years. These results, taken in combination, lend support to a reconsideration of the forceful advice offered by some, albeit few, that professionals and the courts should leave well enough alone and wait for the child to take the lead—that things will spontaneously improve in time (Wallerstein, Lewis & Blakeslee, 2000), a point we return to in the next chapter.

Baker noted that the results of her retrospective and qualitative study, while sobering, must be treated cautiously, as she had no comparison group of adult children of divorce who did not experience parental alienation and, furthermore, that not all children experienced all reported reactions. Consequently, one cannot conclude that the outcomes are due to an alienation process *per se*, and that they may have been a result of the divorce itself, of parental pathology or other precursors. Nevertheless, Baker concluded that the voices and felt experiences of these adult children deserve to be heard and provide a good foundation for future well-designed research.

In this chapter, we discussed the prevalence, definition, and causes of child alienation, differentiating various types of parent-child contact problems. We summarized the characteristics and psychopathology in alienating parents, and provided an overview of the impact of alienation on children and adult children. In the next chapter, we turn our discussion to practical issues that arise when conducting assessments in these situations, including protocols for differentiating parent-child contact problems and the possible clinical and legal remedies.

Chapter 7

Child Custody Assessments, Recommendations and Judicial Remedies Regarding Alienated Children

[P]arental alienation occurs along a continuum of behaviors and . . . it is not necessary to find a certain number of indicia before such a conclusion is appropriate. . . it does not have to be proven that the child hates the mother before intervention is warranted. . . it is very damaging and destructive to the child to be put into a position where they have to dislike the other parent and align with the alienating parent, and the sooner a remedy is implemented, the better. It is clear that encouraging negative feelings towards one parent may impede the normal emotional development of the child and deprive that child of love and support.

Martin, J. (Alberta Queen's Bench) (2007)[1]

In this chapter we: (1) review specific issues relevant to the assessment of alienation, including children's views and preferences and the role of rejected parents; (2) elaborate on various assessment protocols for differentiating parent-child contact problems; (3) discuss possible recommendations that assessors can make, including models of intervention and the role of the court in these, treatment approaches and goals, and custody reversal; and (4) provide an overview of judicial responses to alienation and problems with access enforcement, as illustrated by case law. In general, over the past decade judges have demonstrated greater understanding of the issue of alienation and a greater willingness to respond.

Assessing Cases Involving Allegations of Child Alienation

A thorough assessment is necessary when questions arise about whether or not it is in a child's best interests to spend time with one parent over that child's resistance or objections.[2] Recommendations

---

1 *L. (R.A.) v. R. (R.D.)*, 2007 CarswellAlta 183, 2007 ABQB 79, [2007] A.J. No. 163 (Alta. Q.B.), at para. 156.

2 See our companion book (Birnbaum, Fidler & Kavassalis, 2008) for further elabo-

range from not intervening and letting matters take their own course, to seeking a reversal of custody, with many options in between. It is necessary to evaluate the risks and benefits of all options. It is, however, often difficult to be certain of the effect of any intervention before it is tried, and it is not uncommon for the "attempted solution to become the problem" (Waltzlawick, Weakland & Fisch, 1974), or in other words, for our effor to assist to have its own negative effects. An assessment should always include an examination of any previous efforts through legal or mental health channels that failed to resolve the situation and, in turn, recommend alternative options.

The assessment first identifies whether the child is in fact refusing or resistant to contact. If that is the case, the various types of parent-child contact problems and the degree or level of difficulty—mild, moderate, or severe—must then be differentiated. In addition to what is typically reflected in any assessment (Birnbaum, Fidler & Kavassalis, 2008), the existence of a parent-child contact problem requires that the report include the reasons for the child's rejection of a parent along with an examination of the dynamic interplay between the various contributing factors. It is useful for the assessor to explore the various hypotheses relating to the different types of rejection and elucidate the reasons and supporting evidence for dismissing one type and accepting another. More specifically, the report needs to address whether the rejection is irrational or unjustified (pathological), and primarily the result of the alienating parent's behaviour (overt or covert, conscious or unconscious) or, rather, a realistic estrangement that results from the child's being neglected, abandoned, abused or witness to domestic violence. Even when there is a realistic estrangement, the matter is likely to be complicated to the extent that there may also be alienating behavior. Here, the rejected parent's flaws are exaggerated and, in effect, exploited to further polarize the child's feelings.

An expeditious assessment is necessary in these cases, because the longer a child is pathologically alienated, the harder it becomes to remedy the situation. It often takes considerable time for lawyers to agree on a suitable assessor and then for that assessor to begin and complete an assessment, during which time the alienation is likely to

---

ration of child custody assessment methodology more generally. See also Chapters 3, 4 and 5 in this book for further elaboration on the assessment specifically relevant to cases involving allegations of child sexual abuse and domestic violence. Additional useful references include: the diagnostic tables in Gardner (1998b, 1999d); Gould (2006); Gould and Martindale (2007); Kelly and Johnston's reformulated model (2001); decision trees provided by Garber (2007) and Drozd and Olesen (2004); Jaffe, Lemon and Poisson (2003); Johnston (2005b, 2006); Lee and Olesen (2001); Stahl (1999); and Warshak (2002).

become entrenched, while the rejected parent may react in ways (i.e., by being passive, counter-rejecting, or both) that may well reinforce the alienation (Lee & Olesen, 2001). Further, the alienation may advance (become iatrogenic) as a direct result of the assessment process itself, with the children and alienating parent needing to "up the ante" to justify their positions.

Children's Stated Wishes: Clinical and Legal Perspectives

It is important to consider a child's views and preferences, but the stated wishes of a child are not determinative of the child's best interests or the decision of a court, even when expressed by an older child or adolescent. While most would agree that children should be encouraged to express their feelings and wishes during custody and access assessments, the opportunity to be heard (voice) is not equivalent to a right to make decisions (choice). Further, there are cases in which directly soliciting the child's views in an assessment may be harmful to the child's well-being.

Children's wishes need to be assessed for the impact of loyalty conflicts and undue influence, and then interpreted and weighed by taking into account many factors, including age, competence, maturity, coping skills, family dynamics and the nature of the parent-child relationship. As previously noted and supported in the existing research, children in cases involving domestic violence can be coerced and intimidated by abusive parents who alienate them against the victim parent (Johnston, Walters & Olesen, 2005b; Warshak, 2003b). Sometimes these children identify with the aggressor.

In our companion book, we discussed more thoroughly the role and assessment of children's stated wishes and preferences in child custody assessments.[3] Notwithstanding the importance of giving children a voice, consideration needs to be given to the possibility that the risks of soliciting preferences, even if these could be reliably obtained, may outweigh the benefits in high-conflict separating and divorcing families (Warshak, 2003b). It is important to keep in mind that a child's wishes are not necessarily consistent with what is in their best interests. Providing children with the final authority to determine what constitutes reasonable time with a rejected parent, *after* risk and harm of emotional and physical safety are ruled out, is not likely to be in their best interests, given the risks associated with being burdened by this responsibility (Gardner, 1998c; Johnston & Kelly, 2004a; Lund, 1995; Warshak, 2003b). Such responsibility is

---

[3] See Chapter 3 in Birnbaum, Fidler and Kavassalis (2008).

likely to frighten and overwhelm children, inducing considerable feelings of guilt. Furthermore, this responsibility may reinforce their unrealistic sense of power and encourage disrespectful behaviour, phobic concerns and/or distortions of reality. In many alienation cases, removing children from the role of decision-maker allows the child to save face, in effect the needed excuse, to rebuild their relationship with the target parent (Gardner, 2001c; Johnston, 2001; Warshak, 2003b).

We can, however, rely on what Warshak terms "the collective voice of children", as revealed in research on the impact of separation and divorce on them (Warshak, 2003b). Children of divorced parents usually want to spend time with both parents. Furthermore, many want more, rather than less, time with the non-custodial parent (Fabricius & Hall, 2000; Laumann-Billings & Emery, 2000; Parkinson, Cashmore & Single, 2005; Rosen, 1979; Wallerstein & Kelly, 1980; Warshak & Santrock, 1983). For example, some retrospective studies (Fabricius, 2003; Fabricius & Hall, 2000) report that 75 per cent of a sample of now-adult children of divorce longed for more time with their non-custodial parents. Findings from the separate studies of Emery and Hetherington also underscore children's feelings of pain and abandonment by their non-custodial parents (Emery, 2000, 2005; Hetherington & Kelly, 2002; Laumann-Billings & Emery, 2000). More recently, as summarized in the previous chapter, research on the long-term negative effects of being alienated from a parent is sobering (Baker, 2005a, 2005b, 2006).

Specific to alienation cases, one large-scale study indicated that the vast majority of children (80 per cent) frequently wished for the alienating conduct to stop (Clawar & Rivlin, 1991). Also relevant to this issue are Amy Baker's findings that adults who were alienated as children distinctly remembered, as children, secretly wanting their hated parent to pursue a relationship with them (Baker, 2005b).

Judges have long held that children's stated wishes are but one consideration in determining their best interests. Justice Mesbur's statements in the 2007 Ontario case of *Figliano v. Figliano*[4] aptly summarizes current judicial thinking:

> At trial, there was a great deal of discussion about the children expressing a wish to live with their father. I want to make clear at the outset that the children do not have to choose which parent to live with. That is not their job. It is their parents' responsibility to make that decision, in their best interests. When their parents cannot agree, then the responsibility falls to the court. My role is to take on that task, and to make the decision of what is best for the children. Their wishes are

---

[4] 2007 CarswellOnt 773, 35 R.F.L. (6th) 71, [2007] O.J. No. 530 (Ont. S.C.J.).

> only one factor to consider. What children say they want is not necessarily what is best for them. What children say they want does not necessarily reflect their real wishes. It is important that both of the parents, the children, and both extended families understand this.[5]

For many reasons, children's wishes may not be true reflections of their genuine and deeper feelings. In cases where alienation is a concern, the court is not bound by the wishes of a child, regardless of how consistent and fervent these wishes may be.

In *P.S.-M. v. A.J.-L.C.*,[6] Gomery J. of the Quebec Superior Court was presented with a case of four children caught up in a heated custody dispute between their parents. Although both parents worked during the marriage, the mother was the primary caretaker of the children. Following separation, the children went to live with their father and refused all further contact with their mother. When the mother attempted to exercise her right of access, the children called the police to remove her. After psychological assessments attesting to the alienation of the children from their mother and several interim court orders attempting to re-establish their contact, all of which were sabotaged by the father, the children were finally put into foster care by child protection authorities. When foster care was no longer available, the children returned home to their father. Once with their father, it became impossible for the children to engage with their court-appointed lawyer, and the various mental health professionals, including the court-appointed psychologist, who had been working with the children. At the conclusion of the trial, the two older children were permitted to remain with their father, as it was evident they would run away if they were made to live with their mother. The two youngest, however, were placed in the custody of their mother. Access by the younger two children to the father and the two older children in his care was suspended for a period of six months to allow them to stabilize in their mother's home. In determining the weight to be given to the desires of the children, Justice Gomery stated:

> In determining questions of custody, the court must be guided by the best interests of the child. The desires and preferences of each child are factors to be taken into consideration, particularly in cases where the child's wishes are freely expressed and are not influenced by pressure or manipulation. In this case, the wishes of the children, especially the younger children, may be safely ignored because they are a result of distortions of the truth that their father has told them, and the psychological pressure to which they have been subjected. . .

---

[5] *Ibid.*, at para. 3.

[6] Unreported, [1991], SCM 500-12-184613895 (Que. S.C.).

> Children do not always know what is best for them. The law leaves it up to the court to decide this question, when their parents are unable to agree, and the law does not state anywhere that the court must be guided by what the children have to say, although it does require that they should be given an opportunity to be heard. At their request, as it was expressed through their own lawyer, the court has listened to them. What they have said, and the way they have said it, has served to strengthen the court's opinion that it would not be in their best interests to continue to let them have their own way.[7]

In the Ontario case of *Boukema v. Boukema*,[8] the Court was cautioned by the child's counsel about placing emphasis on the child's stated wishes to the exclusion of all other considerations. The parties had entered into Minutes of Settlement that were ultimately incorporated into a judgment of the court. The agreement provided for, amongst other things, joint custody of the parties' then 11-year-old daughter; the child was to have "primary residence" with her father in Toronto. Almost immediately after signing the agreement, the mother, who had relocated to New Jersey to be with her new spouse, disclosed that she would not abide by its terms; after a six-week holiday with the mother, the child expressed a wish to go and live with her in New Jersey. The mother claimed that the child's desire to live with her was a material change in circumstances justifying new custody and residence arrangements. She applied for a variation of the order. An assessment report concluded that the child's views were not arrived at independently, and for this reason the Children's Lawyer declined to advocate based on the child's views, though the lawyer ensured that there was evidence before the court about the child's views as well as about the factors that may have influenced these views. The Court concluded that there was not a sufficient change in circumstances to justify changing the child's primary residence from her father, as had been previously agreed to by the parents, and the mother's application was dismissed. The judge further determined that joint custody was no longer feasible and awarded sole custody to the father. In coming to this conclusion, the Court considered the child's wishes, but as they had been greatly influenced by the mother, attached less weight to them than she might otherwise have done.

Similarly, in the British Columbia case of *Carnahan v. Carnahan*,[9] the Child Advocate considered the contextual circumstances surrounding the children's views and preferences and did not support

---

[7] *Ibid.*, at p. 19.

[8] 1997 CarswellOnt 3115, 31 R.F.L. (4th) 329, 33 O.T.C. 190, [1997] O.J. No. 2903 (Ont. Gen. Div.).

[9] 1986 CarswellBC 841 (B.C.S.C.).

the children's stated wishes, which were to live with their mother and have very limited or no contact with their father. The Court, in making a ruling contrary to the children's wishes, stated:

> I stop here since recounting the children's litany of ridicule and criticism of their father is ultimately offensive and simply lends weight to the various professionals' conclusions that the children have been sadly manipulated, that their relationship with their father has been cruelly crippled, and that the time is now at hand to take every measure to set a new course. I do not consider the children's views to be those of mature, emotionally healthy 12 and 14-year-old children, with any sound perspective or judgment.[10]

In his decision, the trial judge set out a schedule of increasing access to the father that would ultimately include alternating weekends and half of all holidays, despite the children's wishes to have little or no contact with their father.

Observations of Children with Rejected Parents

Interviews and parent-child observations are two key sources of information in any assessment. Concerns may surface about an assessor seeing a child with a rejected parent, or with a parent the child has not seen for a significant period of time. Often, when seen apart from an alienating parent and with a rejected parent, children behave very differently from what might be expected based on their stated wishes and preferences. Parent-child observations may either confirm or disconfirm the reports of the child and alienating parent, as well as those provided by third parties.

It is usually very helpful to observe the parent-child interaction, but there are no uniform rules in such cases, and the assessor will need to gather information before deciding whether to see a child in the presence of a rejected parent. An agreement to undertake an assessment or a court order will usually oblige both parents to comply with the procedures established by the assessor. However, if objections to an observation of a child with their rejected parent persist, the assessor may choose to seek direction from the court; an assessor would be ill-advised to attempt to force contact, notwithstanding agreement that the assessor is to determine procedures.

A comprehensive and accurate assessment of the risks and benefits to a child of contact with a rejected parent is not possible if the child is not observed interacting with each parent. In our experience, barring imminent risk to child, most, albeit not all, situations warrant

[10] *Ibid.*, at p. 5.

seeing a child with a rejected parent. If this, for any reason, cannot be arranged, the assessor should elaborate on the process that led to making this determination, and further indicate that any conclusions or recommendations provided need to be considered in the context of this missing information.

The Role of the Rejected Parent

No parent is perfect. The assessor must carefully consider the role, if any, of the rejected (or alienated) parent in any parent-child relationship problem. A detailed inquiry into the nature and extent of that parent's participation in parenting both before and after the separation is required. Does the rejected parent's behaviour and parenting history warrant the degree of hate, vilification, and rejection exhibited by the child?

Also important to assess is how the parent responds to the child's resistance or rejection. Rejected parents often react in ways that maintain or reinforce alienation. For example, some rejected parents react with passivity or withdrawal. The withdrawal and passivity often observed in rejected parents may be their way of coping with the conflict between the parents both before and after the separation. These reactions may only serve to reinforce the allegations made against them by the alienating parent and the child, including abandonment, disinterest, and poor parenting (Baker, 2006; Gardner, 2001d; Kelly & Johnston, 2001; Kopetski, 1998a, 1999b; Vassiliou & Cartwright, 2001).

Some rejected parents act in self-centred and immature ways, with little insight into how their own behavior contributes to the problem and impacts their child. They may have difficulty separating their child's needs and feelings from the motivations and behaviours of the alienating parent, quickly concluding—and voicing—that the child is simply mimicking what they have heard and been told. On the surface, rejected parents may look more disturbed than alienating parents. Further, if the rejected parent does not capitulate, the conflict escalates (Kopetski, 1998a; Lee & Olesen, 2001).

Other rejected parents, lacking appropriate empathy, may be counter-rejecting, harsh and even angry with their child, although this response may not rise to the level of emotional or physical abuse. They may become strongly offended and react similarly to their children by being aggressive and disrespectful. It is not uncommon to observe rejected parents vacillating between passivity and confrontational behaviour (Baker, 2006; Kopetski, 1998b; Kelly & Johnston, 2001; Warshak, 2002). While a rejected parent's behaviour may perpetuate or reinforce alienation and be harmful to the child, a distinction must be made between the initial cause of the alienation, and what has become a reaction to a very difficult circumstance that may well have begun before the separation (Gardner, 1992a; Turkat, 1994; Warshak, 2003a).

Differentiating Parent-Child Contact Problems

As previously discussed, since children may resist or refuse contact for many reasons (i.e., affinities, alignments, realistic estrangement, pathological alienation), the assessor must determine if a child is truly, that is, pathologically alienated, or if the child is realistically estranged, or in some other condition. The task involves assessing the relative involvement of several complex and interacting factors.[11]

Table 14 lists five factors described by Warshak (2002) that distinguish a child whose behaviour is not typical of severely alienated, but rather due to a resistance or rejection for other reasons.

Table 14:
Five Factors that Distinguish Rejection/Resistance for Other Reasons from Severe Alienation—Warshak (2002)

Reaction:
1. is temporary and short lived, rather than chronic;
2. is occasional, rather than frequent;
3. occurs in some, but not all situations;
4. occurs along with expressions of genuine love and affection;
5. is directed at both parents.

Relying on the different types of information obtained from various sources, the assessor must investigate several hypotheses by asking questions. For example:

(1) Has either parent, through covert pressure and innuendo, or more overt indoctrination, influenced the child's preferences?

(2) Is there a role reversal in which the child attempts to take care of the parent whom he or she perceives is lonely, unstable, without support, unhappy and/or angry about the separation?

[11] Ellis (2007) provides a useful 3-step process for the evaluating children for parental alienation. This is an instructive approach that includes specific strategies and questions that may be used with the child and alleged alienating parent to identify 15 proposed criteria for alienation. Also, see Ellis (2000).

(3) Are the child's needs for empathy conditional on sharing the distorted perceptions of the humiliated parent?

(4) To cope (for self-protection), does the child placate the angry parent by negatively distorting time spent with the other parent?

(5) Is the child concerned about losing one parent the way the other parent was seemingly lost?

(6) Is the child's reluctance to leave one parent and go to the other a developmentally expected age- or gender-related affinity to the preferred parent, or a preference due to familiarity and shared interests?

(7) Are the child's fears and anxieties understandable reactions to the non-preferred parent's inept, rigid, and/or insensitive parenting?

(8) Are there divorce-specific reasons for the child's rejection of the parent, such as anger and hurt for initiating separation or a premature introduction to a new partner and step-siblings?

(9) Has the favoured parent exploited the child's hurt and angry feelings about the separation, thereby cementing the child's alignment against the other parent? If so, how and to what extent?

(10) How long has the rejection been occurring?

(11) How amenable does the favoured parent seem to be intervention or discussion by the assessor?

(12) Is the child's alliance related to the preferred parent's having few, if any, expectations or offering more material rewards?

(13) Is the child's resistance or refusal a justified reaction and trauma-coping mechanism in reaction to being abused by that parent, and/or having witnessed that parent's violence and abuse with the preferred parent?

In addition, obtaining complete individual histories of both parents is critical to understanding their family-of-origin experiences, their own attachments, and any possible childhood traumas that may be relevant to their parenting and to current family circumstances. If the parents have problems in other areas of their lives, such as with friends, fellow workers, school personnel or other family members, these issues should be pursued, as they may, for example, be symptomatic of a personality disorder.

It is important to ask questions relating to the child's experiences of parenting and their manner of reasoning as well. For example:

(1) What was the child's experience of parenting before and after the separation?

(2) To what extent was each parent involved in the child's care?

(3) Was one parent more of a disciplinarian?

(4) What was the nature of the child's emotional relationship with each parent before and after the separation?

(5) Did either parent's behaviour change significantly after the separation?

(6) Does the rejected parent have positive relationships with any of the children?

(7) Is the child's reaction long-standing or recent?

(8) Does the child reject the parent consistently or only occasionally?

(9) Does the child express some ambivalence, or are their feelings and attitudes fixed and unambivalent?

(10) What is the sequence and context surrounding the rejection?

(11) Can the child consider positive qualities in the rejected parent and negative ones in the preferred parent?

(12) Does the child reject obvious facts: for example, their evident enjoyment as captured in a video or photograph?

In addition, the assessor may choose to ask the child interpretive questions such as: "Did someone tell you to say that?"; "How do you know that?"; or "Who told you to tell me that?".[12]

Transition Difficulties due to Development and Separation Anxiety

Children cope differently with their parents' separation depending on their age and stage of development (Hetherington, Cox & Cox, 1985; Pruett, Williams, Insabella & Little, 2003; Wallerstein & Kelly, 1976, 1980). It is not uncommon for toddlers and preschool-age chil-

[12] See Clawar and Rivlin (1991) for important suggestions for interviewing children suspected of being alienated.

dren, due to their developing internal regulation and, irrespective of the effects of marital separation or divorce, to exhibit anxieties when separating from the parent they are with at the time. For infants, the rule is "out of sight, out of mind"—they are unable to retain or draw on an internal representation of their attachment figures that would help maintain a sense of security. Infants and toddlers are unable to conceptualize time adequately, and have difficulty grasping the rhythm and predictability of parenting time schedules, at least initially. At times of transition, then, these young children may become upset and protest or regress with crying and temper tantrums when separated from a parent.

Sometimes short-lived difficulties occur before or after transitions, especially with younger children; for example, the child may not want to get ready for the parenting time, or may have trouble sleeping, eating or toileting before or after contact. Some children, depending on their temperament, may have more accentuated difficulties handling stress, new situations, or changes, such as sleeping in an unfamiliar bed or environment, while this does not faze others. Difficulties such as these, which may occur before, during and after transitions, are typically the result of normal maturation rather than an alienation process. In fact, they are usually a positive indication that the child is developing normally; the difficulties have more to do with separating from one parent than with being with the other. While this reaction usually occurs with both parents, it may be stronger with one parent. Once the child is with the less familiar or preferred parent for a short period, they are usually able to settle in and adapt. Transition difficulties are usually short-lived, and especially so if the child has a reasonably secure attachment to both parents.

Understanding parent-child relationships requires that the assessor activate the parent-child attachment system (Lee & Olesen, 2001).[13] Observations by the assessor before, during, and after transitions are likely to be especially informative. The assessment of each parent's ability to soothe and prepare a child for transitions to and from the other parent is imperative. Some parents thoroughly prepare a child for a new play date, babysitter or daycare, but they provide absolutely no warmth, support or encouragement for transitions to the parent who is held in disfavour; some refuse, for instance, to allow the child to take along a favourite toy, transitional object, or pet.

---

[13] We elaborate on assessment methodology and protocols for assessing parenting in Chapters 2 and 3 of our companion book, *Child Custody Assessments: A Resource Guide for Legal and Mental Health Professionals* (Birnbaum, Fidler, & Kavassalis, 2008).

Others are attuned to their child's emotional needs and prepare them sensitively, often knowing the critical period when it is best to start preparing the child for the transition—just as they would when making any other transition, such as going to daycare, school, shopping, or a doctor's appointment. It is saddening to observe a parent stand by passively while a child cries and protests, and then scornfully state to the assessor: "See, I told you this happens!"

Out of concern and protectiveness, rather than a conscious attempt to thwart the other parent, some parents may conclude that their child should not have to endure these upsetting transitions (i.e., separation reactions). However, parental protectiveness can be counterproductive and the degree to which it is so requires careful assessment. Parents of vulnerable children, such as those with a preexisting illness, disability, vulnerability, or a school or learning problem, may be particularly protective, and understandably so. In other cases, the protective parent may over-interpret the child's reactions out of an emotional dependency on a child who serves as a substitute for a former spouse; every time the child leaves, the parent experiences a renewed sense of being rejected or abandoned. At these times, the protective parent may become visibly upset or perhaps even quietly tense, in turn reinforcing the child's distress, which further reinforces the parent's state of upset, resulting in a mutually and dysfunctional reinforcing feedback loop (the "snowball effect"). This dynamic serves to sabotage the child's relationship with the other parent. What's more, the receiving parent observing the protective parenting may jump to the false conclusion that the other parent is intentionally alienating the child; such a reaction, along with the other parent's anxiety, concern, and protective behaviour, often reinforce the child's separation difficulties.

Explaining these normal developmental separation difficulties may assist both the aligned parent, worried about the child's distress, and the other parent, who may have prematurely concluded that the first parent is turning the child against him or her. In addition, educating the parents about attachment, and how both parents can better soothe the child through these transitions, including overnights, is likely to be helpful. For infants and toddlers, it is preferable for a child not to be apart from either parent for too long, with schedules that allow for frequent contacts of a shorter duration (Kelly & Lamb, 2000; Lamb & Kelly, 2001).[14] When recommending a parenting time

---

[14] Solomon and Biringen (2001) critique the recommendations of Lamb and Kelly (2001) for the introduction of overnights with a parent for very young children and recommend that there should not be overnights for children under 3 years of age. Others maintain there is value in having both parents regularly involved in the

schedule, the assessor must consider all the changes and other separations the child may be experiencing. The impact of several stressors occurring simultaneously is greater than the impact of each individual stress (Rutter, 1979). Stated differently, the "whole is greater than the sum of its parts". Accordingly, a gradual approach to increasing time away from the usual caregiver and to developing parenting time schedules is advised, keeping in mind that without any time, a child will not be able to either develop, or further enhance, their existing attachment to that parent. One should also keep in mind that toddlers who are used to daily contact with both parents might do best to gradually work toward a schedule that reduces the frequency of contact, rather than having to experience an abrupt change from daily contact to twice weekly contact (Kelly, 2005; Warshak, 1992). Introducing multiple changes all at once and too quickly may only serve to deter the desired outcome for increases in parenting time and a good relationship with the other parent.

Underdeveloped Parent-Child Relationships

When a child exhibits a preference or affinity toward one parent because of comfort or familiarity with that parent, the assessor needs to consider that the non-preferred parent may not be a bad or incapable parent, but rather may be inexperienced and minimally involved. Assuming the non-preferred parent is not abusive, time and experience are likely to remedy this circumstance. Furthermore, the reasons that one parent has remained relatively uninvolved are also important to consider in an assessment. The parenting arrangement during cohabitation, with one parent doing more of the child care, for instance, and the other being the "breadwinner", may have been understood and agreed to as best for the family while the parents lived together. Typically, these understandings, explicit or not, accepted willingly or reluctantly, change after separation.

Regardless of the reason for one parent being more involved than the other while they lived with one another, each is required to take on new roles and tasks once separation occurs, and their child's relationship with each of them will undergo changes. For example, upon

---

aspects of care associated with overnights, such as bathing, bedtime storytelling and putting the child to bed, and further that there is no harm to overnights for this age group providing that there is a consistent schedule and competent parenting. We tend to agree with the recommendations of Lamb and Kelly over those of Solomon and Biringen. For a comprehensive summary of the "overnight" debate and other related issues, such as the "primary parent presumption" and the "approximation rule", see Chapter 5 of our companion book (Birnbaum, Fidler & Kavassalis, 2008; Fidler, 2007). See also the articles in Volume 1, Number 2 of *Child Development Perspecectives* (2007).

separation with its accompanying feelings of loss and sadness for both spouses, a parent working outside the home and relatively uninvolved with the children often begins to realize the need and desire to become more involved in their children's lives. Previously uninvolved or minimally involved parents, while perhaps on a learning curve, will be required after separation to be full-service parents, irrespective of the amount of time the children are in their care. Similarly, a parent doing most of the parenting during cohabitation may either want or be required to return to work outside the home, and will have less time to spend with the child. Changes are inevitable in any family, even when separation does not occur.

The assessor needs to investigate the newly involved parent's willingness and ability to learn, and his or her openness to suggestions and guidance. In addition, the assessor needs to explore the extent to which the more familiar and experienced parent focuses on the other parent's limited involvement, inexperience and parenting weaknesses to the exclusion of the child's need for a good relationship with both parents. The experienced parent's recognition of the other parent's strengths as both a person and parent (i.e., a good friend to others, strong work ethic, good provider to the family, loving son, etc.) is also an important factor to consider.

Another type of parent-child relationship that is underdeveloped or compromised, and not necessarily due to an alienation process *per se*, occurs when a child is distressed and blames one parent for breaking up the family and thereby hurting both the child and the remaining parent. The child may be upset and angry with the departing parent for having a new partner too soon afterwards or for having had an extramarital affair. Similarly, the child may be upset or angry when one parent remarries, even if the new relationship began years after the separation (Warshak, 2000a). The child may occasionally refuse contact in such cases, but not always. For example, the child may be willing to see the parent as long as the new girlfriend or boyfriend is not there. Exacerbating the problem, the non-preferred parent may lack parenting skills (although not to the degree of abuse or neglect) and react defensively, becoming either passive or outwardly angry and counter-rejecting. These reactions are likely to be counterproductive to the extent that they reinforce the child's negative feelings about the offending parent.

The assessor needs to consider whether a child's resistance or refusal may be a means to cope with their hurt and anxiety, and thus be temporary. While some flexibility is necessary on the part of the rejected parent, letting the situation simmer for too long without efforts towards resolution—that is, allowing for a "cooling off period"—is likely to reinforce the rejection. Maintaining appropriate contact and counselling may help to heal the effects of the separation and improve the parent-child relationship problem. Undoubtedly, a child's feelings of hurt, pain and anger in these situations are likely to concern the preferred parent. In fact, not being concerned or not acting in a protective fashion could be construed as poor parenting and dismissive of a child's feelings. While a parent may be exercising good parenting skills, such as active listening and validating the child's feelings, they may be unwittingly reinforcing the child's distress and anger in these circumstances. In these situations, protective parenting is counterproductive. These protective-type reactions, while understandable to a point, may precipitate an incorrect labelling of the protective parent as alienating (Klass & Klass, 2005). The assessment of a protective parent is challenging, and requires that the assessor investigate not only how the preferred parent responds, but also how they do not respond to the child's reactions and emotional needs. Leaving aside for now the debate about whether or not children should be forced to spend time with a rejected parent, the options are not limited to seeing or not seeing the parent. The assessor must question whether in addition to validating the child, the protective parent genuinely recognizes the child's need for a good relationship with the other parent, and furthermore, the extent to which the parent assists the child to develop strategies and coping skills to hopefully resolve the parent-child relationship difficulties. The following questions tap areas of inquiry about the preferred parent that should be investigated:

(1) Does the parent's concern translate into more than just listening and validating?

(2) Does the parent do more than pay lip service to the child's need for a relationship with the other parent?

(3) If so, what does the preferred parent suggest happen to resolve the parent-child relationship problem?

(4) Does the parent propose giving the child indefinite space and time, presumably believing that the problem will improve in time without doing anything?

(5) Would the parent be as passive if the child was repeatedly upset about other concerns, such as a problem with a teacher, coach, grandparent, other relative, or a same-age friend?

(6) Does the parent agree and share with the child the notion that indeed the other parent abandoned them both (i.e., did not want to continue to work on the marriage) and in so doing reinforce the child's hate and rejection?

(7) Does the parent claim that they had a similar experience and know how the child feels, and assert that the child is justified and should not be forced to see the other parent?

(8) Does the parent exploit the child's feelings in the service of lending validation to their own feelings about the other parent?

Preferred (and sometimes non-preferred) parents may make incorrect assumptions and prematurely jump to false conclusions based on a child's behaviour and statements, which may be exaggerated, distorted and reported out of context. A parent may assume that if a child is quiet and does not want to talk about the other parent and about the time spent with them, it is because something bad happened, or the child is uncomfortable with the other parent or the child did not have a good time, when this may not be the case. The child may, in fact, be concerned about their parent's comfort level when hearing positives about the other parent.

A child may tell negative stories about one parent or a situation to gain approval and placate the parent they are with at the time. In telling these stores, a child may have limited ability or inclination to explain the full context of a situation. Vulnerable, hurt and humiliated parents looking for evidence to confirm their own strongly held negative feelings and attitudes often take a child's statements at face value without the appropriate degree of critical thinking or appreciation of the limits of the child's thinking processes and communication abilities. Over-relying on these statements, the parent reacts with concern, disapproval, and sometimes anger, and in so doing further promotes the child's need to appease. Quickly, the child learns to say what they think that parent wants or needs to hear, in order to gain the parent's approval *and* often to avoid their disapproval (and anger and rejection), whether perceived or actual. In such situations, the child does not feel comfortable sharing positive feelings about one parent with the other. The parent's ability and willingness to consider the complexity of these matters, along with alternatives to their assumptions and conclusions, are important to assess.

Realistic Estrangement and Pathological Alienation

As required in cases where domestic violence is alleged (Austin, 2000b, 2001; Bow & Boxer, 2003; Jaffe, Crooks & Bala, 2005; Johnston, 2006), alienation cases require specialized assessment and differential intervention. In cases where allegations of physical or sexual abuse are made, the matter is complicated even further; the assessor must attempt to differentiate *bona fide* and false allegations, keeping in mind the distinction between false but truly believed allegations, and fabricated and malicious allegations.

As we elaborated in Chapters 3 and 4, not all cases of domestic violence are the same (Emery & Laumann-Billings, 1998; Jaffe, Crooks & Bala, 2005; Jaffe *et al.*, 2008; Johnston, 2006; Johnston & Campbell, 1993a). The nature, context, effects and pattern of domestic violence are important considerations. For example, a long-standing pattern of battering (coercive controlling violence) is different from a single incident of mutual pushing at the point of the marital separation. Furthermore, while domestic violence involves conflict, not all high-conflict issues, including power and control struggles, involve domestic violence (Dalton, Carbon & Olesen, 2003; Zibbell, 2005).

Similarly, the more recently developed approaches, decision trees, and rubrics that include the differentiation of various types of parent-child contact problems, including realistic estrangement from pathological alienation, will aid the assessor (see for example, Austin, 2000b, 2001; Drozd & Olesen, 2004; Drozd, Kuehnle, & Walker, 2004; Ellis, 2007; Gardner, 1999d; Jaffe, Crooks & Bala, 2005; Lee & Olesen, 2001).

Drozd and Olesen's (2004) decision tree assists the assessor to differentiate genuine allegations of abuse and neglect from child alienation. Exploring three specific hypotheses will inform decisions regarding avenues to pursue during the assessment, the results of which will inform the recommendations. These hypotheses include:

(1) normal developmental process of the parent-child relationship (ranging from affinity to alliance to alignments with each parent);

(2) the poor-parenting hypothesis (assessing parenting style and fit); and

(3) the abuse hypothesis (asking a number of specific questions that target the issue of whether or not abuse has occurred).

Each hypothesis leads the assessor into different dimensions to further assess both the child and parent variables in a holistic manner. The decision tree also helps describe the range of effects on the child and which recommendation may be most appropriate based on the decision.

Differentiating the symptoms of post-traumatic stress disorder that result from child maltreatment and exposure to domestic violence (i.e., flashbacks, hyper-vigilance, dissociation, numbing, fear of people who resemble the alleged abuser, trauma-specific dreams) from the symptoms of pathological alienation is extremely challenging, even for the most seasoned assessor. In some cases, it may be impossible to formulate a definitive opinion.

Summarizing the literature, Rand (1997a) identified the following motivations for one parent to alienate a child from the other: (a) never having been married and feeling threatened by a possible loss of custody; (b) either parent's having a new partner; (c) narcissistic vulnerability; (d) a need to conceal parental deficits; (e) vulnerability to separation and loss; (f) revenge; and (g) a need for control and domination.

Alienating behaviours range from mild to severe. Table 15 summarizes the literature listing frequently exhibited behaviours of the alienated child, the alienating parent, and the rejected parent.

Table 15: Pathological Alienation: Warning Signs of Behaviours Exhibited by Child, Alienating Parent and Rejected Parent

Child Behaviours:

- View of parents one-sided, all good or all bad; idealizes one parent and devalues the other
- Vicious vilification of target parent; campaign of hatred
- Trivial, false and irrational reasons to justify hatred
- Reactions and perceptions unjustified or disproportionate to parent's behaviours
- Talks openly to anyone about rejected parent's perceived shortcomings
- Extends hatred to extended family and pets (hatred by association)
- No guilt or ambivalence regarding malicious treatment, hatred, etc.
- A stronger, but not necessarily healthy, psychological bond with alienating parent than with rejected parent

- ➢ Anger at rejected parent for abandonment; blames him/her for divorce
- ➢ Speech is brittle, a litany; obsessed; has an artificial quality; affect does not match words; no conviction; unchildlike, uses adult language; has a rehearsed quality
- ➢ Stories are repetitive and lacking in detail and depth
- ➢ Mimics what siblings report rather than own experience
- ➢ Denial of hope for reconciliation; no acknowledgement of desire for reconciliation
- ➢ Expresses worry for preferred parent, desire to care for that parent; or, defensive denial that child is indeed worried about parent

Alienating Parent Behaviours:

- ➢ Allows and insists that child makes decisions about contact
- ➢ Rarely talks about the other parent; uninterested in child's time with other parent after contact; gives a cold shoulder, silent treatment, or is moody after child's return from visit.
- ➢ No photos of target parent; removes reminders of the other parent
- ➢ Refusal to hear positive comments about rejected parent; quick to discount good times as trivial and unimportant
- ➢ No encouragement of calls to other parent between visits; rationalizes that child does not ask
- ➢ Tells child fun things that were missed during visit with other parent
- ➢ Indulges child with material possessions and privileges
- ➢ Sets few limits or is rigid about routines, rules and expectations
- ➢ Refuses to speak directly to parent; refuses to be in same room or close proximity; does not let target parent come to door to pick up child
- ➢ No concern for missed visits with other parent
- ➢ Makes statements and then denies what was said
- ➢ Body language and nonverbal communication reveals lack of interest, disdain and disapproval
- ➢ Engages in inquisition of child after visits

- ➢ Rejected parent is discouraged or refused permission to attend school events and activities
- ➢ Telephone messages, gifts and mail from other parent to child are destroyed, ignored or passed on to the child with disdain
- ➢ Distorts any comments of child that might justify accusations
- ➢ Doesn't believe that child has any need for relationship with other parent
- ➢ When child calls and is quiet or non-communicative, parent wrongly assumes pressure from target parent, or that child is not comfortable with target parent; evidence of bad parenting; does not appreciate that child is uncomfortable talking to alienating parent about target parent
- ➢ Portrays other parent as dangerous, may inconsistently act fearful of other parent in front of child
- ➢ Exaggerates negative attributes of other parent, and omits anything positive
- ➢ Delusional false statements repeated to child; distorts history and other parent's participation in the child's life; claims other parent has totally changed since separation
- ➢ Projection of own thoughts, feelings and behaviours onto the other parent
- ➢ Does not correct child's rude, defiant and/or omnipotent behaviour directed towards the other parent, but would not permit child to do this with others
- ➢ Convinced of harm, when there is no evidence
- ➢ False or fabricated allegations of sexual, physical and/or emotional abuse
- ➢ Denigrates and exaggerates flaws of rejected parent to child
- ➢ Says other parent left "us", divorced "us" and doesn't love "us"
- ➢ Over-involves child in adult matters and litigation
- ➢ Child required to keep secrets and spy or report back on other parent
- ➢ Child required to be messenger
- ➢ Overt and covert threats to withdraw love and affection from child unless other parent is rejected
- ➢ Extreme lack of courtesy to rejected parent

- Relocation for minor reasons and with little concern for effects on child

Parental Behaviours of the Target (Rejected) Parent that Perpetrate Rejection or Alienation:

- Harsh, rigid and punitive parenting style
- Outrage at child's challenge to his/her authority
- Passivity or withdrawal in face of conflict
- Immature, self-centred in relation to child
- Loses temper, angry, demanding, intimidating character traits, but not to level of abuse
- Counter-rejecting behaviour
- Lacks empathic connection to child
- Inept and unempathic pursuit of child, pushes calls and letters, unannounced or embarrassing visits
- Challenges child's beliefs and/or attitudes and tries to convince them otherwise
- Dismissive of child's feelings and negative attitudes
- Induces guilt
- May use force to reassert parental position
- Vents rage, blames alienating parent for brainwashing child and takes no responsibility

Often there is a kernel of truth to a child's complaints and allegations about a rejected parent. In these "mixed" cases, there may be good reasons for the child to reject the parent, while there is also a definite alienation process occurring. How the preferred parent reacts may make or break the relationship with the other parent.

Some preferred parents are hypersensitive and psychologically vulnerable, having experienced their own trauma and deprivation as children coupled with the more recent separation, which has left them feeling hurt, angry and humiliated (Jaffe *et al.*, 2008). These parents may lean on their children for emotional support and use them as weapons to punish their former spouse. Consciously or unconsciously, and out of feelings of betrayal, rejection and humiliation associated with the separation, the preferred parent (and many times their family and friends) may reinforce the child's complaints to the point of exaggeration, which may even result in distortion in their own and the child's memories (Johnston, 2006).

The child may have been abused or subjected to poor parenting; however, the rejection of a parent sometimes results more from the influence of the other parent than "the incident" itself (Johnston, 2001; Warshak, 2002). Before the separation, there may have been traumatic incidents, sometimes only one, which end up forming a basis for the child's estrangement from the perpetrator. Johnston (2006) explains that after separation, traumatic events may be repeatedly evoked, and even used strategically by the preferred parent and other family members to advance litigation and in effect keep the other parent from the child. Using Johnston's term, the incident becomes a "legend" that lives on through the aforementioned "snowball effect" that arises from a mutually reinforcing feedback loop. The incident may become embellished to the extent of distortion. In these situations, the child may display a mixture of realistic and unrealistic fear, anger, and avoidance that needs to be carefully pursued by the assessor.

As noted previously, the assessor must investigate how each parent has responded and not responded to such incidents. For example:

(1) In the case of an isolated incident, did the preferred parent attempt to protect the child from exposure to the incident?

(2) How did the preferred parent comfort the child?

(3) Did the preferred parent attempt to protect the child from their own emotional reaction, or did that parent emphasize the perceived trauma to the child in order to gain support, and in effect be parented by the child?

(4) Did the preferred parent help the child to not only identify and express their feelings, but also to cope with them by resolving and repairing the relationship with the other parent?

(5) Does the rejected parent acknowledge the transgression, apologize, and proceed to learn from their mistakes, or does the parent remain defensive, externalize responsibility, and repeat the same mistakes?

As previously noted, just as the assessor must consider that there may be valid reasons relating to maltreatment or domestic violence for a child to reject a parent, the assessor must also consider that these allegations may be false or substantially exaggerated, whether intentionally or unintentionally. The memory and child development literature confirms that children can be easily manipulated. Children are susceptible to creating false memories and to believing and repeating suggestions implanted by adults and adult interviewers, especially if the adult is a respected authority figure, like a parent (Ceci & Bruck, 1995; Ceci & Friedman, 2000; Kuehnle, Greenberg & Gottlieb, 2004; Poole & Lindsay, 1995; Pool & White, 1991, 1993). Assessors must have knowledge of and experience in child-interview techniques as well as knowledge about the suggestibility of children, memory, persuasion and influence.[15]

An example of a case where the father claimed that the child was alienated but the court concluded that a child was justifiably estranged from a parent is the 2008 Ontario case of *Azimi v. Mirzaei*.[16] Justice Horkins accepted the evidence of a social worker from the Office of the Children's Lawyer that the reason for a nine year old girl not wanting to see her father was that he had been emotionally abusive towards her, for example yelling at her during her piano practicing. Further, he had assaulted and verbally abused the mother prior to the parent's separation, causing the child to be frightened of him. Finally, he moved from the family home without warning and failed to communicate with the mother and child for several weeks. Thereafter, the child was reluctant to see him, and she resisted spending time with him during supervised visits. The judge accepted that the girl was aligned with her mother, but concluded that she was not brainwashed as she had her own understandable reasons for both fearing her father and feeling rejected by him. Even though her safety could be assured by having supervised visits, it was contrary to her best interests to force her to visit with her father. However, the judge directed that the mother, who had limited means, was to try to obtain appropriate publicly funded counselling for the child with a view to having the relationship with the father re-established and was to regularly provide information to the father, and further ordered that the court would retain jurisdiction over the case with a case conference to be held after a year if access was not resumed.

---

[15] For further information see Chapters 2 and 3 in our companion book (Birnbaum, Fidler & Kavassalis, 2008). For further information on the assessment of sexual abuse, see Bala, Mitnick, Trocmé and Houston, (2007b); Bernet (2006); Bruck, Ceci and Hembrooke (1998); Rand, (1993); Doris (1991); Gardner (1987, 1992b); Gould (2006); Gould and Martindale (2007); Hewitt (1999); Kuehnle (1996, 2003); Ney (1995), Poole and Lamb (1998); Wakefield (2006); and Zaragoza, Graham, Hall, Hirschman and Ben-Porath (1995).

[16] 2007 CarswellOnt 2999, [2007] O.J. No. 1824 (Ont. S.C.J.).

The Need for Early Intervention

The literature consistently stresses the need for prevention and early intervention in cases involving parent-child contact problems. A majority of researchers reject the view advanced by a few (see Bruch, 2001a; Faller, 1997; Wallerstein & Blakeslee, 1989) that rejection of any kind—especially for the older child, is a normal part of divorce and that it is best to leave well enough alone, as the child will "come around".

As previously noted in our discussions of children's views and preferences, research indicates that children of divorced parents usually want to spend time with both parents, and many long at the time or in hindsight for more, rather than less, time with the non-custodial parent (Fabricius & Hall, 2000; Laumann-Billings & Emery, 2000; Rosen, 1979; Wallerstein & Kelly, 1980).

Most writers agree that unjustified alienation is a form of emotional abuse that should be addressed. Preliminary data on the long-term negative effects of alienation from a parent are sobering (Baker, 2005a, 2005b, 2006). Johnston writes that "alienating behaviour by parents is a malignant form of emotional abuse of children that needs to be corrected, whether a parent agrees or not" (Johnston, 2005a, p. 770). She and other writers have pointed to the growing body of literature documenting the negative effects of psychological control and intrusive parenting on children (see for example Barber, 2002).

Child protection legislation, such as Ontario's *Child and Family Services Act* ("CFSA"),[17] specifies that emotional abuse is a form of child abuse that must be reported to child protection authorities. This includes emotional abuse, if sufficiently severe, arising from adult conflict. Amendments to the Ontario legislation enacted in 2000 established a lower threshold for emotional abuse than previously existed. Reflecting this legislative provision, Section 3 (Emotional Harm), Scale 2 (Child Exposure to Adult Conflict) of the 2000 Ontario Child Welfare Eligibility Spectrum (2000), a tool that was used to determine whether child protection services should be provided, included the statement about situations of emotional abuse:

> The verbal aggression between the caregivers and the attempts to have the child align with one caregiver versus another is having a significant emotional effect on the child, such that the child is demonstrating serious anxiety, depression, withdrawal, self-destructive or aggressive behaviour, or delayed development. Neither caregiver is acting in a way to

---

[17] R.S.O. 1990, c. C.11, as amended; see s. 37 (2) subsections (a), (b), (f) (f.1), (g) and (g.1).

> address the emotional well-being of the child or to provide services to remedy the situation. (p. 60)

Unfortunately, the October 2006 version of the Spectrum removed the reference to alignment with one parent, though retaining within the eligibility criteria cases where there is the risk of emotional harm due to significant conflict or violence between marital partners as a result of a custody dispute over a child (p. 65). While the more recent version confirms there is a risk of emotional harm in custody-disputing families, we find this change regrettable. The change does, however, reflect the reality that child protection agencies, with their limited resources, are reluctant to become involved in high conflict divorces that raise issues of alienation and emotional abuse but do not involve allegations of domestic violence or physical abuse.

In family law cases the courts have recognized that alienating behaviour is emotionally abusive to children. Children in the midst of custody disputes tend to protect their parents, and are themselves emotionally injured when matters like parental alienation, coaching, or exposure to adult-oriented discussions occur. The Court of Appeal in British Columbia considered the issue in *A. (A.) v. A. (S.N.)*[18] In this case, the trial judge found that it would be "emotionally detrimental" for a ten year old child to remain with her mother, as the Court appointed assessor and trial judge found her to be a "highly manipulative" and "intransigent" parent, "blind to [the child's] interest". The actions of the mother and maternal grandmother foreclosed any positive relationship between the child and the father while the child remained in the care of the mother. Despite all of this, the trial judge awarded custody to the mother, as the child stated that she did not want to see her father. The appellate court, in reversing the trial decision and awarding the father custody, determined, based on the trial judge's findings that it was almost certain that the child, if she remained in the care of the mother with contact with the grandmother, would continue to suffer psychological and emotional harm. The appeal court concluded that:

> . . . the trial judge erred in law in not favouring [the child's] . . . long-term best interests in having a stable home with her father and his extended family over the destructive kind of care that has been provided by the mother and grandmother.[19]

---

18 2007 CarswellBC 1591, 2007 BCCA 363, [2007] B.C.J. No. 1474, 40 R.F.L. (6th) 248 (B.C. C.A.).

19 *Ibid.*

Reviews of social science literature clearly reveal that children are better off psychologically and developmentally in two-parent families than in single-parent families, and further that the effects of father loss due to separation or divorce are greater than that due to paternal death (Amato, 2001; Lamb, 1999). Related findings indicate that children of divorce generally benefit from meaningful relationships with both parents (Kelly & Emery, 2003).

Warshak (2006) astutely points out that in non-divorced families, in the absence of neglect or abuse, it is unlikely for a parent-child contact problem to be ignored, or for contact between the child and the hated parent to be suspended. Even if the problem appears mild and is in the early stages, intervention of some sort, usually involving immediate efforts to restore contact, is warranted to prevent the development of a more severe problem. Delays are likely to reinforce the child's phobic rejection of the parent (Cartwright, 2006; Clawar & Rivlin, 1991; Lowenstein, 2005a; Rand, Rand & Kopetski, 2005; Gardner, 2001b; Johnston, 2005a; Warshak, 2002).

Interim orders are made based on documents filed with the courts, including affidavits from the parties and an assessment report, if one has been prepared. Because there is generally no oral testimony or opportunity for cross-examination of witnesses, judges are generally reluctant to make orders upsetting the status quo at the interim stage. However, in making interim orders, the courts sometimes recognize the need for early intervention in moderate or severe alienation cases, especially where there is an assessment report available recommending such action. For example, in the 2008 Ontario of *Cojbasic v. Cojbasic*[20] where the father claimed that the mother was alienating the three children from him and brought an interim motion for joint custody, Justice Mackinnon observed: "There is clear authority for awards of joint custody and equal residential care, if necessary, in order to protect a child's relationship with a parent. . . However, it is true to say that most such decisions are made following a trial of the issues."[21] The judge noted that as she was faced with conflicting evidence at the motion, she would not make an interim order varying custody. However, she was satisfied that the mother's home environ ment was clearly "negative towards the father" and extended his access at the interim stage in the hope that this would be "adequate to offset the influences in the mother's home and to recognize the importance of the father-son relationship" (para. 13).

---

[20] 2008 CarswellOnt 1230, 52 R.F.L. (6th) 191 (Ont. S.C.J.).

[21] *Ibid.*, at para 2.

In the 2007 Ontario case of *Pettenuzzo-Deschene v. Deschene*,[22] Whalen J. was satisfied at an interim motion that there was a need for "urgent intervention", relying significantly on the views of a court appointed assessor to conclude that the mother was alienating the two children, aged seven and almost four, from their father. The children were refusing visits because the mother had projected her beliefs about father onto children with result that they were afraid of father. The judge ordered that the children were to immediately be placed in the interim care of their father, with the mother to have no access for 10 days, and thereafter supervised access for up to two hours a week, with a judicial review after 6 weeks. The expectation of Whalen J. was that this was to be a temporary arrangement, to alter the attitudes of the children and mother in the five months before a full trial. He observed:

> If all goes well, I would expect that the children might be returned to the primary care of the wife with reasonable generous access, including overnight and a fair share of holidays and special occasions, being granted to the husband. I perceived that the husband does not want to tear the children from the wife on a permanent basis and that he recognizes their attachment to her. The restoration of joint custody on an interim basis is not intended to signal anything more than that the parties are both parents of these children and that both are able to provide care. In any event, I do not regard my present order setting or contemplating a permanent situation beyond the purposes of the reintroduction and adjustment expressed. (para. 65)

Given the need for early intervention and the inevitability of a delay in securing an assessor and completing a full assessment (not to mention the financial cost), an assessor may choose to explore treatment alternatives with the lawyers during the referral stage. This is an important consideration, as it is not uncommon for treatment to be recommended in any event. As previously noted, alienation is likely to worsen the longer it remains unaddressed, and because of the assessment itself.

We have found that if parents, in the early stages of mild and sometimes moderate cases of parental alienation, can agree that it is indeed in their child's best interest to have contact with the rejected parent, a treatment intervention may be preferable to a court-ordered assessment. If parent-child contact is warranted and both parents agree, it should be clearly delineated in an on-consent court order. In such cases a more limited assessment would be undertaken for the

---

[22] 2007 CarswellOnt 5095, 40 R.F.L. (6th) 381, [2007] O.J. No. 3062 (Ont. S.C.J.).

purposes of therapy, which could result in a recommendation being made for a full court-ordered assessment (to be carried out by another professional) if serious allegations of abuse emerge. A safeguard is that the therapist would be required to report to the child protection authorities any reasonable suspicions of abuse or neglect. However, when such an agreement is not possible (or genuine) and a parent continues to dispute whether it is indeed in the child's best interests to have contact with the rejected parent, a comprehensive custody assessment will be necessary.

The Role of the Courts in Intervention and Treatment

Separation agreements, minutes of settlement, and court orders containing custody and access provisions for high-conflict families often lack sufficient detail and precision. Ambiguities and insufficient detail in court orders or parenting plans only serve to exacerbate parental conflict. In alienation cases, any opportunity for the alienating custodial parent to control the access schedule may be exploited. Incomplete or ambiguous parenting plans provide one such opportunity. Although more recently agreements and court orders detailing parenting plans have tended to provide more breadth and specificity, the need for highly structured and specified orders in high-conflict families cannot be overstated (Fidler, 2007).[23] In order for a judgment of the court to be effective in cases of alienation, the order must be detailed, explicit, and comprehensive; these are sometimes referred to as "multi-directional" orders, with directions not only for both parents, but also for third parties such as schools and health care providers (Bala *et al.*, 2007a; Sullivan & Kelly, 2001; Turkat, 1994).

Under s. 28 of the *Children's Law Reform Act*[24] and s. 16(6) of the *Divorce Act*, the court has the authority to impose terms and condi-

---

[23] We elaborate more fully on parenting plans for high-conflict families in our companion book (see Chapter 5 in Birnbaum, Fidler & Kavassalis, 2008). These need to include and address many issues, including: principles of good parenting, rules of engagement and direction to keep children out of parental conflict; detailed parenting-time schedules for both regular and holiday periods; precise start and stop times for parenting times; the location of transitions; who transports the children, and in which direction; parental behaviour during transitions; who cares for the children when they become ill in the morning before school and during school; precise and unabmbiguous rules about parental communication and information exchange; rules about travelling out of jurisdiction; provisions for how day-to-day (i.e., extra-curricular activities, information exchanges, clothing and belongings, etc.) and major (health/medical, education, religion) child-related decisions are made; parent–child telephone and email contact; procedures for making temporary changes to the schedule, and so on.

[24] R.S.O. 1990, c. C.12, as am.

tions to a custody or access order and, the jurisdiction to order a parent to provide a child with counselling as an "incident of custody or access" (Bala, Fidler, Goldberg & Houston, 2007a). There is debate, however, regarding the court's authority to order counselling for parents in the absence of their consent (Epstein, 2007). Case law reveals that some judges have ordered counselling for parents without the consent of the parties, in some cases as an element of a custody or access order, and in other cases as part of a sentence for contempt of an access order.[25] In other cases, judges may encourage parents to attend counselling and to incorporate their consent into an order.

In the 2008 Ontario case of *L. (J.K.) v. S. (N.C.)*,[26] Justice Turnbull did not accept the arguments from the father's lawyer that the 13-year old boy could not be forced to participate in counseling and the Family Workshop for Alienated Children (FWAC), provided by Drs. Rand and Warshak, without first providing his consent. The child's wishes were not considered to be a valid reason for not participating in counselling. In addition to noting the need to consider the rationality of the wishes and the presence of undue influence on these, Justice Turnbull noted that courts order children to participate in counselling regularly. In this particular case, the judge had granted custody to the rejected mother and held that, as the parent with custody, she had the discretion to seek the involvement of FWAC. The Court also ordered that, assuming that the workshop had been completed by the child, the alienating (former custodial) parent was to undertake reintegration counselling with the child. Justice Turnbull stated:

> I do not consider, as submitted by the respondent [the alienating father], that the *Health Care Consent Act, 1996*, S.O. 1996, c. 2, was intended to trump the discretion of the court under sections 16 and 17 of the *Divorce Act* . . . in issues of custody and access. They have different legislative purposes.[27]

He further noted that the *Health Care Consent Act* is not meant to apply to a situation involving the need to remedy a severe alienation (or any conduct) where the best interests of the child are violated.

---

[25] See *Kramer v. Kramer*, 2003 CarswellOnt 1228, 37 R.F.L. (5th) 381, [2003] O.J. No. 1418 (Ont. S.C.J.), *Gendreau v. Campbell*, 2005 CarswellMan 372, 198 Man. R. (2d) 297, 2005 MBQB 224, 20 R.F.L. (6th) 270 (Man. Q.B.); and *Kaplanis v. Kaplanis*, 2005 CarswellOnt 266, 10 R.F.L. (6th) 373, 194 O.A.C. 106, 249 D.L.R. (4th) 620, [2005] O.J. No. 275 (Ont. C.A.), reversing 2003 CarswellOnt 2593, 42 R.F.L. (5th) 373 (Ont. S.C.J.).

[26] 2008 CarswellOnt 2903 (Ont. S.C.J.).

[27] *Ibid.*, para. 192.

The involvement of the court is critical, not only for the effective implementation of a parenting plan (parenting time and decision making), but also for the effective implementation of any treatment or intervention plan in alienation cases (Bala *et al.*, 2007a; Baris *et al.*, 2000; Cartwright, 2006; Everett, 2006; Gardner, 1998c, 2001d; Johnston, Walters & Friedlander, 2001; Lee & Olesen, 2001; Lund, 1995; Lowenstein, 2005a; Rand & Warshak, 2006; Sullivan, 2004; Sullivan & Kelly, 2001; Warshak, 2006; Walsh & Bone, 1997). Given the difficulties of effectively implementing and obtaining compliance with treatment, it is advisable that terms for treatment be translated into an order. Table 16 lists the suggested components of such an order, some of which we elaborate below.

Table 16: Court Order Requirements for Intervention and Counselling

1. Provide structured and specified parenting plan
2. Identify objectives of therapy/intervention
3. Identify minimum period for therapy/intervention
4. Identify the names of professionals who will provide therapy/intervention; failing that, a process for selecting professionals in the event the parents cannot agree[28]
5. Clarify the terms for the parents' withdrawal from services and the procedures for selecting new therapists
6. Identify the specific role of each professional, including scope of decision-making powers, if any
7. Name any specific seminars or educational programs parents are to attend
8. Name the family members who are to participate in the therapy/intervention
9. State that the professionals are entitled to communicate with each other as deemed necessary by the therapist and that the parents will execute any necessary authorizations to allow for the exchange of information
10. State that the parents will cooperate with the therapist
11. Clarify the limits of confidentiality, if any, including reporting requirements to court
12. Identify enforcement clauses (i.e., sanctions, consequences for non-compliance, options to prevent change of custody, etc.)
13. Specify any grievance procedures
14. Clarify details of payment for services

[28] To prevent "therapist shopping", this may include a term that there will not be any unauthorized involvement of new therapists.

Articulating the goals of intervention and counselling in the court order is imperative. As we have noted previously, children living in these circumstances often, although not always, experience many problems, not only those relating to a rejected parent. It is likely that the alienating parent will find the notion of treatment more palpable and in turn will be more amendable to ensuring the child attends if the goals recognize the child's global needs and the benefits of treatment. Specifically, Johnston (2006) and others have advised that there are other goals of treatment that should be identified in addition to implementing court-ordered parenting time for a child and rejected parent. These may include: (a) protecting and removing the child from parental conflict; (b) fostering the child's healthy relationship with *both* parents; (c) restoring the parents' adequate functioning and appropriate roles; (d) correcting the various cognitive distortions, polarization and splitting present in parents and child; (e) augmenting the child's coping skills and improving appropriate expression of the child's affect; (f) replacing inaccuracies and distortions with more realistic perceptions that reflect the child's actual experience with both parents; and (g) improving the child's peer relationships. In other words, treatment involves assisting children to differentiate themselves from others, become autonomous and, in effect, reach their own conclusions about both parents and their relationships with relatives. Sometimes, with explanation and education, an older child may come to understand how and even why the alienation occurred; how they came to believe what they did (Rand & Warshak, 2006; Warshak, 2006).

It is imperative that the order specifically name the persons required to participate in the therapy or intervention, as it is not uncommon for an alienating parent to refuse to attend, claiming that it is the rejected parent who has problems. The alienating parent may also claim an inability to force a child to attend against their will. Regardless of who has caused the problem, or the relative contributions of each parent, both parents are important components of the solution. A family-systems approach, involving various family members and sometimes extended family in various combinations, is the preferred model for treatment (Sullivan & Kelly, 2001).

The steps for assigning a new therapist must be articulated in the order if the duration of service is not indicated, to address the possibility that one parent may refuse to participate, or if the therapist resigns. The order also needs to clarify that there is no confidentiality amongst family members, the therapist and the various professionals involved. While the therapist can and does use discretion, he or she cannot promise, that information provided by one parent will not be communicated to the other parent. Lack of vigilance regarding these common scenarios can cause delays and in all likelihood contribute to prolonging, if not exacerbating, the parent child relationship problems.

Whether or not treatment ought to remain confidential, and thus out of court, is debatable. A confidential process has the benefit of avoiding the negative impacts of public shame and humiliation on the alienating parent. The risk lies in shielding the personality disorders and negative characteristics of parents who tend to show blatant disregard for authority and court orders (Bernstein, 2007; Greenberg, Gould, Schnider, Gould-Saltman & Martindale, 2003; Johnston & Campbell, 1993b; Johnston & Roseby, 1997; Johnston, Walters & Friedlander, 2001; Lebow & Rekart, 2007; Sullivan, 2004; Sullivan & Kelly, 2001). Circumstances vary, and a confidential process may be indicated for some families and not for others. Our experience is that in most moderate and severe cases, the benefits to the child of the therapist's having the possibility of reporting back to the court directly or to a parenting coordinator or arbitrator—with some procedures for preserving the child's confidences—exceed any benefits associated with confidentiality.

While reporting to the court and full exchange of information amongst the team of professionals is potentially important, work with children can be compromised if the therapist does not use discretion in disclosing information. When a parenting coordinator is involved (see elaboration that follows), therapists, collateral sources and children alike are free to communicate with the coordinator, who in turn reports to the court. The parenting coordinator may in some instances be able to protect the participants by using different sources of information to formulate any opinions provided to the court and/or delivery of any awards (Johnston, 2001; Sullivan, 2004; Sullivan & Kelly, 2001).

Models of Intervention

Various intervention models, ranging from the involvement of a single professional to the participation of a team of professionals, are available. Each of these models requires careful consideration when trying to meet the varied needs of each family. Irrespective of the model chosen, it is imperative that each professional involved has a written agreement, preferably made into an on-consent order for services.[29]

If only one professional (not the assessor) is employed, that person is often relied upon to assume multiple roles, including individual

[29] See Appendix B for a sample agreement for services.

therapist to one or more of the family members, visitation facilitator, family therapist, or parenting coordinator. In these roles, the professional may simultaneously provide reunification or reconciliation therapy, as well as family therapy and individual therapy to one or more members, while also being responsible for monitoring the implementation of a court-ordered parenting plan, reporting to court, making recommendations, and/or making decisions with respect to parenting time or other related matters. Taking on such multiple roles often leads to complications and poses ethical dilemmas.

Roles involving decision-making or arbitrating commonly fall under the title of parenting coordinator or mediator/arbitrator in Ontario (Special Master in California) (Association of Family and Conciliation Courts, 2005; Baris *et al.*, 2000; Boyan & Termini, 2004; Coates, 2003; Coates, Deutsch, Starnes, Sullivan, & Sydlik, 2004; Garrity & Baris, 1994). Coates *et al.* (2004) define parenting coordination as an intervention for high-conflict families in which the coordinator helps the parents implement their parenting plan, most typically one that has already been determined by agreement of the parties or the court. Parenting coordinators are usually retained for a term that lasts between 18 and 24 months.[30]

The single-professional model was more common during the earlier development of intervention models in cases involving alienation (see for example, Garrity & Baris, 1994), and is sometimes still used where resources are limited. It is often very difficult, if not impossible, for one professional to achieve the desired objectives and meet all of the various, complex and often competing needs of family members, let alone assume additional roles, such as arbitration, that may compromise the practitioner's effectiveness and neutrality in the eyes of the family. Similar to the problems inherent in an individual parent's or child therapist's offering recommendations in a custody case (Greenberg & Gould, 2001; Greenberg & Shuman, 1997), being a therapist and decision maker of whatever sort amounts to assuming a dual role that poses serious ethical issues (Greenberg, Gould, Schnider, Gould-Saltman & Martindale, 2003; Kirkland & Kirkland, 2006; Ontario Psychological Association, 1998; Sullivan, 2004). The model we are proposing permits the role of the family therapist (or the visitation facilitator) to remain distinct from that of the parenting coordinator or mediator/arbitrator.

---

[30] See Association of Family and Conciliation Courts (AFCC) Task Force on Parenting Coordination, (2003) and Parenting Coordination: Implementation Issues, *Family Court Review* (2003), *41,* 533–564.) Also see *Guidelines for Parenting Coordination* developed by the AFCC Task Force on Parenting Coordination, May, 2005, which can be found at: http://www.afccnet.org. See Fidler and Epstein (2008).

When it is not possible to engage more than one professional, caution should be exercised in having a therapist or visitation facilitator also assume the role of decision-maker (arbitrating parenting time beyond minor or temporary changes), because the two roles may work at cross-purposes. More specifically, if the child and the alienating parent believe the therapist/facilitator has the authority to determine whether or not access occurs, there is little likelihood of progress to achieve the stated objectives of the work. It is far preferable for a therapist/facilitator to be able to say that they understand that the child does not want to see the parent, while also noting that they have no control over parenting time schedule/orders. The therapist/facilitator can then advise the child that their role is to assist in implementing the court-ordered parenting time and to work towards making this time be as good as it can possibly be. The child is then invited to participate by expressing their concerns and providing their ideas about how to make that time manageable and enjoyable.

Just as there is no confidentiality between participants and with respect to reporting to the court, there cannot be restrictions on the ability of the various professionals to exchange information with each other and this must be explicitly stated in the court order for the intervention. A parenting coordinator's function as case manager is imperative when there is more than one professional actively involved with the family. In this role, the parenting coordinator attempts to ensure team consistency and continuity in an effort to avoid the splitting or pitting of one professional against the other, as polarization of professionals is frequently seen in high-conflict families, particularly in alienation cases. As case manager, the parenting coordinator directs and manages the team of professionals, defines *consistent* treatment goals, and facilitates the ongoing exchange of information amongst the team members, while being mindful not to undermine the client's relationship with their therapist. The parenting coordinator's scope of decision-making may include the appointment of additional members to the professional team when parents cannot agree.

Naturally, the family's financial resources are an important consideration. In addition to criticism for being intrusive and inappropriately leaving decisions to those other than the judiciary (Bruch, 2001a), the significant costs of the various treatment models preclude many families from receiving these services.

Treatment Modality

Notwithstanding the controversy surrounding issues relating to child alienation, there is considerable consensus about not only the need for counselling and intervention, but also about the treatment modality for mild and some moderate cases of alienation. Experienced assessors typically recommend a *family-systems approach* to intervention by an experienced and trained therapist for milder cases.[31] Notwithstanding the reported need for a family approach, survey results reported by Bow, Gould and Flens (2006) indicate that, in cases of alienation, the most common recommendation of assessors is for individual therapy for the child and the parents. In our practices, we frequently receive referrals for individual child therapy from lawyers, judges, assessors and therapists. A family-systems approach involves the participation of the entire family in various combinations, sometimes including other relatives such as step-parents, step-siblings, and grandparents (Everett, 2006; Cartwright, 2006; Gardner, 1998a, 1998c, 2001c; Lee & Olesen, 2001; Lowenstein, 1998; Johnston, 2005b; Johnston, Walters & Friedlander, 2001; Sullivan & Kelly, 2001). It may also include other professionals who have been involved with the family. Individual therapy for the child by either the same or a different therapist working as a member of a team, without the inclusion of other family members, is likely to deter the effectiveness of the intervention.[32]

Gardner identified three types or levels of PAS—mild, moderate, and severe—to qualify both the child's and alienating parent's symptoms, along with different management and treatment interventions for each of the three levels.[33] In mild cases, there is some alienating conduct by the custodial parent, but parent-child contact is not seriously disrupted and the child manages transitions without too much difficulty. The child has a reasonably healthy relationship with the both parents.

In moderate cases, there is a significant degree of alienating conduct by the custodial parent, along with significant struggles around contact with the other parent. While difficulties are encountered at transitions, the child usually settles down in reasonably short order and enjoys the time with the parent available at the time. In addition, the bond between alienating parent and child appears reasonably healthy, although the two still share a conviction that the rejected parent is essentially bad or unworthy.

---

[31] This requires training and experience in systemic therapies, high-conflict, separation/divorce, alienation, custody/access-disputing families, and personality disorders.

[32] Frequently, therapists not familiar with high-conflict and custody-litigating families may be of the mistaken view that only individual therapy for the child (or one or both of the parents) is indicated.

[33] See Gardner (2004), p. 619; Gardner (2006), p. 8–10.

One of the goals for therapy in both mild and moderate cases of alienation is to implement a court-ordered parenting time schedule, preferably detailed and unambiguous, in which allotted times for the rejected parent may gradually increase. Specifying that an alienating parent is to retain legal custody if the court-ordered parenting time is followed, may provide the much needed reassurance to the parent and decrease insecurities to the extent that the parent, in addition to participating meaningfully in the treatment intervention, will also actively encourage the child to do so as well, and further, outwardly support the child's relationship with the other parent (Gardner, 2001d; Rand, 1997a; Warshak, 2001b). Further, an explicit message from the court to the custodial (alienating) parent about the need for them to comply with court orders and alter behaviour if custody is to be retained may encourage compliance with the treatment plan.

Initially, a child's contact with a rejected parent may be limited to therapy sessions (also referred to as "therapeutic access" or "reintegration therapy or counseling"). Depending on the degree of the child's reaction and alienation, individual sessions (not individual therapy) may help the child prepare for eventual sessions with a rejected parent. For example, the court order may require that the child will attend three individual sessions, followed by three months of therapeutic access (sessions with the rejected parent, with the alienating parent's participation as directed by the therapist). Also, the therapist's office can be used as a transitional site where the therapist meets with family members (including the alienating parent) both before and after parent-child contact. The ultimate goal is for the court-ordered parenting time to occur without the need for the therapist's involvement. Sessions before and soon after parent-child contact can monitor and assess the family's progress, and provide expedient intervention where required.

In some cases, the therapist (or parenting coordinator, if there is one) is given the authority to adjust the pacing of the implementation of the parenting time by either increasing it or decreasing it depending on how the treatment is progressing. As previously noted, it is important that the therapist *not* be in a position to determine the parenting-time schedule beyond some minor tweaking; this should be the responsibility of the court or a separate arbitrator. Alternatively, an assessor could make recommendations to the court, relying as well on the reports of the therapist and parenting coordinator where relevant. When there is no assessor, the therapist or parenting coordinator would report on the process and progress, both positive and negative, to counsel and court as required.

Another option, short of reversing custody, is for the order to include a prolonged period of contact with the rejected parent—for example, over the summer school break period—coupled with intervention and restricted time with the alienating parent. This arrangement may be more palatable than reversing custody permanently, while also affording the child and rejected parent the uninterrupted time needed to repair and rebuild their relationship. Peggy Ward and her colleagues have developed a 3-day summer camp where the family, in various combinations, participates in an intervention program along with other families also experiencing parent-child contact problems (Peggy Ward, personal communication 2007).

Once any risk of harm has been ruled out, it is important that the reunification or reconciliation of a child with a rejected parent not be referred to as "supervised access", and that it not take place at a supervised access centre identified as such, as this is likely to reinforce the child's irrational fears (Johnston, 2005a, 2006).

Specific intervention strategies in mild and moderate cases of alienation are based on the individual needs of the family and the degree of aleination demonstrated. An overview of specific intervention strategies for child, alienated and alienating parent and any dyads, etc. is beyond the scope of this chapter.[34]

Deciding to Give Up

In some cases, giving up the struggle to maintain a relationship may be the least detrimental alternative for children who have been severely alienated. This may be especially true for cases involving older children, or situations where the rejected parent is unsuitable or unwilling to have custody, and no measures other than custody reversal will have an effect on the alienation. There are also many cases in which the rejected parent will lack the emotional or financial resources to continue the struggle.

In some of these cases, the access parent may voluntarily give up the effort to seek to enforce access rights. Occasionally, the judge may decide that it is not appropriate to order or enforce access,[35] or may offer comments suggesting that continuing efforts to enforce access may not be in the child's best interests,[36] and ceasing the effort to

---

[34] See: Carey, Sullivan and Ward (2007), Coates, *et al.* (2004), Freeman, Abel, Cooper-Smith and Stein (2004), Gardner (1999c, 2001d), Everett (2006), Johnston (2005a, 2005b), Johnston, Walters and Friedlander (2001), Sullivan and Kelly (2001), Ward and Harvey (1993), Warshak (2001b), De Vries and Niemi (2007).

[35] See *Bailey v. Bailey*, [1996] O.J. No. 4891 (Ont. Gen. Div.); *Roda v. Roda*, 2000 CarswellOnt 3558, [2000] O.J. No. 3786 (Ont. S.C.J.).

[36] See *P. (J.E.) v. W. (H.J.)*, 1987 CarswellSask 68, 11 R.F.L. (3d) 136 (Sask. Q.B.), where a six year old girl had an aversion towards her father because of the mother's hostility to him. The mother was opposed to access, despite mediation efforts. The court refused to order access, at least until "the child is considerably older". See also

continue the relationship may be the "least detrimental alternative". In the 2006 Ontario case of *El-Murr v. Kiameh*,[37] Katarynch J. commented:

> Perhaps this boy is best served at this time in his life by being left in peace. He has been given to opportunity open himself to a reunion with his father. He has declined the opportunity.
>
> . . . There is no benefit for the father at this time—just a faint hope. It is cruel to keep alive hope that is faint, when there is no indication on the evidence that this child is likely to open himself to his father in the near future. . .
>
> Whatever the benefit, it is no more than a potential. At this point in this child's life, his actuality is that he has moved on to establish a father-and-son relationship with his stepfather. From his perspective, he does not need any other father-and-son relationship. (paras. 28-31)

In these situations, the children will likely feel abandoned under such circumstances, notwithstanding any stated wishes and protestations of hate and rejection. It may be appropriate for the rejected parent to have a "final" visit with the child, even if the child seems reluctant to attend. That parent, perhaps accompanied by a mental health professional, can meet the child, allowing the parent to tell the child why access is being discontinued, and express the hope that a relationship may be resumed at some point in the future.[38] These sentiments may also be put in a letter to the child. Leaving the lines of communication open in whatever manner possible, such as occasional letters, cards, gifts, email, etc., may permit positive memories that could pave the way for a future reconciliation, a better alternative than providing no trail of resolution for the grown child (Baker, 2005b; Cartwright, 2006). There may also be a third party, like a therapist or lawyer for the child, who can serve as a conduit for continuing exchange of correspondence or gifts.

At least in some instances, children do resume a relationship with a rejected non-custodial parent after a long period without contact and missed opportunities, though sometimes only in adulthood. In other cases a relationship may never be re-established.

It must be appreciated that giving up the struggle is not likely to be a short term proposition. A "cooling off" period is not likely to

---

Katz v. Katz, 1989 CarswellOnt 260, 21 R.F.L. (3d) 167 (Ont. U.F.C.), *per* Wallace U.F.C.J.

37 2006 CarswellOnt 2058, 2006 ONCJ 111 (Ont. C.J.).

38 See Richard Warshak, "Bringing Sense to Parental Alienation: A Look at the Disputes and the Evidence" (2003), 37:2 Fam. L.Q. 273, at 282; and M.J. Sullivan & J.B. Kelly, "Alienated Children in Divorce: Legal and Psychological Management of Cases With An Alienated Child" (2001), 39 Fam. Ct. Rev. 299, at 311.

improve such a situation in the foreseeable future, and may in fact exacerbate an already difficult situation, as an alienated parent requires time with a child to ensure that contact is not completely lost. Unlike cases of child abuse, where a break from an abusive parent may assist in repairing a damaged relationship, time away from an alienated parent during childhood is only likely to further the alienation.

Custody Reversal: One Option

Perspectives for and against Custody Reversal

Notwithstanding the considerable degree of agreement regarding the need for court involvement, irrespective of the level or extent of parental alienation, controversy surrounds the suitability of assessor recommendations or judicial threats and orders to transfer custody to a rejected parent. There is consensus though that a reversal of custody may be warranted in some severe alienation cases. However, debate continues about how to identify the cases severe enough and appropriate to warrant a custody change. The courts have struggled with cases where the custodial parent is, without justification and in contravention of one or more court orders, influencing the child to resist contact and denying access to the non-custodial parent. The appropriate solution to remedy the harm caused by such alienating behaviour is the elusive goal of having the judicial system entrusted with the duty to ensure that the best interests of children are recognized and promoted.

Severe cases of alienation involve emotional abuse, with a subset of these including repeated malicious and unsubstantiated allegations of abuse against the rejected parent (Johnston, 2005a; Gardner, 1998c; Rand, 1997a, 1997b; Sullivan & Kelly, 2001; Warshak, 2003a). While Gardner[39] and the Johnston group (as well as others) maintain that a change in custody is likely to be warranted in severe cases—providing the rejected party is fit to parent—the Johnston group may be less inclined than Gardner and his followers to identify

[39] Gardner identifies two categories of recommendations for the moderate type of alienation (1998a, 1998c). In the milder of the moderate type (Plan A in his tables), custody remains with the alienating parent, and orders include therapy and threats of various sanctions if there is non-compliance. As in the severe cases, in the more severe of the moderate type (Plan B in his tables), he calls for a change in custody and a significant decrease in access to the alienating parent. In these situations, the children may still be visiting the rejected parent, but the alienating parent is tenacious, possibly paranoid and delusional, and imparting these traits to the child. The child must be removed, according to Gardner, since therapy while remaining in the home of the custodial (alienating) parent will not work.

the cases as severe and in turn to recommend a custody reversal. Johnston (2001) notes that such cases are rare, and may include a psychotic or severely character-disordered custodial parent, accompanied by false or fabricated allegations of abuse. Alienating parents may be paranoid, and there may be evidence of a folie à deux or Munchausen's by Proxy Contemporary Type (Rand, 1993).

While disagreeing with Johnston about the court's involvement more generally, Bruch (2001a) cites Johnston to support the view that reversing custody is ill advised. As previously noted, Bruch and Wallerstein each maintain that these children will "come around" eventually, and further that there is no evidence that ordering contact or expensive treatment is effective.[40] In addition, these writers have questioned the benefits to children involved in high conflict parental separation of having relationships with both parents. Bruch maintains that enforced access, treatment, and custody reversal are likely to be counterproductive and to reinforce a child's hatred for the alienated parent, adding further stress to already vulnerable children. The child may subsequently be at risk for running away and self-destructive behaviour. Further, they argue that an abrupt and lengthy separation from a primary attachment figure, even when the relationship is unhealthy, is believed to place the child at greater risk than losing contact with a rejected parent. The implication appears to be that the more dysfunctional (i.e., hostile-dependent) the relationship with the custodial parent, the greater the risk there is in separating the child from that parent.

In addition, Bruch (2001a) and Wallerstein and Tanke (2006) assert that children's stated wishes deserve careful consideration, and should be respected in many cases. Paradoxically, the writers who stress the importance of heeding children's stated wishes, while objecting to the court's involvement in mandating treatment and access enforcement (see for example Bruch, 2001a; Faller, 1997; Walker, Brantley, & Rigsbee, 2004a, 2004b), glaringly exclude any mention of the many studies of children and adult children of divorce, some of whom may have been alienated, reporting a longing to have had more time with their non-custodial fathers (see for example Ahrons & Tanner, 2003; Hetherington & Kelly, 2002; Fabricius, 2003; Fabricius & Hall, 2000; Laumann-Billings & Emery, 2000; Parkinson, Cashmore & Single, 2005; Parkinson & Smyth, 2004).

Qualitative case studies and experienced clinicians supporting recommendations and/or orders to reverse custody maintain that

---

40 To support her claim, Bruch cites a newspaper report and telephone conversation with Judith Wallerstein on her follow-up of 25 young adults (Wallerstein, Lewis & Blakeslee, 2000).

therapy simply does not work in severe and even in some moderate alienation cases. Moreover, therapy may even make matters worse; the alienated child and preferred parent feel the need to dig in their heels and prove their point, thereby further entrenching their distorted views (Clawar & Rivli, 1991; Dunne & Hedrick, 1994; Kopetski, 1998a, 1998b, 2006; Lampel, 1996; Lowenstein, 2006; Lund, 1995; Gardner, 2001b; Rand, 1997b; Rand, Rand & Kopetski, 2005). Clearly, and most regrettably, this is the experience of many seasoned clinicians, including the authors. The reality is that we have many more treatment failures than successes when it comes to our intervention with some moderate and all severe cases. We identify the need for two important future developments. The first is for further development of treatment models and specific strategies that will hopefully increase our effectiveness in restoring children's relationships with the rejected parent and extended family with the mild and some moderate cases. The second is for the better agreement on and early identification of the more severe cases where treatment is unlikely to be effective, leaving custody reversal as the least detrimental option.

Those advocating for custody reversal maintain that court intervention is justified to protect a child from what all agree is emotional abuse, just as it is in child-protection cases, even when parents may not be conscious of their attempts to turn the child against other parent. Of significant concern are issues of exploitation, indoctrination, and the induction of fear and hatred and, in some cases, paranoia, in children.

Supporters of custody reversal note that we do not let 14- and 15-year-old children decide whether or not they attend a health care professional, receive medical treatment, or go to the doctor or to school. Likewise, these children should not be permitted to decide to opt out of having a relationship with one parent, grandparents and other relatives. These mental health professionals maintain that the risks of staying with a paranoid parent are far greater than the risks of changing custody when the rejected parent is an adequate parent, especially since many children adapt very quickly once the custody change occurs and they are free of indoctrination.

Furthermore, assessors and the courts need to consider carefully what poses the greatest risk to the child, noting the likely detrimental effects, both short-term and long-term, of living in a distorted reality. For some, the least detrimental long-term option is to place the child with the parent more likely to promote a healthy relationship with the other parent and healthy psychological development more generally. The importance of focusing on the long-term welfare of children, notwithstanding the short-term risks, was recognized by the British Columbia Court of Appeal in its 2007 judgment in the previously mentioned case of *A. (A.) v. A. (S.N.)*,[41] where, reversing the trial decision, the Court of Appeal ordered that custody of a ten year old girl be transferred from her alienating mother to her rejected father, with a suspension of access, to the mother and maternal grandmother, including telephone access, until otherwise recommended by the court-appointed professional, or by a court order. In addition, the mother and grandmother were prohibited from contacting the child's school without a court order. The Court of Appeal wrote:

> The trial judge was indeed faced with a "stark dilemma"—albeit one created largely by the custodial parent. . .
>
> . . . the trial judge wrongly focused on the likely difficulties of a change in custody—which the only evidence on the subject indicates will be short-term and not "devastating"—and failed to give paramountcy to M.'s long-term interests. Instead, damage which is long-term and almost certain was preferred over what may be a risk, but a risk that seems necessary if M is to have a chance to develop normally in her adolescent years. . . The obligation of the Court to make the order it determines best represents the child's interests cannot be ousted by the insistence of an intransigent parent who is "blind" to her child's interests.
>
> While it is obvious that no court should gamble with a child's long-term psychological and emotional well-being, the trial judge's findings show that the status quo is so detrimental to M that a change must be made in this case. Although M has not been permitted to have a normal relationship with her father for two years, the expert opinion suggests she will succeed in adjusting, although the process will be difficult. In this regard, it is important to note that Mr. A. has shown sensitivity to the feelings of insecurity and anxiety M is likely to experience should he be given custody of the child. . . We also note that M is by all accounts a bright girl who has shown a "desire to connect with others" when she is out of her mother's control, and that the chances she will weather this change, if it is properly carried out, seem good.[42]

There was a similar recognition of the dilemmas facing the court in alienation cases in the Ontario case of *Reeves v. Reeves*,[43] where Mossip J. had to decide between two options—leaving the adolescent

---

41 *Supra*, at note 18.

42 *Ibid.*, at paras. 26-28; see also 2007 CarswellBC 1592, 2007 BCCA 364, 40 R.F.L. (6th) 261 (B.C. C.A.). It is noteworthy, that notwithstanding the child's adamant wishes before the trial not to see the father, at the appeal hearing, only five days after the transfer of custody from the mother to the father, the Court found that the child was managing the transition well. This observation is consistent with the social science literature reporting that in many cases alienated children adapt well and quickly once they are removed from the alienating parent and environment.

43 2001 CarswellOnt 277, [2001] O.J. No. 308 (Ont. S.C.J.).

boys where they were with their father, or moving them to live with their mother. In analyzing these, she stated:

> Both choices are fraught with difficulties; however, only the second option, I find, offers any hope that Brandon and Nicholas might grow into healthy adults. I am choosing the option that will no doubt cause the most immediate pain, for what I perceive to be the long-term best interests of the children. I find this is a clear case of parental alienation by the father, which has resulted in obvious harm to the Reeves children. Sometimes it takes years for the harm resulting from children being denied their right to have a relationship with both parents to surface. In the case before me, there is already evidence of deep and ongoing harm because of parental alienation.[44]

In determining that a change in custody was in the children's best interests, Justice Mossip went on to state:

> The results of parental alienation by the father against their mother on these children are observable now, and according to the Children's Lawyer social worker, the children are being adversely affected at a rapid and increasing rate.
>
> Rarely does a court have such unequivocal evidence as to the adverse effects on the children to remain with one parent as is set out in the two affidavits of the Children's Lawyer social worker. It would, in my view, be a grave disservice to the Reeves children not to act promptly and effectively on her advice and recommendations in this case.[45]

Justice Turnbull, in the 2008 Ontario case of *L. (J.K.) v. S. (N.C.)*,[46] which concerned the parties' 13 year old son, quoted from Justice Reilly, in his reasons for a finding of contempt, in an earlier proceeding in the same case. Justice Turnbull cited Justice Reilly's admonition of the alienating father:

> contact with even a flawed parent, a parent who has more flaws than, by your perception [the child's] mothers has in this case, is better for a child than no contact at all. To cut off contact is a devastating thing for a child and can have serious long-term consequences.[47]

A change of custody in an alienation case is often accompanied by suspended or restricted access, at least initially, with an alienating

---

44 *Ibid.*, at para. 26

45 *Ibid.*, at paras. 27-28. Eventually, the boys chose to return to live with their father, which illustrates the difficulty in dealing with alienation cases.

46 *Supra*, at note 26.

47 *Ibid.*, at para. 64.

parent, because restoring the relationship with the rejected parent and re-educating the child, like that of extricated cult members, requires separation and isolation from the source of influence (Baker, 2006; Gardner, 1999c, 2001b; Rand, 1997b; Rand & Warshak, 2006). For a successful transition back to the rejected parent, the child's contact with the alienating parent almost invariably needs to be temporarily suspended. The order should include precise specification of the access for the alienating parent after the cessation, which in some cases may be supervised access, recommended by the assessor, with the court retaining jurisdiction. Based on our experience, alienating parents and their children, not only parents accused of domestic violence or child abuse, may need to have their visits supervised at supervised access centers. In other cases, where the alienating parent continues to pose a threat to the emotional well-being of the child, the least detrimental option for the child may be an indefinite suspension of contact. In cases that require monitoring, it is highly desirable for the same judge to remain seized of the case.

To illustrate orders where contact with the alienating parent was restricted we summarize some of these cases. In *Wedsworth v. Wedsworth*,[48] the Nova Scotia Court of Appeal upheld the trial judge's decision to transfer custody from mother to father. The trial judge found that the mother had "demonized" the father to the children and as a result damaged the relationship between the father and children. Although it was expected that the children would "suffer some immediate trauma and grief" from the change in custody, the judge concluded that this was one of those "rare cases" where drastic action was required. To limit the possibility of the mother's undermining the new custodial arrangement, she was not allowed any access to the children for a four-week period; the judge also retained jurisdiction thereafter to deal with access.[49]

Similarly, in the Quebec case of *P.S.-M. v. LJ-A.C.*,[50] the judge, in transferring custody of the two youngest children from their alienating father to the rejected mother, also ordered that there was to be no access to the father and two older children for a period of six months. Justice Gomery found that this case represented an extreme example of parental alienation. "Hatred," he stated, "is not an emotion that comes naturally to a child. It has to be taught. The person who taught the C. children to hate is their father. They would be better

48 2005 CarswellNS 301, 745 A.P.R. 366, 2005 NSCA 102, 234 N.S.R. (2d) 366, [2005] N.S.J. No. 275 (N.S. C.A.) affiming 2005 CarswellNS 7, 2005 NSSF 2, 229 N.S.R. (2d) 168, 725 A.P.R. 168 (N.S. S.C.).

49 See also *Pettenuzzo-Deschene v. Deschene*, *supra*, at note 22.

50 *Supra*, at note 6.

off if he were removed totally as an influence upon their development until they are able to withstand and reject his negative attitudes."[51]

As noted previously when we discussed the court's jurisdiction to order counseling to parents and children, the case of *L. (J.K.) v. S. (N.C.)*[52] involved a blatant and severe case of alienation, where the alienating father had been in breach of many court orders. The 13 year old boy, who had previously testified against the mother at a criminal hearing (she was found not guilty of assault of the father), was refusing all contact with her. The Court relied heavily on a comprehensive court-ordered assessment as well as expert testimony from a local psychiatrist, and from the internationally known alienation expert, Dr. Richard Warshak. The Court ordered a transfer of custody to the mother whose contact with the 13-year old son at the time was limited to observing him occasionally at his sport events. As the sole custody parent, the mother then, had the responsibility for making all healthcare decisions; the judge suggested that the mother might want to take the boy to an intensive alienation-directed therapeutic program, since the Court heard evidence about the program, but indicated that this decision was to be made by the custodial mother. A restraining order was put in place and the father was to have no contact with his son for the next four months. The order included terms for the police to enforce the court's order, that the immediate transfer of custody occur at the courthouse in the absence of the father, and for the judge to remain seized of the matter with a return to court in four months. Finally, there was an order for counselling to occur later to help the father re-establish his relationship with the child.

In some moderate cases and in most severe cases of alienation, when a custody change has not occurred, a warning that in the event of non-compliance with the order in its fullness, a change of custody is likely to occur, may suffice to ensure compliance (Bala & Bailey, 2004; Gardner, 1998a; Johnston & Kelly, 2004b; Lee & Olesen, 2001; Sullivan & Kelly, 2001). In other cases, however, a change in custody is required to ensure the ongoing relationship between the child and the alienated parent.

In severe cases where children refuse contact and threaten to run away or harm themselves or someone else, a program such as the Rand and Warshak Family Workshop may help the family safely adjust to the court orders. In other cases, transfer to a transitional placement may be indicated before the rejected parent and child are united for further intervention (Gardner, 1998c, 2001c; Gotlieb,

[51] *Ibid.*, at p. 21.

[52] *Supra*, at note 26.

2006). Here the child is separated from both parents for a short time before reintegrating with the rejected parent. Sites vary in degree of control required, ranging from placement with a friend or relative to being placed in a treatment centre or hospital. After the child's relationship with the rejected parent is restored, a gradual reintroduction of the alienating parent is carefully monitored to ensure that the alienation does not resume.

Summary of Social Science Research

To date, there has been little well controlled research on the outcomes, either positive or negative, of ordering access or reversing custody in alienation cases. However, experienced clinicians and those reporting on their qualitative research using case studies, report on the benefits of changing custody in severe alienation cases (Clawar & Rivlin, 1991; Dunne & Hedrick, 1994; Gardner, 2001c; Lampel, 1996; Rand & Warshak, 2006; Rand, Rand & Kopetski, 2005).

For example, Clawar and Rivlin (1991) reported an improvement in 90 per cent of cases in children's relationships with rejected parents and in other areas of their functioning in the 400 cases where an increase in parent-child contact was court-ordered—half of these orders over the objection of the children. They further reported that children interviewed after the court-ordered increased time expressed relief, saying they could not have reestablished the relationship on their own. As previously noted, Clawar and Rivlin's findings are consistent with those subsequently reported by Baker (2005b), indicating that adult children who were alienated recall distinctly hoping the rejected parent would realize they were not stating their true feelings when they refused contact.

Lampel (1996) reported that in the 18 cases she analyzed, improvement was observed where there was a change in custody. In another clinical study of 26 cases, 16 of these meeting Gardner's criteria for severe PAS, Dunne and Hedrick (1994) reported that alienation was eliminated in four of the 26 children, for three of whom the court ordered a custody reversal and restricted contact with the alienating parent. In the remaining 22 cases, where there was no change in custody, improvements were not forthcoming with therapy alone.

Gardner (2001c) conducted a qualitative follow-up of 99 children from 52 families he had previously diagnosed with PAS. He stated:

> The court chose to either restrict the children's access to the alienator or change custody in 22 of the children. There was a significant reduction or even elimination of PAS symptomatology in all 22 of these cases. This represents a 100 percent success rate. The court chose not to transfer

> custody or reduce access to the alienator in 77 cases. In these cases there was an increase in PAS symptomatology in 70 (90.9 percent). In only 7 cases (9.1 per cent) of the nontransferred was there spontaneous improvement. Custodial change and/or reduction of the alienator's access to the children was found to be associated with a reduction in PAS symptomatology (§2(df=1)=68.28, p.<.001)" (Gardner 2001b, p. 39).

He reported a spontaneous reconciliation in four cases and no reduction in PAS symptoms in the seven children (nine per cent) for whom contact with the rejected parent was not increased. However, in all of the 22 instances in which custody was changed or the alienating parent's contact was restricted, PAS was eliminated or reduced. There are limitations to Gardner's follow-up: the same individual who formulated the hypotheses and diagnoses (Gardner) also conducted the follow-up interviews, and only the rejected parents—and neither the children nor the alienating parents—were interviewed.

Rand, Rand and Kopetski (2005) reported similar findings in their follow-up study of the 45 children from 25 families Kopetski had studied over 20 years starting in 1976. A range of moderate to severe PAS characterized these cases. Alienation was interrupted for 20 children from 12 families where there was enforced visitation or a change of custody. For those in the treatment group where there were orders for therapy and gradually increased access, alienation remained uninterrupted and in some cases became worse. Those in the first group maintained better relationships with both parents unless the alienator was too disturbed. This group included those subject to both enforced visitation and custody reversal, and consequently it remains unclear the extent to which each of these factors was successful in alleviating the alienation. The authors note that these follow-up results are consistent with other previously mentioned studies reporting on various interventions. They conclude that an assessor's recommendations and subsequent court decisions can make a difference between interrupted and completed alienation in more severe cases.

In the early 1990s, psychologist Dr. Randy Rand developed the previously mentioned specialized family-reunification program, now called the Family Workshop. Dr. Richard Warshak and Dr. Deidre Rand with Dr. Randy Rand as a team implemented this workshop, which is *one* option to consider *after* a court determines that a change in custody to a rejected parent, coupled with a shielding (hopefully only temporarily) of the child from a favoured parent, was in the child's best interest (Rand & Warshak, 2008). The workshop usually takes four days, and at the time of writing, usually takes place in California, sometimes other locations.

The program helps the entire family—alienated and alienating parents and children—adjust to custody reversal. Stated briefly, the goals of the program go beyond improving the child's relationship with the rejected parent. They include: (a) facilitating, repairing and strengthening the child's healthy relationships with both parents; (b) improving the child's critical thinking skills; (c) removing the child from parental conflicts; (d) protecting the child from becoming pathologically alienated in the future; (e) helping the child to maintain balanced and realistic views and perceptions of both parents and of themselves; (f) helping children develop a compassionate view of each parent's actions rather than an excessively harsh or critical one; (g) strengthening the family communication and conflict resolution skills; and (h) improving parenting skills and ability to nurture while also setting and enforcing appropriate limits. These goals are achieved through an education-based intervention (usually four days) intended to repair the relationship with the alienated parent; and immediate and longer term aftercare, which involves efforts to sustain the child and previously alienated parent's relationship in their home community and to resume the child's relationship with the favoured parent.[53] Warshak maintains that when the child and parents are made aware of the court's expectations for the child to reintegrate with the alienated parent notwithstanding the child's resistance or refusal, the child is freed up to participate meaningfully in the program. Further, experience from these workshops indicates that children usually feel relief at having the decision to choose one parent over the other taken away from them.

Rand and Warshak (2008) report that to date more than 70 families and 130 children (ranging in ages from 11 to 21) have completed the program with success. In addition, while not as high a number as one would hope for, about one third of the favoured parents began to support their child's relationship with the formerly rejected parent. Rand and Warshak note that enforcing custody orders is imperative, as the few cases (about 10 per cent) where the intervention was ineffective involved situations where the child had contact with the alienating parent notwithstanding a court order to the contrary.

Clearly, it would be desirable to have well designed research, including longitudinal designs comparing children who change custody with those who do not. Conducting such research however, is very difficult, if not impossible. Still, decisions need to be made without the benefit of good research. Further, an individualized approach is required in child custody determinations since we cannot base

---

53 See *L. (J.K.) v. S. (N.C.)*, *supra*, at note 26, for further elaboration of the FWAC 74/07.

decisions for any one child and their family on the aggregate data. Consequently, a careful investigation and risk-benefit analysis of each case is required, as would be the case even if good research was available. In the next section, we discuss enforcement issues and judicial remedies, starting with the least intrusive and concluding with a discussion of the jurisprudence in cases where alienation was found, some of these resulting in a custody reversal, and others in the status quo being maintained, as the court determined it was in the best interests of the children to remain with the alienating parent.

Enforcement Issues and Judicial Remedies

Non-compliance with court orders in high conflict cases is to be expected, given the high incidence of personality disorders in this population (Jenuwin & Cohler, 1999; Grych & Fincham, 1999). To not implement sanctions against an alienating parent only reinforces their narcissism, false sense of power, and disregard for authority (Gardner, 2001c; Johnston, 2005a; Rand, Rand & Kopetski, 2005). As Justice Mossip stated in *Reeves v. Reeves*:[54]

> The most difficult issue with respect to parental alienation and changes in custody with regard to older children is that such orders are very difficult to enforce. There is no point in me taking the difficult path that I have unless I do everything possible to ensure the order is complied with. This order is in the best interests of Brandon and Nicholas. I must ensure that the father and his mother obey this court order.[55]

In cases of high conflict involving alienating behaviour, the greater the degree of specificity in the order, the higher the likelihood of success in carrying out the terms as envisioned by the judge. As stated earlier in this chapter, the order must be detailed, explicit, unambiguous and comprehensive.

Depending on the circumstances, a parent who has been alienated has a range of legal options, but it is important to appreciate that it is up to that parent to decide what remedies, if any, to seek. Unlike with child support, which is often enforced by a government agency without charge to the recipient, parents must enforce custody and access orders, which can require significant financial resources and emotional energy; many rejected parents simply give up trying to maintain a relationship with their children. If the problem is that the alienating parent is not honouring an existing order, then the rejected

---

[54] *Supra*, at note 43.

[55] *Ibid.*, at para. 37

parent must prove that there has been contempt of court—a willful violation of the court order. The rejected parent may also seek variation of the existing custody and access order, perhaps to increase access, or require counselling, or to seek variation. Both types of proceedings may be joined together. In practice there are invariably a number of court appearances before a matter is concluded, and the judge is likely to try to persuade the parties to resolve the matter, often urging the custodial parent to respect the rights of the access parent and promote their child's best interests by supporting the relationship with the other parent.

Legal responses and penalties for non-compliance with court orders include:

- compensatory parenting time ("makeup time");
- compensatory driving to facilitate contact;
- paying the legal costs of the rejected parent, including costs of an assessment;
- payment for any financial expenses incurred but lost (i.e., airfare);
- paying for treatment;
- posting a bond; and
- probation, community service or a fine payable to the government.

Finally, a court may vary custody in cases of non-compliance with an access order, though this must not be done to sanction the alienating parent, but only if it will promote the child's best interests.

Despite this range of options, family court judges typically exercise restraint when an application is made to finding a parent in contempt for failing to comply with an access order, particularly in regard to sentencing. There are a number of reasons for this judicial caution. First, courts recognize that "the law of contempt . . . is a blunt instrument that is not particularly well suited to the complex emotional dynamics of access disputes."[56] In other words, it may not help to secure compliance with the order to find a parent guilty of contempt, especially in the long term. Second, and perhaps more important, is the concern about the effect of the contempt finding on the welfare of the child. As Veit J. said in an access enforcement proceeding: "Chil-

---

[56] *Payton v. Shymkiw*, 1996 CarswellMan 553, 26 R.F.L. (4th) 22, [1996] M.J. No. 569 (Man. Q.B.), at para. 34.

dren are better off if their parents are not in jail or paying fines."[57] Even if there is a finding of contempt, the judge may suspend imposing a sanction to give the alienating parent a final opportunity to comply.

There is a consensus that judicial enforcement of court orders is vitally important in alienation cases, though there is considerable debate over the nature and extent of appropriate sanctions (Bala & Bailey, 2004; Clawar & Rivilin, 1991; Gardner, 2001c; Lund, 1995; Sullivan, 2004; Sullivan & Kelly, 2001; Stahl, 1999; Turkat, 1994; Warshak, 2006).[57] Some maintain that the penalties which courts have customarily imposed for violation of access orders are far too lenient, while others argue that some penalties, such as incarceration and having to pay fines are excessive and ultimately not in a child's best interest. Furthermore, such actions may be counterproductive to the extent that the punished alienating parent is then portrayed to the child as a martyr, which in turn only serves to reinforce the child's negative reaction and alienation.

Case Management

Judicial continuity and short adjournments (or conditional adjournments if the parenting time does not occur) are especially valuable in cases where there are parent-child contact problems and non-compliance with previous orders (Bala *et al.*, 2007a; Bala & Bailey, 2004; Epstein, 2002). Judicial exhortations and threats in particular are more likely to be effective when the parents return to a judge who will have had an opportunity to get to know the parties and their issues. Legal commentaries note that wherever there is no case-management system, a judge may rule that he or she remains seized of the matter to address future problems. This may be especially useful in a contempt proceeding in order to enable judicial monitoring of a parent's willingness and ability to comply with the existing order (Epstein, 2002).[59] Bala and Bailey (2004) note that while there will

---

[57] *Salloum v. Salloum*, 1994 CarswellAlta 577, [1994] A.J. No. 304, 154 A.R. 65 (Alta. Q.B.), at para. 19.

[58] See sharp criticisms presented by Bruch (2001a), Faller (1997) and Walker, Brantley and Rigsbee (2004a), who in addition to objecting to court-ordered treatment and the appointment of parenting coordinators and case managers, renounce orders enforcing parenting time. Concerns about parenting coordinators relate to their quasi-judicial authority and what is likely to be the mental-health professionals' limited understanding of the law.

[59] Opportunity to purge contempt by complying with the terms of the access order: see *K. (D.) v. K. (D.)*, 2003 CarswellOnt 2559 (Ont. S.C.J.); *Starzycka v. Wronski*, 2005 CarswellOnt 7576, 27 R.F.L. (6th) 159, [2005] O.J. No. 5569 (Ont. C.J.); *Moudry v. Moudry*, 2005 CarswellOnt 2630, [2005] O.J. No. 2655 (Ont. S.C.J); *Amaral v. Myke*,

always be exceptions, many parents will heed the advice and warnings of the judge who has control over their case. Notwithstanding the numbers who comply, in our experience the number of exceptions remains high.

Penalties for Contempt: Financial Consequences, Counselling Orders and Jail

The court can impose a number of monetary remedies in cases of contempt of court with respect to orders of custody and access to children. In Ontario, for example, section 38 of the *Children's Law Reform Act* provides judges of the Ontario Court of Justice with the ability to impose monetary fines of up to $5,000 in addition to their other powers in respect of contempt. This limit does not apply to justices of the Superior Court, who can impose higher fines.

In *Cooper v. Cooper*,[60] Justice Snowie of the Ontario Superior Court of Justice ordered the mother who was found in contempt of an access order, to pay a fine of $10,000 to government. In this case, the father had not had access since the date of separation. Fifteen orders had been made over several years to address the father's access to his children. Despite tremendous efforts by the case-management judge and mental health professionals involved, the mother had successfully manipulated the situation to sabotage all contact between children and father. In finding the mother to be in contempt, Justice Snowie stated:

> I am satisfied beyond a reasonable doubt that Mrs. Cooper's actions and lack thereof constituted the offence of civil contempt. It is also clear that the actions of the respondent were contrary to the best interests of all three children. These children, as all children do, needed a mother and a father. It is the right of all children to have a relationship with their mother and their father. There is no evidence before this court that would indicate that Mr. Cooper was anything but a good father, a loving father, and a father who throughout the last seven years wanted to be involved in any capacity in his children's lives. He has admirably and heroically been before this court on at least 15 occasions trying, unsuccessfully, to

---

1992 CarswellOnt 293, 42 R.F.L. (3d) 322 (Ont. U.F.C.); *C. (A.J.) v. C. (R.)*, 2003 CarswellBC 1172, [2003] B.C.J. No. 1150, 2003 BCSC 664 (B.C. S.C.), *per* Bennett J.; *Thomas v. Pearcy*, 1993 CarswellOnt 352, 48 R.F.L. (3d) 407 (Ont. Gen. Div.); *Badry v. Badry*, 2002 CarswellBC 1622, 2002 BCSC 1006, [2002] B.C.J. No. 1577 (B.C.S.C.); *Poitras v. Bucsis*, 2003 CarswellBC 443, 2003 BCSC 299, [2003] B.C.J. No. 460 (B.C.S.C.); *Duggan v. Huskins*, 2003 CarswellNS 154, 2003 NSSF 10, 214 N.S.R. (2d) 42, 671 A.P.R. 42, [2003] N.S.J. No. 142 (N.S.S.C.).

60 2004 CarswellOnt 5255, [2004] O.J. No. 5096 (Ont. S.C.J.).

> obtain access with his children. He still continues valiantly to attempt to have a relationship with his children.[61]

In *Cooper,* as is common in contempt proceedings in alienation cases, the alienating mother offered as a defence that she was prepared to comply with the order but it was the children who were refusing contact. Some courts have responded to this argument by articulating a positive obligation for the custodial parent to encourage the children to attend for access visits. In *Cooper*, the custodial mother was found in contempt for having "willfully and deliberately sabotaged"[62] telephone access between the children and their father. Although she made the children "available" by having them at home when the father called at the appointed time, she would neither answer the telephone nor, in her words, "put the telephone to the children's ears".[63] The Court rejected her argument that "it was up to the children to decide whether or not they would answer the phone" and found her in contempt for "shirking her responsibility and obligation directly, and . . . indirectly conveying to the children her disapproval of telephone access."[64]

In addition to finding the mother in contempt and imposing a fine of $10,000, Justice Snowie ordered that the mother was to arrange immediately and be supportive of counselling for one of the children. The purpose of this counselling was the reintegration of the father into the child's life. Justice Snowie ordered the mother to take the child to counselling twice a month without exception for the following six months. Additionally, if the mother breached any part of the order requiring her to take the child to counselling, directly or indirectly, the Court stated that it would consider this to be a contempt of court and the mother would be required to pay a fine for $15,000. The judge also threatened to impose imprisonment penalties if the breach continued. In this case, Justice Snowie granted further relief that specified penalties with respect to possible "future" breaches of her order. The jurisdictional basis for the court to make such prospective orders is questionable, as it is not possible to impose a sentence for contempt on a prospective basis, but the judge wanted to send the mother a clear message.

Justice McSorley of the Ontario Court of Justice dealt with the issue of contempt in *K. (L.M.) v. R. (E.P.)*.[65] The judge found that the alienating behaviour of the mother disrupted access to and interfered

---

[61] *Ibid.*, at para. 57

[62] *Ibid.*, at para. 42, *per* Snowie J.

[63] *Ibid.*

[64] *Ibid.*, at para. 42-43.

[65] 2005 CarswellOnt 7984, 2005 ONCJ 505, [2005] O.J. No. 5782 (Ont. C.J.).

with the relationship the children should have with their father. Justice McSorley felt that the mother required some form of incentive to comply with the court order and so fined her $500, suspending payment for a period of 24 months on the condition that the mother complied with the access terms as set out.

In the Ontario case of *Fernandes v. Vukovic*,[66] a mother repeatedly denied the father access and on several occasions, the police were required to enforce the access order. The father was granted interim custody by the court, but the mother continued to interfere. She made more than 30 calls to the police with unfounded child abuse allegations and over 35 calls to the Children's Aid Society. The father applied for and was granted a final order of custody. The Court concluded that the mother repeatedly failed to act in the child's best interests, and that she presented with emotional problems affecting her capacity to care for the child. Additionally, the mother was found to be in contempt of an earlier order. Justice Snowie ordered the mother to pay a fine of $5,000.

Justice Gauthier dealt with contempt of court and appropriate penalties in the Ontario case of *Korwin v. Potworowski*.[67] In this case, three children were to remain in the matrimonial home with the father; however, a short time later, the eldest child refused to return to the father's residence and remained in the mother's care. The mother was found to be in contempt and the child was ordered to return to the father's care, with police involvement if required. The mother brought an application for sole custody of all three children. Ultimately, custody of the two youngest children was granted to the father and custody of the oldest child was granted to the mother. In addition to making the custody orders, Justice Gauthier also dealt with the issue of contempt. The mother had previously been found in contempt, and several fines had been imposed. None of these seemed to have any effect on her, as her conduct did not change significantly. In the end, Justice Gauthier ordered the mother to pay $5,000 into the existing RESP for the children. He also ordered that she pay an additional $5,000 into court as a conditional penalty. Upon a breach of the order, the father could apply to the court for payment to him of the funds. If the mother complied with the order, the money would eventually be returned to her.

In the British Columbia case of *Mugford v. Cartocci*,[68] Justice Prowse dealt with the issue of alienating behaviour and concurrent breaches of access on the part of the mother in a unique manner. She

---

66 2006 CarswellOnt 159 (Ont. S.C.J.).

67 2006 CarswellOnt 3436, 31 R.F.L. (6th) 164 (Ont. S.C.J.).

68 2006 CarswellBC 3343, 2006 BCSC 1989 (B.C. S.C. [In Chambers]).

was ordered to pay $10,000 into trust, with the monies used for the preparation of an independent custody and access report. The assessor was to do an analysis of the situation and make recommendations as to how the parties might facilitate their relationship with one another so that they could work together in the best interests of their child.

In addition to imposing fines, courts have also made orders requiring that the aggrieved party be reimbursed for expenses, such as the purchase of an airline ticket, when these expenses were incurred due to access not taking place as ordered. In *Poitras v. Bucsis*,[69] the principal issue for the court was whether the evidence supported a finding of contempt against a custodial father for not complying with an order requiring him to facilitate child access. The father lived in Saskatchewan and the order required that he send the child to British Columbia for Christmas access. The judge found that civil contempt had been proven, and in addition to ordering additional access for the plaintiff in April of that year, the Court ordered the father to pay her $1,500 for her legal costs. Additionally, the father was ordered to pay the costs of air travel for the April visit. Similarly, in *Payton v. Shymkiw*,[70] the mother was ordered to reimburse the father for expenses incurred because of a wrongful denial of access. Additionally, she was ordered to attend a parenting session and to file with the court a letter confirming her attendance at the session.

In *Remus v. Remus*,[71] the Court was faced with a situation where the mother seriously violated an order requiring her, amongst other things, to equalize the father's time with the children. In the five months following the judgment of Justice Wright, the mother had been in serious breach of the order. The Court cited the details of the mother's contempt as follows:

- She failed to equalize the time with the children in contravention of the judgment.
- She has obstructed the father's communication with the children in contravention of the judgment.
- She has failed to communicate with the father in a timely fashion regarding the children in contravention of the judgment.
- She has failed to release to the father the recreational cloth-

---

[69] *Supra*, at note 59.
[70] *Supra*, at note 56.
[71] 2004 CarswellOnt 3755, [2004] O.J. No. 3793 (Ont. S.C.J.).

ing, sports equipment, musical instruments, and other personal property in contravention of the judgment.

- She has failed to maintain health care coverage and benefits for the father in contravention of the judgment.

- She has failed to provide proof of paid up insurance of at least $250,000 with the children as beneficiaries for the year 2004 in contravention of the judgment.[72]

In a desire to send a very clear message to the mother that continued breaches would not be tolerated by the Court, the judge ordered that all missed access, then amounting to 47 days, was to be made up on or before a specified date and that the mother would forthwith pay to the father the sum of $1,500 for costs payable on or before a date specified by the Court. Furthermore, Justice Smith stated that if the mother failed to abide by the terms of this order, she would be incarcerated for a period of ten days, and the custody provisions would be varied to provide that the father was to have sole custody of the children, with access to the mother.

Although there is great judicial reluctance to impose a jail sentence for violation of an access order, in some extreme cases concerns about the need to maintain the integrity of the administration of justice result in this sanction. In *McMillan v. McMillan*,[73] the Court noted that the father had to bring four separate contempt motions to enforce an access order and re-establish contact with his children. Quinn J. remarked:

> . . . there is a period of time immediately following the separation of spouses when emotions run high and otherwise sensible people are prone to act like vengeful lunatics. A court order deliberately breached during that delicate time frame may attract the compassion of the court. However, a court order which is willfully, deliberately and repeatedly breached many years after such compassions can reasonably be expected to extend, is an entirely different matter.[74]

In light of the repeated defiance of the access order, Quinn J. held that this was an appropriate case to impress upon the custodial mother, and upon other parents involved in a judicial process that "court orders are to be obeyed".[75] In weighing the appropriate sen-

72 *Ibid.*, at para.2

73 1999 CarswellOnt 1028, 44 O.R. (3d) 139, [1999] O.J. No. 1285 (Ont. Gen. Div.).

74 *Ibid.* at para. 24.

75 *Ibid.* at para. 23.

tence, he concluded that the most important factor was: "the need to preserve the integrity of the administration of justice; and that, as I see it, can only be achieved through a sentence of incarceration"[76] which in the circumstances called for a sentencing of five days in jail.

Police Enforcement

The majority of Canadian provinces have legislation that allows the judiciary to include provisions in custody or access orders directing the police to apprehend and deliver a child to a person entitled to custody or access. Even where legislation does not explicitly provide for this type of police assistance, superior court judges have included "police enforcement clauses" in their orders based on their inherent *parens patriae* jurisdiction. An order for police involvement is not be made in every case; however, where there is a significant history of non-compliance with custody and access orders, many judges will be prepared to make police enforcement orders if requested.

Accordingly, the inclusion of police-enforcement clauses in an order may be necessary. Although the police may assist in the enforcement of an access order even without specific provision in the order, the police are often reticent to become involved in what they perceive to be a non-criminal matter. The judiciary has noted concerns about the intrusiveness of this remedy and its potential to be upsetting and traumatic for the child (Bala & Bailey, 2004).

In deciding the matter under the Ontario *Children's Law Reform Act*, Mazza J., in *Allen v. Grenier*,[77] stated:

> It is clear that an order under subsection 36(2) is an order of last resort. Courts must make such orders sparingly and in the most exceptional circumstances. It is an order that can only be made once a court is satisfied that a party is unlawfully withholding a child from a person entitled to custody of or access to the child.[78]

In the Alberta case of *N. (R.J.) v. N. (L.J.M.)*,[79] a father applied to the court for an order seeking police enforcement of his access rights. In dismissing his application, Justice Lee stated:

> I conclude that there is enough concern raised regarding the husband's own behaviour as it relates to access that a police enforcement clause is not necessary to protect his specified access rights. It appears

[76] *Ibid*. at para. 29.

[77] 1997 CarswellOnt 934, [1997] O.J. No. 1198, 145 D.L.R. (4th) 286 (Ont. Gen. Div.).

[78] *Ibid*., at para. 38.

[79] 2003 CarswellAlta 970, 2003 ABQB 591, [2003] A.J. No. 867 (Alta. Q.B.).

> that the access has never been fully exercised in any event. In fact, the wife deposes that the husband has only taken the children for the full-allowed access time once in a almost five years.
>
> It also appears that the children of the marriage do not want to go with the husband, and they are old enough now to have some input into that decision. . .
>
> Accordingly, I will not be imposing any police enforcement clause to protect the husband's access rights.[80]

Imposing Joint Custody

Although the courts have generally held that joint custody should not be ordered unless there is some history of cooperation between the parents,[81] in some cases of alienation judges are prepared to make an order of joint custody as a way to "send a message" to the custodial parent and child that further resistance to the child's relationship with the other parent may result in a reversal of custody. This approach minimizes the instability in the child's life and signals to the alienating parent and third parties that they should respect the roles of both parents. In *Cox v. Stephen*,[82] the Ontario Court of Appeal affirmed a lower court decision that made such a joint custody order, commenting: "[the lower court judge] fashioned a remedy . . . that took appropriate account of the risk of alienation by awarding joint custody to [the father], yet protecting the child's sense of stability by not requiring him to leave his lifelong home and family."[83]

In *Mikan v. Mikan*,[84] the parties' 11-year-old daughter refused to see the father. The mother had armor-coated tinting placed on the windows of the matrimonial home, changed the locks and installed security apparatus and surveillance cameras. The Court found that the father was not a threat to the safety of the child or mother, and concluded that the mother's clear message to the child was that she should fear and reject her father. Justice Langdon observed that in light of s. 16(10) of the *Divorce Act*, the mother "scarcely qualifies as a suitable sole custody parent" and that "prompt, decisive and perhaps radical steps" need to be taken to "put a stop to this alienation".[85] Accordingly, the Court made an interim order of joint "week-about" custody, with an authorization for the father to use "reasonable force"

---

80 *Ibid.*, at paras. 13-16.

81 See *Roy v. Roy*, 2006 CarswellOnt 2898, 27 R.F.L. (6th) 44, [2006] O.J. No. 1872 (Ont. C.A.); *Lawson v. Lawson*, 2006 CarswellOnt 4789, 81 O.R. (3d) 321, 29 R.F.L. (6th) 8 (Ont. C.A.).

82 2003 CarswellOnt 4554, [2003] O.J. No. 4371, 47 R.F.L. (5th) 1 (Ont. C.A.).

83 *Ibid.*, at para. 3; see also *Mulder v. Mulder*, [2003] O.J. No. 2236 (Ont. S.C.J.).

84 2004 CarswellOnt 772, [2004] O.J. No. 740 (Ont. S.C.J.).

85 *Ibid.*, at paras. 21-22.

to have the daughter comply, including a direction for police assistance if requested.

Judicial Decisions for Custody Reversal in Alienation Cases

In some more severe alienation cases, the courts are prepared to order a reversal of custody. This will generally only be done if there is evidence from an assessor or other mental health experts that there has been alienation, that the alienated parent is capable of caring for the child, and that the benefits of the change in custody outweigh the inevitable emotional distress that the child will experience from such a change in living arrangements. Although the courts are reluctant to take this step, which can be very disruptive to the children involved, more and more judges are recognizing that a change in custody may be the only effective way of dealing with the emotional and psychological harm caused by an alienating parent (Epstein, 2007).

This increasing recognition extends for cases involving very young children. In the case of *Donald v. Leyton*,[86] the child was only 2.5 years old. The parents met over the internet and their marriage was short. The Court found that the mother, with her own mother's assistance, had continued to frustrate the child's contact with the father, and further, that the mother had violated court orders for access and was persistent in her unwillingness to communicate with the father about the child's needs. The Court awarded sole custody to the father, who was found to be a capable parent, with good extended family support, and better able to put the child's needs in the forefront and to support the child's relationship with the mother. A similar result occurred in the Alberta case of *S. (T.) v. T. (A.V)*[87] involving a four year old boy. The parents had never married and lived together only briefly. A number of professionals and community agencies, including the police were involved. The mother, who was observed to be overly involved with the child, was given many opportunities to change her alienating behaviour. After at least 14 applications for access, and a finding of alienation by the mother, accompanied by her unrelenting false allegations of physical and sexual abuse against the father, the Court granted sole custody and primary residency to the father. Initially, access of the mother to the child was limited to webcam, with the judge remaining seized of the matter to address further access in the future.

---

86 2008 CarswellOnt 1967 (Ont. S.C.J.).

87 2008 CarswellAlta 353, 2008 ABQB 185 (Alta. Q.B.)

In *Rogerson v. Tessaro*,[88] the Court of Appeal for Ontario upheld a lower court's decision to transfer custody of twin boys, aged five years at the time of trial, to their father based on evidence that the mother was persistently attempting to undermine the relationship between the children and father. The Court acknowledged that the remedy of changing custody was a "drastic one", but it approved the trial judge's structuring of the order as it was gradual, and thus likely to "cause as little disruption as possible for the children".[89]

Similarly, relying on the assessor's recommendations in *Rospendek v. Rzyskiewicz*,[90] the Court transferred primary care of the parties' six-year-old son to the father because of the mother's unwillingness not only to facilitate access of father to son, but also to accept that contact between father and son was beneficial to the child. The parties in this case had separated when the child was approximately one-and-a-half-years old. Although the family had been residing in Oregon, the father allowed the mother to relocate to Toronto with the child. The parties entered into a separation agreement whereby the child would remain in the care and control of his mother and the father would have access approximately once a month depending on his ability to travel to Toronto. Neither party had custody under the separation agreement. The evidence at trial was that the mother continually thwarted the father's access to the child and made several unsubstantiated allegations of abuse to the Children's Aid Society and the police. Additionally, in an attempt to curtail the father's ability to cross the border, she filed a report with immigration authorities alleging that the father had attempted to kidnap the child. An assessment was highly critical of the mother and her parental judgment. Justice Seppi placed significant weight on the evidence of the assessors, who recommended that the child be placed in the primary care of the father, with sole authority granted to him to make major decisions for the child. The judge found that the father was a loving parent who understood the importance for his son to have a strong bond with both parents. As difficult as the initial adjustment may have been to the child, the judge concluded that the boy needed to leave his mother's home in order to develop normally into a healthy adult. Justice Seppi placed the child in the primary care of his father,

---

88 2006 CarswellOnt 2777, [2006] O.J. No. 1825 (Ont. C.A.); see also *Pettenuzzo-Deschene v. Deschene*, *supra*, at note 22; *G. (C.J.) v. G. (R.C.)*, 2007 CarswellBC 215, 2007 BCSC 161, [2007] B.C.J. No. 212 (B.C. S.C.); *S. (T.) v. T. (A.V.)*, *supra*, at note 87; *Savage v. Savage*, 2007 CarswellOnt 448, [2007] O.J. No. 312 (S.C.J.); *Polsfut v. Polsfut*, 2008 CarswellSask 160, 2008 SKQB 63, [2008] S.J. No. 160 (Sask. Q.B)

89 *Ibid.*, at para. 8.

90 2006 CarswellOnt 1514, 28 R.F.L. (6th) 55 (Ont. S.C.J.), aff'd 2007 CarswellOnt 2924, 2007 ONCA 352, 37 R.F.L. (6th) 168 (Ont. C.A.).

with regular access to the mother. The Court of Appeal for Ontario affirmed Justice Seppi's order.

In *Starzycka v. Wronski*,[91] the Court, after a protracted initial proceeding in the year following separation, granted custody to the mother of the children; the father was granted alternate weekend and mid-week access to both children, even though only the youngest was the biological child of the father. Some eight years after separation, when the boy was nine years of age, the father claimed he was being denied access to his son with increasing frequency, and eventually that he was unable to exercise any access to his son. An order was made appointing the Office of the Children's Lawyer to investigate and report to the court on the issues of custody and access. The mother refused to cooperate with the Children's Lawyer's office, although she had been previously ordered to do so, and she continued to disobey court orders, despite several findings against her for contempt. After citing the mother for contempt, the Court ordered that the father should get interim custody to facilitate an investigation by the Office of the Children's Lawyer. In transferring interim custody of the son to the father and denying access to the mother, the Court concluded that "[t]he applicant (mother) has refused to follow any orders of this court for the past year and has been found to be in contempt of this court. She has refused numerous opportunities to purge her contempt by cooperating with the children's lawyer and by following the directions of this court."[92] The judge did grant her custody of the oldest child, for whom the father had not persisted in his claims for access, perhaps because he was not the biological parent. Justice Wolder was clear that had it not been for the one child who was to remain in her custody, he would have considered incarcerating the mother.

In Alberta case of *W. (S.L.) v. W. (W.N.)*[93] the case-management judge, on her own motion, made an emergency interim order transferring custody from the alienating mother to the father after receiving a copy of a psychologist's report and evidence from the mother's own computer transmissions confirming her ongoing alienation of her children from their father. The Court concluded that the father was more likely to abide by the access provisions of the emergency order than the mother was if the stay were removed. Further, the Court concluded that an irreparable harm concern would arise if the children remained with their mother. Justice Acton of the Alberta Queen's Bench refused to stay the order transferring custody to a father.

---

91 *Supra*, at note 59.

92 *Ibid* at para. 29.

93 2007 CarswellAlta 875, 2007 ABQB 420, [2007] A.J. No. 705 (Alta. Q.B.).

In *Moudry v. Moudry*,[94] the Court was faced with a mother who not only undermined her daughter's relationship with the father, but also attempted to manipulate the court system and deprive the court of helpful evidence. The Court found that "when all of the evidence was considered, there was a pattern of conduct" by the mother which disregarded the child's best interests."[95] The Court, in transferring custody to the child's father, concluded that in his care, the daughter would have a loving relationship with both parents, and that the court-ordered access would occur. The Court did not have the same confidence in the mother.

The Nova Scotia court in *Anderson v. Anderson*[96] was faced with determining appropriate custodial arrangements for the children in the face of the apparent unwillingness on the part of the custodial mother, to make any change that was not forced upon her. The Court was uncertain that the mother would carry out anything ordered by the Court was concerned that if she did, she would put the narrowest possible construction on any access provisions, all of which would lead to more interventions by the courts. The Court found that only if the children were to reside with the father would both parents have an opportunity to play a part in the children's lives. In making this finding, the Court stated, "It is important to remember that children usually benefit from having positive relationships with both of their parents since such involvement typically improves their self-esteem and reassures them that they are valued and loved despite the fact that their parents are no longer together. Positive relationships with both extended family members are important as well."[97] Although the Court had determined that it would be transferring custody to the father, it was concerned about the trauma that would be caused by removing the children from their primary caregiver. The Court believed that the transition would be difficult for the children as they had been conditioned to hate their father. The Court concluded that while a change in custody would no doubt be disruptive to the children in the short term, it was the long-term best interests that were of utmost importance.[98] The Court ordered that there should be a transition period and that custody should be changed incrementally over two months, with the children placed permanently with their father at the end of the school year.

---

[94] 2007 CarswellOnt 2782, [2007] O.J. No. 1735 (Ont. S.C.J.).

[95] *Ibid.*, at para. 85.

[96] 2005 CarswellNS 197, 2005 NSSC 94, 232 N.S.R. (2d) 371, 737 A.P.R. 371 (N.S. S.C.).

[97] *Ibid.*, at para. 99.

[98] *Ibid.*, at para. 102.

In *D. (N.) v. P. (T.)*,[99] Justice Jardine placed little weight on the wishes of an 11-year-old and a 13-year-old in determining appropriate custodial arrangements. In this case, the parties had separated in 1997 and litigated until 1999, when they entered into court-related mediation. A new arrangement was negotiated varying the previous orders of the court. The new agreement contained provisions whereby the parents would share the children on an alternating-year basis. The agreement seemed to work somewhat well for the parents and the children until 2005. In 2006, however, the mother commenced an application seeking custody of the elder child. Three months later, she amended her application to seek custody of the younger child as well. The father sought custody of both children. The children became heavily involved in the litigation, with the mother obtaining letters and tape recordings from the children to file as exhibits, expressing their wishes to live with their mother and blaming their father for taking their mother to court. Justice Jardine declined to place much weight on the statements or letters of the children, suggesting that the children were "directed, educated, and assisted in what to write or say".[100] The judge found that the mother's feelings towards the father influenced the children's views of him and his new wife. The judge ordered custody to the father, with specified access to the mother during holiday and vacation periods, as the distance between the parents' residences did not make weekend access possible. In an attempt to ensure that further alienation did not take place during the extended access and to ensure continuity, the judge seized himself of the case for a further two years.

Judicial Decisions against Custody Reversal When Alienation is Present

In some cases the courts conclude that despite alienating behaviour by the custodial parent, a child should not be removed from the care of the alienating parent as, on balance, it is not in the best interests of the child to do so. Even if the courts conclude that there has been severe alienation that will continue without a change in custody, they may decide not to vary custody. In some cases, a court is faced with a difficult situation in which an older child is steadfastly refusing contact with one parent.

In the Nova Scotia case of *Corkum v. Corkum*,[101] the Court had to decide the appropriate custodial arrangements for a 14-year-old

---

[99] 2007 CarswellBC 2073, 2007 BCPC 288, 42 R.F.L. (6th) 423, [2007] B.C.J. No. 1966 (B.C. Prov. Ct.).

[100] *Ibid.*, at para. 138.

[101] 2005 CarswellNS 235, 2005 NSSC 135 (N.S. S.C.).

girl who was unwilling to see her father. The father had had little access to his daughter in the preceding three years, and in the prior two years had had no contact with her despite several findings of contempt against the mother. An assessment was conducted, and the assessor found that although the child was thriving academically and socially, her emotional and psychological needs were not being met in the mother's home. The assessment report concluded that if the child continued to remain with her mother, she was at risk of mental-health difficulties and continued emotional harm; it was recommended that she be placed in the care of the child-welfare authorities. The child-welfare authorities declined to intervene, and so the trial judge was left to decide between placing the girl with a father she terrified, or leaving her with a mother who was causing her emotional harm. In making the decision, the Judge stated:

> I cannot find that it is Michelle's best interest to take her from a place she feels safe and put her with someone which will cause her great fear and anxiety. She is fourteen years old and I doubt she would go or stay if I made such an order. The option proposed by the IWK Health Centre allowed Michelle to feel safe in a neutral place while she received counselling to deal with her mother's mental health and to reunite her with her father. This is the option that I find would be in Michelle's best interest. However, it is not available to me.[102]

The judge ordered that the parents have joint custody of the child with primary residence granted to the mother and all decision-making authority resting in the hands of the father. The mother could obtain emergency medical treatment for the child, but all other consents were to be signed by the father. The child was to have counselling and the father's access was to be as recommended by the counsellor in the interim. Lastly, the court ordered the parties to return to court in six months, sending a clear message to the mother that their progress was to be monitored.

Similarly, in *Korwin v. Potworowski*,[103] the Court reluctantly felt that it had no alternative but to allow a 13-year-old to remain with his mother despite finding that she would not promote the relationship between the children and their father if the children were in her custody. In allowing the 13-year-old child to remain with his mother, Justice Gauthier stated: "There is no means of forcing this thirteen-year-old boy to remain in his father's home, short of locking him up. He is now of an age where, even if he may be too immature to appreciate what is best for him, he cannot be physically forced to remain

---

[102] *Ibid.*, at para 19

[103] *Supra*, at note 67.

where he does not want to be."[104] The two younger children were placed in their father's custody with access granted to their mother. The judge had envisioned a situation where the children would be together every weekend, but left the oldest boy's access subject to his wishes, given that access to a child of that age is virtually unenforceable.

In *S. (D.) v. S. (S.T.)*,[105] the mother sought sole custody of her son, aged nine, and a daughter, aged five, and a termination of all access to the father on the basis that he had sexually and emotionally abused the son. Psychological assessments of the children, however, indicated that abuse had likely not occurred, but that the mother had influenced the son's feelings toward the father. One expert advised the court that even if abuse had occurred, it was in the children's best interests to re-establish a relationship with their father through a therapeutic process rather than have them go through life hating him. The Court found that the mother lacked credibility and had alienated the children from their father. The Court stated if there was a viable alternative available, it would have awarded custody of the children to someone other than the mother, who was unable to accept that the children's anxieties and relationship with the father had to be resolved in a manner that would enable to develop emotionally intact. The Court ordered joint custody, with primary residence being with the mother. The judge stated that the order for joint custody gave the wife discretion to care for the children, but limited that discretion in the area of the children's relationship with their father, whose involvement in their lives was necessary. The father was to have immediate access to his daughter, and access to the son was subject to the alleviation of the son's fears by therapy.

In *P. (G.T.) v. P. (M.C.)*,[106] although the Court found that the mother had systematically attempted to alienate the children from their father, the Court dismissed the father's application for custody but on specific terms as to access and counselling. The Court observed that despite the alienation, the mother was more available to the children on a daily basis. Additionally, a change of residence might be counter-productive to any therapy, particularly to the oldest child who was most alienated from the father. The Court concluded that the children should remain with the mother on terms that gave the father the sole responsibility to make decisions about mental health counselling and liberal scheduled access. The father, though, was to have sole responsibility for making decisions about the children's

---

[104] *Ibid.*, at para. 145.

[105] 1997 CarswellOnt 3973, 40 O.T.C. 321, [1997] O.J. No. 4061 (Ont. Gen. Div.).

[106] 1997 CarswellOnt 6070 (Ont. Gen. Div.).

mental health, including the choice of counsellors, and access to the children for purposes of appointments. The Court gave the mother a clear message that her conduct was unacceptable and that her continued custody of the children was conditional upon her attending any counselling required by the children's therapist.

Conclusion

Building on the literature discussing prevalence, definition, causes and the impact of alienation summarized in Chapter 6, in this chapter we focused on assessment considerations and issues, including children's wishes and preferences, the role of the rejected parent and protocols for differentiating parent-child contact problems. We then provided an overview of different options for assessment recommendations, including interventions and treatment and the role of the court in these, and custody reversal. We concluded the chapter with an overview of enforcement issues and various judicial remedies, illustrating these with case law examples. Although the courts are not always able to deal effectively with alienation cases, in recent years they have shown a greater recognition of the problem and a greater willingness to respond. The most common initial response is to try to persuade alienating parents to cease their emotionally harmful conduct and to support actively the child's relationship with the other parent. However, in more severe cases where parents persist in defying an access order there may be a sanction for contempt of court or even reversal of custody for both younger children and adolescents.

Conclusion

Child custody and access custody assessments, also referred to as parenting plan assessments, frequently involve allegations of intimate partner violence, sexual abuse and child alienation or requests for relocation. At times only one of these issues will be present, but often, more than one will arise. While it is common to encounter these issues in child custody disputes, each is complex and challenging, often controversial. Each requires both legal and mental health practitioners to have specialized knowledge of the social science literature and research and of the legal trends and case law.

In our Introduction, to provide the legal context, we briefly discussed the laws in Canada relating to custody and access of children. In Chapter 1, we provided the social science context, summarized the literature on the impact of divorce on children, including factors that mediate adjustment, which can be applied to relocation cases as well as those involving allegations of intimate partner violence, sexual abuse and child alienation. For each of these issues, we summarized the relevant social science and research literature, discussed the various assessment considerations, protocols and options for the assessor's recommendations. Finally, we reviewed the court's approach, legal trends and remedies for each of these issues to assist legal and mental health practitioner in their appreciation for what the judiciary considers in their final decision-making about children's best interests.

As we have emphasized in this book and our earlier companion book, a competent assessment involves a painstaking examination of the family and a careful investigation of the allegations advanced by both parties. A multi-method, multi-source approach must be employed during which the assessor develops hypotheses that are both research and fact based. The assessor then looks for confirming and disconfirming data to either support or refute these allegations. In many cases, a single set of best interest recommendations regarding the parenting plan will be made, while in other cases, several alternatives will be presented to the court.

In addition to being aware of the continually growing literature available, the task of conducting parenting plan assessments is further complicated by the fact that there is no empirical data on assessment methods and protocols. There are virtually no well-controlled studies on outcomes for which parenting plans and arrangements are best for which circumstances, though it must be noted that for many issues it is not practical or ethically possible to conduct valid and reliable research. We do though have the benefit of a large and relevant literature as well as our own professional experience. We concur with others who have asserted that child custody assessments involve both science and art. Notwithstanding the lack of definitive data, we need to rely on the information that we do have, which includes well-controlled research from which we can extrapolate combined with our professional experience, to make best effort recommendations that can ultimately be used by the parties to come to a settlement, or failing that by the court to make decisions. Further research is required into both assessment methodology and differentiated parenting plans best suited for a particular set of circumstances.

Each of the four areas discussed in this book give rise to significant debate and controversy, and unfortunately, in some cases strong criticisms levelled by (or at) professionals. Highly politicized gender issues touch the core of issues relating to relocation, intimate partner violence, sexual abuse allegations and child alienation. Complicating matters further are dwindling resources for families in need. We applaud recent efforts towards multidisciplinary collaboration, like the Wingspread Conference on Domestic Violence Issues in Custody Cases, where experienced professionals have attempted to bridge gaps with respect to our understanding of these issues, develop appropriate and differentiated interventions, and provide direction for much needed future research.

It is no longer acceptable or useful for legal and mental health professionals to treat issues like domestic violence as unitary phenomena without differentiating on the basis of the family dynamics, the context and the consequences. As we have summarized, there are different types of violence, different types of parent-child contact problems, and different scenarios relative to cases involving sexual abuse allegations. Similarly, in relocation cases there are different sets of circumstances that need to be considered before making recommendations and decisions about best interest parenting plans for children. Clearly, a one size fits all model directed by presumptions is insufficient. Unpacking each of these issues is necessary to tailor the interventions so that the specific needs of specific children and their specific families can be better met.

As in common in life, and painfully evident for many who work in the complex and challenging area of child custody disputes, more often than not, the more that we know, the more we realize what we do not know. Further, knowing what we do not know is often more important than knowing what we do know. As John Tukey (1915-2000) said "Far better an approximate answer to a right question, which is often vague, than an exact answer to the wrong question, which can always be made precise."[1]

[1] Tukey, J.W. "The Future of Data Analysis" *Annals of Mathematical Statistics 33:1* (1962), 13-14.

Appendix A

A Comparison of Provincial and Territorial Custody and Access Legislation and Past Parental Conduct and Violence[1]

PROVINCE/ STATUTE	FACTORS – CUSTODY APPLICATIONS	FACTORS – ACCESS APPLICATIONS	ADDITIONAL FACTORS – PAST PARENTAL CONDUCT AND VIOLENCE	PARTIES
Alberta Family Law Act S.A. 2003, C.F.-4.5	s.18 (1) In all proceedings under this Part, the court shall take into consideration only the best interests of the child. (2) In determining what is in the best interests of the child, the court shall (a) ensure the greatest possible protection of the child's physical, psychological and emotional safety, and (b) consider all the child's needs and circumstances, including (i) the child's physical, psychological and emotional needs, including the child's need for stability, taking into consideration the child's age and stage of development. (ii) the history of care for the child, (iii) the child's cultural, linguistic, religious upbringing and heritage, (iv) the child's views and preferences, to the extent that it is appropriate to ascertain them.	Factors – s. 18(2)	ss. 18(2)(vi); 18(3) ; 18(4)	

[1] Adapted from www.canlii.org.

PROVINCE/ STATUTE	FACTORS – CUSTODY APPLICATIONS	FACTORS – ACCESS APPLICATIONS	ADDITIONAL FACTORS – PAST PARENTAL CONDUCT AND VIOLENCE	PARTIES
	(v) any plans proposed for the child's care and upbringing, (vi) any family violence, including its impact on (A) the safety of the child and other family and household members (B) the child's general well-being (C) the ability of the person who engaged in the family violence to care for and meet the needs of the child, and (D) the appropriateness of making an order that would require the guardians to cooperate on issues affecting the child, (vii) the nature and strength of the relationship (A) between the child and each person residing in the child's household and any other significant person in the child's life, and			

PROVINCE/ STATUTE	FACTORS – CUSTODY APPLICATIONS	FACTORS – ACCESS APPLICATIONS	ADDITIONAL FACTORS – PAST PARENTAL CONDUCT AND VIOLENCE	PARTIES
	(B) between the child and each person in respect of whom an order under this Part would apply, (viii) the ability and willingness of each person in respect of whom an order under this Part would apply (A) to care for and meet the needs of the child, and (B) to communicate and co-operate on issues affecting the child. (ix) taking into consideration the views of the child's current guardians, the benefit to the child of developing and maintaining meaningful relationships with each guardian or proposed guardian, (x) the ability and willingness of each guardian or proposed guardian to exercise the powers, responsibilities and entitlement of guardianship, and (xi) any civil or criminal proceedings that are relevant to the safety and well-being of the child.			

PROVINCE/ STATUTE	FACTORS – CUSTODY APPLICATIONS	FACTORS – ACCESS APPLICATIONS	ADDITIONAL FACTORS – PAST PARENTAL CONDUCT AND VIOLENCE	PARTIES
British Columbia *Family Relations Act*, R.S.B.C. 1996, c. 128 as amended	Best Interests s. 24(1) Factors: (a) the health and emotional well-being of the child including any special needs for care and treatment; (b) if appropriate, the views of the child; (c) the love, affection and similar ties that exist between the child and other persons; (d) education and training for the child: and (e) the capacity of each person to whom guardianship, custody or access rights and duties may be granted to exercise these rights and duties adequately. s. 1.1 persons in s.1(c)(d) defined as parents, grandparents, other relatives of the child and persons who are not relatives of the child	Best Interests - s.24 (1)	s.24(3) If the conduct does not substantially affect a factor set out in (1) or (2), the court must not consider that conduct. s.24(4) If under (3) the conduct of a person may be considered by a court, the court must consider the conduct only to the extent that the conduct affects a factor set out in (1) or (2). s. 37 On application, a court may make an order: (a) restraining any person from molesting, annoying, harassing, communicating or attempting to molest, annoy, harass or communicate with the applicant or a child in the lawful custody of the applicant or both; and (b) require person named in the order under (a) (i) to enter into a recognizance, with or without sureties, or to post a bond, and (ii) to report to the court or a person designated by the court, at the times and places and for the periods of time the court directs. s. 38(1) If a court makes a custody order or separation agreement is enforceable by a court the court may	s. 34 mother, father and any parent (as defined in s. 1).

PROVINCE/ STATUTE	FACTORS – CUSTODY APPLICATIONS	FACTORS – ACCESS APPLICATIONS	ADDITIONAL FACTORS – PAST PARENTAL CONDUCT AND VIOLENCE	PARTIES
			(a) order person not to enter premises where child resides from time to time, including premises owned by person , or right to possession by person; (b) order person must not make contact or endeavour to make contact or interfere with the child or any person who has custody or access to the child, or (c) where court is concludes that person named in custody order may not comply with order under (a) or (b) court may further order person to: i) enter into a recognizance, with or without sureties, in any reasonable amount that court thinks necessary ii) report to court or person designated for period of time and at times and places as court considers necessary iii)deliver up to court, or a person designated by court, any documents that court thinks fit, or	

PROVINCE/ STATUTE	FACTORS – CUSTODY APPLICATIONS	FACTORS – ACCESS APPLICATIONS	ADDITIONAL FACTORS – PAST PARENTAL CONDUCT AND VIOLENCE	PARTIES
			iv)transfer specific property to a trustee named by the court to be held subject to the terms and conditions specified in the order; or any combination of these. s.45 court may exercise jurisdiction to make or vary custody/ access order if: (a) child physically present in province; and (b) court is satisfied that on a balance of probabilities, suffer serious harm if child (i) remains in custody of person legally entitled to custody; (ii) returned to custody of person legally entitled to custody; **(iii)** is removed from province. **S. 38 (2) The Provincial Court must not make an order under subsection (1) (c) (iv).** **(3) In an order under subsection (1) (c) (iv), the court may specify terms and conditions for the return or the disposition of the property that the court considers appropriate.**	

PROVINCE/ STATUTE	FACTORS – CUSTODY APPLICATIONS	FACTORS – ACCESS APPLICATIONS	ADDITIONAL FACTORS – PAST PARENTAL CONDUCT AND VIOLENCE	PARTIES
			(4) A court, or a person designated by the court in an order under subsection (1) (c) (iii), must hold documents delivered in accordance with the order in safekeeping in accordance with any directions set out in the order. **(5) In an order under subsection (1), a court may give any directions it considers appropriate in respect of the safekeeping of the documents or property.**	
Manitoba *The Family Maintenance Act*, CC.S.M. 1997, c. F.20 as amended	Best Interests (s. 2(1) may include: s. 2(2) Views and preferences of the child considered where child able to understand the nature of the proceedings and court considers would not be harmful to the child. s. 3 Court may direct investigation by a qualified third party to determine best interests.	Best Interests s. 2(1) Factors s. 2(2) Investigation to determine best interests s. 3	s. 39(3) conduct considered in custody or access application only if court satisfied that the evidence bears directly on the parent's ability to care properly for the child. s.10(1)(c&d) REPEALED S.M. 1998, c.41, s.29 (allowed orders to restrain entrance to premises of other spouse and restraining from molesting, annoying, harassing spouse or child) s. 10.1(2) when a protection order or prevention order is made under the Domestic Violence and Stalking prevention, protection and compensation Act in respect of persons	

PROVINCE/ STATUTE	FACTORS – CUSTODY APPLICATIONS	FACTORS – ACCESS APPLICATIONS	ADDITIONAL FACTORS – PAST PARENTAL CONDUCT AND VIOLENCE	PARTIES
The Child Custody Enforcement Act, R.S.M. 1987, c.C360			who are also parties to an order under this Act that includes a provision made under the former clause 10(1)(d) (restraining order clause) of this Act, the provision made by a provincial court judge is revoked and the order made by a magistrate is revoked. s. 8 Upon application, a court may make an order that any person shall not molest, annoy or harass the applicant or a child in the lawful custody of the applicant and may require the respondent to enter into such recognizance, with or without sureties, or to post such bond as the court considers appropriate. s. 14(1) Court may punish contempt of or resistance to its process or orders in respect of custody or of access to a child by a fine of not more than $500 or imprisonment for not more than six months or both	s. 39(2)(a) either parent (biological or adoptive as defined in s. 1; or person so declared under Part II of the Act).
New Brunswick *Family Services Act*, S.N.B. 1980, c. F-2.2, as amended	Best Interests (s. 129(2)) Factors: s. 1: best interests of the child means the best interest of the child under the circumstances taking into consideration:	Best Interests: s.129(2) Factors s. 1.	s.128 Upon application of a person who is living separate and apart from his spouse a court may make an order restraining spouse of applicant from molesting, annoying, harassing or	s. 129(2) either or both parents (i.e. mother or father and any parent as defined in s. 1) or any person.

PROVINCE/ STATUTE	FACTORS – CUSTODY APPLICATIONS	FACTORS – ACCESS APPLICATIONS	ADDITIONAL FACTORS – PAST PARENTAL CONDUCT AND VIOLENCE	PARTIES
	(a) the mental, emotional and physical health of the child and his need for appropriate care or treatment, or both; (b) the views and preferences of the child, where such views and preferences can be reasonably ascertained; (c) the effect upon the child of any disruptions of the child's sense of continuity; (d) the love, affection and ties that exist between the child and each person to whom the child's custody is entrusted, each person to whom access to the child is granted and, where appropriate, each sibling of the child, and, where appropriate, each grandparent of the child; (e) the merits of any plan proposed by the Minister under which he could be caring for the child, in comparison with the merits of the child returning to or remaining with his parents; (f) the need to provide a secure environment that would permit the child to become a useful and productive member of society through the achievement of his full		interfering with applicant or any children in lawful custody of applicant. Court may also require spouse of applicant to enter into such recognizance as court considers appropriate. **129 (1) Unless otherwise agreed by written agreement or unless otherwise ordered by the court, where the child has more than one parent, the parents jointly have custody of their child.** **130 (3) The removal or withholding of a child without the consent of the person having custody of the child does not alter the habitual residence of the child unless there has been acquiescence or undue delay in commencing due process by the person from whom the child is removed or withheld.** **s. 130 (4) Notwithstanding subsection (1) and section 130.2, a court may exercise its jurisdiction to make or to vary an order in respect of the custody of or access to a child where:**	

PROVINCE/ STATUTE	FACTORS – CUSTODY APPLICATIONS	FACTORS – ACCESS APPLICATIONS	ADDITIONAL FACTORS – PAST PARENTAL CONDUCT AND VIOLENCE	PARTIES
	potential according to his individual capacity; and (g) the child's culture and religious heritage.		(a) child is physically present in province; and (b) court is satisfied child would, on balance of probabilities, suffer serious harm if (i) child remained in custody of person legally entitled to custody of child; (ii) child was returned to custody of person legally entitled to custody of child; or (iii) child was removed from province. s. 132 (1) Where court makes custody order or a custody order is enforceable under this Part, court may order that a person (a) shall not enter premises, including premises the person owns or has a right to possession of, where the child resides from time to time, or (b) shall not make contact or endeavor to make contact with or otherwise interfere with either child or any person having custody or access to child.	

PROVINCE/ STATUTE	FACTORS – CUSTODY APPLICATIONS	FACTORS – ACCESS APPLICATIONS	ADDITIONAL FACTORS – PAST PARENTAL CONDUCT AND VIOLENCE	PARTIES
			s. 132 (2) Where court is of the belief that the person named in an order under para. (1)(a) or (b) may not comply court may further order that person to (a) enter into a recognizance, with or without sureties, in such reasonable amount as the court considers necessary (b) report to court or person designated for such period of time, and at such times and places, as court considers necessary and reasonable, (c) deliver up to court such documents as court considers fit. **31 (1) The security or development of a child may be in danger when** . . . **(f) the child is living in a situation where there is domestic violence** **37.1 (1) For the purposes of subsection (2), the security of a person may be in danger when** . . . **(f) the person is living in a situation where there is severe domestic violence**	

PROVINCE/ STATUTE	FACTORS – CUSTODY APPLICATIONS	FACTORS – ACCESS APPLICATIONS	ADDITIONAL FACTORS – PAST PARENTAL CONDUCT AND VIOLENCE	PARTIES
Newfoundland *Children's Law Act*, R.S.N. 1990, c. C-13, as amended	Best Interests (s. 31(1) and s.72). Factors (s. 31(2)): (a) the love, affection and emotional ties between the child and, (i) each person entitled to or claiming custody of or access to the child (ii) other members of the child's family who live with the child, and (iii) persons involved in the care and upbringing of the child; (b) views and preferences of the child, where views and preferences can be reasonably be ascertained; (c) length of time the child has lived in a stable environment; (d) ability and willingness of each person applying for custody of the child to provide the child with guidance and education, the necessaries of life and the special needs of the child; (e) ability of each parent seeking the custody or access to act as a parent; (f) plans proposed for the care and upbringing of the child;	Best Interests -s.31(1) & s.72 Factors s.31(2)	s. 31(3) In assessing a person's ability to act as a parent, the court shall consider whether the person has ever acted in a violent manner towards (a) his/her spouse or child; (b) his/her child's parent; or (c) another member of the household, otherwise a person's past conduct shall only be considered if the court thinks it is relevant to the person's ability to act as a parent. s. 42 Court may make order restraining person from molesting, annoying or harassing the applicant and/or child in lawful custody of the applicant or from communicating with the applicant or children, except as the order provides and may require person to enter into a recognizance or post the bond that the court considers appropriate. (2) A person who contravenes a restraining order is guilty of an offence and upon summary conviction is liable, (a) for 1st offence, to a fine of not more than $1000 or to imprisonment for a term of not more than 3 months or to both;	s. 27 parent of a child or other party. s. 69(4)(b) to (d) other party: (b) a person who has demonstrated a settled intention to treat the child as a child of his or her family; (b).1 a grandparent of the child; (c) a person who had the actual care and upbringing of the child immediately before the application; and (d) another person whose presence as a party is necessary to determine the matters in issue. s. 70(1) a minor who is a parent, without a litigation guardian.

PROVINCE/ STATUTE	FACTORS – CUSTODY APPLICATIONS	FACTORS – ACCESS APPLICATIONS	ADDITIONAL FACTORS – PAST PARENTAL CONDUCT AND VIOLENCE	PARTIES
	(g) permanence and stability of the family unit with which it is proposed that the child will live; and (h) relationship by blood or through an adoption order between the child and each person who is a party to the application. s. 71(1) Where possible, court will take into consideration views and preferences of child to extent that child able to express them.		(b) 2nd or subsequent offence, to a fine of not more than $10 000 or imprisonment for a term of not more than 2 years or both. (3) A police officer may arrest without a warrant a person the police officer believes on reasonable grounds to have contravened a restraining order. s.40 Court may order the supervision of custody or access by a person or a director of child, youth and family services under the *Child, Youth and Family Services Act.* s. 41(4) A denial of access is not wrongful where respondent believes on reasonable grounds that a) child will suffer physical or emotional harm if access exercised; b) he/she might suffer physical harm if access exercised; or c) applicant is impaired by alcohol or a drug at the time of access.	
Northwest Territories *Children's Law Act*, S.N.W.T. 1997, c. 14as amended	Best Interests with a recognition that differing cultural values and practices must be respected (s. 17(1))	Best Interests with respect for differing cultural values - s.17(1) Factors - s. 17(2)	s. 17(3): Court shall also consider evidence that a person seeking custody or access has at any time committed an act of violence against his or her spouse, former spouse, child, child's	s. 20(1) a parent of a child or any other person with leave of the court (s. 20(2)).

PROVINCE/ STATUTE	FACTORS – CUSTODY APPLICATIONS	FACTORS – ACCESS APPLICATIONS	ADDITIONAL FACTORS – PAST PARENTAL CONDUCT AND VIOLENCE	PARTIES
	Factors (s. 17(2)): (a) the love, affection and emotional ties between the child and, (i) each person entitled to or seeking custody or access, (ii) other members of the child's family , and , (iii) persons involved in the care and upbringing of the child; (b) child's views and preferences if they can be reasonably ascertained; (c) child's cultural, linguistic and spiritual or religious upbringing and ties; (d) ability and willingness of each person applying for custody of the child to provide the child with guidance, education, and the necessaries of life and provide for any special needs of the child; (e) ability of each parent seeking custody or access to act as a parent; (f) who, from among those persons entitled to custody or access, has been primarily responsible for the care of the child, including care of the child's daily physical and social		parent or any other member of the person's household or family and any effect that such conduct had, is having, or may have on the child. s.17(4) Subject to (3) a person's past conduct may be considered in respect of custody or access to a child only where the court is satisfied that it is relevant to the person's ability to act as a parent. s.23: Where an order is made for custody of or access to a child, a court may give such directions as it considers appropriate for the supervision of the custody or access by a person who has consented to act as a supervisor.	

PROVINCE/ STATUTE	FACTORS – CUSTODY APPLICATIONS	FACTORS – ACCESS APPLICATIONS	ADDITIONAL FACTORS – PAST PARENTAL CONDUCT AND VIOLENCE	PARTIES
	needs, arrangements for alternative care for the child where it is required, arrangement for the child's health care and interaction with the child though, among other things, teaching,- playing, conversation, reading and discipline; (g) the effect a change of residence will have on the child; (h) permanence and stability of the family unit within which it is proposed that the child live; (i)any plans proposed for the care and upbringing of the child; (j) the relationship, by blood or though adoption, between the child and each person seeking custody or access; and (k) the willingness of each person seeking custody to facilitate access between the child and a parent of the child who is seeking custody or access.			
Nunavut *Children's Law Act (Nunavut)* S.N.W.T. 1997 c. 14 as amended	Best Interests with a recognition that differing cultural values and practices must be respected (s. 17(1))	Best Interests with respect for differing cultural values – s.17(1) Factors s. 17(2)	s. 17(3): Court shall also consider evidence that a person seeking custody or access has at any time committed an act of violence against his or her	s. 20(1) a parent of a child or any other person with leave of the court (s. 20(2)).

PROVINCE/ STATUTE	FACTORS – CUSTODY APPLICATIONS	FACTORS – ACCESS APPLICATIONS	ADDITIONAL FACTORS – PAST PARENTAL CONDUCT AND VIOLENCE	PARTIES
	Factors (s. 17(2)): (a) the love, affection and emotional ties between the child and, (i) each person entitled to or seeking custody or access, (ii) other members of the child's family , and (iii) persons involved in the care and upbringing of the child; (b) child's views and preferences if they can be reasonably ascertained; (c) child's cultural, linguistic and spiritual or religious upbringing and ties; (d) ability and willingness of each person applying for custody of the child to provide the child with guidance, education, and the necessaries of life and provide for any special needs of the child; (e) ability of each parent seeking the custody or access to act as a parent; (f) who, from among those persons entitled to custody or access, has been primarily responsible for the care of the child, including care of		spouse, former spouse, child, child's parent or any other member of the person's household or family and any effect that such conduct had, is having, or may have on the child. s.17(4) Subject to (3) a person's past conduct may be considered in respect of custody or access to a child only where the court is satisfied that it is relevant to the person's ability to act as a parent. s.23: Where an order is made for custody of or access to a child, a court may give such directions as it considers appropriate for the supervision of the custody or access by a person who has consented to act as a supervisor.	

PROVINCE/ STATUTE	FACTORS – CUSTODY APPLICATIONS	FACTORS – ACCESS APPLICATIONS	ADDITIONAL FACTORS – PAST PARENTAL CONDUCT AND VIOLENCE	PARTIES
	the child's daily physical and social needs, arrangements for alternative care for the child where it is required, arrangement for the child's health care and interaction with the child though, among other things, teaching, playing, conversation, reading and discipline; (g) the effect a change of residence will have on the child; (h) permanence and stability of the family unit within which it is proposed that the child live; (i) any plans proposed for the care and upbringing of the child; (j) the relationship, by blood or though adoption, between the child and each person seeking custody or access; and (k) the willingness of each person seeking custody to facilitate access between the child and a parent of the child who is seeking custody or access.			

PROVINCE/ STATUTE	FACTORS – CUSTODY APPLICATIONS	FACTORS – ACCESS APPLICATIONS	ADDITIONAL FACTORS – PAST PARENTAL CONDUCT AND VIOLENCE	PARTIES
Nova Scotia Maintenance and Custody Act, R.S.N.S.1989 c. 160, as amended	s. 18(5) welfare of the child is the paramount consideration. s. 18 Court may require written report from Minister respecting the child and his or her parents or guardian.	Welfare of the child – s. 18(5)	No existing provision.	s. 18(2) parent, guardian or other person authorized by the Ministry (parent defined in s. 18(1).
Ontario *Children's Law Reform Act*, R.S.O. 1990, c.C.12 as amended	Best Interests (s. 24(1)). Factors (s. 24(2)): (a) the love, affection and emotional ties between the child and, (i) each person entitled to or claiming custody of or access to the child, (ii) other members of the child's family who reside with the child, and (iii) persons involved in child's care and upbringing ; (b) views and preferences of child, where such views and preferences can reasonably be ascertained; (c) length of time the child has lived in a stable home environment; (d) ability and willingness of each person applying for custody of the child to provide the child with	Best Interests – s. 24(1) Factors – s.24(2)	s. 24(3) Past conduct of a person is not relevant in custody and/or access application unless the conduct is relevant to the ability of the person to act as a parent of a child. s. 23. A court may exercise its jurisdiction to make or to vary an order in respect of the custody of or access to a child where, (a) child is physically present in Ontario; and (b) court is satisfied that the child would, on the balance of probabilities, suffer serious harm if, (i) the child remains in the custody of the person legally entitled to custody of the child, (ii) child is returned to the custody of person legally entitled to custody of child, or	s. 21 parent of a child or any other person.

PROVINCE/ STATUTE	FACTORS – CUSTODY APPLICATIONS	FACTORS – ACCESS APPLICATIONS	ADDITIONAL FACTORS – PAST PARENTAL CONDUCT AND VIOLENCE	PARTIES
	guidance and education, the necessaries of life and any special needs of the child; (e) any plans proposed for the care and upbringing of the child; (f) permanence and stability of the family unit with which it is proposed the child will live; and (g) relationship by blood or through an adoption order between the child and each person who is a party to the application.		(iii) child is removed from Ontario. s. 34(1) Where an order is made for custody of or access to a child, a court may give such directions as it considers appropriate for the supervision of the custody or access by a person, a children's aid society or other body. s. 35(1) On application, a court may make an interim or final order restraining a person from molesting, annoying or harassing the applicant or children in the applicant's lawful custody and may require the person to enter into the recognizance or post the bond that the court considers (2) A person who contravenes a restraining order is guilty of an offence and on conviction is liable to either or both a fine of $5,000 and imprisonment for a term of not more than three months for a first offence and not more than two years for a subsequent offence. (3) A police officer may arrest without warrant a person the police officer believes on reasonable and probable grounds to have contravened a restraining order.	

PROVINCE/ STATUTE	FACTORS – CUSTODY APPLICATIONS	FACTORS – ACCESS APPLICATIONS	ADDITIONAL FACTORS – PAST PARENTAL CONDUCT AND VIOLENCE	PARTIES
			(4) Subsections (2) and (3) also apply in respect of contraventions, committed after those subsections come into force, of restraining orders made under a predecessor of this section.	
Prince Edward Island *Custody Jurisdiction and Enforcement Act*, R.S.P.E.I. 1988, c. C-33 as amended	Best Interests (s. 2(a)). s. 8(1) where possible, court shall consider the child's views and preferences, to extent that the child is able to express them	Best Interests s. 2(a) Child's views s. 8 (1)	s. 13 Court may make or vary order in respect of custody or access where: a) child physically present in the province, b) court satisfied child would, on balance of probabilities, suffer serious harm if i) child remains in custody of person legally entitled to custody of the child, ii) child is returned to the custody of person legally entitled to custody of the child, or iii) child is removed from province. s. 20 Upon application, court may make order restraining any person from molesting, annoying, harassing applicant or child in the lawful custody of the applicant and may require	s. 7(3) parties include: (a) the mother and father of the child; (b) a person who has demonstrated a settled intention to treat the child as a child of his or her family; (c) a person who had the actual care upbringing of the child immediately before the application; and (d) any other person whose presence as a party is necessary to determine the matters in issue.

PROVINCE/ STATUTE	FACTORS - CUSTODY APPLICATIONS	FACTORS - ACCESS APPLICATIONS	ADDITIONAL FACTORS - PAST PARENTAL CONDUCT AND VIOLENCE	PARTIES
			respondent to enter into such recognizance, with or without sureties, or to post such bond as the court considers appropriate.	
Quebec *Civil Code of Quebec*, S.Q. 1991, c. 64	s. 33 Every decision concerning a child shall be taken in light of the child's interest and the respect of his rights. Consideration is given, in addition to the moral, intellectual, emotional and material needs of the child, to the child's age, health, personality and family environment, and to other aspects of his situation. s. 34 The court shall, in every application brought before it affecting the interest of a child, give the child an opportunity to be heard if his age and power of discernment permit it.	Child's Interests - s. 33 Child's Wishes – s. 34	s. 606 Court may for a grave reason and in interest of the child, on applicant of any interested person, declare the father, the mother or either of them, or a third person on whom parental authority may have been conferred, to be deprived of such authority. Where such a measure is not required by the situation but action is nevertheless necessary the court may declare, instead, the withdrawal of an attribute of parental authority or of the exercise of such authority. The court may also directly examine an application for withdrawal.	s. 605 either parent or a third person.
Saskatchewan *Children's Law Act*, S.S. 1997, c. C-8.2, as amended	Best Interests – s.8(1)(a) Factors s. 8(1)(a): (i) quality of the relationship that child has with person who is seeking custody and any other person who may have a close connection with the child;	Best Interests – s. 9(1)(a) Factors – s. 9 (1) (a) (i) quality of the relationship that child has with person who is seeking access; (ii) personality, character	s. 8(1)(b) Past conduct not considered on custody application or variation unless conduct is relevant to ability of that person to act as a parent of a child s. 9(1)(b) Past conduct not considered on access application or variation unless conduct is relevant to ability of	s. 6(1) parent (as defined in s. 2(1)(j) or other person having a sufficient interest.

PROVINCE/ STATUTE	FACTORS – CUSTODY APPLICATIONS	FACTORS – ACCESS APPLICATIONS	ADDITIONAL FACTORS – PAST PARENTAL CONDUCT AND VIOLENCE	PARTIES
	(ii) personality, character and emotional needs of child; (iii) physical, psychological, social and economic needs of child; (iv) capacity of person who is seeking custody to act as legal custodian of the child; (v) home environment proposed to be provided for child; (vi) plans that person who is seeking custody has for child's future; and (vii) wishes of the child, to the extent that the court considers appropriate, having regard to the age and maturity of child. s.6(5) when making an order for custody and access, the court shall a) give effect to the principle that a child should have as much contact with each parent as is consistent with the best interests of the child and, for that purpose, shall take into consideration the willingness of the person seeking custody to facilitate that contact.	and emotional needs of child; (iii) capacity of person who is seeking access to care for the child during the times that the child is in his or her care; and (iv) wishes of child, to the extent that the court considers appropriate, having regard to the age and maturity of the child. s.6(5) when making an order for custody and access, the court shall a) give effect to the principle that a child should have as much contact with each parent as is consistent with the best interests of the child and, for that purpose, shall take into consideration the willingness of the person seeking custody to facilitate that contact.	the times that child is in his/her care. s. 23(1) Court may make order restraining any person from molesting, annoying, harassing, communicating or otherwise interfering with the applicant or a child in lawful care and custody of applicant. (2) Court may require respondent to enter into any recognizance, with or without sureties, or post any bond that the court considers appropriate. s. 29 Contempt of order under this Act (provision not specific to violence or inadequate parenting) – court may fine, imprison or both.	

PROVINCE/ STATUTE	FACTORS – CUSTODY APPLICATIONS	FACTORS – ACCESS APPLICATIONS	ADDITIONAL FACTORS – PAST PARENTAL CONDUCT AND VIOLENCE	PARTIES
Yukon *Children's Act*, R.S.Y. 2002, c.31 as amended	Best Interests (s. 1 and s. 30(1)) Factors s.30(1): (a) the bonding, love, affection and emotional ties between the child and, (i) each person entitled to or claiming custody of or access of the child, (ii) other members of the child's family who reside with the child, and (iii) persons involved in the care and upbringing of the child, (b) views and preferences of child, where such views and preferences can be reasonably ascertained; (c) length of time, having regard to child's sense of time, that child has lived in a stable environment; (d) ability and willingness of each person applying for custody of child to provide child with guidance, education, necessaries of life and any special needs of the child; (e) any plans proposed for care and upbringing of the child; (f) permanence and stability of family unit with which it is proposed that the child will live, and	s. 1 and s. 30(1)	s. 30(2) Past conduct not relevant unless conduct relevant to ability of person to have care or custody of a child. s. 36 Court may make an order restraining any person from molesting, annoying, harassing the applicant, or a child in the lawful care or custody of the applicant. s. 38 Court may make or vary order where (a) child physically present in Yukon, and (b) court satisfied child would, on balance of probabilities, suffer serious harm if, (i) child remains in custody of person legally entitled to custody; or (ii) child returned to custody of person legally entitled to custody.	s. 33(1) a parent of the child or any other person (parent as defined in s. 4 i.e. father or mother of a child by birth or adoption).

PROVINCE/ STATUTE	FACTORS – CUSTODY APPLICATIONS	FACTORS – ACCESS APPLICATIONS	ADDITIONAL FACTORS – PAST PARENTAL CONDUCT AND VIOLENCE	PARTIES
	(g) effect that awarding custody or care of child to one party would have on ability of the other party to have reasonable access to the child. s.30(3) No presumption of law or fact that best interests of child are, solely by virtue or age or sex of child, best served by placing child in care or custody of a female person rather than a male person or of a male person rather **than a** female person. s. 30(4) In any custody proceedings between mother and father of child, there shall be a rebuttable presumption that court ought to award care of child to one parent or other and all other parental rights associated with custody of child ought to be shared by mother and father jointly.			

Appendix B: Parent-Child Contact Treatment Program Agreement

Between: ________________________ **and** ________________________
(father) (mother)

1. Both parents have agreed that it is in the children's best interests to have meaningful relationships with both parents. To meet this goal they have agreed to engage the services of [insert therapist's name] to restore and/or facilitate contact between _______________ and the children, __________ age ___ ; ______________ , age ___ ; ______________ , age ___ ; ______________ , age ___ .

2. While the parents may have different views about the cause and reason for the children's refusal and or reluctance to see their ____________ , they agree not only on the objectives defined in #1, but also that they each are a part of the solution to meet those objectives.

3. Both parents understand they will be engaged in the therapeutic work necessary to support the children's contact to their ____________ . The therapist may provide consultation to the parents and may coach and educate them about ways to better communicate regarding the children, and about ways to better communicate with each other, all towards the goal of restoring/facilitating the children's contact to their ____________ .

4. Both parents agree and understand that in the best interest of their children the therapist will:

   a) work with each parent and their children toward the goal of identifying and separating each child's needs and views from each parent's needs and views;
   b) assist the parents to fully understand the needs of each of the children and the negative repercussions for the children of a severed and/or compromised relationship with a parent in their young lives and as adults;
   c) work with each family member to help them form more appropriate parent-parent and parent-child roles and boundaries;
   d) help each parent to distinguish valid concerns from those that are overly negative, critical and generalized relating to the other parent.

5. Both parents will overtly support the therapy and the thera-

pist to the children. This includes respecting the children's right *not* to discuss their sessions with the therapist.

6. The therapist will not be making decisions regarding the children's time with each parent and/or legal decision-making. Rather, the therapist will be assisting to implement the previously agreed to and/or court ordered parenting plan. Notwithstanding, we agree that the therapist may [*insert here scope of authority, if any, e.g., to determine the nature of the transitions, e.g. the rules of engagement, location and pacing of the contact, etc.*]. The therapist may make recommendations to the parents, lawyers and the court to the extent that the therapist has obtained sufficient information.

7. The parents have agreed to the involvement of the entire family, in various combinations, as directed by the therapist. The process will include meetings between the therapist and each of the parents and the children individually and jointly as directed by the therapist. The process may include interviews and/or meetings with other family members as deemed necessary by the therapist.

8. The therapist may also choose to contact any other professionals involved with the family to both give and receive information to better meet the aforementioned objectives and goals of the therapy. Toward this end, the parents will sign all releases of information required to implement the process. The parents shall provide all records, documentation, and information requested by the therapist as soon as possible upon request.

9. The therapy shall continue for at least ____________________ . [*Insert term in months or number of sessions, if any. May omit and have #10 only.*]

10. If either parent wishes to withdraw from the process, it is agreed that four (4) weeks notice will be given, with participation by that parent continuing during that period. Should the therapist wish to withdraw from the process, she will make a referral to another therapist after giving 4 weeks notice.

11. The parents understand that the process is not confidential. The therapist may use her discretion to exchange information as necessary between parents, between the parents and the children, and between the children. The therapist shall be free to disclose all information, documentation and corre-

spondence generated by the process with the lawyer for each parent and with the court. The therapist may at her discretion exchange information with other relevant professionals currently or previously involved and may speak with the lawyers ex-parte. This signed agreement serves as the parents' informed consent for [*insert therapist's name*] to obtain information from the Court, counsel and both parents AND for [*insert therapist's name*] to provide information received from all sources to the Court, counsel and the other parent.

12. The parents understand that the therapist is required to report to the appropriate child welfare authority (i.e., Metropolitan Children's Aid Society, Catholic Children's Aid Society, or Jewish Child & Family Service) if she has a reasonable suspicion that a child(ren) are being abused and/or neglected. In addition, the therapist is obliged to notify the proper authorities if she has a "reasonable suspicion" that a client may harm himself or herself or the other parent.

13. Father and Mother shall pay all of the costs at a rate of $ _______ per hour. Fees are applied to all time expended in any/all professional activities, including administrative matters. This includes time spent in reviewing documents and correspondence, writing memos to the file, writing reports, voice-mail, e-mail, meetings, and contacts/telephone calls with the parents, their counsel and other professionals involved. Also included are any unpaid fees charged retroactively from the time that services are initially requested and the file is opened. This also includes disbursements paid to collateral sources for verbal and/or written reports and agency/hospital reports.

14. Fees related to preparation for court are billed at $ _______ hour. Fees for testifying in court are billed by minimum half-day rate of $ _______ . Court-related fees (i.e., preparation time, attendance and travel) shall be by retainer in advance of any services rendered by the parent requesting the therapist's attendance at court. A separate contract for these services (detailing cancellation policy etc.) will apply and be provided at the time of any request.

15. Record keeping requirements make it necessary to log each e-mail, telephone call and/or message and make a record of even the briefest telephone call. For this reason, contacts in excess of 5 minutes are charged at the pro-rated hourly rate stipulated in the service agreement.

16. Mother shall pay ____ % and Father shall pay ____ % of the fees. Father and Mother will each provide a retainer of ____ hours of services, that is, $ ________ . At all times each parent shall maintain a retainer of at least $ ________ (two hours) in the account of [insert therapist's name], who shall advise in advance when a further retainer is required. A statement of account will be provided to the parents from time to time. If the above terms are not satisfied, [*insert therapist's name*] will postpone all services until the retainer terms are met. Non-payment of fees shall be grounds for the resignation of [*insert therapist's name*].

17. Appointments cancelled without at least 48 (forty-eight) hours advance notices may be charged at full fee independent of the reason for the cancellation. Monday and Tuesday appointments must be cancelled by 5:00 p.m. on the previous Friday. The parents will each be responsible for bills arising from his or her own cancellation with insufficient notice and/or failure to attend a scheduled appointment.

TO EVIDENCE THEIR AGREEMENT, FATHER AND MOTHER HAVE SIGNED THIS AGREEMENT BEFORE A WITNESS. CERTIFICATES OF INDEPENDENT LEGAL ADVICE ARE ATTACHED.

DATE: ______________________________

______________________________ ______________________________

Witness *Father*

DATE: ______________________________

______________________________ ______________________________

Witness *Mother*

References

Ackerman, M.J. *Clinician's Guide to Child Custody Evaluations* (New Jersey: John Wiley & Sons, 2006).

Adam, E. & Chase-Lansdale, P.L. "Home Sweet Home(s): Parental separations, residential moves, and adjustment problems in low-income adolescent girls" *Developmental Psychology* 38:5 (2002), 792-805.

AFCC Model Standards of Practice for Child Custody Evaluation (Task Force for Model Standards of Practice for Child Custody Evaluation 2004, revised 2007).

Agar, S. "Interventions for children who witness intimate partner violence: A literature review." The British Columbia Institute Against Family Violence: Vancouver, BC (2004).

Ahrons, C.R. "Family ties after divorce: Long-term implications for children" *Family Process* 46:1 (2007), 53-65.

Ahrons, C. & Tanner, J.L. "Adult children and their fathers: Relationship changes 20 years after parental divorce" *Family Relations* 52 (2003), 340-351.

Ainsworth, M.D.S., Blehar, M.C., Waters, E. & Wall, S. *Patterns of Attachment: A Psychological Study of the Strange Situation* (Hillsdale, NJ: Erlbaum, 1978).

Allen, S. & Daly, K. *The effects of father involvement: An updated research summary of evidence.* (Centre For Families, Work & Well-Being, University of Guelph, 2007).

Allen, S.M. & Hawkins, A.J. "Maternal gatekeeping: Mothers' beliefs and behaviors that inhibit greater father involvement in family work" *Journal of Marriage and the Family* 61 (1999), 199-212.

Amato, P.R. "Family processes in one-parent, stepparent and intake families: The child's point of view" *Journal of Marriage and the Family* 49 (1987), 327-337.

Amato, P.R. "Father-child relations, mother-child relations, and offspring psychological well-being in early adulthood" *Journal of Marriage and Family* 56 (1994), 1031-1042.

Amato, P.R. "The consequences of divorce for adults and children" *Journal of Marriage* and *Family Therapy* 62:1 (2000), 269-288.

Amato, P.R. "Children of divorce in the 1990's: An update from Amato and Keith (1991) meta-analysis" *Journal of Family Psychology* 15 (2001), 355-370.

Amato, P.R. "Reconciling divergent perspectives: Judith Wallerstein, quantitative family research, and children of divorce." *Family Relations* 52 (2003), 332-339.

Amato, P.R. & Afifi, T.D. "Feeling caught between parents: Adult children's relations with parents and subjective well-being" *Journal of Marriage and Family* 68 (2006), 222-235.

Amato, P.R. & Booth, C. "A prospective study of parental divorce and parent-child relationships" *Journal of Marriage and Family* 58 (1996), 356-373.

Amato, P.R. & Cheadle, J. "The long reach of divorce: Divorce and child well-being across three generations" *Journal of Marriage and Family* 67 (2005), 191-206.

Amato, P.R. & Gilbreth, J.G. "Nonresident fathers and children's wellbeing: A meta-analysis" *Journal of Marriage and Family* 61:3 (1999), 557-574.

Amato, P.R. & Keith, B. "Parental divorce and the well-being of children: A meta-analysis" *Psychological Bulletin* 110:1 (1991), 26-46.

Amato, P.R., Loomis, L. & Booth, A. "Parental divorce, marital conflict, and offspring well-being during early adulthood" *Social Forces* 73:3 (1995), 895-915.

Amato, P.R. & Rezac, S. "Contact with residential parents, interparental conflict and children's behaviour" *Journal of Family Issues* 15 (1994), 191-207.

American Academy of Child and Adolescent Psychiatry. Perspective: Guidelines for the Clinical Evaluation of Child and Adolescent Sexual Abuse (Adopted by the Council of the American Academy of Child and Adolescent Psychiatry June 11, 1988).

American Academy of Child and Adolescent Psychiatry. *Practice Parameters for the Forensic Evaluation of Children and Adolescents Who May Have Been Physically or Sexually Abused* (1997).

American Professional Society on the Abuse of Children. *Guidelines for Psychosocial Evaluation of Suspected Sexual Abuse in Young Children* (1990).

American Psychological Association Committee on Professional Practice and Standards. *Guidelines for Psychological Evaluations in Child Protection Matters* (Washington, DC: American Psychological Association, 1998).

Anderzén, I., Arnetz, B. B., Söderström, T. & Söderman, E. "Stress and sensitization in children: A controlled prospective psychophysiological study of children exposed to international relocation" *Journal of Psychosomatic Research* 43:3 (1997), 259-269.

Appel, A.E. & Holden, G.W. "The co-occurrence of spouse and physical child abuse: A review and appraisal" *Journal of Family Psychology* 12:4 (1998), 578-599.

Aquilino, W. S. "The noncustodial father-child relationship from adolescence into young adulthood" *Journal of Marriage and Family* 68 (2006), 929-946.

Archer, J. "Sex differences in physical aggression to partners: A reply to Frieze (2000), O'Leary (2000), and White, Smith, Koss, & Figueredo (2000)" *Psychological Bulletin* 126:5 (2000), 697-702.

Association of Family and Conciliation Courts, Parenting Coordination Guidelines (May 2005) (afcc@afccnet.org).

Attala, J., Hudson, W.W. & McSweeney, M. "A partial validations of two-short-form partner abuse scales" *Women and Health* 21:2/3 (1994), 125-139.

Austin, W.G. "A forensic psychology model of risk assessment for the child custody relocation law" *Family and Conciliation Courts Review* 38 (2000a), 192-207.

Austin, W.G. "Assessing credibility in allegations of marital violence in the high-conflict child custody case" *Family and Conciliation Courts Review* 38:4 (2000b), 462-477.

Austin, W.G. "Relocation law and the threshold of harm" *Family Law Quarterly* 34 (2000c), 1-13.

Austin, W.G. "Risk reduction interventions for the child custody relocation case" *Journal of Divorce and Remarriage* 33 (2000d), 65-72.

Austin, W.G. "Partner violence and risk assessment in child custody evaluations" *Family Court Review* 39:4 (2001), 483-496.

Austin, W.G. "Guidelines for utilizing collateral sources of information in child custody evaluation" *Family Law Review* 40 (2002), 177-184.

Austin, W.G. "Partner violence and risk assessment in child custody evaluations" *Domestic Violence, Essays from the Family Court Review: An Interdisciplinary Journal, Special Issue* (2005a), 104-117.

Austin, W.G. "The child and family investigator's evaluation for the relocation case". In R.M. Smith (Ed.), *The role of the child and family investigator and the child's legal representative in Colorado.* (pp. C9-1-C9-28), Denver: Colorado Bar Association, 2005b.

Austin, W.G. "The child and family investigator's evaluation for the relocation case". In R.M. Smith (Ed.), *The role of the child and family investigator and the child's legal representative in Colorado.* (pp. C9-1-C9-20), Denver: Colorado Bar Association, 2006.

Austin, W.G. "The child and family investigator's evaluation for the relocation case". In R.M. Smith (Ed.), *The role of the child and family investigator and the child's legal representative in Colorado.* (pp. C9-1-C9-24), Denver: Colorado Bar Association, 2007.

Austin, W.G. "Relocation, research, and forensic evaluation, Part 1: Effects of residential mobility on children of divorce" *Family Court Review* 46:1 (2008a), 137-150.

Austin, W.G. "Relocation, research, and forensic evaluation: Part II: Research in support of the relocation risk assessment model. *Family Court Review* 46:2 (2008b), 347-365.

Austin, W.G. & Gould, J.W. "Exploring three functions in child custody evaluation for the relocation case: Prediction, investigation, and making recommendations for a long-distance parenting plan" *Journal of Child Custody* 3:3/4 (2006), 63-108.

Austin, W.G. & Kirkpatrick, H.D. "The investigation component in forensic mental health evaluations: Considerations in the case of parenting time evaluations" *Journal of Child Custody 1* (2004), 23-43.

Awad, G., A. "The assessment of custody and access disputes in cases of sexual abuse allegations" *Canadian Journal of Psychiatry* 32 (1987), 539.

Ayoub, C., Deutsch, R. & Maranganore, A. "Emotional distress in children of high-conflict divorce" *Family and Conciliation Courts Review* 37:3 (1999), 297-314.

Bachman, R. & Saltzman, L.E. *Violence Against Women: Estimates from the Redesigned National Crime Victimization Survey* (U.S. Department of Justice, Bureau of Justice Statistics Report No. NCJ-154348, 1995).

Bagby, R.M., Nicholson, R.A., Buis, T., Radovanovic, H. & Fidler, B.J. "Defensive responding on the MMPI-2 in family custody and access evaluations" *Psychological Assessment* 11:1 (1999), 24-28.

Baker, A.J.L. "Parent alienation strategies: A qualitative study of adults who experienced parental alienation as a child" *Journal of Forensic Psychology* 23:4 (2005a), 41-64.

Baker, A.J.L."The long-term effects of parental alienation on adult children: A qualitative research study" *The American Journal of Family Therapy* 33 (2005b), 289-302.

Baker, A.J.L: "Patterns of parental alienation syndrome: A qualitative study of adults who were alienated from a parent as a child." *The American Journal of Family Therapy* 34 (2006), 63-78.

Baker, A.J. *Adult Children of Parental Alienation Syndrome: Breaking the Ties that Bind.* (New York: W. W. Norton & Company, Inc., 2007).

Bala, N. (2003). "Spousal abuse & children: Family law issues." Presentation at the National Family Law Program: La Malbaie, QC.

Bala, N. & Bailey, N. "Enforcement of access and alienation of children: Conflict reduction strategies and legal responses" *Canadian Family Law Quarterly* 23:1 (2004), 1-61.

Bala, N., Bertrand, M.C., Paetsch, L.D., Knoppers, J.J., Hornick, J.P., Noel, J., Boudreau, L. & Miklas, S.W. *Spousal Violence in Custody and Access Disputes: Recommendations for Reform* (Ottawa, ON: Status of Women Canada, 1998).

Bala, N., Fidler, B.J., Goldberg, D.L., & Houston, C. "Alienation children and parental separation: Legal responses in Canada's family courts" *Queen's Law Journal* 38 (2007a), 79-138.

Bala, N. & Harris, J. "Parental relocation: Applying the best interests of the child test in Ontario" *Canadian Journal of Family Law* 22 (2006), 127-170.

Bala, N., Jaffe, P. & Crooks, C. "Spousal violence and child-related cases: Challenging cases requiring differentiated responses" *Canadian Family Law Quarterly* 27 (2007), 1- 113.

Bala, N., Jaffe, P.G., Johnston, J.R. & McIntosh, J. "Domestic violence in separating families: Debates and dilemmas in developing appropriate parenting plans" Plenary Session presented at the 45th Annual Conference, Association of Family and Conciliation Courts (Vancouver, B.C.: May 28-31, 2008).

Bala, N., Mitnick, M., Trocme, N. & Houston, C. "Sexual abuse allegations and parental separation: Smokescreen or fire?" *Journal of Family Studies* 13 (2007b), 26-56.

Bala, N., & Schuman, J. "Allegations of sexual abuse when parents have separated" *Canadian Family Law Quarterly* 17 (1999), 191-241.

Bancroft, L. & Silverman, J.G. "Assessing abusers' risks to children" in P.G. Jaffe, L.L. Baker & A. Cunningham (Eds.) *Protecting Children from Domestic Violence: Strategies for Community Intervention* (New York: Guilford Press, 2004), 101-119.

Bancroft, L. & Silverman, J. *The Batterer as Parent: Addressing the Impact of Domestic Violence on Family Dynamics* (Thousand Oaks, CA: Sage Publications, 2002b).

Barber, B.K. "Reintroducing parental psychological control" In B.K. Barber (Ed.), *Intrusive Parenting* (Washington, DC: American Psychiatric Association, 2002a), 2-14.

Baris, M.A., Coates, C.A., Duvall, B.B., Garrity, C.B., Johnson, E.T. & LaCrosse, R.R. *Working with High Conflict Families of Divorce: A Guide for Professionals*. (New Jersey: Jason Aronson Publishers, 2000).

Baris, M. & Garrity, C. *Children of Divorce: Guidelines for Residence and Visitation* (DeKalb, IL: Psytec, Inc., 1988).

Bathurst, K., Gottfried, A.W. & Gottfried, A. E. "Normative data for the MMPI-2 in child custody litigation" *Psychological Assessment* 9 (1997), 205-211.

Baumrind, D. "Current patterns of parental authority" *Developmental Psychology Monograph 4:1* (1971), Part 2.

Bauserman, R. "Child adjustment in joint-custody versus sole-custody arrangements: A meta-analytic review" *Journal of Family Psychology 16* (2002), 91-102.

Behnke, D.A. & Connell, M. "Child custody evaluations in cases involving sexual abuse: A view from the bench" *Journal of Child Custody* 3:2 (2005), 121-136.

Belsky, J. "Child maltreatment: An ecological integration" *American Psychologist* 35 (1980), 320-335.

Belsky, J. "Etiology of child maltreatment: A developmental-ecological analysis" *Psychological Bulletin* 114:3 (1993), 413-434.

Benedek, E. & Schetky, D. "Allegations of sexual abuse in child custody and visitation disputes" in E. Benedek & D. Schetky (Eds.) *Emerging Issues in Child Psychiatry and Law* (New York: Brunner/Mazel, 1985), 145-156.

Benotto, M.L. "Ethics in family law: Is family law advocacy a contradiction in terms?" Paper presented at the Ontario Advocates Society Conference in Nassau, Bahamas, 2 December 1995.

Berkman, M., Casey, R.L., Berkowitz, S.J. & Marans, S. "Police in the lives of children exposed to domestic violence" in G.P. Jaffe, L.L. Baker & A.J. Cunningham (Eds.) *Protecting Children from Domestic Violence: Strategies for Community Intervention* (New York: The Guilford Press, 2004), 153-170.

Berman, M.E., McCloskey, M.S., & Broman-Fulks, J.J. (2003). "Biopsychosocial Approaches to Aggression." In E.F. Coccaro, *Aggression: Assessment and treatment into the 21st century*, pp. 61-74. New York, NY: Marcel Dekker, Inc.

Bernet, W. "Sexual abuse allegations in the context of child custody disputes" in R.A. Gardner, S.R. Sauber & D. Lorandos (Eds.) *The International Handbook of Parental Alienation Syndrome: Conceptual, Clinical and Legal Considerations* (Springfield, IL: Charles C Thomas, 2006), 242-263.

Berns, S. "Parents behaving badly: Parental alienation syndrome in the family court—Magic bullet or poisoned chalice?" *Australian Journal of Family Law 15:3* (2001), 191-214.

Bernstein, A.C. "Re-visioning, restructuring, and reconciliation: clinical practice with complex postdivorce families" *Family Process 46:1* (March 2007), 67-78.

Biller, H.B. *Fathers and Families: Paternal Factors in Child Development* (Westport, CT: Auburn House, 1993).

Birnbaum, R. "Court outcomes in child legal representation and clinical evaluations in child custody disputes" *Canadian Family Law Quarterly 24:2* (2005), 167-189.

Birnbaum, R. "Rendering children invisible: The forces at play during separation and divorce in the context of family violence" in R. Alaggia & C. Vine (Eds.) *Cruel but Not Unusual: Violence in Canadian Families* (Waterloo: Wilfrid Laurier University Press, 2006), 267-324.

Birnbaum, R., Fidler, B.J. & Kavassalis, K. (2008). *Child Custody Assessments: A Resource Guide for Legal and Mental Health Professionals*. Toronto: Thomson Carswell.

Black, T., Trocmé, N., Fallon, B. & MacLaurin, B. "The Canadian child welfare system response to exposure to domestic violence investigations" Child Welfare Information Sheet No. 39E. (Centre of Excellence for Children's Well-being, 2006).

Blush, G.J. & Ross, K.L. "Sexual allegations in divorce: The SAID Syndrome" *Conciliation Courts Review* 25:1 (1987), 1-11.

Boat, B. W. & Forman, S.B. "Consider the source: A commentary of incest and parental contact" *Journal of Child Sexual Abuse* 17:1 (2008), 13-19.

Bond, R. "The lingering debate over the parental alienation syndrome phenomenon" *Journal of Child Custody* 4:1/2 (2007), 37-54.

Booth, A. & Amato, P. "Divorce, residential change and stress" *Journal of Divorce and Remarriage* 18:1/2 (1992), 205-13.

Bow, J.N. & Boxer, P. "Assessing allegations of domestic violence in child custody evaluations" *Journal of Interpersonal Violence* 18:12 (2003), 1394-1410.

Bow, J. N., Gould, J. W. & Flens, J. R. *Examining Parental Alienation in Child Custody Cases: A Survey of Mental Health and Legal Professionals*. Association of Family and Conciliation Courts, 7th International Symposium on Child Custody Evaluations. Atlanta, Georgia, October 19-21, 2006.

Bow, J.N., Quinnell, F.A., Zaroff, M. & Assemany, A. "Assessment of sexual abuse allegations in child custody cases" *Professional Psychology: Research and Practice* 33:6 (2002), 566-575.

Bowlby, J. *Attachment and Loss, Vol. 1 Attachment* (New York: Basic, 1969).

Boyan, S.M. & Termini, A. *The Psychotherapist as Parent Coordinator in High Conflict Divorce: Strategies and Techniques* (New York: The Haworth Clinical Practice Press, 2004).

Brennan, P.A., and Raine, "A biosocial bases of antisocial behavior: Psycho-physiological, neurological, and cognitive factors. Psycho-physiological protective factors for males at high risk for crime." *Clincial Psychology Review* 17 (1997) 589-604.

Briere, J. *Trauma symptom inventory (TSI),* (Odessa, FL.: Psychological Assessment Resources, 1995).

Briere, J. *Trauma symptom checklist for children (TSCC)*, (Odessa, FL.: Psychological Assessment Resources, 1996).

Briere, J. Detailed *assessment of posttaumatic stress (DAPS)*. Odessa, Fl.: Psychological Assessment Resources, 2001)

Briere, J.N. & Elliot, D.M. "Immediate and long-term impacts of child sexual abuse" *The Future of Children: Sexual Abuse of Children* 4:2 (1994), 54-69.

Braver, S.R., Ellman, I.M. & Fabricius, W.V. "Relocation of children after divorce and children's best interests: New evidence and legal considerations" *Journal of Family Psychology* 17:2 (2003), 206-219.

Braver, S.R. & O'Connell, D. *Divorced dads: Shattering the myths*. (New York: Tarcher Putnam, 1998).

Brody, B. "Criticism of PAS in courts of law: How to deal with it and why it occurs" in R. A. Gardner, S. R. Sauber & D. Lorandos (Eds.) *The International Handbook of Parental Alienation Syndrome: Conceptual, Clinical and Legal Considerations* (Springfield, IL: Charles C Thomas, 2006a), 372-377.

Brody, B. "The misdiagnosis of PAS" in R. A. Gardner, S. R. Sauber & D. Lorandos (Eds.) *The International Handbook of Parental Alienation Syndrome: Conceptual, Clinical and Legal Considerations* (Springfield, IL: Charles C Thomas, 2006b), 209-227.

Brown, T. "Fathers and child abuse allegations in the context of parental separation and divorce" *Family Court Review* 41 (2003), 367-380.

Browne, A. & Finkelhor, D. "Impact of child sexual abuse: A review of the research" *Psychological Bulletin* 99 (1986), 66-77.

Brownridge, D.A. "Violence against women post-separation" *Aggression and Violent Behavior* 11 (2006), 514-530.

Bruch, C. "Parental alienation syndrome and parental alienation: Getting it wrong in child custody cases" *Family Law Quarterly* 35 (2001a), 527-552.

Bruch, C. "Parental alienation syndrome: Junk science in child custody determinations" *European Journal of Law Reform* (2001b), 383-404.

Bruch, C.S. (2002). Amica Curiae Brief of Dr. Carol S. Bruch, J.D., Dr. Filed in Case No. S107355, Marriage of LaMusga, Supreme Court of the State of California, August, 19, 2002.

Bruch, C.S. & Bowermaster, J.M. "The relocation of children and custodial parents: Public policy, past and present" *Family Law Quarterly* 30 (1996), 245-265.

Bruck, M., Ceci, S.J. & Hembrooke, H. "Reliability and credibility of young children's reports: From research to policy and practice" *American Psychologist* 53:2 (1998), 136-151.

Buchanan, C., Maccoby, E. & Dornbusch, S. "Caught between parents: Adolescents' experience in divorced homes" *Child Development* 62 (1991), 1008-1029.

Buchanan, C., Maccoby, E. & Dornbusch, S. *Adolescents After Divorce*. (MA: Harvard University Press, 1996).

Buckley, H., Whelan, S. & Holt, S. *Listen to me: Children's experience of domestic violence* (Trinity College, Dublin: Children's Research Centre, Research for Children and Young People, 2006).

Buerkle, K. "Mobile children and families qualitative and quantitative explorations of the meaning and "impact of residential mobility and school changes" Dissertation Abstracts International Section A: Humanities & Social Sciences 58:6-A (1997), 2067.

Bumpass, L.L., Martin, T.C. & Sweet, J.A. "The impact of family background and early marital factors on marital disruption" *Journal of Family Issues* 12 (1991), 22-42.

Burrill, J. "Descriptive statistics of the mild, moderate, and severe characteristics of parental alienation syndrome" in R. A. Gardner, S. R. Sauber & D. Lorandos (Eds.) *The International Handbook of Parental Alienation Syndrome: Conceptual, Clinical and Legal Considerations* (Springfield, IL: Charles C Thomas, 2006a) 49-55.

Burrill, J. "Reluctance to verify PAS as a legitimate syndrome" in R. A. Gardner, S. R. Sauber & D. Lorandos (Eds.) *The International Handbook of Parental Alienation Syndrome: Conceptual, Clinical and Legal Considerations* (Springfield, IL: Charles C Thomas, 2006b), 323-330.

Campbell, J.C. "Prediction of homicide of and by battered women" in J.C. Campbell (Ed.) *Assessing the Risk Dangerousness: Potential for Further Violence of Sexual Offenders, Batterers, and Child Abusers* (Newbury Park, CA: Sage, 1995), 96-113.

Campbell, J.C. "Safety planning based on lethality assessment for partners of batterers in intervention programes" in R.A. Geffner and A. Rosenbaum (Eds.) *Domestic Violence Offenders: Current Interventions, Research, and Implications for Policies and Standards* (New York: The Haworth Press, 2001), 129-143.

Carbon, S.B., Dunford-Jackson, J.D., Frederick, J.D., Jaffe, P.G., Johnston, J.R. & Salem, P. "Beyond windspread: Domestic violence and differentiation" Workshop presented at the 45th Annual Conference, Association of Family and Conciliation Courts (Vancouver, B.C.: May 28-31, 2008).

Carey, P.M., Sullivan, M.J. & Ward, M. "Complexities of child alienation: From assessment to options for intervention" Workshop presented at the 44th Annual Conference, Association of Family and Conciliation Courts (Washington, D.C.: June 2, 2007).

Carlson, B. E. "Children exposed to intimate partner violence: Research findings and implications for intervention" *Trauma, Violence and Abuse* 1:4 (2000), 321-342.

Carlson, M.J. "Family structure, father involvement, and adolescent behavioural outcomes" *Journal of Marriage and Family* 68 (2006), 137-154.

Cartwright, G.F. "Expanding the parameters of parental alienation syndrome" *American Journal of Family Therapy* 21:3 (1993), 203-215.

Cartwright, G.F. "Beyond parental alienation syndrome: Reconciling the alienated child and the lost parent" in R. A. Gardner, S. R. Sauber & D. Lorandos (Eds.) *The International Handbook of Parental Alienation Syndrome: Conceptual, Clinical and Legal Considerations* (Springfield, IL: Charles C Thomas, 2006), 286-291.

Ceci, S. J. & Bruck, M. "The suggestibility of the child witness: A historical review and synthesis" *Psychological Bulletin* 113 (1993), 403-439.

Ceci, S., & Bruck, M. *Jeopardy in the Courtroom: A Scientific Analysis of Children's Testimony* (Washington, D.C.: American Psychological Association, 1995).

Ceci, S.J. & Bruck, M. "The ontogeny and durability of true and false memories: A fuzzy trace account" *Journal of Experimental Child Psychology* 71 (1998), 165-169.

Ceci, S.J. & Friedman, R.D. "The suggestibility of children: Scientific research and legal implications" *Cornell Law Review* 86 (2000), 35-108.

Chase, N. "Parentification: An overview of theory, research, and society issues" in N. Chase (Ed.) *Burdened Children: Theory, Research and Treatment of Parentification* (New York: Sage Publications, 1999).

Cherlin, A.J., Furstenberg, F.F., Jr., Chase-Lansdale, P.L., Kiernan, K.E., Robines, P.K., Ruane Morrison & D., Teitler, J.O. "Longitudinal studies of effects of divorce on children in Great Britian and the United States" *Science* 252 (1991), 1386-1389.

Clarke-Stewart, K.A. & Hayward, C. "Advantages of father custody and contact for the psychological well-being of school-age children" *Journal of Applied Developmental Psychology* 17 (1996), 239-270.

Clarke-Stewart, K., Vandell, D., McCartney, K., Owen, M. & Booth, C. "Effects of parental separation and divorce on very young children" *Journal of Family Psychology* 14:2 (2000), 304-326.

Clawar, S. & Rivlin, B. *Children Held Hostage: Dealing with Programmed and Brainwashed Children.* (American Bar Association Section of Family Law, 1991).

Coates, C. "Parenting coordination: Implementation issues" *Family Court Review* 41:4 (2003), 533-564.

Coates, C., Deutsch, R., Starnes, H., Sullivan, M.J. & Sydlik, B. "Parenting coordination for high conflict families" *Family Court Review* 42:2 (2004), 246-262.

Conger, D. & Finkelstein, M. "Foster care and school mobility" *The Journal of Negro Education* 72:1 (2003), 97-103.

Conte, J.R. & Berliner, L. "The Impact of Sexual abuse on children: Empirical findings" In L.E. Walker (Ed.) *Handbook on Sexual Abuse of Children: Assessment and Treatment Issues* (New York: Springer, 1988).

Crossman, A.M., Powell, M.B., Principe, G.F. & Ceci, S.J. "Child testimony in custody cases: A review" *Journal of Forensic Psychology Practice* 2:1 (2002), 1-32.

Cummings, E.M. & Davies, P.T. *Children and Marital Conflict.* (New York: Guildord, 1994).

Dalton, C., Kelly, J.B., Ver Steegh, N. & Kruzick, E.R. "Domestic violence, differentiation and family court: Tensions, terminology and collaboration" Opening session presented at the 45th Annual Conference, Association of Family and Conciliation Courts (Vancouver, B.C.: May 28-31, 2008).

Dalton, C. "When paradigms collide: Protecting battered parents and their children in the family court system" *Special Essays from the Family Court Review: An Interdisciplinary Journal* (2005), 10-33.

Dalton, C., Carbon, S. & Olesen, N. "High conflict divorce, violence, and abuse: Implications for custody and visitation decisions" *Juvenile and Family Court Journal* (2003), 11-33.

Dalton, C., Drozd, L.M. & Wong, F.Q.F. *Navigating custody and visitation evaluations in cases with domestic violence: A judge's guide* (National Council of Juvenile and Family Court Judges, 2006).

Dammeyer, M.D. "The assessment of child sexual abuse allegations: Using research to guide clinical decision-making" *Behavioural Sciences and the Law* 16 (1998), 21-34.

Darnell, D. "A broader definition of parental alienation" Downloaded from http://www.parentalalienation.com/PASfound2.htm (1997).

Darnell, D. *Divorce Casualties: Protecting Your Children from Parental Alienation* (Dallas, TX: Taylor Publishing Co., 1998).

Darwish, D., Esquivel, G.B., Houtz, J.C. & Alfonso, V.C. "Play and social skills in maltreated and non-maltreated preschoolers during peer interactions" *Child Abuse and Neglect* 25 (2001), 13-31.

Dauvergne, M. "Homicide in Canada" *Juristat* 24:8 (2003).

Davis, K.E. "Interparental violence: The children as victims" *Issues in Comprehensive Pediatric Nursing* 11 (1988), 291-302.

De Bellis, M.D. "Developmental traumatology: The psychobiological development of maltreated children and its implications for research, treatment, and policy" *Developmental and Psychopathology* 13 (2001), 539-564.

De Vries, S. & Niemi, J.D. "Reintegration of disrupted parent-child relationships" Workshop presented at the 44th Annual Conference, Association of Family and Conciliation Courts (Washington, D.C.: June 2, 2007).

Debele, G. "A children's rights approach to relocation: A meaningful best interests standard" *Children's Rights* 15 (1998), 74-118.

DeKeserdy, W.S. & Schwartz, M.D. "Definitional issues" in C.M. Renzetti, J.L. Edleson & R.K. Bergen (Eds.) *Sourcebook on Violence Against Women* (Thousand Oaks, CA: Sage, 2001), 23-34.

DeWIt, D. "Frequent childhood geographic relocation: Its impact on drug use initiation and the development of alcohol and other drug-related problems among adolescents and young adults" *Addictive Behaviours* 23:5 (1998), 623-634.

Diler, R.S., Avci, A. & Seydaoglu, G. "Emotional and behavioural problems in migrant children" *Swiss Medical Weekly* 23:5 (2003), 623-634.

Dobash, R.E. & Dobash, R. *Violence Against Wives* (New York: The Free Press, 1979).Doris, J. (Ed.) *The Suggestibility of Children's Recollections: Implications for Eyewitness Testimony* (Washington, DC: American Psychological Association, 1991).

Drozd, L.M. "DVCC protocol" *Journal of Child Custody* 4:3/4 (2007), 19-31.

Drozd, L., Kuehnle, K. & Walker, L. "Safety first: A model for understanding domestic violence in child custody and access disputes" *Journal of Child Custody* 1:2 (2004), 75-103.

Drozd, L., & Olesen, N. "Is it abuse, alienation, and/or estrangement? A decision tree" *Journal of Child Custody* 1:3 (2004), 65-106.

Duncan, K. *Healing from the Trauma of Childhood Sexual Abuse.: The Journey of Women* (Westport, CT: Praeger, 2004).

Dunford-Jackson, B.L. & Jordan, S. "Context is everything: Domestic violence in the real world" *Synergy* 10:1 (2006), 7-8.

Dunn, J., Cheng, H., O'Connor, T.G. & Bridges, L. "Children's perspectives on their relationships with their non-resident fathers: Influences, outcomes and implications" *Journal of Child Psychology* 45:3 (2004), 553-566.

Dunne, J. & Hedrick, M. "The parental alienation syndrome: An analysis of sixteen selected cases" *Journal of Divorce and Remarriage* 21 (1994), 21-28.

Dutton, D.G. "Domestic abuse assessment in child custody disputes: Beware the domestic violence research paradigm" *Journal of Child Custody* 2:4 (2005), 23-42.

Dutton, D. G. "A briefer reply to Johnson: Re-affirming the necessity of a gender-neutral approach to custody evaluations" *Journal of Child Custody* 3:1 (2006), 67-69.

Dutton, D.G. "The complexities of domestic violence" *American Psychologist* 62:7 (October 2007), 708-709.

Dutton, M.A. *Empowering and Healing the Battered Woman: A Model for Assessment and Intervention* (New York: Springer, 1992).

Edleson, J.L. "Do batterers' programs work? Minnesota Center Against Violence and Abuse" (1995) available online at: www.mincava.umn.edu/documents/batterer-program/battererprogram.html

Edleson, J.L. "Children's witnessing of adult domestic violence" *Journal of Interpersonal Violence* 14:8 (1999a), 839-870.

Edleson, J.L. "The overlap between child maltreatment and woman battering" *Violence Against Women* 5:2 (1999b), 134-154.

Edleson, J.L., Gassman-Pines, J. & Hill, M.B. "Defining child exposure to domestic violence as neglect: Minnesota's difficult experience" *Social Work* 51:2 (2006), 167-174.

Edleson, J.L., Mbilinyi, L.F. & Shetty, S. *Parenting in the Context of Domestic Violence.* (San Francisco: Judicial Council of California, Administrative Office of the Courts, Center for Families, Children & the Courts, 2003). Available online at: www.courtinfo.ca.gov/programs/cfcc/resources/publications.

Edleson, J.L. & Syers, M. "The relative effectiveness of group treatments for men who batter" *Social Work Research and Abstracts* 26 (1990), 10-17.

Edleson, J.L. & Syers, M. "The effects of group treatment for men who batter: An 18-month follow-up study" *Research in Social Work Practice* 1 (1991), 227-243.

Ehrenberg, M.F. & Elterman, M.F. "Evaluating allegations of sexual abuse in the context of divorce, child custody, and access disputes" in Tara Ney (Ed.) *True and False Allegations of Child Sexual Abuse: Assessment and Case Management* (New York: Brunner/Mazel Publishers, 1995), 209-230.

El-Sheikh, M. & Harger, J. "Appraisals of marital conflict and children's adjustment, health, and physiological reactivity" *Developmental Psychology* 37:6 (2001), 875-885.

Ellis, D. "Divorce and the family court: What can be done about domestic violence?" *Family Court Review* 46:3 (2008), 531-536.

Ellis, D. & Stuckless, N. "Pre-separation abuse, marital conflict mediation and post-separation abuse" *Mediation Quarterly* 9 (1992), 205-225.

Ellis, D. & Stuckless, N. *Mediating and Negotiating Marital Conflicts* (Thousand Oaks, CA: Sage, 1996).

Ellis, D. & Stuckless, N. "Domestic violence, dove, and divorce mediation" *Family Court Review* 44:4 (2006), 658-671.

Ellis, D., Stuckless, N. & Wright, "Separation, domestic violence, and divorce mediation" *Conflict Resolution Quarterly* 23:4 (2006), 461-485.

Ellis, E. *Divorce Wars: Interventions with Families in Conflict* (Washington, D.C.: American Psychological Association, 2000).

Ellis, E. "A stepwise approach to evaluating children for parental alienation syndrome" *Journal of Child Custody* 4:1/2 (2007), 55-78.

Emery, R. E. "Interparental conflict and the children of discord and divorce" *Psychological Bulletin* 92 (1982), 310-333.

Emery, R.E. "Family violence" *American Psychologist* 44 (1989), 321-328.

Emery, R.E. "Changing the rules for determining child custody in divorce cases" *Clinical Psychology: Science and Practice* 6 (1999a), 323-327.

Emery, R.E. *Marriage, Divorce and Children's Adjustment, 2nd Ed.* (New York: Sage Publications, 1999b).

Emery, R.E. "Post-divorce family life for children: An overview of research and some implications for policy" in R.A. Thompson & P.R. Amato (Eds.) *The Post-Divorce Family* (Thousand Oaks, Ca: Sage, 1999c).

Emery, R.E. "Distress among young adults from divorced families" *Journal of Family Psychology* 14:4 (2000), 671-687.

Emery, R.E. "Children's voices: Listening—and deciding-is an adult responsibility" *Arizona Law Review* 45 (2003), 621-627.

Emery, R.E. *The Truth about Children and Divorce: Dealing with Your Emotions So You and Your Children Can Thrive* (NY: Penguin, 2004).

Emery, R.E. "Parental alienation syndrome: Proponents bear the burden of proof" *Family Court Review* 43:1 (2005), 8-13.

Emery, R.E. & Laumann-Billings, L. "An overview of the nature, causes, and consequences of abusive family relationships: Toward differentiating maltreatment and violence" *American Psychologist* 53 (1998), 121-135.

Epstein, P. "Enforcement of access: Judicial management of interference with access" Paper presented at the Law Society of Upper Canada 6-Minute Lawyer Lecture Series (Toronto, Canada, 2002), 32.

Epstein, P. "Judicial management of interference with access" Paper presented at the Saskatchewan Trial Lawyers Association Fall Conference: Gaining an Edge (Regina, Canada, November 2007).

Everett, C. A. "Family therapy for parental alienation syndrome: Understanding the interlocking pathologies" In R. A. Gardner, S. R. Sauber & D. Lorandos (Eds.), *The International Handbook of Parental Alienation Syndrome* (Springfield, IL: Charles C Thomas Publisher, Ltd., 2006) 228-241.

Fabricius, W.V. "Listening to children of divorce: New findings that diverge from Wallerstein, Lewis & Blakeslee (2000)" *Family Relations* 52 (2003), 385-396.

Fabricius, W.V., Braver, S.L. & Deneau, K. "Divorced parents' financial support of their children's college expenses" *Family Court Review* 41 (2003), 224-241.

Fabricius, W.V. & Braver, S.L. "Relocation, parent conflict, and domestic violence: Independent risk factors for children of divorce" *Journal of Child Custody* 3:3/4 (2006), 7-27.

Fabricius, W.V. & Hall, J. "Young adults' perspectives on divorce: Living arrangements" *Family & Conciliation Courts Review* 38:4 (2000), 446-461.

Fabricius, W.V. & Luecken, L.J. "Postdivorce living arrangements, parent conflict, and long-term physical heahl correlates for children of divorce." *Journal of Family Psychology* 21:2 (2007), 195-205.

Fagan, J. & Barnett, M. "The relationship between maternal gatekeeping, paternal competence, mothers' attitudes about the father role, and father involvement" *Journal of Family Issues* 24 (2003), 1020-1043.

Fahn M.S. "Allegations of child sexual abuse in custody disputes: Getting to the truth of the matter" *Family Law Quarterly* 25 (1991), 193 -216.

Faller, K. "Possible explanations for child sexual abuse allegations in divorce" *American Journal of Orthopsychiatry* 61:1 (1991), 86-91.

Faller, K. "The parental alienation syndrome: What is it and what data support it?" *Child Maltreatment* 3 (1997), 100-115.

Faller, K.C. "Research and practice in child interviewing: Implications for children exposed to domestic violence" *Journal of Interpersonal Violence* 18:4 (2003), 377-389.

Faller, K. "Coaching children about sexual abuse: A pilot study of professionals' Perceptions" *Child Abuse & Neglect* 31 (2007), 947-959.

Faller , K.C. & DeVoe, E. "Allegations of sexual abuse in divorce" *Journal of Child Sexual Abuse* 4:4 (1995), 1-25.

Fantuzzo, J. W. & Lindquist, C.U. "The effects of observing conjugal violence on children: A review and analysis of research methodology" *Journal of Family Violence* 4 (1989), 77-94.

Fantuzzo, J. W. & Mohr, W. K. "Prevalence and effects of child exposure to domestic violence" (1999) Retrieved May 11, 2006, from www.futureofchildren.org/usr_doc/vol9no3Art2.pdf

Fantuzzo, J.W., Mohr, W.K. & Noone, M.J. "Making the invisible victims of violence against women visible through university/community partnerships" *Journal of Aggression, Maltreatment and Trauma* 3:1 (2000), 9-23.

Feinberg, R., & Greene, T. "The intractable client: Guidelines for working with personality disorders in family law" *Family and Conciliation Court Review* 35:3 (1997), 351-365.

Fidler, B.J. "Developing parenting time schedules: Conundrums and considerations" In Martha Shaffer (Ed.) *Contemporary Issues in Family Law: Engaging with the Legacy of James G. McLeod* (Toronto: Thomson Carswell, 2007).

Fidler, B.J. & Birnbaum, R. "Child custody disputes: Private and public assessments." *Canadian Family Law Quarterly*, 25(2) (2006) 137-167.

Fidler, B., & Epstein, P. "Parenting coordination in Canada: An overview of legal and practice issues" *Journal of Child Custody* 5:1/2 (2008), 53-87.

Finkelhor, D. "The sexual abuse of children: Current research reviewed" *Psychiatric Annals* 17:4 (1987), 233-241.

Finkelhor, D. "The international epidemiology of child sexual abuse" *Child Abuse & Neglect* 18:5 (1994), 409-417.

Finkelhor, D. "The legacy of the clergy abuse scandal" *Child Abuse & Neglect* 27 (2003), 1229-1229.

Finkelhor, D. & Browne, A. "The traumatic impact of child sexual abuse: A conceptualization" *American Journal of Orthopsychiatry* 55:4 (1985), 530-541.

Finley, G. E. & Schwartz, S. J. "Father involvement and young adult outcomes: The differential contributions of divorce and gender" *Family Court Review* (in press).

Fischer, K., Vidmar, N. & Ellis, R. "The culture of battering and the role of mediation in domestic violence cases" *SMU Law Review* 46 (1993), 2117-2174.

Frederick, L. "Questions about family court domestic violence screening and assessment" *Family Court Review* 46:3 (2008), 523-530.

Frederick , L. & Tilly, J. *Effective Intervention in Domestic Violence Cases: Context is Everything* (Minneapolis, MN: Battered Women's Justice Project, 2001).

Freeman, R., Abel, D., Cooper-Smith, M. & Stein, L. "Reconnecting children with absent parents: A model for intervention" *Family Court Review* 42:3 (2004), 439-459.

Friedrich, W.N. "Correlates of sexual behavior in young children" *Journal of Child Custody* 3:20 (2005), 41-55.

Friedrich, W.N., Gully, K.J. & Trane, S.T. "Re: It is a mistake to conclude that sexual abuse and sexualized behaviour are not related: A reply to Drach, Wientzen and Ricci" *Child Abuse and Neglect* 29:4 (2005), 297-302.

Friedman, M. "The so-called high-conflict couple: A closer look" *The American Journal of Family Therapy* 32 (2004), 101-117.

Furstenberg, F.F., Morgan, S.P. & Allison, P.D. "Paternal participation and children's well-being after marital dissolution" *American Sociological Review* 52:5 (1987), 695-701.

Furstenberg, Jr., F.F., Nord, C.W., Peterson, J.L. & Zill, N. "The life course of children of divorce: Marital disruption and parental contact" *American Sociological Review* 48 (1983), 656-658.

Ganley, A.L. & Schechter, S. *Domestic violence: A national curriculum for child protective services* (San Francisco, CA: Family Violence Prevention Fund, 1995).

Garbarino, J. "The human ecology of child maltreatment: A conceptual model of research" *Journal of Marriage and the Family* (1977), 721-735.

Garbarino, J. & Stott, F.M. *What Children Can Tell Us: Eliciting, Interpreting and Evaluating Critical Information from Children* (San Francisco: Jossey-Bass Publishers, 1992).

Garber, B. "Parental alienation in light of attachment theory: Consideration of the broader implications for child development, clinical practice, and forensic process" *Journal of Child Custody* 1:4 (2004), 49-76.

Garber, B.D. "Conceptualizing visitation resistance and refusal in the context of parental conflict, separation and divorce" *Family Court Review* 45:4 (2007), 588-599.

Gardner, R. "Recent trends in divorce and custody litigation" *The Academy Forum* 29:2 (1985), 3-7.

Gardner, R. *The PAS and the Differentiation Between Fabricated and Genuine Child Sex Abuse* (Cressskill, New Jersey: Creative Therapeutics, 1987).

Gardner, R. *The Parental Alienation Syndrome: A Guide for Mental Health and Legal Professionals* (Cresskill, New Jersey: Creative Therapeutics, Inc., 1992a, with updated addenda in 1994 and 1996).

Gardner, R. *True and False Allegations of Child Sex Abuse* (Cresskill, New Jersey: Creative Therapeutics, Inc., 1992b).

Gardner, R.A. *Protocols for the Sex-abuse Evaluation* (New Jersey: Creative Therapeutic, Inc., 1995).

Gardner, R. "Recommendations for dealing with parents who induce a parental alienation syndrome in their children" *Journal of Divorce and Remarriage* 28 (1998a), 1-23.

Gardner, R. "The Burgess decision and the Wallerstein brief" *Journal of the American Academy of Psychiatry and the Law* 26 (1998b), 425-431.

Gardner, R. *The Parental Alienation Syndrome, 2nd Ed.* (Cresskill, NJ: Creative Therapeutics Inc., 1998c).

Gardner, R.A. "Assessment for the stronger, healthier psychological bond in child custody evaluations" *Journal of Divorce & Remarriage* 31:1/2 (1999a), 1-14.

Gardner, R. "Differentiating between the parental alienation syndrome and bona fide abuse/neglect" *The American Journal of Family Therapy* 27 (1999b), 97-107.

Gardner, R.A. "Family therapy for the moderate type of Parental Alienation Syndrome" *The American Journal of Family Therapy* 27 (1999c), 195-212.

Gardner, R.A. "Guidelines for assessing parental preference in child custody disputes" *Journal of Divorce and Remarriage* 30:1/2 (1999d), 1-9.

Gardner, R.A. "Rebuttal to Carol S. Bruch's article 'Parental Alienation Syndrome and parental alienation: Getting it wrong in child custody cases'" *Family Law Quarterly* 35:3 (2001a), 527-552.

Gardner, R. "Should courts order PAS children to visit/reside with the alienated parent? A follow-up study" *The American Journal of Forensic Psychology* 19:3 (2001b), 61-106.

Gardner, R. "The empowerment of children in the development of parental alienation syndrome" *The American Journal of Forensic Psychology* 20:2 (2001c), 5-29.

Gardner, R.A. *Therapeutic Interventions for Children and Parental Alienation Syndrome* (Cresskill, NJ: Creative Therapeutic, Inc., 2001d).

Gardner, R.A. "Denial of the parental alienation syndrome (PAS) harms women also" *The American Journal of Family Therapy* 30:3 (2002a), 191-202

Gardner, R.A. "Parental alienation syndrome vs. parental alienation: Which diagnosis should evaluators use in child custody disputes?" *The American Journal of Family Therapy* 30 (2002b), 93-115.

Gardner, R.A. "Commentary on Kelly and Johnston's 'The alienated child: A reformulation of Parental Alienation Syndrome'" *Family Court Review* 42:4 (2004), 611-621.

Gardner, R.A. "Introduction" (written May 2003) In R. A. Gardner, S. R., Sauber & D. Lorandos (Eds.), *The International Handbook of Parental Alienation Syndrome:*

Conceptual, Clinical and Legal Considerations (Springfield, IL: Charles C Thomas, 2006), 5-11.

Gardner, R.A., Sauber, S.R. & Lorandos (Eds.), *The International Handbook of Parental Alienation Syndrome: Conceptual, Clinical and Legal Considerations* (Springfield, IL: Charles C Thomas, 2006).

Garrity, C. & Baris, M. *Caught in the Middle: Protecting the Children of High-Conflict Divorce* (Toronto: Maxwell Macmillan Canada, 1994).

Geffner, R.A., Jaffe, P.G. & Suderman, M. *Children Exposed to Domestic Violence: Current Issues in Research Intervention, Prevention, and Policy Development* (New York: The Haworth Maltreatment & Trauma Press, 2000).

Geffner, R.A. & Rosenbaum, A. *Domestic Violence Offenders: Current Interventions, Research, and Implications for Policies and Standards* (New York: The Haworth Maltreatment & Trauma Press, 2001).

Gelles, R.J. "Child abuse as psychopathology: A sociological critique and Reformulation" *American Journal of Orthopsychiatry* 43 (1973), 611-621.

Gelles, R.J. "Violence in the family: A review of research in the seventies" *Journal of Marriage and the Family* 42:4 (1980), 873-885.

Gewirtz, A.H. & Edleson, J.L. "Yong children's exposure to intimate partner violence: Towards a developmental risk and resilience framework for research and intervention" *Journal of Family Violence* 22 (2007), 151-163.

Ghetti, S., Goodman, G.S., Eisen, M.L., Qin, J. & Davis, S.L. "Consistency in children's reports of sexual and physical abuse" *Child Abuse & Neglect* 26 (2002), 977-995.

Gindes, M. "The psychological effects of relocation for children of divorce" *Journal of the American Academy of Matrimonial Lawyers* 15 (1998), 119-148.

Goldstein, J., Freud, A. & Solnit, A J. *Beyond the Best Interests of the Child* (New York: Free Press, 1973).

Goldstein, J. Freud, A. & Solnit, A.J. *In the Best Interests of the Child* (New York: Free Press, 1986).

Gondolf, E.W. "Who are these guys? Toward a behavioral typology ofbatterers" *Violence and Victims* 3 (1988), 187-203.

Gordon, M.L. "Supervised access: Why, when, how long" *Canadian Family Law Quarterly* 22 (2004), 185-218.

Gottfried, S. "Virtual visitation: The wave of the future in communication between children and non-custodial parents in relocation cases" *Family Law Quarterly* 36:3 (2002), 475-485.

Gould, J.W. "Evaluating the probative value of child custody evaluations: A guide for forensic mental health professionals" *Journal of Child Custody* 1:1 (2004), 77-96.

Gould, J.W. *Conducting Scientifically Crafted Child Custody Evaluations, 2nd ed.* (Sarasota, Florida: Professional Resource Exchange, Inc., 2006).

Gould, J.W. & Martindale, D.A. *The Art and Science of Child Custody Evaluations* (New York: Guilford Press, 2007).

Gould, J.W, Martindale, D.A. & Eidman. "Assessing allegations of domestic violence" *Journal of Child Custody* 4:1/2 (2007), 1-37

Graham-Bermann, S.A. "Designing intervention evaluations for children exposed to domestic violence: Applications of research and theory" in S.A. Graham-Bermann & J.L. Edleson (Eds.) *Domestic Violence in the Lives of Children: The Future of Research, Intervention, and Social Policy* (Washington, DC: American Psychological Association, 2002), 237-267.

Green, A. "True and false allegations of sexual abuse in child custody disputes" *Journal of the American Academy of Child Psychiatry* 25 (1986), 449-456.

Greenberg, L.R. & Gould, J.W. "The treating expert: A hybrid role with firm boundaries" *Professional Psychology: Research and Practice* 32:5 (2001), 469-478.

Greenberg, L.R., Gould, J.W., Schnider, R.A. Gould-Saltman, D.J. & Martindale, D.A. "Effective intervention with high-conflict families: How judges can promote and recognize competent treatment in family court" *Journal of the Center for Families, Children and the Courts* 4 (2003), 49-65.

Greenberg, L., Martindale, D., Gould, J. & Gould-Saltman, D. "Ethical issues in child custody and dependency cases: Enduring principles and emerging challenges" *Journal of Child Custody* 1:1 (2004), 7- 30.

Greenberg, L.R., Gould-Saltman, D.J. & Schnider, R. "The problem with presumptions-A review and commentary" *Journal of Child Custody* 3:3/4 (2006), 139-172.

Greenberg, S.A. & Shuman, D.W. "Irreconcilable conflict between therapeutic and forensic roles" *Professional Psychology: Research and Practice* 28:1 (1997), 50-57.

Grych, J. H. "Interparental conflict as a risk factor for child maladjustment: Implications for the development of prevention programs" *Family Court Review* 43:1 (2005), 97-108.

Grych, J. & Fincham, F. "Marital conflict and children's adjustment: A cognitive-contextual framework" *Psychological Bulletin* 108 (1992), 267-290.

Gunnoe, M. & Braver, S.L. "The effects of joint legal custody on mothers, fathers, and children" *Law and Human Behaviour* 25:1 (2001), 25-43.

Hamberger, L.K., Lohr, J.M., Bonge, D. & Tolin, D.E. "A large sample empirical typology of male spouse abusers and its relationship to dimensions of abuse" *Violence and Victims* 11 (1996), 277-292.

Hamel, J. & Nicholls, T. "Domestic violence: A gender-inclusive conception" in J. Hamel & T. Nicholls (Eds.) *Family Approaches to Domestic Violence: A Guide to Gender-Inclusive Research and Treatment* (New York: Springer Publishing, 2006).

Hanks, S.E. "Translating theory into practice: A conceptual framework for clinical assessment, differential diagnosis, and multi-modal treatment of martially violent individuals, couples, and families" in E.C. Viano (Ed.) *Intimate Violence Interdisciplinary Perspectives* (pp. 157-176). (Washington, D.C.: Hemisphere Publishing Corporation, 1992).

Haour-Knipe, M. "International employment and children: Geographical mobility and mental health among children of professionals" *Social Science Medicine* 28:3 (1989), 197-205.

Hardesty, J.L. & Chung, G.H. "Intimate partner violence, parental divorce, and child custody: Directions for intervention and future research" *Family Relations* 55 (2006), 200-210.

Haugaard, J.J. "The challenge of defining child sexual abuse" *American Psychologist* 55:9 (2000), 1036-1039.

Haveman, R., Wolfe, B. & Spaulding, J. "Childhood events and circumstances influencing high school completion" *Demography* 28:1 (1991), 133-157.

Herman, S. "Improving decision-making in forensic child sexual abuse investigations" *Law and Human Behaviour* 29 (2005), 87-120.

Hester, M., Pearson, C. & Harwin, N. *Making an Impact: Children and Domestic Violence, A Reader* (London: Jessica Kingsley Publications, 2000).

Hetherington, E.M., Bridges, M. & Insabella, G.M. "What matters? What does not? Five perspectives on the association between marital transitions and children's adjustment" *American Psychologist* 53 (1998), 167-184.

Hetherington, E.M., Cox, M. & Cox, R. "Effects of divorce on parents and children" in M.E. Lamb (Ed.) *Nontraditional Families: Parenting and Child Development* (Hillsdale, NJ: Lawrence Erlbaum, 1982), 233-288.

Hetherington, E.M., Cox, M. & Cox, R. "The long-term effects of divorce and remarriage on the adjustment of children" *Journal of the American Academy of Child Psychiatry* 24 (1985), 518-530.

Hetherington, E. M. & Kelly, J.B. *For Better or for Worse: Divorce Reconsidered* (New York: Norton & Company, 2002).

Hetherington, E.M. & Stanley-Hagan, M. "The adjustment of children with divorced parents: A risk and resiliency perspective" *Journal of Child Psychology and Psychiatry* 40 (1999), 129-140.

Hewitt, S.R. *Assessing Allegations of Sexual Abuse in Preschool Children: Understanding Small Voices* (Thousand Oaks, CA: Sage Publications, 1999).

Hickman, J.A. & Reynolds, C.R. "Effects of False Allegations of Sexual Abuse on Children and Families" In Threatt, B. (Ed.) (1994). *Evaluating Children's Allegations of Sexual Assault.* (Austin, TX, 1994)

Higgins, D.J. & McCabe, M.P. "Multitype treatment and long-term adjustment of adults" *Child Abuse Review* 9 (2000), 6-18.

Hodges, W.F. "The Cumulative Effect of Stress on Preschool Children of divorced and intake families" *Journal of Marriage and the Family* 46 (1984), 611-617.

Holtzworth-Munroe, A. & Stuart, G.L. "Typologies of male batterers: Three subtypes and the differences among them" *Psychological Bulletin* 116 (1994), 476-497.

Hoppe, C. & Kenney, L. "A Rorschach study of the psychological characteristics of parents engaged in child custody/visitation disputes" Paper presented at the 102nd Annual Convention of the American Psychological Association (Los Angeles, August 1994).

Hudson, W.W. & McIntosh, S.R. "The assessment of spouse abuse: Two quantifiable dimensions" *Journal of Marriage and Family* 43 (1981), 873-885.

Hughes, H.M., Graham-Bermann, S.A. & Gruber, G. "Resilience in children exposed to domestic violence" in S.A. Graham-Bermann & J.L. Edleson (Eds.) *Domestic Violence in the Lives of Children: The Future of Research, Intervention, and Social Policy* (Washington, DC: American Psychological Association, 2002), 67-90.

Hovestad, W., Tonmyer, L., Hubka, D. & De Marco, R. "The Canadian incidence study of reported child abuse and neglect: Implications for federal responses to child maltreatment" *International Journal of Mental Health* 7:4 (2004), 6-13.

Ingersoll, G., Scamman, J. & Eckerling, W. "Geographic mobility and student achievement in an urban setting" *Educational Evaluation and Policy Analysis*, 11:2 (1989), 143-149.

Jacobson, N. & Gottman, J. *When Men Batter Women* (New York: Simon & Schuster, 1988).

Jaffe, P.G., Austin, G.W. & Poisson, S. "Violence in Custody and Access Disputes" Paper presented at the 4th International Family Violence Research Conference, July 1995: Durham, NH.

Jaffe, P.G., Baker, L.L. & Cunningham, A.J. *Protecting Children from Domestic Violence: Strategies for Community Intervention* (New York: The Guilford Press, 2004).

Jaffe, P., Crooks, C.V. & Bala, N. *Making Appropriate Parenting Arrangements in Family Violence Cases: Applying the Literature to Identify Promising Practices* (Department of Justice Canada: September 7, 2005).

Jaffe, P.G., Crooks, C.V. & Wolfe, D.A. "Legal and policy responses to children exposed to domestic violence: The need to evaluate intended and unintended consequences" *Clinical Child and Family Psychology Review* 6:3 (2003), 205-213.

Jaffe, P.G., Johnston, J., Crooks, C., & Bala, N. "Custody disputes involving allegations of domestic violence: The need for differentiated approaches to parenting plans" *Family Court Review* 46:3 (2008), 500-522.

Jaffe, P.G., Lemon, N., & Poisson, S. *Child Custody and Domestic Violence*. (Thousand Oaks, CA: Sage, 2003).

Jaffe, P.G., Lemon, N., Sandler, J. & Wolfe, D.A. *Working Together to End Domestic Violence* (Tampa, Florida: Mancorp Publishing, Inc., 1996).

Jaffe, P.G., Wolfe, D.A. & Wilson, S. *Children of Battered Women* (Newbury Park, CA: Sage Publications, 1990).

Jalongo, M. "Helping children to cope with relocation" *Childhood Education* 71:2 (1994), 80-85.

Jenuwine, M.J. & Cohler, B.J. "Major parental psychopathology and child custody" In R. Galatzer-Lary & L. Kraus (Eds.) *The Scientific Basis of Child Custody Decisions* (Wiley, 1999) 285-318.

Johnson, M. P. "Violence Against Women in the American Family: Are There Two Forms?" Paper presented at the annual pre-conference Theory Construction and Research Methodology Workshop, National Council on Family Relations: Baltimore, MD (1993).

Johnson, M. P. "Patriarchal terrorism and common couple violence: Two forms of violence against women" *Journal of Marriage and the Family* 57:2 (1995), 283-294.

Johnson, M. P. "Violence against women in the family: The United States and Vietnam" in K. Barry (Ed.), *Vietnam's Women in Transition* (New York: St. Martin's Press, 1996), 287-296.

Johnson, M.P. "Apples and oranges in child custody disputes: Intimate terrorism vs. situational couple violence" *Journal of Child Custody* 2 (2005a), 43-52.

Johnson, M.P. "Domestic violence: It's not about gender—Or is it?" *Journal of Marriage and Family* 67:5 (2005b), 1126-1130.

Johnson, M. P. "Conflict and control: Gender symmetry and asymmetry in domestic violence" *Violence Against Women* 12 (2006), 1003-1018.

Johnson, M. P. & Ferraro, K. J. "Research on domestic violence in the 1990's: Making distinctions" *Journal of Marriage and the Family* 62:4 (2000), 948-963.

Johnson, T.C. & Friend, C. "Assessing young children's sexual behaviours in the context of child sexual abuse evaluations" in Tara Ney (Ed.) *True and False Allegations of Child Sexual Abuse: Assessment and Case Management* (New York: Brunner/ Mazel Publishers, 1995), 49-72.

Johnston, J.R. "Children of divorce who refuse visitation in nonresidential parenting" In C. Depner and J. Bray (Eds.) *New Vistas in Family Living* (Newbury Park, CA: Sage Pub., 1993).

Johnston, J.R. "High conflict divorce" in *The Future of Children: Children and Divorce* (Los Altos, CA: David and Lucille Packard Foundation, 1994), 165-182.

Johnston, J. R. "Domestic violence and parent-child relationships in families disputing custody" *Australian Journal of Family Law* (1995a), 12-25.

Johnston, J.R. "Research update: Children's adjustment in sole custody compared to joint custody families and principles of custody decision-making" *Family and Conciliation Courts Review* 33:4 (1995b), 415-425.

Johnston, J.R. "Building Multidisciplinary Professional Partnerships with the Court on Behalf of High-conflict Divorcing Families and Their Children: Who Needs What Kind of Help?" Paper presented at Children of Embattled Divorce Symposium: Little Rock, AK (1999).

Johnston, J.R. "Rethinking parental alienation and redesigning parent-child access services for children who resist or refuse visitation" Paper presented at the International Conference on Supervised Visitation (Munich, Germany, 2001).

Johnston, J. "Developing Group Interventions for Families at Impasse" Unpublished report (San Jose: San Jose State University, Administration of Justice Department, 2002).

Johnston, J.R. "Parental alignments and rejection: An empirical study of alienation in children of divorce" *Journal of the American Academy of Psychiatry and Law* 31 (2003), 158-170.

Johnston, J.R. "Children of divorce who reject a parent and refuse visitation: Recent research and social policy implications for the alienated child" *Family Law Quarterly* 38:4 (2005a), 757-775.

Johnston, J. R. "Clinical work with parents in entrenched custody disputes" In L. Gunsberg & P. Hymowitz (Eds.) *A Handbook of Divorce and Custody: Forensic, Developmental, and Clinical Perspectives* (Hillsdale, NJ: The Analytic Press, 2005b).

Johnston, J. R. "A child-centered approach to high conflict and domestic violence families: Differential assessment and interventions" *Journal of Family Issues* 12:1 (2006), 15-36.

Johnston, J.R. & Campbell, L.E. *Impasses of Divorce: The Dynamics and Resolution of Family Conflict* (New York: The Free Press, 1988).

Johnston, J.R. & Campbell, L.E. "A clinical typology of interparental violence in dispute-custody divorces" *American Journal of Orthopsychiatry* 63:2 (1993a), 190-199.

Johnston, J.R. & Campbell, L.E. "Parent-child relationships in domestic violence families disputing custody" *Family and Conciliation Courts Review* 31:3 (1993b), 252-298.

Johnston, J.R. & Kelly, J.B. "Commentary on Walker, Brantley, and Rigsbee's (2004) "A critical analysis of parental alienation syndrome and its admissibility in the family court" *Journal of Child Custody* 1:4 (2004a), 77-89.

Johnston, J.R. & Kelly, J.B. "Rejoinder to Gardner's commentary on Kelly and Johnston's 'The alienated child: A reformulation of Parental Alienation Syndrome'" *Family Court Review* 42:4 (2004b), 622-628.

Johnston, J.R., Lee, S., Olesen, N.W. & Walters, M.G. "Allegations and substantiation of abuse in custody disputing families" *Family Court Review* 43:2 (2005), 283-294.

Johnston, J.R. & Roseby, V. *In the Name of the Child: A Developmental Approach to Understanding and Helping Children of Conflicted and Violence Divorce* (New York: The Free Press, 1997).

Johnston, J.R, Walters, M. & Friedlander, S. "Therapeutic work with alienated children and their families" *Family Court Review* 39:3 (2001), 316-333.

Johnston, J.R., Walters, M.G. & Olesen, N.W. "Clinical ratings of parenting capacity and Rorschach protocols of custody-disputing parents: An exploratory study" Submitted for publication in the *Journal of Child Custody* 2:1-2 (2005a), 159-178.

Johnston, J.R., Walters, M.G. & Olesen, N.W. "Is it alienating parenting, role reversal or child abuse? A study of children's rejection of a parent in child custody disputes" *Journal of Emotional Abuse* 5:4 (2005b), 191-218.

Johnston, J.R., Walters, M.G. & Olesen, N.W. "The psychological functioning of alienated children in custody disputing families: An exploratory study" *American Journal of Forensic Psychology* 23:3 (2005c), 39-64.

Juby, H., Le Bourdais, C. & Marcil-Gratton, N. "Sharing roles, sharing custody? Couples' characteristics and children's living arrangements at separation" *Journal of Marriage and Family* 67 (2005), 157-172.

Katz, A. "Junk science v. novel scientific evidence: Parental alienation syndrome, getting it wrong in custody cases" *Pace Law Review* 24 (2004), 239-243.

Kelly, J.B. "Current research on children's adjustment: No simple answers" *Family and Conciliation Courts Review* 31:1 (1993), 29-49.

Kelly, J.B. "The determination of child custody" in The Future of Children: Children and Divorce (Los Altos, CA: David and Lucille Packard Foundation, 1994), 121-142.

Kelly, J.B. "Children's adjustment in conflicted marriage and divorce: A decade review of research" *Journal of the American Academy of Child and Adolescent Psychiatry* 39 (2000), 963-973.

Kelly, J.B. "Changing perspectives on children's divorce adjustment following divorce: A view from the United States" *Childhood* 10:2 (2003), 237-254.

Kelly, J.B. "Children's living arrangements following separation and divorce: Insights from empirical and clinical research." *Family Process* 46:1 (2007), 35-52.

Kelly, J.B., & Emery, R. "Children's adjustment following divorce: Risk and resilience perspectives" *Family Relations* 52 (2003), 352-362.

Kelly, J.B. & Johnson, M.P. "Differentiation among types of intimate partner violence: Research update and implications for interventions" *Family Court Review* 46:3 (2008), 476-499.

Kelly, J.B. & Johnston, J.R. "The alienated child: A reformulation of parental alienation syndrome" *Family Court Review* 39:3 (2001), 249-266.

Kelly, J.B. & Lamb, M.E. "Using child development research to make appropriate custody and access decisions for young children" *Family and Conciliation Courts Review* 38:3 (2000), 297-311.

Kelly, J.B. & Lamb, M.E. "Developmental issues in relocation cases involving young children: When, whether and how?" *Journal of Family Psychology* 17:2 (2003), 193-205.

Kelly, J.B. "Developing beneficial parenting plan models for children following separation and divorce" *Journal of American Academy of Matrimonial Lawyers* 19:2 (2005), 237-254.

Kerr, S.G. & Jaffe, P. "The clinical pitfalls in adopting the 'Parental Alienation Syndrome' in child custody disputes and 'Parental Alienation Syndrome' and family law" National Family Law Program (affiliated to) the Federation of Law Societies and Canadian Bar Association (1998).

Kerr, S.G. & Jaffe, P.G. "Legal and clinical issues in child custody disputes involving domestic violence" *Canadian Family Law Quarterly* 17:1 (1999), 1-37.

Kilpatrick, K.L., Litt, M. & Williams, L.M. "Post-traumatic stress disorder in child witnesses to domestic violence" *American Journal of Orthopsychiatry* 67 (1997), 639-644.

Kilpatrick, K.L. & Williams, L.M. "Potential mediators of post-traumatic stress disorder in child witnesses to domestic violence" *Child Abuse & Neglect* 22:4 (1998), 319-330.

King, V. "Variation in the consequences of nonresident father involvement for children's well-being" *Journal of Marriage and the Family* 56 (1994), 176-189.

King, V. "The antecedents and consequences of adolescents' relationships with stepfathers and nonresident fathers" *Journal of Marriage and Family* 68 (2006), 910-928.

King, V. & Heard, H.E. "Nonresident father visitation, parental conflict, and mother's satisfaction: What's best for child well-being?" *Journal of Marriage and Family* 61 (1999), 385-396.

King, V. & Sobolewski, J.M. "Nonresident fathers' contributions to adolescent well-being" *Journal of Marriage and the Family* 68 (2006), 537-557.

Kirkland, K. & Kirkland, K. E. "Risk Management and aspirational ethics for Parenting Coordinators" *Journal of Child Custody* 3:2 (2006), 23-43.

Klass, J. & Klass, J. "Threatened Mother Syndrome (TMS): A diverging concept of Parental Alienation Syndrome (PAS)" *American Journal of Family Law* 18:4 (2005), 189-191.

Kline, M., Johnston, J.R. & Tschann, J.M. "The long shadow of marital conflict: A model of children's post divorce adjustment" *Journal of Marriage and the Family* 53 (1991), 297-309.

Kneale, A. *Supporting Children and Young People Affected by Family Violence* (Melbourne: Annie North Inc., Victorian Government Department of Human Services, 1999).

Knopp, P.R., Hart, S.D., Webster, C.D. & Eaves, D. *Manual for the spousal assault risk assessment guide, 2nd ed.* (Vancouver, British Columbia: British Columbia Institute on Family Violence, 1995).

Koch, D.R. & Pincolini-Ford, A. "Parenting coordination in domestic violence Cases" *Synergy* 10:2 (2006), 2-5.

Kolbo, J.R., Blakely, E.H. & Engleman, D. "Children who witness violence: A review of the empirical literature" *Journal of Interpersonal Violence* 11:2 (1996), 281-293.

Kopetski, L. "Parental alienation syndrome: Recent research" Paper presented at the Fifteenth Annual Child Custody Conference (Keystone, Colorado, 1991).

Kopetski, L. "Identifying cases of parent alienation syndrome: Part I" *The Colorado Lawyer* 29:2 (1998a), 65-68.

Kopetski, L. "Identifying cases of parent alienation syndrome: Part II" *The Colorado Lawyer* 29:3 (1998b), 63-66.

Kopetski, L. M. "Commentary: Parental alienation syndrome" In R. A. Gardner, S. R. Sauber & D. Lorandos (Eds.) *The International Handbook of Parental Alienation Syndrome: Conceptual, Clinical and Legal Considerations* (Springfield, IL: Charles C Thomas, 2006), 378-390.

Kopetski, L. M., Rand, D. C. & Rand, R. (2006). "Incidence, gender, and false allegations of child abuse: Data on 84 parental alienation syndrome cases" In R. A. Gardner, S. R. Sauber & D. Lorandos (Eds.) *International Handbook of Parental Alienation Syndrome: Conceptual, Clinical and Legal Considerations* (Springfield, IL: Charles C Thomas, 2006), 65-70.

Kruttschnitt, C., McLaughlin, B.L. & Petrie, C.V. (2004). *Advancing the federal research agenda on violence against women* (Washington, D.C.: National Academics Press). Available online. Accessed February 24, 2007 at http://www.nap.edu/catalog/10849.html

Kuehnle, K. *Assessing Allegations of Child Sexual Abuse* (Sarasota, FL: Professional Resource Press, 1996).

Kuehnle, K. "Child sexual abuse evaluations: The scientist-practitioner model" *Behavioural Sciences and the Law* 16 (1998), 5-20.

Kuehnle, K. "Child sexual abuse evaluations" In A. M. Goldstein, I. B. Weiner (Eds.) *Handbook of Psychology, Volume 11: Forensic Psychology* (Hobokon, NJ: John Wiley & Sons, 2003), 437-460.

Kuehnle, K., Greenberg, L. & Gottlieb, M. "Incorporating the principles of scientifically based child interviews into family law cases" *Journal of Child Custody* 1:1 (2004), 97-114.

Kuehnle, K. & Kirkpatrick, H.D. "Evaluating allegations of child sexual abuse within complex child custody cases" *Journal of Child Custody* 2:3 (2005), 3-38.

Kuehnle, K. & Walker, L.E.A. *Children Exposed to Domestic Violence (Home Study Continuing Education Program)* (Sarasota, FL: Professional Resource Press, 2003).

Lamb, M.E. "The investigation of child sexual abuse: An interdisciplinary consensus Statement" *Child Abuse & Neglect* 18:12 (1994), 1021-1028.

Lamb, M.E. "The development of father-infant attachments" in M.E. Lamb (Ed.) *The Role of the Father in Child Development (3rd ed.)* (New York: John Wiley, 1997), 104-120; 332-342.

Lamb, M.E. "Non-custodial fathers and their impact on the children of divorce. In R.A. Thompson & P.R. Amato (Eds.) *The Post-divorce Family: Research and Policy Issues* (Thousand Oaks, CA: Sage, 1999) 105-25.

Lamb, M.E. "Noncustodial fathers and their children" in C.S. Tamis-LeMonda & N. Cabrera (Eds.) *Handbook of Father Involvement: Multidisciplinary Perspectives* (Mahwah, NJ: Erlbaum, 2002), 169-184.

Lamb, M.E. & Kelly, J.B. "Using the empirical literature to guide the development of parenting plans for young children: A rejoinder to Solomon and Biringen" *Family Court Review* 39 (2001), 365-371.

Lamb, M., Sternberg & Thompson, R. "The effects of divorce and custody arrangements on children's behaviour, development, and adjustment" *Family and Conciliation Courts Review* 35:4 (1997), 393-404.

Lamb, M. E., Sternberg, K. J., Esplin, P. W., Hershkowitz, I. & Orbach, Y. "Assessing the credibility of children's allegations of sexual abuse: Insights from recent research" *Learning and Individual Differences* 9 (1997), 175-194.

Lampel, A. "Post-divorce therapy with high conflict families" The Independent Practitioner, Bulletin of the Divisions of Psychologists in Independent Practice, Division 42 of the American Psychological Association 6:3 (1986), 22-26.

Lampel, A. "Child's alignment with parents in highly conflicted custody cases" *Family and Conciliation Courts Review* 34 (1996), 232-235.

Lampel, A. "Assessing for alienation and access in child custody cases: A response to Lee and Olesen" *Family Court Review* 40:2 (2002), 232-235.

Laumann-Billings, L. & Emery, R.E. "Distress among young adults in divorced families" *Journal of Family Psychology* 14 (2000), 671-687.

LaViolette, A. *Assessing Dangerousness in Domestic Violence Cases*. (San Jose, CA: California Statewide Dispute Resolution Institute, 2005).

Law Society of British Columbia Gender Bias Committee (1992), *Gender Equality in the Justice System*

Lawson, A., Gardiner, S., Johansson, B. & MacLaurin, B. (2006). "Addressing the effects of child maltreatment through the lens of domestic violence" Accessed December 3, 2007 at www.cecw-cepb.ca.

Lebow, J. & Rekart, K.N. "Integrative family therapy for high-conflict divorce with disputes over child custody and visitation" *Family Process* 46:1 (2007), 79-91.

Lee, S. M. & Olesen, N.W. "Assessing for alienation in child custody and access evaluations" *Family Court Review* 39:3 (2001), 282-298

Lehr, R. & MacMillan, P. "The psychological and emotional impact of divorce: The noncustodial fathers' perspective" *Families in Society* 82:4 (2001), 373-383.

Lemon, N.K.D. "The legal system's response to children exposed to domestic Violence" *The Future of Children* 9:3 (1999), 67-83.

Leon, K. "Risk and protective factors in young children's adjustment to parental divorce. A review of the research" *Family Relations* 52 (2003), 258-270.

Leonoff, A. & Montague, R. (1996). *Guide to Custody and Access Assessments*. (Toronto: Carswell, 1996).

Leving, J. M. "The parental alienation syndrome and gender bias in the courts" In R. A. Gardner, S. R. Sauber & D. Lorandos (Eds.) *The International Handbook of Parental Alienation Syndrome: Conceptual, Clinical and Legal Considerations* (Springfield, IL: Charles C Thomas, 2006) 391-396.

Lieberman, A. & Van Horn, P. "Attachment, trauma and domestic violence: Implications for child custody" *Child Adolescent Psychiatric Clinic of North America* 7 (1998), 423-443.

Litvack, A. *Best practices with families experiencing high conflict separation and divorce* (Toronto: Jewish Family and Child Services in conjunction with The High Conflict Forum, 2008).

Logan, T.K. & Walker, R. "Separation as a risk factor for victims of intimate partner violence: Beyond lethality and injury, A response to Campbell" *Journal of Interpersonal Violence* 19:12 (2004), 1478-1486.

London, K., Bruck, M., Ceci, S.J. & Shuman, D.W. "Disclosure of child sexual abuse: What does the research tell us about the ways that children tell?" *Psychology, Pubic Policy, and Law* 11:1 (2005), 194-226.

Lorandos, D. "Parental alienation syndrome: Detractors and the junk science vacuum" In R. A. Gardner, S. R. Sauber & D. Lorandos (Eds.) *The International Handbook of Parental Alienation Syndrome: Conceptual, Clinical and Legal Considerations* (pp. 397-418). (Springfield, IL: Charles C Thomas, 2006) 397-418.

Lowenstein, L.F. "Parent alienation syndrome: A two step approach toward a solution" *Contemporary Family Therapy* 20:4 (December 1998), 505-520.

Lowenstein, L.F. "Attempting to solve child contact disputes (Recent research)" *Parental Alienation: Southern England Psychological Services* (2005a) Retrieved January 8, 2006 from http://www.parental-alienation.info/publications/36-atttosolchicondisrecres.htm.

Lowenstein, L.F. "How can one overturn the programming of a child against a parent?" *Parental Alienation: Southern England Psychological Services* (2005b) Retrieved February 9, 2006 from http://www.parental-alienation.info/publications/30-howcanoneovetheproofachiagaapar.htm.

Lowenstein, L.F. "Part IV - Dealing with and treatment of parental alienation syndrome or parental alienation" *Parental Alienation: Southern England Psychological Services* (2005c) Retrieved January 8, 2006 from http://www.parental-alienation.info/publications/28-deawitandtreofparalisynorparali.htm.

Lowenstein, L.F. "The psychological effects and treatment of the parental alienation syndrome worldwide" In R. A. Gardner, S. R. Sauber & D. Lorandos (Eds.) *The International Handbook of Parental Alienation Syndrome: Conceptual, Clinical and Legal Considerations* (Springfield, IL: Charles C Thomas, 2006) 292-301.

Lund, M. "A therapist's view of parental alienation syndrome" *Family and Conciliation Courts Review* 33 (1995), 308-316.

Maccoby, E.E. & Mnookin, R.H. Dividing the Child: Social and Legal Dilemmas of Custody (Cambridge, MA: Harvard University Press, 1992).

Mahoney, M.R. "Legal images of battered women: Redefining the issue of Separation" *Michigan Law Review* 90:1 (1991/1992), 1-94.

Margolin, G. "Children's exposure to violence: Exploring developmental pathways to diverse outcomes" *Journal of Interpersonal Violence* 20:1 (2005), 72-81.

Margolin, G. & Gordis, E.B. "The effects of family and community violence on Children" *Annual Review of Psychology* 51 (2000), 445-479.

Masten, A.S. & Coatsworth, J.D. "The development of competence in favorable and unfavorable environments: Lessons from research on successful children" *American Psychologist* 53:2 (1998), 205-220.

Mears, D.P. & Visher, C.A. "Trends in understanding and addressing domestic violence" *Journal of Interpersonal Violence* 20:2 (2005), 204-211.

McCloskey, L.A. & Stuewig, J. "The quality of peer relationships among children exposed to family violence" *Developmental and Psychopathology* 13 (2001), 83-96.

McCloskey, L.A., Figuerdo, A.J. & Koss, M.P. "The effects of systematic family violence on children's mental health." *Child Development* 66 (1995), 1239-1261.

McGill, J.C., Deutsch, R.M. & Zibbell, R.A. "Visitation and domestic violence: A clinical model of family assessment and access planning" *Family and Conciliation Courts Review* 37:3 (1999), 315-334.

McGleughlin, J., Meyer, S. & Baker, J. "Assessing sexual abuse allegations in divorce, Custody, and visitation disputes" in Robert M. Galatzer-Levy and Kraus, Louis (Eds.) *The Scientific Basis of Child Custody Decisions* (New York: John Wiley & Sons, Inc., 1999), 357-388.

McIntosh, J. "Thought in the face of violence: A child's need" *Child Abuse and Neglect* 26 (2002), 229-241.

McIntosh, J. "Children living with domestic violence: Research foundations for early intervention" *Journal of Family Studies* 9:2 (2003a), 219-234.

McIntosh, J. "Enduring conflict in parental separation: Pathways of impact on child development. A synopsis of recent research" *Journal of Family Studies* 9:1 (2003b), 63-80.

McIntosh, J.E., Wells, Y.D., Smyth, B.M. & Long, C.M. "Child-focused and child-inclusive divorce mediation: comparative outcomes from a prospective study of post-separation adjustment" *Family Court Review* 46:1 (2008), 105-124.

McLanahan. S.S. "Father absence and the welfare of children" in E.M. Hetherington (Ed.) *Coping* with Divorce, Single Parenting, and Remarriage: A Risk and Resiliency Perspective (Hillsdale, NJ: Erlbaum, 1999), 117-145.

McLanahan, S. & Sandefur, G. *Growing Up With a Single Parent: What Hurts, What Helps*. (Cambridge, MA: Harvard University Press, 1994).

McLeod, G. "Relocation for dummies" (paper presented to the Law Society of Upper Canada, Six Minute Family Law Lawyer, Continuing Legal Education Program, (Nov. 30, 2004) 10-14.

McLoyd, V., Harper, C. & Copeland, N.K. "Does gender moderate the effects of marital conflict on children?" in J. Grych & F. Fincham (Eds.) *Interparental Conflict and Child Development* (New York: Cambridge University Press, 2001), 9-38.

Menning, C. L. "Nonresident fathering and school failure" *Journal of Family Issues* 27:10 (2006), 1356-1382.

Meritt-Bair, M.H., Blackstone, M. & Feudtner, C. "Physical health outcomes of Childhood exposure to intimate partner violence: A systemic review" *Pediatrics* 117 (2006), 278-290.

Mertin, P. & Mohr, P. "Incidence and correlates of post-traumatic symptoms in children from backgrounds of domestic violence" *Violence and Victims* 17:5 (2002), 555-567.

Milner, J.S. *The Child Abuse Potential Inventory-Second Edition* (De Kalb, Illinois: Psytec Corporation, 1986).

Minuchin, S. *Families and Family Therapy* (MA: Harvard University Press, 1974).

Mohr, W.K., Noone Lutz, M.J. Fantuzzo, J.W. & Perry, M.A. "Children exposed to family violence: A review of empirical literature from a developmental-ecological perspective" *Trauma, Violence, & Abuse* 1:3 (2000), 264-283.

Moloney, L., Smyth, B., Weston, R., Richardson, N., Qu, L., & Gray, M. *Allegations of family violence and child abuse in family law children's proceedings: A pre-reform exploratory study*. Research Report #15 (Government of Australia Australian Institute of Family Studies, 2007).

Mullender, A., Hague, G., Iman, U., Kelly, L., Malos, E. & Regan, L. *Children's Perspectives on Domestic Violence* (London: Sage, 2003).

Mullender, A., Kelly, L., Hague, G., Malos, E. & Inman, N. *Children's Needs, Coping Strategies and Understanding of Woman Abuse* (Coventry, UK: Economic and Social Research Council, 2000).

Murphy, J.C. & Robinson, R. "Domestic violence and mediation: Responding to the challenges of crafting effective screens" *Family Law Quarterly* 39:1 (2005), 53-85.

Myers, J.E.B. "Expert testimony describing psychological syndromes" *Pacific Law Journal* 24 (1993), 1449-1464

Nash, M., Hulsey, T., Sexton, M., Harralson, T. & Lambert, W. "Long-term sequel of childhood sexual abuse: Perceived family environment, psychopathology, and dissociation" *Journal of Consulting and Clinical Psychology* 61:2 (1993), 276-283.

Neilson, L.C. *Spousal Abuse, Children and the Legal System: Final report for Canadian Bar Association, Law for the Futures Fund* (Muriel McQueen Fergusson Centre for Family Violence Research, University of New Brunswick, 2001).

Neilson, L. "Assessing mutual partner-abuse claims in child custody and access cases" *Family Court Review* 42:3 (2004), 411-438.

Nelson, P., Simoni, J. & Adelman, H. "Mobility and school functioning in early grades" *The Journal of Educational Research* 89 (1996), 365-369.

Nemark, L., Harrell, A. & Salem, P. "Domestic violence and empowerment in custody and visitation cases" *Family and Conciliation Courts Review* 33 (1995), 30-62.

Neustein, A. & Leshner, M. *From Madness to Mutiny: Why Mothers Are Running From the Family Courts - and What Can be Done About It* (Lebanon NH : Northeastern University Press, 2005)

Ney, P., Fung, T. & Wickett, A. "The worse combinations of child abuse and neglect" *Child Abuse & Neglect* 18 (1994), 705-714.

Ney, T. (Ed.) *True and False Allegations of Child Sexual Abuse: Assessment and Case Management* (New York, NY: Brunner/Mazel, 1995).

Nord, C.W., Brimhall, D. & West, J. (1997). Fathers' Involvement in Their Children's School, U.S. Department of Education, National Center for Educational Statistics (NCES #98-091)

O'Leary, K.D., Smith Slep, A.M. & O'Leary, S.G. "Co-occurrence of partner and parent aggression: Research and treatment implications" *Behaviour Therapy* 31 (2000), 631-648. Ontario Child Welfare Eligibility Spectrum (2000 and 2006).

Oats, R.K., Jones, D.P.H., Denson, D., Sirontnak, A., Gary, N. & Krugman, R.D. "Erroneous concerns about child sexual abuse" *Child Abuse & Neglect* 24:1 (2000), 149-157.

Oddone Paolucci, E., Genuis, M.L. & Violato, C. "A meta-analysis of the published research on the effects of child sexual abuse" *The Journal of Psychology* 135:1 (2001), 17-36.

Office of the Chief Coroner, Province of Ontario. Fourth Annual Report of the Domestic Violence Death Review Committee (2006).

Ontario Psychological Association *Ethical Guidelines for Psychological Practice Related to Child Custody and Access* (1998).

Orbach, Y. & Lamb, M. E. "Assessing the accuracy account of sexual abuse: A case study" *Child Abuse & Neglect* 23:1 (1999), 91-98.

Osofsky, J. "Prevalence of children's exposure to domestic violence and child maltreatment: Implications for prevention and intervention" *Clinical Child and Family Psychology Review* 6:3 (1999), 161-170.

Paolucci, E., Genuis, M.L. & Violato, C. "A meta-analysis of the published research on the effects of child sexual abuse" *The Journal of Psychology* 135:1 (2001), 17-36.

Parkinson, P., Cashmore, J. & Single, J. "Adolescents' views on the fairness of parenting and financial arrangements after separation" *Family Court Review* 43:3 (2005), 429-444.

Parkinson, P. & Smyth, B. "Satisfaction and dissatisfaction with father-child contact arrangements in Australia" *Child and Family Law Quarterly* 16:3 (2004), 289-304.

Pasahow, R. "A critical analysis of the first empirical research study on child relocation" *Journal of the American Academy of Matrimonial Lawyers* 19 (2005), 321-335.

Peled, E. "Secondary victims no more: Refocusing intervention with children" in J.L. Edleson & Z. Eiskovits (Eds.) *Future Interventions with Battered Women and Their Families* (Thousand Oaks, CA: Sage, 1996), 125-152.

Pence, E. & Paymar, M. *Education Groups for Men Who Batter: The Duluth Model.* (New York: Springer, 1993).

Pfefferbaum, B. & Allan, J.R. "Stress in children exposed to violence: Re-enactment and rage" *Child and Adolescent Psychiatric Clinics of North America* 7:1 (1998), 121-135.

Poole, D. A. & Lamb, M. E. *Investigative Interviews of Children: A Guide for Helping Professionals* (Washington, DC: American Psychological Association, 1998).

Poole, D.A. & Lamb, M.E. *Investigative Interviews of Children: A Guide for Helping Professionals* (Washington, D.C.: American Psychological Association, 1998).

Poole, D.A. & Lindsay, D.S. "Interviewing preschoolers: Effects of nonsuggestive techniques, parental coaching and leaving questions on reports of nonexperienced events" *Journal of Experimental Child Psychology* 60 (1995), 129-154.

Poole, D.A. & White, L.T. "Effects of question repetition on the eyewitness testimony of children and adults" *Developmental Psychology* 27 (1991), 975-986.

Poole, D.A. & White, L.T. "Two years later: Effects of question repetition and retention interval on the eyewitness testimony of children and adjusts" *Developmental Psychology* 29 (1993), 844-853.

Pruett, M., Williams, T., Insabella, G. & Little, T. "Family and legal indicators of child adjustment to divorce among families with young children" *Journal of Family Psychology* 17:2 (2003), 169-180.

Putnam, F. "Ten-year research update review: Child sexual abuse" *Journal of the American Academy of Child and Adolescent Psychiatry* 42:3 (2003), 269-278.

Racusin, R. & Copans, S. "Characteristics of families of children who refuse post-divorce visits" *Journal of Clinical Psychology* 50:5 (1994), 792-801.

Rand, D.C. "Munchausen Syndrome by proxy: A complex type of emotional abuse responsible for some false allegations of child abuse in divorce" *Issues in Child Abuse Accusations* 5:3 (1993), 135-155.

Rand, D. "The spectrum of parental alienation syndrome, Part I" *American Journal of Forensic Psychology* 15:3 (1997a), 23-52.

Rand, D. "The spectrum of parental alienation syndrome, Part II" *American Journal of Forensic Psychology* 15:4 (1997b), 39-92.

Rand, D.C., Rand, R. & Kopetski, L. "The spectrum of parental alienation syndrome - Part III: The Kopetski follow-up study" *American Journal of Forensic Psychology*, 23:1 (2005), 15-43.

Rand, R. & Warshak, R. *Overview of the Family Workshop - 2.2* (2008).

Reich, W. *Character Analysis, 3rd ed.* Trans. Theodore P. Wolfe (New York: Orgone Institute Press, 1949).

Reynolds, M.W., Wallace, J., Hill., T., Weist, M.D. & Nabors, L.A. "The relationship between gender, depression, and self-esteem in children who have witnessed domestic violence" *Child Abuse & Neglect* 25 (2001), 1201-1206.

Ricci, I. Mom's House, *Dad's House: Making Shared Custody Work* (2nd ed.). Macmillan, New York. 1997

Ricks, F. *Accountability Case Management* (Victoria, B.C. Canada: Fotoprint, 1991).

Roseby, V. & Johnston, J.R. "Children of Armageddon: Common developmental threats in high-conflict divorcing families" *Child and Adolescent Psychiatric Clinics of North America* 7:2 (1998), 295-309.

Rosen, R. "Some crucial issues concerning children of divorce" *Journal of Divorce* 3 (1979), 19-25.

Rotman, A., Tompkins, R., Schwartz, L. & Samuels, M. "Reconciling parents' and children's interests in relocation: In whose best interest?" *Family and Conciliation Courts Review* 38:3 (2000), 341-367.

Rumberger, R. "The causes and consequences of student mobility" *The Journal of Negro Education* 72:1 (2003), 6-21.

Rutter, M. "Children's responses to stress and disadvantage" In M.W. Kent & J.E. Rolfe (Eds.) *Primary Prevention of Psychopathology, Vol. 3* (Hanover, NJ: University Press of New England, 1979) 49-74.

Sachsenmaier, S.J. "Complex child custody evaluations: Evaluating the alleged incestuous parent" *Journal of Child Custody* 2:3 (2005), 57- 97.

Salem, P. & Dunford-Jackson, B.L. "Beyond politics and positions: A call for collaboration between family court and domestic violence professionals" *Family Court Review* 46:3 (2008), 437-453.

Saunders, D.G. "A typology of men who batter women. Three types derived from cluster analysis" *Journal of Orthopsychiatry* 62 (1992), 264-275.

Saunders, D.G. "Child custody decisions in families experiencing woman abuse" *Social Work* 39 (1994), 51 - 59.

Saunders, D.G. "Posttraumatic stress symptom profiles of battered women: A comparison of survivors in two settings" *Violence and Victims* 9:1 (1994), 31-44.

Saywitz, K. J. & Camparo, L. "Interviewing child witnesses: A developmental perspective" *Child Abuse & Neglect* 22 (1998), 825-843.

Saywitz, K.J. & Goodman, G. "Interviewing children in and out of court: Current research and practice implications" in J. Briere, L. Berliner, J. Bulkly, C. Jenny & T. Reid (Eds.) *The APSAC Handbook of Child Maltreatment* (Thousand Oaks, CA: Sage Publications, 1996).

Schultz, L.G. "The wife assaulter" *Journal of Social Therapy* 6:2 (1960), 103-111.

Schwartz, S.J. & Finley, G.E. "Fathering in intact and divorced families: Ethnic differences in retrospective reports" *Journal of Marriage and Family* 67 (2005), 207-215.

Selzer, J. A. "Consequences of marital dissolution for children" *Annual Review of Sociology* 20 (1994), 235-266.

Shaffer, M. & Bala, N. "Wife abuse, child custody and access in Canada" In R. Geffner, R. S. Ingelman, & J. Zellner (Eds.) *The Effects of Intimate Partner Violence on Children* (New York, NY: Haworth Maltreatment & Trauma Press, 2003) 253-276.

Shear, L.E. "Life stories, doctrines, and decision making: Three high courts confront the move-away dilemma" *Family and Conciliation Courts Review* 34 (1996), 439-458.

Shear, L.E. (2004). *Amici curiae* brief, *In re the marriage of LaMusga*, Supreme Court of California.

Shefts, K. R. "Virtual visitation: The next generation of options for parent/child Communication" *Family Law Quarterly* 36:2 (2002), 303-27.

Shopper, M. "Parental alienation: The creation of a false reality" In L. Gunsberg & P. Hymowitz (Eds.) *A Handbook of Divorce and Custody: Forensic, Developmental, and Clinical Perspectives* (Hillsdale, NJ, US: Analytic Press, Inc., 2005) 109-125.

Siegel, J. "Traditional MMPI-2 validity indicators and initial presentation in custody evaluations" *American Journal of Forensic Psychology* 13:3 (1996), 55-63.

Siegel, J. & Langford, J. "MMPI-2 validity scales and suspected parental alienation syndrome" *American Journal of Forensic Psychologist* 16:4 (1998), 5-14.

Simmons, R., Burgeson, R., Carlton-Ford, S. & Blyth, D. "The impact of cumulative change in early adolescence" *Child Development* 58 (1987), 1220-1234.

Simons, L. G. & Conger, R. D. "Linking mother-father differences in parenting to a typology of family parenting styles and adolescent outcomes" *Journal of Family Issues* 28:2 (2007), 212-241.

Simpson, G. & Fowler, M.G. "Geographic mobility and child's emotional/behavioural adjustment and school functioning" *Pediatrics* 93 (1994), 303-309.

Smith, A.B., Taylor, N.J. & Tapp, P. "Rethinking children's involvement in the decision making after parental separation" *Childhood*, 10 (2003), 210-216.

Smyth, B. "Time to rethink time? The experience of time with children after divorce" *Family Matters* 71 (2005), 4-10.

Sobolewski, J.M. & King, V. "The importance of the coparental relationship for non resident fathers' ties to children" *Journal of Marriage and Family* 67:5 (2005), 1196-1211.

Solomon, J. & Biringen, Z. "Another look at the developmental research" *Family Court Review* 39:4 (2001), 355-364.

Spinetta, J.J. & Rigler, D. "The child abusing parent: A psychological review" *Psychological Bulletin* 77 (1972), 296-304.

Stahl, P. *Conducting Child Custody Evaluations* (CA: Sage Publications, 1994).

Stahl, P. *Complex Issues in Child Custody Evaluation* (New York: Sage Publications, 1999).

Stahl, P.M. "Avoiding bias in relocation cases" Journal of Child Custody 3:3/4 (2006), 109-124.

Statistics Canada. *Family violence*. Ottawa: Statistics Canada, July 25, 2000.

Statistics Canada. *Family violence in Canada: A statistical profile 2005*. Ottawa: Ministry of Industry (2005).

Statistics Canada. *General Social Survey, 2004: Victimization*. Ottawa: Statistics Canada, November 24, 2005.

Statistics Canada, Canadian Centre for Justice Statistics. (2006a). *Family Violence in Canada: A Statistical Profile* (Ottawa)

Statistics Canada, Canadian Centre for Justice Statistics. (2006b) *Measuring Violence Against Women* (Ottawa)

Stern, N. & Oehme, K. "The troubling admission of supervised visitation records in custody proceedings" *Temple Law Review* 75 (2002), 271-312.

Stewart, S. D. "Nonresident parenting and adolescent adjustment" *Journal of Family Issues* 24 (2003), 217-244.

Stolberg, A.L. & Ankers, J.M. "Perceptual and behavioral changes in children resulting from parental divorce and consequent environmental changes" *Journal of Divorce* 7 (1983), 23-41.

Stolberg, A.L., Camplair, C., Currier, K. & Wells, M. "Individual, familial and environmental determinants of children's post-divorce adjustment and maladjustment" *Journal of Divorce* 11:1 (1987), 51-70.

Stoltz, J. & Ney, T. "Resistance to visitation: Rethinking parental and child alienation" *Family Court Review* 40:2 (2002), 220-231.

Straus, M.A. "Ordinary violence, child abuse, and wife beating: What do they have in common?" in M. Straus & R. Gelles (Eds.) *The Dark Side of Families: Current Family Violence Research* (Beverly Hills, CA: Sage, 1983), 213-234.

Straus, M.A. & Gelles, R.J. *Physical Violence in American Families: Risk Factors and Adaptations to Family Violence in 8,145 Families* (New Brunswick, NJ: Transaction Publishers, 1990).

Straus, M.A., Gelles, R.J. & Steinmetz, S. *Behind Closed Doors: Violence in the American Family* (New York: Anchor Books, 1980).

Straus, M.A., Hamby, S.L., Boney-McCoy, S. & Sugarman, D.B. (1996). "The revised Conflict Tactics Scale (CTS2): Development and preliminary psychometric data" *Journal of Family Issues* 17 (1996), 283-316.

Stern, N. & Oehme, K. "The troubling admission of supervised visitation records in custody proceedings" *Temple Law Review* 75 (2002), 271-312.

Sturge, C. & Glaser, D. "Contact and domestic violence-the expert's court report" *Family Law* (September, 2000), 615-629.

Sudermann, M. & Jaffe, P.G. *A Handbook for Health and Social Service Providers and Educators on Children Exposed to Women Violence/Family Violence* (Ottawa, ON: Health Canada, 1999).

Sullivan, M.J. "Ethical, legal and professional practice issues involved in acting as a psychologist coordinator in child custody cases" *Family Court Review* 42:3 (2004), 576-582.

Sullivan, M.J. & Kelly, J.B. "Legal and psychological management of cases with an alienated child" *Family Court Review* 39:3 (2001), 299-315.

Summit, R. (1983). "Child abuse accommodation syndrome" *Child Abuse & Neglect* 14 (1983), 151-163.

Swanson, C. & Schneider, B. "Students on the move: Residential and educational mobility in America's schools" *Sociology of Education* 72:1 (1999), 54-67.

Thoennes, N. & Tjaden, P. "The extent, nature, and validity of sexual abuse allegations in custody/visitation disputes" *Child Abuse & Neglect* 14 (1990), 151-163.

Thompson, R.D.A. "Movin' on: Parental relocation in Canada" *Family Court Review* 42:3 (2004), 398-410.

Thompson, R.D.A. "Ten Years After Gordon: No Law, Nowhere" in Reports of Family Law (Articles) 6th Series (Toronto: Carswell, 2007).

Thompson, R. & Amato, P.R. (Eds.) *The Postdivorce Family: Research and Policy Issues* (Beverly Hills, CA: Sage, 1999).

Tjaden P & Thoennes N. *Full report of the prevalence, incidence, and consequences of violence against women: findings from the national violence against women survey*. Report NCJ 183781 (Washington: National Institute of Justice, 2000).

Tonmyr, L., De Marco, R., Hovstad, W.E. & Hubka, D. "Policy makers' perspectives on the utility of a national study of child maltreatment" *Child Maltreatment* 9:2 (2004), 304-308.

Tonmyr, L., Fallon, B. & Trocmé, N. (2003) "Canadian incidence study of reported child abuse and neglect (CIS)" in Statistics Canada 2006 *Family violence in Canada: A statistical profile* (Ottawa: Ministry of Industry), pp.35-36.

Trocmé, N.M. & Bala, N. "False allegations of abuse and neglect when parents separation" *Child Abuse & Neglect* 29 (2005), 1333-1345.

Trocmé, N.M., Tourigny, M., MacLaurin, B. & Fallon, B. "Major findings from the Canadian Incidence Study of Reported Child Abuse and Neglect" *Child Abuse & Neglect* 27 (2003), 1427-1439.

Troxel, W.M. & Matthews, K.A. "What are the costs of marital conflict and dissolution to children's physical health?" *Clinical Child and Family Psychology Review* 17:1 (2004), 29-57.

Tucker, C.J., Marx, J. & Long, L. "Moving on: Residential mobility and children's school lives" *Sociology of Education 71* (1998), 111-129.

Tukey, J.W. "The future of data analysis" *Annals of Mathematical Statistics* 33:1 (1962), 13-14.

Turkat, I.D. "Child visitation interference in divorce" *Clinical Psychology Review* 14 (1994), 737-742.

Turkat, I. D. "Relocation as a strategy to interfere with the child-parent Relationship" American Journal of Family Law 11 (1996), 39-41.

Turkat, I.D. "Divorce-related malicious parent syndrome" *Journal of Family Violence* 14 (1999), 95-107.

Van Horn, P. & Lieberman, A. *Domestic violence and parenting: A review of the literature.* (San Francisco: Judicial Council of California, Administrative Office of the Courts, Center for Families, Children & the Courts, 2002).

Vassiliou, D. & Cartwright, G. "The lost parent's perspective on parental alienation syndrome" *American Journal of Family Therapy* 29:3 (2001), 181-193.

Ver Steegh, N. "Differentiating types of domestic violence: Implications for child Custody" *Louisiana Law Review* 65 (2005), 1379-1431.

Ver Steegh, N. & Dalton, C. "Report from the Wingspread Conference on Domestic violence and Family Courts" *Family Court Review* 46:3 (2008), 454-475.

Vernberg, E. M. "Experience with peers following relocation during early adolescence" *American Journal of Orthopsychiatry* 60 (1990), 466-472.

Vogel, C.A., Bradley, R.H., Raikes, H.H., Boller, K. & Shears, J.K. "Relation between father connectedness and child outcomes" *Parenting Science and Practice* 6:2 (2006), 189-209.

von Boch-Galhau, W. & Kodjoe, U. (Trans. Christian T. Dum) "Psychological consequences of PAS indoctrination for adult children of divorce and the effects of alienation on parents" In R. A. Gardner, S. R. Sauber & D. Lorandos (Eds.) *The International Handbook of Parental Alienation Syndrome: Conceptual, Clinical and Legal Considerations* (Springfield, IL: Charles C Thomas, 2006), 310-322.

Wakefield, H. "Guidelines on investigatory interviewing of children: What is the consensus in the scientific community?" *Journal of Forensic Psychology* 24:3 (2006), 57-74.

Waldron, K. "A review of the social science research on post divorce relocation" *Journal of the American Academy of Matrimonial Lawyers* 19 (2005), 337-372.

Waldron, K.H. & Joanes, D.E. "Understanding and collaboratively treating parental alienation syndrome" *American Journal of Family Law* 10:3 (1996), 121-133.

Walker, L. *The Battered Women Syndrome* (New York: Springer, 1984).

Walker, L., Brantley, K. & Rigsbee, J. "A critical analysis of parental alienation syndrome and its admissibility in the family court" *Journal of Child Custody* 1:2 (2004a), 47-74.

Walker, L., Brantley, K. & Rigsbee, J. "Response to Johnston and Kelly critique of PAS article" *Journal of Child Custody* 1:4 (2004b), 91-97.

Walker, R., Logan, T., Jordan, C. E. & Campbell, J. C. "An integrative review of separation in the context of victimization: Consequences and implications for women" *Trauma Violence Abuse* 5 (2004), 143-193.

Wallerstein, J. S. "Tailoring the intervention to the child in the separating and divorced family" *Family and Conciliation Courts Review* 29:4 (1991), 448-459.

Wallerstein, J.S. (1995). *Amicus Curiae* Brief of Dr. Judith S. Wallerstein, Ph.D. filed in Cause No. SO46116, *In re Marriage of Burgess*, Supreme Court of the State of California, December 7, 1995.

Wallerstein, J.S. (2003). Misrepresentation of findings in psychology study by APA. American Psychological Association Journal of Family Psychology. Press Release. www.thelizlibrary.org/lamusga/braver.htm.

Wallerstein, J. S. & Blakeslee, S. *Second Chances: Men, Women, and Children a Decade After Divorce* (New York, NY: Ticknor & Fields, 1989).

Wallerstein, J.S. & Kelly, J.B. "The effects of parental divorce: Experiences of the child in later latency" *American Journal of Orthopsychiatry* 46:2 (1976), 256-269.

Wallerstein, J.S. & Kelly, J.B. *Surviving the Breakup: How Children and Parents Cope with Divorce* (New York: Basic Books, 1980).

Wallerstein, J.S., Kernberg, P.F., Silberg, J.L., Lewis, J.M., Sikorski, J.B. & Dallam, S.J. (2004). *Amici curiae* brief, *In re the marriage of LaMusga*, Supreme Court of California.

Wallerstein, J.S. & Lewis, J. "The long-term impact of divorce on children" *Family and Conciliation Courts Review* 36:3 (1998), 368-383.

Wallerstein, J.S., Lewis, J. & Blakeslee, S. *The Unexpected Legacy of Divorce: A 25-year Landmark Study* (New York: Hyperion, 2000).

Wallerstein, J.S. & Tanke, T. "To move or not to move" *Family Law Quarterly*, 30:4 (2006), 1-18.

Walsh, R. & Bone, M. "Parental alienation syndrome: An age-old custody problem" *The Florida Bar Journal* LXXXI:6 (1997), 93-96.

Waltzlawick, P., Weakland, J. & Fisch, R. *Change: Principles of Problem Formation and Problem Resolution* (New York: W.W. Norton & Company, 1974).

Ward, P. (2007). Personal Communication.

Ward, P. & Harvey, J. "Family wars: The alienation of children" *New Hampshire Bar Journal* 34:1 (1993), 30-40.

Warshak, R.A. *The Custody Revolution: The Father Factor and the Motherhood Mystique* (New York: Poseidon Press, 1992).

Warshak, R.A. "Remarriage as a trigger of parental alienation syndrome" *American Journal of Family Therapy* 28 (2000a), 229-241.

Warshak, R.A. "Social science and children's best interests in relocation cases: Burgess revisited" *Family Law Quarterly* 34 (2000b), 83-113.

Warshak, R.A. "Current controversies regarding parental alienation syndrome" *American Journal of Forensic Psychology* 19:3 (2001a), 29-59.

Warshak, R.A. *Divorce Poison: Protecting the Parent-child Bond from a Vindictive Ex* (New York: Regan Books, 2001b).

Warshak, R.A. "Misdiagnosis of parental alienation syndrome" *American Journal of Forensic Psychology* 20:2 (2002), 31-52.

Warshak, R.A. "Bringing sense to parental alienation: A look at the dispute and the evidence" *Family Law Quarterly* 37:2 (2003a), 273-301.

Warshak, R.A. "Payoffs and pitfalls of listening to children" *Family Relations* 52:4 (2003b), 373-384.

Warshak, R. A. "Social science and parental alienation: Examining the disputes and the evidence" In R. A. Gardner, S. R. Sauber & D. Lorandos (Eds.) *The International Handbook of Parental Alienation Syndrome: Conceptual, Clinical and Legal Considerations* (Springfield, IL: Charles C Thomas, 2006) 352-371.

Warshak, R.A., Braver, S.L., Kelly, J.B., Bray, J.H., et al. (2004). Amici Curiae Brief, *In re the Marriage of LaMusga*, Supreme Court of California.

Warshak, R.A. & Santrock, J.W. "The impact of divorce in father-custody and mother-custody homes: The child's perspective". In L. Kurdek (Ed.), *Children and Divorce*. (San Francisco: Jossey-Bass, 1983).

Weiner, I.B. "Rorschach assessment in child custody cases" *Journal of Child Custody* 2:3 (2005), 99-119.

Weisman, H.N. "Forensic psychological examination of the child witness in cases of alleged sexual abuse" *American Journal of Orthopsychiatry* 61:1 (1991), 48-58.

Weisman, N. (1992). "On access after parental separation" 36 *Reports of Family Law* 3d (1992), 35-77.

White, L. & Gilbreth, J.G. "When children have two fathers: Effects of relationships with stepfathers and noncustodial fathers on adolescent outcomes" *Journal of Marriage & Family* 63:1 (2001), 155-167.

Whitechurch, G. & Constantine, L. "Systems theory" in P. Boss, W. Doherty, R. LaRossa, W. Schumm & Steinmetz (Eds.) *Sourcebook of Family Theories and Methods: A Contextual Approach* (New York: Plenum Press, 1993).

Whiteside, M.F. & Becker, B.J. "Parental factors and the young child's postdivorce adjustment: A meta-analysis with implications for parenting arrangements" *Journal of Family Psychology* 14 (2000), 5-26.

Williams, F. S. "Preventing parentectomy following divorce" Paper presented at the Fifth Annual Conference: National Council for Children's Rights (Washington DC, October 20, 1990).

Williams, J. "Should judges close the gate on PAS and PA?" *Family Court Review* 39:3 (2001), 267-281.

Wolfe, D.A. & Jaffe, P.G. "Emerging strategies in the prevention of domestic Violence" *The Future of Children* 9 (1999), 133-144.

Wolfe, D.A., Zak, L., Wilson, S. & Jaffe, P.G. "Child witnesses to violence between parents: Critical issues in behavioural and social adjustment" *Journal of Abnormal Child Psychology* 13 (1986), 95-104.

Wood, D., Halfon, N., Scarlata, D., Newacheck, P. & Nessim, S. "Impact of family relocation on children's growth, development, school function, and behavior" *Journal of the American Medical Association* 270:11 (1993), 1334-1338.

Young, L. "AIF v AMS - The high court and relocation" *Australian Journal of Family Law* 13:3 (1999), 264-270.

Zaragoza, M. S., Graham, J. R., Hall, G. C. N., Hirschman, R. & Ben-Porath, Y. S. (Eds.) *Memory and Testimony in the Child Witness* (Thousand Oaks, CA: Sage Publications, 1995).

Zibbell, R.A. "Common couple aggression: Frequency and implications for child custody and access evaluations" *Family Court Review* 43:3 (2005), 454-465.

Zill, N., Morrison, D.R. & Coiro, J.J. "Long term effects of parental divorce on parent-child relationships, adjustment and achievement in young adulthood" *Journal of Family Psychology* 7 (1993), 91-103.

Zirogiannis, L. "Evidentiary issues with parental alienation syndrome" *Family Court Review* 39:3 (2001), 334-343.

Index